Dirty
Tricks
or
Trump
Cards

Dirty Tricks
or
Trump Cards

U.S. Covert Action &
Counterintelligence

**Roy
Godson**

With a new introduction by the author

Transaction Publishers
New Brunswick (U.S.A.) and London (U.K.)

Sixth printing 2008
New material this edition copyright © 2001 by Transaction Publishers, New
Brunswick, New Jersey. Originally published in 1995 by National Strategy
Information Center, Inc.

This book is printed on acid-free paper that meets the American National
Standard for Permanence of Paper for Printed Library Materials.

Library of Congress Catalog Number: 00-023427
ISBN: 978-0-7658-0699-4
Printed in the United States of America

Library of Congress Cataloging-in-Publication Data

Godson, Roy, 1942-
    Dirty tricks or trump cards : U.S. covert action and counterintelligence
l. Roy Godson.
        p. cm.
    Originally published: Washington : Brassey's, c1995, in series: Brassey's
intelligence and national security library. With new introd.
    Includes bibliographical references and index.
    ISBN 0-7658-0699-1 (pbk. : alk. paper)
    1. Intelligence service—United States. 2. United States—Politics and
government—1945-1989. 3. United States—Politics and government-
1989-   I. Title.

JK468.I6 2000
327.1273—dc21   00-023427

Give me twelve good men who mean what they say
and say what they mean

From a headstone in a London cemetery

Contents

Introduction to the Transaction Edition   *xi*
Preface   *xliii*

1 Neglected Elements in American Intelligence   **1**
    INTEGRATING THE ELEMENTS   3
    NEGLECTED ELEMENTS   6
    COUNTERINTELLIGENCE   9
    COVERT ACTION   18

2 Steps and Missteps: Covert Action Since 1945   **27**
    HALCYON DAYS   32
        Consensus: Stopping Communism   35
        A Sometime Instrument of Policy   39
        Successes   42
        Missteps   46
        Exposé   50
    THE WIND SHIFTS   51
        Congressional Assertiveness   53
        The Central American Drama   55
    COVERT ACTION IN THE 1990s   58
        The Current Ethos   64

3 Building and Rebuilding:
Counterintelligence Since World War II   **66**
    BUILDING THE COLD WAR CONSENSUS   67
        The FBI   74
        Collection   76
        Analysis   81
        Exploitation   82
        The CIA   85
        Military Counterintelligence   95
    BREAKING THE MOLD   100
    REBUILDING   102
        The FBI   107

The CIA 111

The Military 115

4 Handmaiden of Policy: Principles of Covert Action **120**

FIRST PRINCIPLES 121

POLICY, OPPORTUNITY, AND PEOPLE 122

The Infrastructure 126

Personnel 126

Material Support 129

Question of Values 130

Symbiosis 132

Ends, Means, and Historical Lessons 134

Political Action 135

Agents of Influence 139

Helping Organizations 145

Movement of Money and Support 147

Covert Propaganda 151

Paramilitary Operations 158

Assassination 159

Terrorism 161

Guerrillas and Resistance Movements 164

Safe Haven 170

Materiel Support for Paramilitary Operations 171

Special Forces 173

Coups d'Etat 175

Intelligence Support 177

COUNTERTERRORISM: SYNERGY IN ACTION 180

5 Offensive Defense: Principles of Counterintelligence **184**

CENTRAL COORDINATION AND STRATEGY 185

COUNTERINTELLIGENCE ANALYSIS 187

Triage of Targets 188

Assessing Vulnerability 190

Adversaries: Targets and Competence 191

Counterdeception Analysis 192

Support for Operations 195

Counterintelligence Analysis and Positive Intelligence 199

COUNTERINTELLIGENCE COLLECTION 201

    Integration of Sources 201

    Collection from Open Sources 203

    Clandestine Collection from Human Sources 207

        Defectors 211

        Physical Surveillance 216

        Access Agents 218

        Double Agents 219

        Liaison 220

        Illegals 221

    Technical Counterintelligence 224

EXPLOITATION 226

    On the Offensive 231

        Deception and Offensive Counterintelligence 235

    Positive Intelligence 237

6 In Pursuit of Effective Intelligence **241**

    VARIABLES AT PLAY 241

    The Pace of Modernization and Technological Innovation 241

    Government Structure and Bureaucratic Culture 243

    The Perception of Political Circumstances 246

    The Nature of the Regime 249

    PUTTING THE PIECES TOGETHER 251

    FOR THE FORESEEABLE FUTURE 252

Notes **257**

Glossary of Terms and Abbreviations **303**

Bibliography **309**

Index **327**

Introduction to the Transaction Edition

WORLD POLITICS AND INTELLIGENCE have evolved throughout human history. Perhaps the sharpest breaks in the evolution are between premodern and modern societies and the way intelligence has been used in them. As we enter the late modern or postmodern era, with all three types of societies coexisting, there will be a complex mix of intelligence practices and challenges.

Before addressing these contemporary intelligence challenges, the major characteristics of the values, institutional actors, and intelligence practices in each of these types of societies will be differentiated. It will be suggested that there are significant similarities but also significant differences between the intelligence practices of premodern, modern, and late modern societies. If indeed we are moving into a late modern or postmodern era, we should not be surprised to see continuities in intelligence, but also differences. Americans, and others, need to understand and anticipate the characteristics of the players or actors in each society, and the resulting intelligence environment that they are facing.

The introduction concludes by drawing major implications of these challenges for U.S. intelligence, and particularly U.S. counterintelligence and covert action. To preempt the conclusion, just as these clandestine arts were and remain useful to premodern actors, and, at times, to states in the modern era, there will be ample opportunities and challenges for the effective use of these instruments in the early twenty-first century.

Premodern Societies

Sharp differences can be found in the paramount values,[1] institutions, and strategies employed to achieve the objectives of each of these societies. Premodern people have been most characteristic of humankind—from the appearance of primitive man and local groups about 500,000 years ago (of which little is known), to the more established agricultural societies of about 10,000 years ago, to the great multiethnic civilizations that began to emerge, often in river valleys, approximately 5,000 years ago. The primitive and traditional prevailed almost everywhere until the dramatic changes associated with the Reformation, Renaissance, and later the Enlightenment and Industrial Revolution—the period we call early modern.[2] Modern society in turn spawned a mainstream of liberal as well as quasi-liberal and deviant, totalitarian, systems in the twentieth century.

The spread of the modern and the clash with the traditional—the acute conflicts amongst moderns in the twentieth century and their appeals for allies in traditional societies—has been the dominant political struggle in recent world history. These struggles in turn have played a large role in shaping (and in part have been shaped by) what we now call intelligence— a term that was uncommon in most societies, modern and premodern, prior to the twentieth century.

Premodern societies, for the most part, were characterized by traditional values and institutions. In private, some of the elites may have been uncharacteristically "modern," but in public the traditional prevailed. The past was the model for the present. Nature controlled man, who sought to achieve harmony with its forces through religion. Rigid hierarchies prevailed. Society was ascriptive: people were born into their roles in life. Familial, hierarchal loyalty was the predominant norm.

The rulers' values shaped the institutions of politics, government, and intelligence practices. The primary political unit was the local family, clan or tribe, and religious unit, which often overlapped. This strong religion-based authority decided where and when one lived, worked, and went to war.

From time to time, multiethnic societies and empires were established. Yet almost all of them—the Hellenic, Roman, Turkish, and Arab empires, for example, established ethnic hierarchies within their multiethnic domains. Some empires tended toward modernity, creating permanent or semipermanent bureaucracies, and allowing for the establishment of commercial relations, private property, and nongovernmental organizations. Others became "oriental despotisms," with strong religious/political elites, a powerful agro-bureaucracy, weak private property and weak, legal, nongovernmental organizations. Han China is an example.

In these kinds of societies, intelligence was designed to serve the interests of the rulers. Although often powerful and strong, they trusted few individuals, not their own families, not their subjects, and especially not the leaders and populations of other territories. This basic mistrust was mutual. Rival leaders feared each other. For them, the collection of intelligence information and what we would call counterintelligence and covert action were important instruments of statecraft. Counterintelligence, they believed, was necessary to identify, neutralize, and manipulate disloyal family members, rivals, and their secret agents. Covert action was useful to secretly manipulate the allegiance of rival leaders, their deputies, and their military commanders.

There are remarkable similarities in the theoretical and historical writings of the advisors to the rulers in the more advanced of traditional societies, and the memoirs of those who came into contact with these societies before they were crushed by, or became subservient to, modern society.[3] Among the most famous are the works of the Chinese Sun-tzu,[4] the Indian Kautilya,[5] the Seljuc Nizam al Mulk,[6] Venetian ambassadors in the late medieval era,[7] and accounts by Spanish missionaries in the fifteenth and sixteenth centuries.[8]

What is remarkable is that all stressed the utility to the ruler of secret intelligence to manipulate and to identify and neutralize manipulation by others. Intelligence usually was centralized under the ruler's direct control. There was little discussion of the elements of intelligence such as counterintelligence and covert action as came to be characteristic of modern liberal states in the twentieth century. In addition to foreign actors—tribal, cities, and empires—the targets of intelligence were the ruler's own family and his officials, as well as rival families in the ruler's society. There was little distinction between war and peace or between enemies at home and those abroad. In contrast to the dominant pattern of modern liberal societies after the Westphalian and Grotian state systems, the use of violence against rivals was more or less normal. Genuine peace was abnormal. Intelligence functioned most if not all the time. Collecting information and preventing oneself from the penetration and manipulation of rivals was standard practice.

And in premodern society there were few if any limits on what intelligence could do. The most benign to the most insidious and cruel means were regularly used. This was not an era of human rights, rule of law, or respect for human dignity. Techniques of secret intimidation and persuasion—bribery, torture, maiming, kidnapping, and rape—and every covert technique of violence—from straightforward assassination, to terrorism, to the use of poisons (the biological weapons of the day)—were employed to weaken, persuade, deter, and defeat rivals at home and abroad.

Intelligence in the era prior to modern international relations emphasized the clandestine arts—counterintelligence and covert action. Rulers used these capabilities both offensively and defensively, and often. Secret agents and sympathizers of rivals were identified and neutralized—at home and abroad. Covert means were employed to deceive, manipulate, weaken, and defeat real and perceived enemies—rival clans, ethnic groups, religious leaders, as well as bandits.

Evolving Modernity

As modern societies evolved and values, institutions, and techniques changed, so too did intelligence. The shift was gradual and uneven, much like the evolution of modernity itself. The belief that the past did not control the present and future, that nature could be understood and made to serve man, had a huge impact on the growth of science and technology. In the twentieth century it had a major impact on intelligence. Understanding the laws of physics and manipulating aspects of the electromagnetic spectrum—particularly light, heat, and radio waves—brought about the era of signals intelligence (SIGINT), imagery (IMINT), and other forms of technical collection now known generically as MASINT.[9] Indeed it could be maintained that this is one of the most significant changes in the "second oldest profession"—which earlier had relied so much on human beings.

Other major changes in intelligence were to come with the growing modern belief in social equality as opposed to hierarchy—ascriptive class and ethnic status, and family and religious loyalty. The impact of the ideas embodied in the Enlightenment and set down in such documents as the Declaration of Independence, and the U.S. and French constitutions, over a century or two began to transform hierarchal, religious, ethnic-based authority. Governmental institutions and instruments, in theory if not always in practice, were to serve the interest of the people, irrespective of their ascriptive status.

The growth of the sovereign state, initially owned and ruled by a person (a sovereign), then the development of the state owned by the people in the state (the impersonal nation state), and the doctrine of national self-determination—was revolutionary. Starting in northwestern Europe at the end of the eighteenth century, the doctrine spread slowly on the continent.

Its growing popularity there coincided ironically with European imperialism, and thus the dissemination of these ideas, very slowly and often incompletely, to much of the traditional world.[10]

Not all of Europe's traditional rulers and societies accepted these values. The leaders of the Russian and Austro-Hungarian Empires resisted them. Some European elites accepted modern values opportunistically, to rally their multiethnic and multireligious societies to overthrow imperialism in the nineteenth century. Others may have subscribed to beliefs in the equal rights of all individuals living in the state and the rule of law, but in practice they found it difficult to maintain authority in their heterogeneous societies. The transition was longer for some than others. In the twentieth century, there were also many deviations, particularly in the Soviet Union, Fascist Italy, Spain, Portugal, and Nazi Germany. After major Western hot and cold wars, some lasting four years and others more than seventy-five years, the modern liberal societies, adhering to the belief if not always the practice of the rule of law, in the main, won out.

In the traditional non-Western world, dominated for centuries as societies were by ambivalent European rule, the process is taking much longer. Non-Western elites, some educated at Western schools and universities and some embracing Western trade unionism, rallied heterogeneous populations against Western imperialism. In the name of national self-determination, and nation statehood, they established "quasi" and micro states—states that were recognized as sovereign entities by other states and by international organizations such as the United Nations. In reality, few had the internal attributes of nation-states. Their populations, in the main, held traditional beliefs, and key institutions were traditional, with a veneer of modern statehood. The governments of these states—representing particular personal, subnational, or class interests—could not control much of their territory, nor compel the allegiance of many of their "countrymen"; tax collection and enforcement were feeble and ineffective; bureaucratic and police structures were weak; regional and local traditional strongmen confronted their authority. Nonetheless, they were recognized internationally as "modern nation-states."[11]

Where the modern pattern was truly institutionalized, the state came to be guided by what has been called the "Clausewitzian Trinity"—the distinction between the state, the military, and the people.[12] In most of Europe, North America, and Japan, there was an impersonal sovereign bureaucratic state, whose interests were recognized by other sovereign states. The professional military preserved the interests of the state, according to laws adhered to by sovereign states, international law, and the international rules of war. The military was to protect the state against other states, and the military instruments that threatened state interests. A small intelligence collection capability sometimes was established in the military to target the military of other states, but only rarely was there a professional intelligence organization. The police and criminal justice system were to deal with citizens or bandits that did not accept the authority of the state. The remainder of the population was *hors de combat,* separate from the military, and with some exceptions, unarmed. The military did not target the population unless it became involved in directly supporting the war machine of another state. As liberal states became institutionalized in Europe and North America in the latter half of the nineteenth century, states usually did not target their own citizens. Unless they violated criminal laws, or were suspected of supporting the efforts of a foreign state, they were not intelligence targets either.

The Clausewitzian Trinity sometimes broke down during the wars between liberal democracies and the modern deviants. The Bolsheviks, Fascists, and Nazis broke the trinity when they seized power. They perceived their enemies to be internal as well as external, and created counterintelligence services to root them out, even in their own military. The party elites were permanently at war with both internal and external enemies; they did not shrink from using mass murder, genocide, and purges against their own citizens, and indeed against their own party members. Covert action and counterintelligence were their tools of choice to undermine their enemies, wherever they might be. With the outbreak of war, the liberal democracies responded to foreign intelligence practices by the deviant moderns. During WWI and WWII, as will be described in subsequent chapters, the democracies developed robust intelligence bureaucracies, which then declined precipitously at war's end. As the democracies began to wage the Cold War in earnest after 1947, once again they built up their intelligence services and their capabilities for counterintelligence and covert action.

The trinity was also severely strained in the anticolonial struggles in the non-Western world, particularly the violent struggles of the post WWII era. Colonial suppression of the independence movements, the resulting reliance on clandestine organizations, and the secret relations that these non-Western movements had with both the Soviet bloc and the United States, led the Europeans to target the non-Western civilian population.

Intelligence practices, and the absence of restraints on the means used, by both the colonialists and some parts of the independence movements, were often reminiscent of premodern society.[13]

Except for conflicts among the moderns and the anticolonial struggles, by and large the trinity held up. Major components of the national security apparatus of modern liberal states was focused on foreign states, perceptions of their national interests, and their military. Ninety percent of the resources, human and national, were focused on foreigners, not on the citizenry. The use of counterintelligence and covert action, on the whole, was circumscribed. Limits were imposed. Intelligence bureaucracies, even when they existed, were decentralized. By and large the focus of intelligence was on states, their interests, their military, and to some extent their economic instruments.

These Enlightenment driven concepts became so deeply ingrained that when universities started to teach about "national security" in the 1950s, the focus was on the state, its military instruments, and on modern technologies. Intelligence, and especially the clandestine arts, was almost nowhere to be found in university curricula, war colleges, or indeed in almost any institution except the training centers of intelligence agencies themselves. Even there the focus was on the collection and analysis of information, rather than counterintelligence and covert action. This was particularly true in the post-World War II United States. The state centric model of world politics, international relations, and "national" security studies remained dominant in academic and government circles until quite recently.[14]

Contemporary World Politics

But even before the end of the Cold War, a variety of tendencies known as globalization, the information age, and postmodernity were emerging. Opinions and interpretations of what is taking place differ widely, as reflected in the terminology used by the various proponents—"the end of history,"[15] "the clash of civilizations,"[16] "Jihad vs. McWorld,"[17] or "the coming anarchy."[18] To be sure, this is not the first time that the demise of the modern nation state has been predicted. However, there is a considerable body of inductive and deductive evidence to indicate a new era is emerging, even if its contours are only dimly understood as yet.

Arguing by the authority of contemporary statesmen, a new era of world politics appears to be upon us, however. Few would claim that modern values, institutions, and instruments have passed from the scene. But many argue that something different is brewing—an unfamiliar combination of the known and the new. Moreover, they suggest that this blend poses new security threats, which requires–some acknowledge openly–new intelligence approaches. Thus far, there is little clamoring to make greater use of those neglected instruments counterintelligence and covert action. However, the logical implications of their arguments point in this direction.[19]

Leaders and specialists in many regional and global governmental, and nongovernmental bodies also are beginning to shift their thinking. Regional bodies such as the European Union, the Council of Europe, the Organization of American States, and global bodies such as the United Nations, the International Money Fund, and the IBRD (World Bank) have started to increase their capabilities to identify and counter new security threats, and to incorporate this into planning. Changing values, actors, institutions, and instruments, which they and the world community must confront, are shifting long prevailing viewpoints and policies. These actors have begun to realize that sustainable development cannot be achieved without security, although none have yet recommended the use of intelligence in pursuit of security.

Students and informed observers of world politics and security are coming to similar conclusions, although there are considerable differences, too.[20] Given the nature of the world environment at the beginning a twenty-first century—whatever the era is called—a new mix of security techniques and capabilities will be required. Specialists in international relations, usually focus on external variables, and remain state centric. They study the threat and the use and management of forces by states. A few consider foreign intelligence practiced by states. Even here the focus is on collection and analysis as inputs into decision making. Rarely is it on the clandestine arts. Yet the dominant state centric paradigm cannot explain major aspects of contemporary world politics. The main theories used to explain international relations—particularly realism and idealism, and their recent variations, neorealism and neoliberalism—rarely help us to understand what forces are leading to globalization, integration, the fragmentation and breakdown of the state, or ungovernability and violence in key regions, such as Central Asia, the Balkans, the Andes, and key states such as Russia.

Among specialists in comparative politics, who usually focus on internal variables there is growing recognition that local and regional politics cannot be explained exclusively with the dominant concepts and theories of the past. By and large, their concern is with the institutions, processes, and domestic policy of states. Regional specialists tend to be more sensitive to fissiparous tendencies and instability. They are aware that traditional and modern values, institutions, and practices are at play and intermingle with modern and even postmodern forces, a phenomenon they seek to explain. However, many still reflect the developmental perspective, or liberal Western paradigm. Increasing modernization and globalization, they believe, are leading to liberal, democratic, modern nation-states, and the intellectual tools and concepts of Western political science, and instrumentalities of the modern state are adequate to understand and guide the process.[21] Specific instruments of violence, such as terrorism by state and nonstate forces, or the uses and abuses of intelligence are included by some specialists, as is crime. But local, regional, and transnational security threats, and the use of intelligence, let alone the clandestine arts, are rarely touched upon.

Nevertheless, there is ferment. What is changing?

It is far from easy to measure changing values, beliefs, and expectations, particularly on a global scale. But, there is evidence of shifting patterns. Some have identified these patterns as late modern, postmodern, or antimodern.[22] The shifts appear to be affecting the governability of modern states, and the security challenges that have come to the fore. Some trends are leading to greater fragmentation of states, some to greater integration causing the nation-state to lose its predominance as the leading global actor in favor of both smaller and larger actors.[23]

Among the fissiparous trends are:

1. Indigenization—people in various parts of the world are increasingly identifying with pre-traditional or tribal roots. This has been referred to as the "4th World Movement" and can be seen on several continents.[24]

2. Nationalization or ethnic separatism—increasing identity based on "blood," race, ethnicity, or perceived historical roots, and rejection of heterogeneous, formal citizenship. Again the pattern can be widely discerned.[25]

3. Regionalism—substate regions are attracting the loyalty and identity. There is a weakening of the national project in many parts the world.[26]

4. Immigration and Minority Ethnification—increasing immigration and the movement of people, which has not been accompanied by assimilation. Large diasporas are being transformed into segregated communities in many parts the world.[27]

At the same time, other trends integrate people across state boundaries, and this tends to undermine nation-states and their governments. One of the most pervasive is "cosmopolitanism" in which certain types of people in various parts of the world are beginning to identify with each other.

Most notably, elites in modern societies, and modernized elites in basically traditional cultures and quasi states, are beginning to share worldviews. Various explanations have been put forward for the growth of this type of cosmopolitanism, particularly globalization, and information and communication technology. These elites, often highly educated, no longer view their identity as inextricably tied to their nation-state or to their ethnic origins. Traditional and modern identities and loyalties are becoming diluted. These elites are becoming "cosmopolitan," traveling, living, moving, working, and raising their children in various parts the world. Most learn to converse in English. They see themselves as a "new class," representative of "world culture," and "humanity."[28]

A contributing factor to late postmodernity also may be a radical brand of postmodern philosophy sometimes called decon-structionism. This intellectual movement undercuts national myths or "stories." In both traditional and modern societies, it undercuts religious and Enlightenment doctrines that lead to both traditional and modern identities and institutions. Few outside academic circles have the time, patience, and inclination to read or even become aware of the main theoreticians of this brand of postmodernism. However, like the major ideologies of the past, the major themes of deconstructionism are slowly passing from elite into popular culture, through art, films, literature, and television.[29]

At the same time, belief in free, democratic societies, the rule of law, and free markets—liberal internationalism—has grown. If there is a dominant ideology now, since communism faded, then liberal internationalism is probably the most potent force. Fostered both by modern states, particularly the United States, and by transnational and globalizing companies, internationalism has adherents in many parts the world. It has yet to become well established in many of the societies formerly ruled by communism or in former colonial regions.[30] Moreover, countervailing pressures, sometimes taking an anti-Western form, such as Islamism or "anti-Americanism," also have surfaced in various parts of the world.

These contradictory forces are producing a ferment of values often pulling in different directions. Forces of integration and fragmentation are at work simultaneously, and at many levels of society. Some are supportive of liberal, modern nation statehood and the rule of law, but others undermine it.

On one hand, modern nation-states have been strengthened. The doctrine of national self-determination remains strong. Although many millions move, travel, and live in various parts of the world, they still remain loyal to a national homeland. Some cosmopolitans may be loyal to Sony, Seagrams, or Motorola, however, many if not most people still support the idea of modern nation-states. They may be reluctant, but they appear to pay taxes, follow the laws, and even to die for their "national" independence. The number of breakaway and new states has risen dramatically over the past twenty years and shows only a few signs of slowing—from 150 in 1975 to 193 in 1997—but many in these breakaway units aspire to modern nation statehood.

On the other hand, nation-state loyalty cannot be taken for granted. There has been a dramatic growth in substate and transstate actors that command various degrees of loyalty and commitment, some legal, some not. Another discernable trend is the growth or strengthening of regional, as opposed to national, governmental actors.

The growth of legal and illegal new actors, often with regional and global reach, is staggering —and shows little signs of slowing. Some are formal organizations–with a hierarchy, bureaucracy, and budgets, and even a capacity for defensive and offensive violence. Other actors also are more informal, "horizontal," networks–people who work together periodically, some using violence and intimidation.[31]

One index of this trend is the increase in the number of international governmental organizations (IGO) and international nongovernmental organizations (INGO). On the eve of World War I there were 49 IGOs and 170 INGOs. These numbers had grown to 300 IGOs and 2,400 INGOs by the mid-1970s, and in 1988 there were 4,518 INGOs. The INGOs have continued to grow at a rate of 3-5 percent annually, and some now estimate the number is more than 25,000.[32]

These formal and informal actors are economic, ethnonational, multi or single purpose, religious, and criminal. Economic players, particularly multinational corporations and transnational manufacturing, service, financial, and communications companies have attracted the most attention. They now control a considerable share of the world's resources and productive capacity. At this level, their activities have the potential to make or break economic, social, and political stability in many parts of the world.[33] Some have their own intelligence, counterintelligence, and covert action capabilities. Few, if any, states control them.

Ethnonational groups can be divided into two groups: those that seek separate nation-states or self-government through any means, including secret intelligence infrastructures and violence, and those with more limited objectives and more circumscribed means. In recent years, the more ambitious and violent have been concentrated in a few geographic areas, particularly the former Yugoslavia and Soviet Union. There are many other examples on most continents. In almost all regions, their relative influence has increased and the power and authority of the state has declined.

Religious movements also sometimes overlap with ethnonational ones. Some are separate. Islamists (extreme fundamentalists) have regional and sometimes broader aspirations and reach. Some are independent of state support. They have human and financial resources, secret infrastructures, and are capable of using violence in many parts of the world. Some, like the Japanese-based Aum Shinrykyo, which operated also in Russia and the United States, are transstate actors with a covert infrastructure and capability to use violence and even weapons of mass destruction.

The growing number of INGOs with global reach is difficult to categorize. Perhaps the term cosmopolitan is useful. Some are promoting single issues while others seek global governance. Some, like the international labor movement have been around for decades and have played a significant role in twentieth-century world politics. Others are relatively new. Some are very well funded and organized on traditional lines, such as Transparency International, which focuses on anticorruption, and Amnesty International, which seeks to protect human rights and, in effect, the rule of law. These latter organizations operate legally and overtly. Others are more loosely organized, even secretive. Yet, even relatively mainstream groups may occasionally resort to physical intimidation and violence, for example, some of the more radical environmental organizations and networks. Some members of Greenpeace, a worldwide organization with the elements of traditional structure, have also been known to use such tactics.

Criminals, by the very nature of their activities are compelled to be secretive. Their organizations have been powerful in some areas such as Sicily and parts of Southeast Asia for decades. But in recent years, criminal organizations have mushroomed, and they have gone transnational. There are few areas of the world where they are not found. Some regions are "source" or "sanctuary" countries, for example, the Andes, Southeast and Southwest Asia, Nigeria, Russia, and Mexico, the stronghold of the organization and often the source of its raw materials, for example drugs or people. Other areas serve as transit zones through which the criminals and their products move; Central Asia, Turkey, and the Caribbean fall into this category. Still other areas provide services that help criminals to evade national laws. These include covert financial arrangements, money laundering, the provision of passports and other documents. Some areas such as the micro states and offshore havens in Europe are no longer merely tax havens and have expanded their offerings. Others in the South Pacific, and the Caribbean are of recent origin, stimulated by the growing underground criminal economy. All told, estimates of the annual criminal economy range from $500 billion to $1 trillion, or larger than the GNP of more than half of the states in the world.[34]

Much of the illegal proceeds are derived from the target regions—the richer more developed areas of North America, Europe, Australia, and Japan. Organized crime has added new levels of sophistication to the operation of traditional vice such as drugs, prostitution, gambling and loan sharking. In addition, it has moved into other types of crime such as illegal migration. Some governments and research institutes estimate that as many as one million people per year are illegally transported by criminals, often transnationally, netting their organizations $5 to $7 billion annually.[35] Other lucrative and widespread criminal enterprises include kidnapping, car theft, and ecocrime such as illegal dumping of toxic waste, and stealing and transporting prohibited fauna, flora, and endangered species. Although they are also trafficking in weapons, as far as is known, this has not yet included weapons of mass destruction. However, should they so choose, many criminal organizations probably have the capability to do so.

Their activities reduce economic development, illegally siphon off money from productive uses, harm the environment, and abuse the rights of many hundreds of thousands of individuals. However, another major challenge to liberal society is posed by organized crime: the clandestine nexus—symbiosis and collaboration—between professional criminals and political actors. On one hand, established organized criminals covertly cooperate with state authorities—the executive, legislative, and judicial branches at various levels—and the nongovernmental sector—political parties, financial institutions, lawyers, and others. Criminals also collaborate secretly with "illegitimate" or illegal political players, such as enthnonational and religious groups, particularly violent ones.

This is by no means a new problem, but the present scale of this collaboration is without precedent. This is true almost in all continents and in areas of particular concern to the United States, such as Mexico, Russia and the CIS, Turkey, Nigeria, and South Africa. Because of the interconnectedness of the source, transit, service, and target areas, almost all now suffer from some degree of political-criminal collaboration, and the problem has assumed worldwide significance. Global organizations such as the United Nations and the World Bank, as well as regional organizations such as the Organization of American States and the European Union, and the G-8 now regard organized crime, political-criminal collaboration, and corruption as one of the most serious security challenges of the next decade.[36]

In sum, modern liberal society increasingly is being challenged by nonstate forces. This is not to suggest that the era of nation-states, and quasi and micro states, is past. Rather, it suggests that for individuals to get what they want, at the local, national, regional, or global level, there are a variety of ways to do this. There is a choice of working through the governments of nation-states, or through nonstate actors, legal and illegal, formal and informal.

As values and actors have become more mixed, strategies, instruments, and techniques used also have been undergoing change. This was happening even in the move from premodern to modern society. In traditional societies, the elites of local and multiethnic empires were more important than the "state" or "society." Assassinations of kings or emperors, alliances with the family of rival rulers, through marriage or force, corruption of chief advisors and generals of rival rulers were all standard practices before the institutionalization of the Westphalian system both in the nineteenth and twentieth centuries.

Statecraft largely changed, however, with the advent of the modern national state system. The focus became "national interests" rather than the personal interests of rulers, increasing the military capability of the state, and mobilizing the power of other states. On the whole, the state monopolized violence. The distinction between the state and its instruments and society or the population at large was sharpened. To be sure, in an effort to undercut or influence rival governments, there were occasioned appeals or threats to the population of other states. Overt and covert instruments, sometimes importantly, were directed at the population or society, particularly in the wars and battles waged by and against the deviant moderns such as Nazis and ruling communist parties. Sometimes nonstate institutions, such as labor, religious, and cultural organizations, were created or penetrated by state actors. However, the main instruments, military, economic, and diplomatic, were monopolized and used by states against other states to enhance the national interests.

The shift or mix of late modern/postmodern societies and actors also has coincided with the changes in technology, strategy, and instruments.[37] On one hand, states, particularly liberal modern states, remain particularly capable of mobilizing resources to achieve ends. In the near-term, over the next ten years or so, there is also likely to be an asymmetric power relationship between the United States and other states. The United States, more than any other state, will be able to mobilize major resources–military, economic, and political–and to be capable of deploying them in most regions of the world.

On the other hand, other modern, quasi, and micro states as well as nonstate actors, are capable of challenging the security of the United States and other liberal societies. To begin with, some of these states, however weak, are ruled by personal and familial concerns. They and a host of illegal actors are not bound by the Clausewitzian Trinity. The distinction between the state and the population no longer prevails there, if it ever did. As a result, the rulers of both liberal and not so liberal state and nonstate actors, and their families, once again are potential targets of assassins, extortion, bribery, and corruption. There is also a breakdown of the distinction between the bureaucracy of the state, particularly its military, police, and intelligence agencies, and the rest of the population. The leaders of many quasi and weak states as well as nonstate actors are commonly using paramilitary organizations and militias. Sometimes these forces have uniforms to distinguish themselves from the regular military, but not always. They may wear civilian clothes, and even mask their identities. They may or may not live separately from the population. They may or may not be disciplined. They certainly do not conform to uniform codes of military justice, nor follow the rules of war on the treatment of prisoners, the care of wounded, or the treatment of civilians. The regional and local commanders of these organizations, whether state or nonstate, live "off the land," extorting and stealing from the local population. They "tax" both legal businessmen, peasants, workers, and travelers, as well as 'license' illicit activities, such as smuggling drugs, arms, people, cars—for a fee. Some local leaders also organize criminal activities to enrich themselves personally or to support their forces with the proceeds. These forces may be no match militarily for even the conventional forces of the United States or others. However, they have a variety of local advantages or capabilities that jeopardize the interests of, and in some cases neutralize the advantages of, the ostensibly stronger liberal democracies.

The United States, and other democracies, have widespread interests in regions where these new actors and strategies are significant. No state in history has had so many of its citizens, assets, and raw materials located abroad, as does the United States. Many are in regions occupied by weak states and unregulated nonstate actors. Furthermore, these regions are used as sanctuaries, service and transit areas, for attacks inside the territory of the United States and other democracies.

Some of these areas also are of strategic concern. Some governments in these regions now have or soon will have weapons of mass destruction and a capability to deliver them regionally or to North America, Europe, and Japan. Should the United States or others become involved in local regional conflicts, these governments will be able to threaten various types of retaliation. Other political players will not be leaders of states trying to protect state interests. Instead they will be leaders of tribes, clans, fiefdoms, and criminals, or combinations of the above, many with little sense of representing the interests of a responsive citizenry.

Modern technologies also present new opportunities to damage adversaries. In addition to conventional terrorism–primarily bombs and guns–some political players also are taking an interest in what is called infowar or cyberwar. The critical infrastructures of the more developed societies–telecommunications, transportation, financial, and health systems, for example–are vulnerable to what some have termed "weapons of mass disruption." For example, interfering with the energy supply of the United States, or the water supply of a key region, such as Mexico City, would create havoc. As familiarity and expertise increase, the vulnerabilities of liberal societies–to protect their citizens and assets abroad, as well as at home–will become increasingly apparent.

Adversaries also are likely to realize that to develop, protect, and use effectively technologies of both mass destruction and disruption requires a secret infrastructure, that is, counterintelligence and covert action capabilities. The information revolution offers opportunities to identify those developing these techniques, it also offers myriad opportunities to hide and deceive. Conceivably the leaders of failing rogue, weak, quasi and micro states, about half of the governments of the world, as well as nonstate players–ethnonationalists, terrorists, and criminals–on their own or in collaboration with other political actors, also will have the capacity to use these instruments.[38]

The Role of Intelligence

World politics is in flux. There are still leaders, institutions, and instruments of traditional society at play. There are modern liberal states that in the main follow Clausewitzian rules. And, there are late modern trends in values, institutions, and techniques, operating in local, regional, and global contexts that undermine the power and influence of states and governments. Developing coherent policy and strategy in this era will not be easy.

What are the intelligence implications of this?

As is argued in this book (and others)[39] the four major elements of intelligence–collection, analysis, counterintelligence, and covert action–are symbiotically related to each other and to overall policy and strategy. In times of strategic and policy coherence, for example, during the era of post WWII containment, the mission and priorities of these elements of intelligence are usually defined more precisely, and resources are allocated to serve them. The elements tend to operate symbiotically, supporting each other to achieve strategic objectives. Even in the face of consensus on a centralized adversary, such as the Soviet bloc, this ideal state of affairs does not always obtain. As will be shown, a variety of variables or conditions affect the functioning and effectiveness of intelligence. In a period of global change, uncertainty, and complexity, such as we are now experiencing, it is especially difficult to develop coherent intelligence to achieve strategic objectives. Clear-cut intelligence guidelines from the policymakers are not always forthcoming. Even if they are, effective implementation will mean reorienting or recalibrating means to desired ends.

Collectors and analysts will be faced with understanding the competing value orientations of innumerable actors and the strategies and instruments they are using. These multiple players sometimes will operate in the same region, sometimes across regions, and sometimes globally. The challenge will be to determine the objectives of the many players, and the instruments they are using, both overt and covert, to achieve them. Whether or not the strategy of their political masters is coherent, collectors and analysts will be required to anticipate, if not predict, trends in threats and policy opportunities.

Counterintelligence and covert action, as they have in the past, will provide significant advantages to those who can use them effectively in the service of policy, as well as collection and analysis. The clandestine arts will not only be able to help identify threats and opportunities, but they can also serve as instruments of policy and strategy. Their work can protect their own societies and intelligence systems from being penetrated and manipulated, and provide capabilities to weaken adversaries and assist coalitions of friendly forces.

Counterintelligence

The primary mission of counterintelligence is to identify, neutralize, and exploit the intelligence or secret infrastructures of others. It is by its very nature both a defensive and offensive tool. Defensively, it collects and analyzes information about the intelligence and clandestine infrastructure of adversaries in order to protect military, diplomatic, technical, and intelligence secrets and to protect the state from being penetrated, deceived or manipulated by the secret activities of others. Offensively, counterintelligence helps to advance strategy and policy through knowledge about adversary intelligence and exploit an adversary's vulnerabilities to weaken or manipulate them to advantage. In reality, only the counterintelligence bureaucracies of liberal states are in a position to provide these defensive and offensive services both at home and abroad. The law enforcement, diplomatic, economic, and cultural tools of the state can work with the intelligence service in both parts of this counterintelligence mission. The private sector also can be helpful in preventing the penetration and utilization of its resources. But only counterintelligence, and particularly those parts of the counterintelligence community that operate abroad, has the mission and the capabilities to understand, defend against, and exploit an adversary's secret intelligence.

For example, in liberal society law enforcement usually is reactive, with good reason. Following the rule of law, it can and often does play a major role in identifying professional criminals, as well as terrorists, and proliferators of weapons of mass destruction. But the primary responsibility or mission of law enforcement in democracies is to burden–to arrest and prosecute past and current violators of their state's criminal laws. With exceptions, law enforcement agencies do not focus on violations of foreign laws. They have little impetus to develop the skills and knowledge for long-term, high-level strategic penetration and neutralization of secret adversary infrastructures, particularly foreign organizations, that may or may not be threatening.

Law enforcement also conducts its affairs largely in the open and is supposed to follow the rule of law. Both its operations and results are subject to public scrutiny. The information law enforcement personnel obtain very often must be presented in discovery proceedings and publicly in court to those being prosecuted. The mission, training, methods, procedures, and culture is not the same as those of intelligence or counterintelligence practitioners who usually are not required to observe foreign law and who do not operate in the glare of public scrutiny. This is not to say that skilled, knowledgeable law enforcement collectors (investigators) and analysts do not make a major contribution to identifying and neutralizing significant aspects of foreign criminal enterprises—particularly when they are targeted on their own state. However, they usually do not have the mission, the capabilities, the resources, and the skills necessary to reach major secret adversary alliances in the contemporary era.

Counterintelligence has a particularly significant role to play in responding to the complex coalitions that have developed between governmental and nonstate actors. The former head of (West) German clandestine operations in the BND recently pointed out that secret collaboration between criminal leaders and political authorities exists in many strategic regions, particularly in the former Soviet Union.[40] The participants in this political-criminal nexus employ numerous former and current intelligence officials to facilitate, solidify, and protect the relationship. Hence, it is extremely difficult for law enforcement outside the region, as well as inside the region, to penetrate these clandestine alliances and infrastructures. There are known instances where local law enforcement, and intelligence and security agencies have been penetrated by these political-criminal coalitions. Honest officials in these regions may be reporting to leaders or political masters who are part of the political-criminal nexus. This experienced senior German practitioner maintains that those best positioned to identify and analyze this challenge are foreign counterintelligence specialists. They are less constrained and more secure than local and foreign law enforcement and local security services. They have the skills, knowledge, and capabilities to understand foreign governmental and nonstate secret collaboration.

Similarly, it is very difficult for law enforcement to penetrate the relationship between criminals and other nonstate actors, such as groups using violence for political/religious purposes. Surveillance and penetration of these usually secret relationships take place both at home and abroad, and often in relatively inaccessible areas. The Eastern slopes of the Andes, the Bekka Valley in Lebanon, areas of Southwest, Southeast, and Central Asia that are not under any real control are difficult territory. When intelligence operations and capabilities of various state and nonstate actors are added to an already secret mix, determining what is really happening is very difficult indeed. Yet identifying the players, understanding their motives, and anticipating techniques that will be employed in these kinds of coalitions are the key challenges facing liberal democracies in the contemporary era.

In addition to helping collectors and analysts identify and protect their societies from adversary coalitions—the defensive counterintelligence function—used offensively counterintelligence can be of even greater strategic significance. Liberal democracies tend to pick up this weapon only in wartime or crisis. In times of peace and prosperity, it is usually on the back burner and the practitioners of offensive counterintelligence are rarely encouraged or supported. Occasionally, states that perceive themselves to be threatened use this instrument, as has Israel for example. Now, in the United States, there may be a greater incentive to use offensive counterintelligence. Contemporary threatening coalitions—criminal, terrorist, and rogue states–and the technologies available to them are very different from older "enemies" such as the Soviet Union. Offensive counterintelligence could exploit knowledge of secret adversary infrastructures to keep adversaries off-balance and to force them to divert critical resources to defend against the offensive thrusts of well-informed enemies. Offensive counterintelligence can also deceive and manipulate the leaders of hostile coalitions, as Western governments did repeatedly in WWII, and in the Gulf War.

Moreover, as it is difficult to arrest and imprison leaders of the adversarial coalition–witness the relatively few terrorists and criminal leaders serving time in jail–so other measures are needed. Just as counterintelligence has been used by democracies at various junctures in the twentieth century, it can be used to address the more difficult threats of the contemporary era. Although almost nothing has appeared publicly on this topic, counterintelligence means (employed by a combination of intelligence and law enforcement) has on occasion severely disrupted and undermined criminal organizations in the Western Hemisphere. Criminals are fundamentally distrustful of one another, with good reason. To exploit this predisposition, sowing distrust among the criminals and their political allies would cause them to spend a good deal of time assessing situations and individuals. By seizing the assets of one group and leading that group to believe that they were seized or betrayed by another, significant resources and energy were diverted. This action did not stop all major criminals in the area. It did, however, weaken them and destroy collaboration between some major political and criminal actors.

These are difficult and dangerous undertakings. Considerable care, planning, and oversight–from outside the ranks of the operatives–is necessary to ensure that programs to prevent or break the link between political, criminal, and terrorist groups are effective and consistent with the norms of liberal society. There will be risks. Violence, murder, and other capital crimes are routine for many of these players. There may be serious, even deadly reactions, if they feel threatened. But the alternatives—allowing for the development of cooperative relationships among a variety of rogues using techniques that threaten mass destruction or mass disruption and which threaten human rights, economic vitality, and democratic government—are not particularly desirable either.

Covert Action

Covert action means influencing conditions and behavior in ways that cannot be attributed to the sponsor. Covert action and counterintelligence both seek to manipulate and control adversaries. But among the major differences is that covert action usually is targeted on non-intelligence players, while counterintelligence is targeted at adversary intelligence operatives and their political masters. Covert action seeks to influence values, and more overt institutions and instruments. It also can target state and nonstate actors.

The twentieth century history of covert action, at least in the liberal democracies, has been varied. Both splendid triumphs and dismal failures can be found in abundance. Decidedly controversial in most liberal democracies, some have established elaborate oversight mechanisms for covert action in the latter part of the twentieth century, primarily to ensure that covert action was used by the state in a manner consistent with democratic values, and only partially to ensure that it was being used effectively.

Liberal democracies tend to develop a distaste for covert action in peacetime, opting instead for overt influences. Where states now publicly allocate resources and maintain mechanisms, such as the National Endowment for Democracy (U.S.), the Westminster Foundation (U.K.), and the German party foundations, to further democratic values, the rule of law, and economic development in other regions, some argue secret means have little utility and many disadvantages. However, many circumstances may be envisioned where covert action is a useful adjunct or complementary tool to overt instruments. As a general rule, covert action is useful when overt mechanisms will harm the beneficiaries of the covert action or assistance, and its sponsor. Both in war and peace, and in the gray area in between, many opportunities arise to harm adversary coalitions and further the interests of friendly coalitions, if the sponsor or direct beneficiary and operatives of specific activities are not acknowledged. As will be discussed in the book, sometimes deep cover will be needed. At other times a thin veneer will suffice.

To illustrate, part of a campaign to reduce the transnational influence of terrorists, proliferators, and other types of criminals and their political allies could be their public exposure. For example, if it became widely believed, based on facts, that a person, group, or cause was involved in what is generally considered a crime against humanity or international banditry, the person or group would probably be exposed to great scrutiny and unable to carry out their activities as before. If exposed, ethnonationalist, revolutionary, or religious leaders that deliberately use crime (such as trafficking in drugs, women and children, or radioactive materials) would become pariahs. Many states and international bodies would condemn them. They and their families would find it more difficult to obtain visas and travel, or to conduct business with legitimate firms and banks. Their propaganda would tend to be disregarded, if not discredited. It would become more difficult for them to act effectively.

Sometimes public exposure can be accomplished openly. If a government overtly maintains that a person or group has committed a certain act and uses the information from overt or clandestine collection to document this, it may be sufficient to minimize the behavior. There are advantages to doing so; however, there are also disadvantages. A covert exposure campaign, perhaps coordinated with a public campaign, would have a number of advantages. It would enable the release of damming pieces of information without indicating who obtained the information and how, to back up more general overt statements, or the denial of visas, etc. Even if there was not an overt campaign, books, articles, videos in a number of countries containing true information that a particular group or politician was consciously involved in and benefits from say organized crime, can have a significant impact on the reputation and influence of the perpetrator, his group, or cause.

Because it is very difficult to conduct an orchestrated campaign effectively by relying exclusively on overt means, only rarely is it possible to develop a near global governmental coalition to do so. Hence, an overt campaign, emanating from one or two capitals, would appear to be, and of course would be, the preoccupation of one or two governments "picking on" particular foreigners. These targets, often with well-placed political connections, also employ lawyers and overt and clandestine public relations specialists who would seek to undermine the charges. In addition, to make the charges credible and to sustain the campaign, in a legal proceeding the government will be tempted or pressured to release information that will endanger its sources–human and technical. Such an overt campaign also may discourage the enlistment of various private sector specialists and organizations. Some in the private sector may be encouraged by overt denunciation of the perpetrators and the information provided. Many others, particularly large institutions at home and abroad, will be unwilling to shoulder the potential legal burdens (for example, libel suits from the perpetrators), their being labeled as tools or lackeys of the United States government, or various threats of retaliation from the perpetrators. Washington's reputation and military umbrella may be important in some contexts, however, it does little to protect–politically and psychologically–foreign nongovernmental actors. Direct association with the American government could be a decided disadvantage.

Finally, a covert campaign would likely limit a government's legal exposure. The United States would not have to risk being drawn into the legal process by the perpetrators in the United States, for example in civil suits, or in other countries. Also, if the United States decided at some point to prosecute the perpetrator, the government may be placed in an awkward position by the detailed information that it had admitted into the public debate.

There are undisputable risks associated with the covert option. The government may be mistaken about the culpability of an individual. That individual will have little means of redress once the damage to his/her reputation has been accomplished. To minimize this risk, special oversight of programs designed to weaken adversaries through public exposure can be adapted.[41] The guidelines, procedures, and general techniques used can be reported to executive and legislative oversight bodies prior to and during such campaigns to minimize mistakes about culpability and to ensure that the measures taken are consistent with values of liberal societies.

There is also danger of retribution by the target. He may go after the managers of the campaign and those involved in the campaign against him. Certainly journalists and others have been targeted and killed many times, but usually irrespective of whether they were part of an overt and covert campaign.

Finally, there is a risk that the covert campaign will be exposed publicly. This would not be a major problem if there is good evidence about culpability, the techniques used in the campaign are consistent with democratic values, and there is a policy consensus about the aims of the program. Exposure of a covert campaign usually is harmful in the short term, but the likelihood, risks, and costs of such exposure are minimal if the covert programs are consistent with public perspectives of the threat, the covert action approval procedures have been followed correctly, and the means do not violate general standards of decency. As is discussed in this book, such campaigns of exposure have been successful in the past in many political contexts, for example, in discrediting political opponents for their affiliation with violence, extremism, and the intelligence activities of hostile governments.

This illustration of how covert action, and the earlier discussion of counterintelligence can be adapted to the contemporary environment is not intended to suggest that security can be enhanced primarily or exclusively by the clandestine arts. Indeed, the thesis of this book is that only rarely has this been the case. However, although branded publicly as "dirty tricks," liberal democracies such as the United States, except in crises or wartime, have been reluctant to do what is necessary to use these instruments strategically. For this to be accomplished in the complex contemporary era of world politics, there would have to be a consensus–domestically, and preferably among democracies–on the basic elements of the threat and on the utility of such instruments. Further, it would be prudent to ensure that such techniques are governed by guidelines consistent with liberal values, and that there will be oversight to ensure compliance with the rules and to ensure effectiveness.

As this consensus develops these clandestine instrumentalities also will have to be integrated into overall policy. (If there is no overall policy, clandestine instruments on their own are unlikely to have significant impact.) Even assuming consensus and integrated policy, in order for the instruments to be effective there is also the requirement for a secret and effective counterintelligence and covert action "infrastructure," described in subsequent chapters. Full-time professionals and part-time assets will have to be recruited, trained, and supported, both materially and psychologically, as they undertake this work. As the history of liberal democracies demonstrates, all too often these managers and specialists are not sought after, adequately trained, and rewarded. Hence, they are not prepared for or inclined to work for extended periods of time in these fields. However, some have been so motivated and stimulated by this work that they were prepared to undertake the risks–physical, political, and psychological–and to forgo salary and promotions. As is discussed in this book, their involvement in the clandestine arts, particularly counterintelligence, often puts them at loggerheads with colleagues inside their organizations who believe them to be counterproductive. Defensive counterintelligence practitioners are often viewed as "brakes" and "foot-draggers," impeding zealous collectors who are rewarded for recruiting agents or otherwise acquiring adversary secrets. There is sometimes merit to these criticisms. But postmortems of failed operations also often indicate that more prudent use of counterintelligence would have been effective.

Offensive counterintelligence and covert action specialists have an additional burden. They are exposed to particular risks, dealing as they do with gray areas, which can be subject to misunderstanding by inspectors or political overseers inside their own governments. These exceptional counterintelligence and covert action officers, who think strategically and offensively, are likely to be few in number, especially in peacetime when the quality of life, rather than life itself, usually is in jeopardy. As a result of swimming against the tide, it will not be difficult for adversaries to identify them and focus offensive operations against them. It should not be surprising if adversaries seek to neutralize them by indicating that those who practice offensive operations are "in their sights" and that someday they will be targeted for retribution. "You may not know how and when," but the veiled threat is there and sometimes will be used. Outside the profession, these complex equations rarely will be visible.

If democracies are to protect and advance their interests in the complex mix of traditional, modern, and late modern societies, they not only will need an underlying policy consensus and strategy, but also overt and covert programs designed to achieve significant results, and the infrastructure to carry out these programs. If they do, the clandestine arts may well be trump cards in the early twenty-first century.

Notes

1. In social science research the term "value orientation" would be more appropriate. See Florence Rockwood Kluckhohn, ed., *Variations in Value Orientation* (Evanston, IL: Row, Peterson, 1961); Clyde Kluckhohn, Edward C. Tolman, et.al., in Talcott Parsons and Edward A. Shils, eds., *Toward a General Theory of Action* (Cambridge, MA: Harvard University Press, 1951); Harold Dwight Lasswell, *Power and Society: A Framework for Political Inquiry* (London: Routledge and K. Paul, 1952).

2. On the emergence of modern attitudes and modernizing transformations, see Alex Inkeles and David Smith, *Becoming Modern: Individual Change in Six Developing Countries* (Cambridge, MA: Harvard University Press, 1974); Daniel Lerner, *The Passing of Traditional Society: Modernizing the Middle East* (Glencoe, IL: Free Press, 1958); and Haim Gerber, *The Social Origins of the Modern Middle East* (Boulder, CO: Lynne Rienner Publishers, 1987).

3. There is a considerable body of original literature available in English on the more famous writers. However, there is much more by Chinese, Persian, Arabic, Turkish, and other writers who were advisers, practitioners, and scholars, most of which has not been translated into English. However, summaries of their writings and references to their works are available in secondary studies.

The single most significant scholar who brought many of these references together and who distinguished between premodern and modern approaches to society, statecraft, and intelligence is Adda B. Bozeman. See Adda B. Bozeman, *Politics and Culture in International History*, Second Edition (New Brunswick, NJ: Transaction Publishers, 1994); see also Adda B. Bozeman, *Strategic Intelligence and Statecraft* (Washington, DC: Brassey's, 1992).

For a useful compendium of Chinese writing on intelligence over several millennia, see Ralf D. Sowyer, *The Tao of Spycraft* (Boulder, CO: Westview Press, 1998). Also useful is Frances Dvornik, *Origins of Intelligence Services* (New Brunswick, NJ: Rutgers University Press, 1974).

4. Sun-tzu, *The Art of War*, translated by Samuel B. Griffith (New York: Oxford, University Press, 1963).

5. Kautilya, *Kautilya's Arthasastra*, 8th Edition, translated by R. Shamasastry (Mysore: Mysore Print and Publishing House, 1967), chapters XI, XII, XIII, and XIV.

6. Nizam al-Mulk, *The Book of Government, or Rules for Kings*, translated by Hubert Darke (New Haven, CT: Yale University Press, 1960), pp. 66-91.

7. Major characteristics of Venetian statecraft are described especially in Bozeman, *Strategic Intelligence and Statecraft*, pp. 464-498, and in Garrett Mattingly, *Renaissance Diplomacy* (New York: Russell and Russell, 1970), chapters XXIV, and XXV.

8. For descriptions of indigenous tribes' diplomatic protocol, refer to accounts of their contact with colonizers in William Hickling Prescott, *History of the Conquest of Peru: With a Preliminary View of the Civilization of the Incas* (Boston: Phillips, Sampson and Co., 1857); William Hickling Prescott, *The Conquest of Mexico* (New York: E.P. Dutton & Co., 1909); and Bartolome de las Casas, *Las Antiguas Gentes del Peru* (Lima, Peru: Libreria Imprenta Gil, S. A., 1939).

9. For a brief discussion of contemporary collection sources, see the former senior British intelligence officer Michael Herman, *Intelligence Power in Peace and War* (New York: Cambridge University Press, 1996). There was some technical collection prior to the twentieth

century, particularly signaling through the use of fire and smoke, and the making and breaking of codes.

10. A classic on the history of the theory of self-determination and its effects on the traditional order can be found in Alfred Cobban, *National Self-Determination* (Chicago: University of Chicago Press, 1948). See also Robert H. Jackson, *Quasi-States: Sovereignty, International Relations, and the Third World* (Cambridge, U.K.: Cambridge University Press, 1990). Chapters 3 and 4 describe the revolutionary impact of the notions of self-determination in formerly colonized states. Also, Karl Deutsch, *Nation Building* (New York: Atherton Press, 1963); and Gianfranco Poggi, *The State: Its Nature, Development, and Prospects* (Stanford, CA: Stanford University Press, 1990).

11. For a general treatment of the differing rates of acceptance of the concept of modern nation statehood, see Barrington Moore, *Social Origins of Dictatorship and Democracy: Lord and Peasant in the Making of the Modern World* (Boston: Beacon Press, 1966); Dankwart A. Rustow, *A World of Nations* (Washington, DC: Brookings Institution, 1967); Rupert Emerson, *From Empire to Nation: The Rise to Self-Assertion of Asian and African Peoples* (Boston: Beacon Press, 1962); and Martin van Creveld, *The Rise and Decline of the State* (Cambridge, U.K.: Cambridge University Press, 1999), pp 264-335.

12. Martin van Creveld, *The Transformation of War* (New York: Free Press, 1991), pp. 33-62.

13. Martin van Creveld notes in *The Transformation of War* that most of the violent struggles in the postwar era were either anticolonial or internal wars. In these conflicts the trinity was diminished, if not abolished. There is no general history on the use of intelligence in these conflicts. There are, however, episodic studies and articles on aspects of intelligence in some of these conflicts. See, for example, the journals: *Intelligence and National Security*, and *The Journal of Intelligence and Counterintelligence*.

14. Roy Godson, "Intelligence and National Security," in Richard Shultz, Roy Godson, and George Quester, eds., *Security Studies for the 21st Century* (Washington, DC: Brassey's, 1997), pp. 323-353.

15. Francis Fukuyama, *The End of History and the Last Man* (New York: Free Press, 1992).

16. Samuel P. Huntington, *The Clash of Civilizations and the Remaking of World Order* (New York: Simon and Schuster, 1996).

17. Benjamin R. Barber, *Jihad vs. McWorld* (New York: Times Books, 1995).

18. Robert Kaplan, "The Coming Anarchy," in *The Atlantic Monthly* 273 (February 1994), pp. 44-46; see also Robert D. Kaplan, *The Ends of the Earth: A Journey at the Dawn of the 20th Century* (New York: Random House, 1996).

19. The U.S. has been the foremost proponent of identifying trends in world politics and their security implications. See, for example, the annual reports issued by the President entitled "A National Strategy for a New Century" (Washington, DC: The White House, Office of the President of the United States, 1997 and 1998). The Director of Central Intelligence and the Director of the Defense Intelligence Agency also have issued public annual threat assessments to the Congress in recent years which reflect similar concerns. G-8 statesmen such as Helmut Kohl, Tony Blair, and Boris Yeltsin have expressed similar views.

Several IGOs have also confirmed the trend, among them, the CSCE. See "CSCE Summit Seeks New Tasks in a Changed World," by Gregor Meyer, *Deutsche Presse-Agentur* (December 2, 1994), International News. Refer also to Brazilian President Fernando Henrique Cardoso's EU Summit welcoming comments in "Brazilian President Opens Latin America-EU Summit in Rio de Janeiro," in *BBC Summary of World Broadcasts* (June 30, 1999), from Radio Nacional da Amazonia, Brasilia, in Portuguese.

20. A number of authors note this emerging theme: Yale H. Ferguson and Richard W. Mansbach, *Polities: Authority, Identities, and Change* (Columbia: University of South Carolina Press, 1996); James N. Rosenau, *Along the Domestic-Foreign Frontier: Exploring Governance in a Turbulent World* (Cambridge, U.K.: Cambridge University Press, 1997); Thomas Risse-Kappen, ed., *Bringing Transnational Relations Back In: Non-State Actors, Domestic Structures, and International Institutions* (New York: Cambridge University Press, 1995); David Bobrow, ed., *International Studies Review: Prospects for International Relations: Conjectures about the Next Millennium* (Malden, MA: Blackwell Publishing, 1999); and Victor D. Cha, "Assessing the Impact of Globalization on the Study of International Security," *Journal of Peace Research*, 37, 5 (May 2000) pp. 391-413.

21. Peter F. Klaren and Thomas J. Bossert, eds., *Promise of Development: Theories of Change in Latin America* (Boulder, CO: Westview Press, 1986); and J. Samuel Valenzuela and Arturo Valenzuela, "Modernization and Dependency: Alternative Perspectives in the Study of Latin American Underdevelopment," *Comparative Politics* (July 1978), pp. 535-556.

22. Alan Swingewood, "Theorizing Culture: Weber, Simmel and Social Action," in Alan Swingewood, *Cultural Theory and the Problem of Modernity* (New York: St. Martin's Press, 1998), pp. 22-52. Those who have attempted to measure values shifts include: Ronald Inglehart, *The Silent Revolution: Changing Values and Political Styles Among Western Publics* (Princeton, NJ: Princeton University Press, 1977); Ronald Inglehart, *Modernization and Postmodernization: Cultural, Economic, and Political Change in 43 Societies* (Princeton, NJ: Princeton University Press, 1997); Robert D. Putnam, Robert Leonardi, and Raffaella Y. Nanetti, *Making Democracy Work: Civic Traditions in Modern Italy* (Princeton, NJ: Princeton University Press, 1993); and Russell Hardin, *One for All: The Logic of Group Conflict* (Princeton, NJ: Princeton University Press, 1995).

For an interesting attempt to explicitly define postmodernism, and its implications for international relations and security studies, see the monograph by British diplomat Robert Cooper, *The Post Modern State and the World Order* (London, U.K.: Demos, 1996).

23. James N. Rosenau, *Along the Domestic-Foreign Frontier: Exploring Governance in a Turbulent World* (Cambridge, U.K.: Cambridge University Press, 1997).

24. Johan Leman, ed., *The Dynamics of Emerging Ethnicities: Immigrant and Indigenous Ethnogenesis in Confrontation* (New York: Peter Lang, 1998); Richard G. Fox and Orin Starn, eds., *Between Resistance and Revolution: Cultural Politics and Social Protest* (New Brunswick NJ: Rutgers University Press, 1997); Faye Ginsburg, "From Little Things, Big Things Grow," in Fox and Starn, *Between Resistance and Revolution*, pp. 118-144; and Eleanor Leacock and Richard Lee, *Politics and History in Band Societies* (Cambridge, U.K.: Cambridge University Press, 1982), especially pp. 307-490. For more information on The Fourth World Movement, see The Center for World Indigenous Studies' website at *http://www.cwis.org/fourthw.html.*

25. See, for example: Benedict Anderson, *Imagined Communities, Revised Edition* (New York: Verso, 1991); Thomas Hylland Eriksen, "Formal and Informal Nationalism," *Journal of Ethnic and Racial Studies* 16:1 (January 1993), pp. 1-25; Charles Kupchan, ed., *Nationalism and Nationalities in the New Europe* (Ithaca, NY: Cornell University Press, 1995); Ted Robert Gurr, *Minorities At Risk* (Washington, DC: United States Institute of Peace Press, 1993); and Ted Robert Gurr, "People Against States: Ethnopolitical Conflict and the Changing System," *International Studies Quarterly* 38 (September 1994), pp. 347-377.

26. For projections on the landscape of the globe given the potential of regionalism to rearrange world order, see Zalmay Kahalilzad and Ian O. Lesser, *Sources of Conflict in the 21ˢᵗ Century: Regional Futures and U.S. Strategy* (Santa Monica, CA: Rand Corporation, 1998); Edward D. Mansfield and Helen V. Milner, "The New Wave of Regionalism," *International Organization* 53, 3 (Summer 1999), pp. 589-627. On the impact of regionalism on Russia, see

Martin Nicholson, *Towards a Russia of the Regions*, Adelphi Paper 330 (New York: Oxford University Press, 1999).

27. On ethnification, refer to Jonathan Friedman, *Cultural Identity and Global Process* (Thousand Oaks, CA: Sage Publications, 1994), p. 234; Richard W. Mansbach, *The Global Puzzle* (Boston: Houghton Mifflin, 1997); and John T. Rourke, ed., *Taking Sides: Clashing Views on Controversial Issues in World Politics* (Guilford, CT: Dushkin Publishing Co., 1998).

28. For an overview on the subject of cosmopolitanism, refer to: Akhil Gupta and James Ferguson, "Beyond 'Culture': Space, Identity, and the Politics of Difference," *Cultural Anthropology* 7,1 (1992), pp. 6-23; Michael Featherstone, ed., *Global Culture: Nationalism, Globalization, and Modernity* (London, U.K.: Sage, 1990); Bruce Robbins, *Secular Vocations: Intellectuals, Professionalism, Culture* (London, U.K.: Verso, 1993); and Bruce Robbins, *Feeling Global: Internationalism in Distress* (New York: New York University Press, 1999). For detailed journalistic accounting of contemporary cosmopolitanism see, for example: Thomas L. Friedman, *The Lexus and the Olive Tree* (New York: Farrar, Straus & Giroux, 1999); and Robert Kaplan, *An Empire Wilderness* (New York: Random House, 1998).

For scholars skeptical of cosmopolitanism, see Louisa Schein, "Forged Transnationality and Oppositional Cosmopolitanism," in Michael Peter Smith and Luis Eduardo Guarnizo, eds., *Transnationalism from Below* (New Brunswick, NJ: Transaction Publishers, 1998), pp. 291-313; and Pheng Cheah and James Clifford, "Mixed Feelings," in Bruce Robbins, ed., *Cosmopolitics: Thinking and Feeling Beyond Nation* (Minneapolis: University of Minnesota Press, 1998), pp. 362-370.

29. On the philosophy and politics of deconstructionism, see, for example: Michel Foucault, in Colin Gordon, ed., *Power/Knowledge: Selected Interviews and Other Writings, 1972-1977* (New York: Pantheon Books, 1980); and Richard Rorty, *Philosophy and the Mirror of Nature* (Princeton, NJ: Princeton University Press, 1979). For secondary sources, see Andrew Ross, ed., *Universal Abandon?: The Politics of Postmodernism* (Minneapolis: University of Minnesota Press, 1988); Robert Hollinger, *Postmodernism and the Social Sciences: A Thematic Approach* (Thousand Oaks, CA: Sage Publications, 1994). For how postmodernism may be affecting international relations, see Robert J. Beck, Anthony Clark Arend, and Robert D. Vander Lugt, eds., "The New Stream," *International Rules: Approaches from International Law and International Relations* (New York: Oxford University Press, 1996), pp. 227-252.

30. For a discussion on economic impact of globalization on the state, see Geoffrey Garrett, "Global Markets and National Politics: Collision Course or Virtuous Circle?," *International Organization* 52, 4 (Autumn 1998), pp. 787-824; Alan Scott, ed., *The Limits of Globalization: Cases and Arguments* (New York: Routledge, 1997); and Michael Peter Smith and Luis Eduardo Guarnizo, eds., *Transnationalism from Below* (New Brunswick, NJ: Transaction Publishers, 1998).

On the political impact of economic globalization on the state, see Dani Rodrik, *Has Globalization Gone Too Far?* (Washington, DC: Institute for International Economics, March 1997); Martin van Creveld, *The Rise and Decline of the State* (Cambridge, U.K.: Cambridge University Press, 1999); and Susan Strange, *The Retreat of the State: The Diffusion of Power in the World Economy* (Cambridge, U.K.: Cambridge University Press, 1996).

For a contrarian viewpoint on the declining power of the state, see Gary Burtless, Robert Z. Lawrence, Robert E. Litan, and Robert J. Shapiro, *Globophobia: Confronting Fears About Open Trade* (Washington, DC: Brookings Institution, 1998); and Linda Weiss, *Myth of the Powerless State* (Cambridge, U.K.: Polity Press, 1998).

31. Sociological and organizational literature in the earlier part of the twentieth century distinguished between more formal hierarchical institutions and informal networks. A few, such as Harold Lasswell, Herbert Simon, and Karl Deutsch applied these ideas to world politics. One of

the growth nodes of recent international relations and security studies focuses on the impact of economic and social change on conflict. Although still largely deductive and speculative, it points to the role of nonstate formal and particularly of informal actors. See, for example, John Arquilla and David Ronfeld, eds., *In Athena's Camp* (Santa Monica, CA: RAND, 1997), especially Part III.

32. Charles W. Kegley and Eugene R. Wittkopf, *World Politics: Trend and Transformation* (New York: St. Martin's Press, 1981). See also Cheryl Shanks, Harold K. Jacobson, and Jeffrey H. Kaplan, "Inertia and Change in the Constellation of International Organization, 1981-1992," *International Organization* 50, 4 (Autumn 1996), pp. 593-627.

33. Evidence for the shift of state control out of the hands of the modern nation state can be found by examining trends in world trade and finance, the percent of state GNP derived from the activity of transnational corporations, the percent of economic capital within a state economy furnished by foreign direct investment, and the rise of off-shore financial activity and Euro-currency markets. For less modern states, one of the best indicators of this trend is the percentage of capital flow provided from sources outside of the state, and particularly of the percentage of that capital flow which is provided by private sources. Refer to discussions of such trends in *Global Development Finance* (Washington, DC: World Bank, 1997), pp. 3-9; *Global Development Finance* (Washington, DC: World Bank, 1999), pp. 23-67; as well as *Private Capital Flows to Developing Countries* (New York: Oxford University Press for the World Bank, 1997).

34. According to President Clinton, criminal syndicates "drain up to $750 billion a year from legitimate economies. That sum exceeds the combined GNP of more than half of the nations in this room [the United Nations General Assembly]." Remarks of the President of the United States to the 52nd Session of the United Nations General Assembly, New York, September 23, 1997. See also United Nations Development Program, *Human Development Report* (New York: Oxford University Press, 1999), p. 5. It is, of course, extremely difficult to estimate with precision the economic impact of organized crime. Some U.S. and foreign academics are skeptical of U.S. and U.N. figures.

35. Jonas Widgren, "Multilateral Co-operation to Combat Trafficking in Migrants and the Role of International Organizations," reproduced in *Trends in Organized Crime*, 2, 2, (Winter 1996), p. 67.

36. The G-8, in general, and the United States, in particular, have been at the forefront of recognizing the threat of political criminal collaboration. See, for example, "A Global Forum on Fighting Corruption: Safeguarding Integrity Among Justice and Security Officials," hosted by Vice President Albert Gore, *Final Conference Report*, Washington, DC, 1999, in *Trends in Organized Crime* 5, 1 (Fall 1999). The journal *Trends in Organized Crime* regularly carries articles on political-criminal collaboration and measures to minimize the trend.

37. One of the best summaries of these threats can be found in the testimony of Lt. General Patrick M. Hughes, Director of the Defense Intelligence Agency, "Global Threats and Challenges: The Decade Ahead," U.S. Senate, Committee on Armed Services, *Hearing on Current and Future Worldwide Threat to the National Security of the United States*, February, 1999. Another summary can be found in U.S. Commission on National Security/21st Century, "New World Coming: American Security in the Twenty-First Century," September 15, 1999, (http://www.nssg.gov/Reports/New_World_Coming/new_world_coming.htm).

38. For a summary of the U.S. perspective on the current and anticipated threat, and for the recognition that much remains to be done to meet that challenge, see the FBI's Michael Vatis, Director of the National Infrastructure Protection Center, *Hearing*, U.S. Senate, Committee of

the Judiciary, Subcommittee on Technology and Terrorism, Washington, DC, October 6, 1999. See also Martin van Creveld, *The Transformation of War* (New York: Free Press, 1991.)

39. See, for example, Abram N. Shulsky and Gary J. Schmitt, *Silent Warfare: Understanding the World of Intelligence,* 2nd Edition (Washington, DC: Brassey's, 1993).

40. Volker Foertsch, *Counterintelligence to Counter Transnational Organized Crime*, Working Group on Organized Crime (Washington, DC: National Strategy Information Center, 2000).

41. Since the 1970s, the United States has pioneered the most extensive mechanisms for overseeing intelligence, in both the Executive and Legislative branches. Little has been written about Executive oversight, such as the work of the President's Foreign Intelligence Advisory Board and the Intelligence Oversight Board. There is, however, extensive literature on many aspects of contemporary Congressional oversight.

Preface

A SENIOR CIA OFFICIAL, reflecting on the conduct of his profession in the Agency's halcyon days of the fifties, suggested that its reality could only be conveyed by fiction. This is a common notion and one that tends to perpetuate the romantic image of intelligence. Without denigrating either that gentleman or the le Carrés and Deightons of the world, the opinion does not hold up.

As William Hood, an experienced practitioner of the clandestine arts, has written,

> . . . spying [is] half waiting and another thirty percent report writing and record keeping. In a good month, a case man could count himself lucky to spend the few remaining hours dealing with agents and contact men. The time committed to stakeouts, peering out of [observation posts], waiting for a safe house telephone to ring, and typing reports is such a significant part of espionage that [he] . . . never understood why even the novelists with some professional experience never thought to mention it.[1]

Although the world of intelligence has its unique aspects, it still reflects and is animated by most of the same rules of human and bureaucratic behavior that affect other endeavors. In short, intelligence may be arcane but is not practiced in a cultural vacuum.

To gain understanding of intelligence, we need no longer confine ourselves to the creative writing genre. Over the last twenty years, serious study about intelligence has grown enormously. The literature on intelligence in English alone is voluminous, and increases steadily. A remarkable number of historical and conceptual studies have made their way into print in recent years, surely far more than even the most optimistic intelligence scholars in the past would have thought possible. The "hidden dimension" of diplomatic history, statecraft, and military affairs is far less hidden today. With more and more material being made available from various government archives around the world, this trend shows no sign of slowing. Although the intelligence equivalents of Sun Tsu or Clausewitz have yet to appear, the study of intelligence is well beyond the early postwar writings of former practitioners or of the journalistic exposés that dominated the field initially.[2]

That said, our knowledge of two of the four fundamental elements of intelligence, counterintelligence and covert action, is sketchy at best. Compared with the elements of collection and analysis, counterintelligence and covert action have received far less systematic and careful study—even while they remain the subject of radical polemics and provide grist for conspiracy buffs and screenwriters. It is my hope that this book will provide some badly needed balance.

Counterintelligence is identifying, neutralizing, and exploiting the intelligence activities of others. Counterintelligence protects a state's secrets from the prying eyes and ears of adversaries. If our adversaries learned these diplomatic, military, technological, and intelligence secrets, the United States would be seriously disadvantaged. Effective counterintelligence also would enable the United States to manipulate hostile states and organizations to our advantage.

Covert action is influencing events in other parts of the world without revealing or acknowledging involvement. Covert action, used skillfully and as part of well-designed policies, could provide the United States with a decisive and winning edge in a dangerous world.

The book begins by briefly discussing why counterintelligence and covert action are in many respects neglected elements of U.S. intelligence and, through the use of historical examples, what the consequences of such neglect can be. Chapters 2 and 3 are accounts of the evolution of counterintelligence and covert action as understood and conducted in the United States from the end of World War II to the present. These are not definitive histories of the subject. Indeed, given the lack of scholarly writing on the subject and the difficulties in accessing most official records, it is impossible to write such a history at present. Nevertheless, the main contours of the story are visible.

With this as background, the book then lays out the "ideal" principles and techniques that, if followed, lead to effective covert action and counterintelligence. These principles are not drawn exclusively from either the U.S. experience or the cold war period. There are invaluable lessons to be learned from world intelligence history, and I have benefited enormously from the wealth of scholarship about other times and places. At the heart of this book, then, is an implicit comparison of how two elements of intelligence have been practiced in the United States, and how they might be conducted in the future to enhance American security. The book concludes with an explanation of the gap between the "ideal" and the contemporary American practice of counterintelligence and covert action, how the gap could be narrowed, and what its continued existence portends about the country's ability to meet the security challenges of the future.

This book could not have been written without the aid of various groups and individuals. My knowledge and understanding of intelligence has been dramatically improved by the members of the Consortium for the Study of Intelligence, as well as by scores of scholars and practitioners from various intelligence agencies who participated in colloquia and seminars over the years, among them Adda Bozeman, Angelo Codevilla, Ken deGraffenreid, Sam Halpern, Walter Jajko, Noel Jones, George Kalaris, Merrill Kelly, David Major, Ernest May, John Millis, James Nolan, Sam Papich, Ray Rocca, Herbert Romerstein, Gary Schmitt, Paul Seabury, Ted Shackley, Abram Shulsky, Richard Shultz, Larry Sternfield, Hugh Tovar, and Ray Wannall. Elizabeth Anderson, Chris Swenson, and Tamara Wittes also provided invaluable research assistance.

A number of foundation executives, publishers, and editors were encouraging and invaluable in their help; among them are Michael Joyce, Hillel Fradkin, David Kennedy, Dick Ware, Tony Sullivan, Les Lenkowsky, Roger Kaplan, Frank Margiotta, Don McKeown, Connie Buchanan, James McCargar, Jeff Berman, and the late Frank Barnett. I am grateful as well to the many people whom I met while working as a consultant to the U.S. government on intelligence matters, notably my colleagues at the National Security Council, and the President's Foreign Intelligence Advisory Board, as well as at the Central Intelligence Agency, the Federal Bureau of Investigation, and the Department of Defense. They gave me insight into the workings of government intelligence and patiently listened to an outsider's questions and suggestions.

Finally, this book could not have been written without my wife's encouragement, and equally important, her intellectual and professional skill.

None of these people, of course, is responsible for the propositions and arguments put forward here. While they all helped directly and indirectly, the responsibility is mine alone. My overall objective is to stimulate thinking about how to improve the long-term effectiveness of U.S. intelligence.

1

NEGLECTED ELEMENTS IN AMERICAN INTELLIGENCE

WHAT IS INTELLIGENCE? This is a question that has many answers.[1] There is no scholarly or professional consensus regarding the theoretical definition of intelligence. One way of defining the subject is to set aside theory and look at the ways in which states practice intelligence in modern times. This approach also leads to different answers. To avoid confusion, it is useful to lay out the basic characteristics of the subject matter. Intelligence is information that is acquired, exploited, and protected by the activities of organizations specifically established for that purpose. Allowing for differences in government systems, political history, and security interests, there appear to be four distinct elements (functions or disciplines) of intelligence: collection, analysis, counterintelligence, and covert action.

A particular state may choose not to adopt this division of intelligence labor or may choose not to perform all four functions. But the decision to forgo or play down one or more of them does not alter the operational logic that associates each with the other, or the fact that the absence of one or more, or poor implementation, will likely impair a state's ability to fulfill its national security requirements. Full-service intelligence consists of four elements.

Collection is the gathering of valued information, much of it by clandestine means. Not all information is considered intelligence—only that which is determined to be valuable by policymakers or intelligence managers. Nor are there any rules to distinguish what is valuable from what is not. Governments take an interest in information only when it relates to something they wish to accomplish, deter, or affect, and different governments want different things at different times. Hence there is no predetermined body of information that can be called intelligence, although there are certain types of information that are valued by almost all governments all the time.

Broadly speaking, intelligence is gathered from three sources: open, technical, and human sources. The information derived from each source has its strengths and its weaknesses.[2]

Analysis is the processing of information, and its end products. Usually intelligence is acquired in "raw" form, for example, a report from an agent or a photograph of a weapon. During analysis, it is processed for intelligibility and meaning. Analysis entails sifting, screening, comparing information with other data, and, ultimately, including it within a larger intelligence context.

Analyzed data can be broad or specific, ranging anywhere from reports on immediate security concerns to predictions about long-term future trends and events.[3]

Counterintelligence, as practiced by most states, is the effort to protect their secrets, to prevent themselves from being manipulated, and (sometimes) to exploit the intelligence activities of others for their own benefit. To protect their secrets, states rely, in part, on security procedures and countermeasures.

Security procedures, which may be more or less passive, involve limiting the number of people with access to secrets, screening those people for signs of unreliability, and instituting accounting systems to trace losses. Countermeasures are security procedures to protect against specific tactics used by foreign intelligence services. Counterintelligence, by contrast, involves active efforts to identify, neutralize, and possibly exploit foreign intelligence services.[4]

Covert action, or, to use the British term, *special political action*, is the attempt by a government or group to influence events in another state or territory without revealing its own involvement. Seeking to influence others is, of course, the stuff of politics and foreign policy. People and governments rarely reveal exactly what they seek to accomplish or how they intend to do it. Their actions are to one degree or another secret (hidden) or covert (disguised).

Covert action is really an American term-of-art that came into use after World War II. Other states do not use the term, even if many at some point seek to exert influence in a covert way. In any case, most states do not make a sharp distinction between overt and covert behavior. While they may create special components within the bureaucracy to deal with some aspects of covert tradecraft, they regard the exertion of influence, with varying degrees of secrecy, as a normal function of statecraft.

Generally, covert action activities fall into one of four areas: propaganda, political action, paramilitary operations, and intelligence assistance.

* *Propaganda* uses words, symbols, and other psychological techniques to influence foreign developments. Most propaganda in the latter half of the twentieth century has been directed at influencing the mass media.
* *Political action* uses political means (advice, agents of influence, information, material support) to influence foreign events. Such efforts can be directed at foreign governments, nongovernmental entities such as labor, intellectual, and religious movements, and nonstate actors such as ethnic groups and criminal cartels.
* *Paramilitary activity* involves the use of force. This includes support for or defense against terrorism, resistance movements, insurgents, other unconventional forces, and the use of force to deny or degrade significant information to adversaries.
* *Intelligence assistance* aids the intelligence activities of another group or government beyond normal liaison. It attempts to influence events or decisions in other countries by training personnel, providing material or technical assistance, or passing information and ideas to achieve intended effects.

Integrating the Elements

The four elements of intelligence can be distinguished by function. Intelligence professionals usually specialize in one area, and experience shows that even those who practice several specialties may tend to favor one over the others.[5] In fact, the elements of intelligence are interdependent. If one is weakened or eliminated, the others are likely to be adversely affected. Counterintelligence and covert action rely for their effectiveness on collection and analysis, and vice versa, each in turn dependent on policy for its impetus and direction.

This symbiosis is not always apparent, nor is its effect necessarily immediate or absolute. But if a state is to develop an effective intelligence system, it must recognize this relationship and understand it as highly complex and often tumultuous.

Analysis and collection depends on policy to specify its goals. Policymakers set policy and determine priorities for collection and analysis. Analysts and collectors may not always adhere to policymakers' priorities or answer the questions policymakers consider most relevant. If they stray too far from policymakers' concerns, they risk losing access to senior officials and having their resources curtailed.

Many intelligence analysts depend heavily on the clandestine services for their raw materials. Although they can meet some of their enormous need for information from open sources, they also rely on human and technical collection. This is primarily what distinguishes them from nonintelligence analysts. It is what makes them unique.

In less obvious ways, analysts and collectors also benefit from covert action. Covert action channels are often unique sources of highly prized information. Why? Because when a government wants to influence a foreign society, it tries to recruit agents from its top echelons. For a state to exert influence, particularly through subtle political maneuvers, its intelligence service must know a great deal about the values and expectations of the target society. Highly placed agents, sources or "assets," are more capable of producing such information, which can be of great value to analysts.

Potentially valuable human sources often hesitate to hand over prized information unless they are persuaded that it will be put to good use. While there are those who spy or give away information for base rewards such as money, others do so because they agree with the policy of the foreign power, or would like to change the policy of their own government. Wanting to influence events in their own country or elsewhere, they find themselves positioned to translate their desires into effective action. In their minds, the end is worth the risk.[6] Sources providing information for reasons of principle enhance the flow of intelligence to the foreign power, boosting analysis as well as collection and counterintelligence.

There is, of course, a potential disadvantage to collection and analysis based exclusively or in large part on information derived from covert action assets. Agents can be self-serving. They tend, naturally, to report information that bolsters their own reputations or encourages the foreign intelligence service in a particular direction. Many collectors and analysts have adopted the principle that information from a covert action asset must be verified by an independent source.

All areas of intelligence benefit from counterintelligence. Counterintelligence protects collection and aims to ensure that hostile intelligence services do not mislead or manipulate collection from open, technical, and human sources. Counterintelligence needs guidance from policymakers. Counterintelligence cannot protect everything. Policymakers need to determine what to defend, what to neutralize, and what to manipulate. This is particularly important to the United States, whose collection task is massive and global. The United States has had to develop extensive technical collection systems to overcome these problems. Enforced reliance on a single type of source makes the United States vulnerable to technical manipulation of the sort practiced by the now-defunct Soviet Union or Iraq. Much of the latter's nuclear weapons program went undetected by American technical sources in the late 1980s.[7]

To prevent themselves from being misled by technical manipulation, analysts and collectors need the support of effective counterintelligence. Counterintelligence can protect collectors from double agents or penetration agents passing calculatedly biased information to distort analysis. Similarly, covert action operations need the protection of counterintelligence. Otherwise, they run the risk of penetration, manipulation, or exposure by hostile foreign services. This often happened to many British and U.S. operations against Communist governments during the cold war—a story that will be told in detail later.

Collection is heavily reliant on the other intelligence areas and on policy. Policymakers, influenced by analysis, set the priorities. They can pose the questions the collectors are to answer. (Like analysts, collectors may not always answer policymakers' questions, and if they fail to produce, or if they stray too far from assigned targets, they may be cut off from budget resources.) Analysts also levy requirements on collectors; like policymakers, analysts ask questions that collectors presumably do their best to answer. And, as already noted above, collection depends heavily on counterintelligence. The deception of collectors by rival intelligence services is a common occurrence that counterintelligence can and should forestall. At the same time, collection is enhanced by covert action programs that, if properly protected by counterintelligence, lead to more and better intelligence. Counterintelligence benefits from good overall collection and analysis, because it too needs information about the objectives, priorities, and concerns of targets.

Covert action programs, of course, require constant counterintelligence for protection. An additional reason for a close association among covert action and the other intelligence areas is command and control. Direction is almost impossible if the areas are not integrated in a single organization under the same leader. If they remain separate and pursue their respective objectives independently, competition for agents abroad is likely to lead to chaos. That fate befell some British covert action and collection operations in World War II and some early postwar U.S. operations. Yet another reason for the close association of covert action with other intelligence areas, specifically collection, is that in many countries those who by virtue of their position and status would make good agents of influence may already be the target of collectors. The latter, in turn, are quite likely to be charged with the development of a covert action infrastructure. Good collection often lies behind successful covert action.

The essence of the symbiotic relationship comes down to this: covert action, counterintelligence, analysis, and collection benefit the *entire* intelligence system, and at the same time the entire intelligence system benefits *each* of them.

If one attempts to define, explain, or alter a national intelligence system at a particular time, it is important to consider the relationship among the areas of intelligence as well as the relationship of each area to policy. Are these relationships understood and taken into account by most practitioners, particularly those in positions of authority? If that is not the case, and if, for example, the intelligence community is torn by turf wars or lulled into complacency, then an ideal, effective, full-service intelligence system will be elusive.

Neglected Elements

Of the four elements of intelligence, collection and analysis have historically caused less consternation in the United States than covert action and counterintelligence. The latter activities are far more likely to generate bold headlines and heated public debate. One reason is that collection and analysis are seen as useful components of rational decision-making. In business or at home, a citizen will routinely collect information, assess the information at hand, and then seek a decision based on the best available analysis. Although collection and analysis done by governments are far more complex and involve esoteric methodologies and special tradecraft, the general concept of collection and analysis is not totally foreign to the average person.

In contrast, counterintelligence and covert action are more arcane activities. Most people don't spend time ferreting out illicit behavior or engaging in elaborate subterfuge. Citizens in liberal democracies generally have the luxury of treating other individuals in a relatively open, honest fashion. In public perceptions, collection and analysis may simply appear less "underhanded" than covert action and counterintelligence. Probably the greatest historical contribution the United States has made to the intelligence business is the innovation and expansion of collection by technical means. A satellite whizzing through space taking photos of a factory below seems infinitely more civilized than suborning a plant manager with money or sex. American reliance on technical means for most of its collection has left the impression that intelligence collection is a relatively "clean" business.

That intelligence analysis is looked upon in the United States as something of an academic endeavor may have heightened this impression. Intentionally insulated from politics and policymakers during much of the post–World War II period, intelligence analysts seek to provide scholarly, objective assessments of the world and world events, their ultimate and higher goal being to keep U.S. government officials "honest" by providing analyses of the security environment as it is, not as administration officials want it to be. With social science as their model, intelligence analysts often feel more at home in the groves of academe, not back alleys and the halls of power.[8]

Compared with periodic efforts to improve analysis and collection, pleas for bolstering American covert action or counterintelligence capabilities are generally greeted with skepticism and suspicion. This can be traced, in part, to the breakdown of the foreign policy consensus in the postwar period. The executive and congressional investigations of U.S. intelligence operations and the ensuing media coverage have sometimes served to intensify negative attitudes. A survey of the reports of two major investigations, the Church Committee and Pike Committee reports in 1976, indicates that the emphasis was on real and purported abuses of "the rights of Americans" by U.S. intelligence, for the most part by counterintelligence.[9] The committees' second major concern was with U.S. covert action operations. Only three percent of the Church report focused on analysis and collection.[10] Both counterintelligence and covert action, as practiced in the United States, have had their share of dubious, and, in a few cases illicit, activities. Even so, there was little balance in the Church Committee's investigation: few successful operations were chronicled, and no real effort was made to match covert action and counterintelligence capabilities to the requirements generated by an assessment of national security interests. As one British scholar noted, the Church Committee report and the intelligence literature of that period tended "to ignore or downplay the threats that intelligence services are designed to counter," and instead focused "on the 'domestic' dimension of intelligence."[11]

In the context of counterintelligence, that provoked a massive debate about the rights and civil liberties of American citizens. The effectiveness and utility of U.S. counterintelligence in neutralizing, let alone manipulating and exploiting, the concerted, sophisticated intelligence collection effort then being run by the KGB, the GRU (Soviet military intelligence), and their allied secret services were virtually ignored.

Similarly, covert action was seen primarily as a secret foreign policy tool of presidents (or, worse, "rogue" agencies) that violated the norms of democratic accountability. Further, without popular assent and proper congressional oversight, covert action was being used for toppling regimes, assassination attempts, and other such purposes that arguably ran counter to the country's moral conscience. Yet, left largely unaddressed was the question of the effectiveness or ineffectiveness of covert action in support of U.S. foreign policy and defense objectives. Samuel Huntington has remarked about this era's discussion of intelligence issues in general and covert action in particular, "In a different atmosphere . . . congressional committees investigating the CIA might have been curious as to why the agency failed so miserably in its efforts to assassinate Lumumba and Castro. But in 1975 no one was interested in the inability of the agency to do what it was told to do, but only in the immorality of what it was told to do."[12] In short, "the arrogance of power was superseded by the arrogance of morality."[13]

Certainly, liberal democratic values are not easily squared with counterintelligence and covert action. But the tensions inherent in this relationship were greatly exacerbated in the early and middle 1970s by the sudden and sharp reordering of the nation's foreign policy perspective. The national security goal that had governed U.S. policy since the start of the cold war—the containment of Communism—was challenged, and with it the various means—military, intelligence, and so forth—that had been built and employed in its support.[14] Not surprisingly, many scholars of intelligence reflected this new and highly critical perspective.[15]

By the late 1970s, events abroad such as the Soviet invasion of Afghanistan and the hostage crisis in Iran had left the American public with a keen sense of the relative decline of U.S. prestige and power; the United States still faced real threats that needed to be addressed. Congressional interest in tightening control over intelligence waned. Proposals emanating from the Church Committee and other congressional quarters to draft a detailed "charter" governing the scope and conduct of the intelligence community's activities were dropped altogether. Nevertheless, the critical perspectives and attitudes about counterintelligence and covert action remained "on the books." The need for the exercise of American power in its various forms was increasingly acknowledged. But, absent a coherent justification for strong covert action and counterintelligence, the view persisted that they are, at best, necessary evils.[16]

Next to collection and analysis, most policymakers and members of Congress have tended to treat covert action and counterintelligence as the "stepchildren" of intelligence. This imbalance was perpetuated in much of the scholarly literature on intelligence, in spite of the flood of material on these subjects that has reached the public domain in recent years.[17] The arguments are of more than academic importance. Historically, those states that have maintained effective covert action and counterintelligence capabilities have gained significant advantages over states that have not.

Counterintelligence

There is no shortage of examples of the negative consequences of ineffective counterintelligence. A state's failure to protect its diplomatic and military secrets from the collection efforts of foreign intelligence services can be disastrous. If an enemy learns these secrets it can damage a nation's strategy, or even neutralize it completely. The story of the U.S. entry into World War I is a striking illustration of this point.

From 1915 on, Imperial Germany sought to prevent the United States from entering the war on the British and French side. At the outset of hostilities, the British cut Germany's transatlantic cable. Thereafter German communications had to travel by radio or over foreign cables that happened to run through British waters, thereby allowing the British to tap the cables and intercept coded German messages. Through the work of "Room 40" (the British Admiralty's code-breaking unit) and the acquisition of German code books elsewhere, they were able to decipher many German messages.

The Germans, ignoring the possible compromise of their code materials and convinced of the inviolability of their ciphers, remained blind to the fact that British intelligence was reading many of their secret military and diplomatic communications. Nor did German intelligence apparently think it necessary to verify whether this confidence was well placed by penetrating British intelligence. In 1917, German foreign minister Zimmermann sent a coded telegram to the German embassy in Washington to be forwarded to Mexico City proposing a Mexican-German alliance against the United States. British intelligence intercepted the telegram and thus helped frustrate Germany's goal of keeping the United States out of the war by proving Germany's hostile intent toward the United States. This operation assisted Britain's own efforts to bring the United States into the conflict on the Allied side.[18]

The British faced a delicate problem in exposing the German scheme to the Americans without revealing their penetration and mastery of German communications. To protect their valuable asset from the Americans, the British apparently stole another copy of the Zimmermann telegram from the Mexican Telegraph Office and presented it to the Americans. When the American government released the text of the telegram (without revealing the British role), the Germans, seeking the origins of the leak, sent messages flying between Berlin, Washington, and Mexico City, all in the same code as the original telegram, and into the hands of the British.

What difference did all this make? If German counterintelligence had been able either to protect German communications or to identify and neutralize British intelligence capabilities, the United States might have further hesitated to join the Allies. Had it joined the Allies at a later date, America probably would not have been able to mobilize quickly enough to turn back the major German offensive of 1918—an offensive that came perilously close to succeeding, and could have changed the outcome of the war.

Poor German counterintelligence and security practices were also vitally important in World War II. Ignoring his past as a radical leftist and the fact that his mother was Russian, Nazi security allowed Richard Sorge, an agent of Soviet military intelligence, to infiltrate the German embassy in Tokyo. Using his position as a reporter for a leading German newspaper, Sorge became fast friends with the ambassador. Through his own efforts and the ring of spies he ran, Sorge gained remarkable access to German and Japanese war plans.[19]

Before his arrest in the fall of 1941, Sorge passed on to Moscow the critical intelligence that Japan had decided, after some debate, not to attack the Soviet Union in the Far East from its bases in Manchuria. Instead, the Japanese would move south in the Pacific against the British and the Americans. This intelligence allowed Stalin to move half of his forces in the east to the western front to face the German army's advance on Moscow. The Nazi offensive was held that winter. In retrospect, it was a key turning point; from that point forward, the Wehrmacht never fully regained the upper hand.

Exploiting an adversary's inadequate security and counterintelligence capabilities can also help a state maintain its strategic power during peacetime. The USSR is an outstanding example of a state that used its positive intelligence capabilities to shift the strategic balance of power more in its favor.

At the beginning of the nuclear age, the USSR was able, through espionage, to get significant help in acquiring the most important military technology of the twentieth century from the United States and the United Kingdom. Through contacts with Western scientists and technicians who were politically sympathetic to the Soviet Union, Moscow learned key secrets about how to make an atomic weapon. Among the most important agents were Klaus Fuchs, Alan Nunn May, Bruno Pontecorvo, and David Greenglass. Ultimately, the Soviet Union would have developed a weapon without this intelligence. However, its effort was far less costly than it would have been otherwise. Moreover, this information gave Stalin an early, strategic card to play in his dealings with the West.

Indeed, in the immediate postwar period, Moscow was heavily dependent on military technology from the West. According to the U.S. government, despite several decades of heavy investment in science, technology, and weapons systems, the USSR continued to use, and, in some instances, depend on the acquisition of militarily significant Western technology to improve its own arsenal.[20]

What is noteworthy is the systematic scheme the Soviet Union established to acquire this technology. Moscow's collection effort has been outlined in several places, including a Department of Defense study, *Soviet Acquisition of Militarily Significant Western Technology: An Update*.[21] Much of the content was derived from information obtained from a KGB officer, code-named "Farewell," recruited by French intelligence in early 1981. Between 1981 and 1982, Farewell provided the French with detailed information on the organization of the Soviet technology acquisition system, annual results of Soviet efforts, and a list of Soviet science and technology officers working in France under diplomatic cover—most of whom were expelled from the country by President Mitterrand in 1983.

According to these reports, the Soviet effort was not haphazard. Through a complex and structured system, the Soviets would produce a technology "shopping list," and then systematically review the success (or failure) of their collection efforts. This system was overseen by the Military Industrial Commission (VPK). Designed to circumvent the inefficiencies in the Soviet economy, the VPK collected and prioritized requirements from key defense industries and then passed those requirements on to "acquisition" organizations: Directorate T of the

KGB, the GRU, the State Committee for Science and Technology (GKNT), and even the Soviet Academy of Sciences. Using both overt and covert operations, this system allowed the Soviets to target advanced technologies, the companies and individuals involved in producing them, and ways in which the desired information or technology might be acquired.

According to the Soviets themselves (as attributed in the DoD study), only about one-third of their list was acquired annually. However, the list itself grew by 15 percent a year. This indicated not only continuing Soviet reliance on Western technology, but also a growing collection effort (including use of Soviet bloc intelligence services) and rising expectations on the part of Soviet users. Acquisition plans had two- and five-year cycles, and it is estimated that during the 1979–80 cycle, four thousand samples and eighty thousand technical documents were obtained each year, with four thousand to five thousand military and industrial projects benefiting.[22] Most of the documents and technology of significance were either classified or under export controls of one sort or another. Again, according to the Soviets themselves, this effort over one four-year period (1976–80) saved the defense and aviation industries $800 million in research costs alone, and some 100,000 man-years of scientific research. In short, in addition to allowing the Soviets to field advanced weapon systems much more rapidly, the collection effort freed up additional resources for other projects and lightened the burden of increasing R&D costs on an already overburdened economy.

For the U.S. defense budget, the flow of technology to the East was substantial and negative.[23] A congressional study argued that NATO forces could have been maintained at a substantially lower cost had the West been able to deny the Soviets this stolen technical knowledge. The defense expenditures of the United States are determined in large part by the level of threat faced, and the threat grew in those years as a result of the USSR's clandestine acquisition of U.S. technology. In wartime, the costs would have been weighed in human lives.

Counterintelligence challenges are not always tangible. Under the right circumstances, clandestine efforts to influence public opinion and decision-making in foreign countries can play an important role in world politics. Covert techniques include the use of nonattributed propaganda, agents of influence, and forgeries or other forms of covert disinformation (deliberately false information circulated without attribution). These are often referred to as "active measures," a translation of a Soviet term. The Soviets waged vigorous "active measures" campaigns in Western Europe after World War II and throughout the cold war, with mixed results. One of Moscow's more successful efforts in the mid-1970s was directed against NATO's decision to modernize its theater nuclear weapons by adding the "neutron bomb." U.S. and Western European indecisiveness in this instance was exploited by a Soviet active measures campaign to influence Western decision-making. The NATO governments did little to counter Soviet bloc overt and covert active measures. The U.S. government estimates that during the campaign, Moscow spent $100 million a year for three years on the support apparatus, including local Communist parties, front organizations, and agents of influence.[24]

Responding to Moscow's deployment in Europe of a new generation of intermediate-range missiles (the SS-20) in 1979, NATO decided to upgrade its own theater nuclear delivery systems with modern cruise missiles and Pershing II rockets. Following the successful anti–neutron bomb campaign, the Soviets mounted one of the largest active measures campaigns ever seen to stop NATO's new deployments. In the end, they failed, in part because European politicians who favored the deployment, particularly in West Germany, the UK, and Italy, won key elections. The stakes were very high. Had they been successful, the Soviets would have weakened NATO militarily and perhaps even destroyed the alliance. But they also failed because Western governments realized their previous mistake in not challenging the Soviet campaign against the neutron warhead more vigorously. This time, the Allies did not hold back. They decided to uncover, expose, and publicize the Soviet campaign against the intermediate nuclear force. In Britain, West Germany, and the United States, Western intelligence poured information into the public domain, which was then picked up by private groups and political parties sympathetic to NATO's modernization decision.[25] It is impossible to assess what would have happened if Western intelligence services had not moved aggressively to identify, expose, and, in some instances, neutralize the Soviet bloc's active measures campaign. What is certain, however, is that their efforts facilitated an outcome that was initially in question but that in time proved to be critical in the history of the alliance.[26]

A key element in developing a counterintelligence capability is understanding the nature of the intelligence threats posed by others. This means collecting information about foreign intelligence activities—of friends and foes. There are many ways to obtain this; among the most important is penetrating adversary intelligence services. To do this, counterintelligence must either recruit someone inside the target foreign service or gain control of someone or something (for example, codes or ciphers) that is already there. At the top of every counterintelligence wish list is recruiting an agent in the most sensitive echelons of the foreign intelligence service, a so-called mole.

A leading twentieth-century example of a successful mole is Harold A. R. "Kim" Philby, a top official in the British Secret Intelligence Service (MI6) in the 1940s and 1950s who was recruited by Soviet intelligence as a young man. Although Philby was part of a left-wing circle while a student at Cambridge University and had married an Austrian Communist while living in Vienna in the 1930s, MI6 never ran a serious background check before asking him to join the organization early in World War II. Successful in his various postings, Philby was promoted to head MI6's counterintelligence branch after the war. In 1949, he was sent to the United States as chief of the Washington station and as principal liaison with the CIA, OPC, and FBI. By that time he was considered a possible future head of MI6. With his access, he was able to give away many Western operations and warned the Soviets about weaknesses in their own operational security for more than ten years.[27]

Philby passed on information about many Western intelligence operations behind the Iron Curtain, which the Soviets subsequently neutralized. He is believed to have compromised from the start the clandestine U.S.-British effort to explore the feasibility of a resistance movement within Albania overthrowing the brutal Communist dictator Enver Hoxha.[28] In 1948, the break between Yugoslavia's Tito and Moscow left Albania physically isolated from the rest of the Soviet bloc. The United States and Britain hoped a success in rolling back Communism in Albania would not only deny the Soviets a submarine base in the Mediterranean (on Albania's island of Sasebo) but might also encourage resistance movements still operating in parts of Eastern Europe and in the Soviet Union. With Philby involved in its planning, the Albanian operation was doomed from the outset. Most of the Albanian agents who initially landed in 1949 and 1950 were killed or captured by Albanian troops. Although, in retrospect, it seems the chances were slim for resistance movements in Albania or any of the other Soviet-allied states, Philby's access to British and American plans closed whatever opportunity did exist.[29]

Poor counterintelligence analysis, in some cases, can cause as much harm as poor security. An example of this is Iraq and its program to develop nuclear weaponry in the 1990s. Although U.S. intelligence was fairly confident such a program was under way, it was only after the Gulf War in 1991, when UN inspection teams had made several trips to the country, that the West learned how massive the Iraqi effort was. In retrospect, it is clear that Iraq, knowing the overall capabilities of U.S. technical collection systems, conducted a thorough and sophisticated campaign to deceive American intelligence. According to the congressional testimony of then Director of Central Intelligence (DCI) Robert Gates, had the Gulf War not taken place, Saddam Hussein's regime would have likely developed a weapon by 1992—not in the late 1990s, as predicted by U.S. intelligence in estimates prepared before the conflict.[30]

Counterintelligence analysis often plays a critical role in catching a major penetration. Take, for example, the mid-1980s, when it became apparent that the KGB was identifying and arresting Soviet agents run by the CIA and FBI. A succession of operational failures suggested that the KGB was aware of the Bureau's and the Agency's clandestine plans and successes. The question for counterintelligence analysts was, how? Was it connected to the defection of former CIA officer Edward Lee Howard in 1985? Or the lapse of embassy security associated with the Marine guard scandal in Moscow? A compromise of a communication channel used by U.S. intelligence? Or perhaps a little of each? Or was it, as analysts ultimately determined, someone within the CIA who had the kind of formal and informal access to cases that Aldrich Ames did as the onetime chief of the Agency's Soviet counterintelligence branch within the Directorate for Operations? Analytically eliminating and narrowing possibilities is at the heart of counterintelligence in such instances. Done well, this process protects a state's intelligence operations; done poorly—or worse, not done at all—it can greatly undermine efforts against an adversary and, in turn, leave a state vulnerable to manipulation by that same adversary. At a minimum, Ames's work for the KGB left the United States largely unable to sustain ongoing espionage operations against the Soviets and later the Russians at a critical period in history.[31]

Countering the intelligence efforts of an adversary is the central function of counterintelligence, but this may involve activities that reach well beyond the defensive. In addition to neutralizing foreign intelligence activities, counterintelligence must sometimes take the offensive and actively seek to manipulate a hostile intelligence service. Typically, the hostile service is led to believe it is operating successfully against another, whereas in reality it is being led down blind alleys or induced to steer its government in desired directions. This kind of deception can be tactical deception, such as masking the true performance characteristics of new aircraft; strategic military deception, such as the Allied landings in Normandy in 1944; or strategic political deception, such as the "Trust" operation in the fledgling Soviet Union in the 1920s.

As one scholar-practitioner notes,

> where no genuine internal opposition organization exists [a security service might] invent one—both to infiltrate the more dangerous émigré organizations abroad in order to blunt or channel their actions, and to surface real or potential internal dissidents. If an internal opposition already exists, it will be infiltrated in an attempt to control it, to provoke opponents into exposing themselves, and to cause the movement to serve state interests.[32]

Sometimes, if circumstances allow and the practitioners are skillful, counterintelligence can target its deception not only at the internal and émigré opposition but also at the intelligence services and governments of foreign adversaries. The Soviet Trust was such an operation. The Trust was created in the early 1920s and completely controlled by the Soviet secret service, the Cheka.[33] Believing they were operating in league with an active and effective anti-Bolshevik movement, opponents of the regime within the USSR and in exile were lured by the Trust into exposing themselves and became targets of Soviet state security. Using that information and controlling communications between Western intelligence agencies, the Russian émigré community, and Russian dissidents inside the country, the Cheka expertly neutralized anti-Communist opposition at home and abroad.

The Trust was also able to use its contacts with Western intelligence services to pass along misleading and false information on the internal state of the Soviet regime to those same services' foreign ministries and governments. Essentially, the West was being told by its intelligence "assets" within the Soviet Union that support for the Bolshevik regime was weakening, and that the Soviet leaders were at heart nationalists who, if left in peace by the West, would gradually turn a state dedicated to revolution at home and abroad into one that would behave in a more traditional and predictable fashion.

This counterintelligence operation was an important covert adjunct to Lenin's general policy during the 1920s to "buy time" for the Soviet regime in order to consolidate the party's control over the country, while simultaneously stabilizing the Soviet economy through the New Economic Policy (NEP). The Trust, and similar deception operations run by Soviet intelligence, distracted the West with unproductive operations against the Soviet Union and reinforced Lenin's effort to establish in the West the view that the Bolsheviks were coming to their senses.[34]

Counterintelligence can also protect sensitive military plans. In 1943, the Allies decided to open another major front against the Nazis. The plan was to invade France in 1944 and then drive into Germany from the west while the Russians were attacking from the east. To protect this plan, and to break through Hitler's daunting Atlantic Wall, the Allies devised a counterintelligence strategy to convince the Nazis that they would not land in Normandy. Even when the Nazis realized that Normandy was in fact a landing site, the plan, code-named Operation Fortitude, was to persuade Hitler that the main landing would come more than a hundred miles to the north, at the Pas de Calais. Thus Hitler, waiting for the "real" Allied landing, would hold back key German reserves instead of directing all the German army's might against the Normandy beaches in an effort to crush the invasion. If Hitler's intelligence had learned of the invasion plan, or of the plan to deceive the Germans into believing the Normandy attack was a feint, it almost certainly would have doomed the landing in 1944. As it happened, the British and Americans succeeded, first, in hiding the real invasion plan from German intelligence, and second, in manipulating German intelligence into believing the Normandy invasion was a ruse, even days after the landing.

Earlier in the war, the British had captured every German agent sent into Britain. The agents were given the choice of working for the British or being shot. Most chose to live. In intelligence jargon, they were "turned" against their former patrons. British counterintelligence then used its radio reports back to Germany to deceive the Nazi high command, an effort known as Operation Double-Cross. The particular advantage the Allies had in carrying out this deception was their ability to verify the effect of the false intelligence they were supplying to the Germans through a "feedback channel." British interception and decoding of German communications, known as Ultra, showed that the Nazis believed the information their agents were reporting from Britain.

What the Double-Cross agents reported to Germany was the apparent extensive preparation for an invasion whose main landing would be at the Pas de Calais. The "preparation" taking place in the west and north of England and in Scotland created a completely false order of battle. British and American commanders set up dummy camps and ship movements, complemented by bogus wireless traffic. There was an entirely fictional army group, the First U.S. Army Group (FUSAG), supposedly commanded by General Patton and supposedly headquartered in East Anglia, facing the Pas de Calais. All this activity was backed by high-level "intelligence" that was allowed to fall into German hands. A captured German map confirmed success of the deception—it depicted the Allied order of battle as of May 15, 1944, as being identical to that fabricated by Operation Fortitude.

Ultra intercepts revealed that Hitler expected the initial assault at Normandy, but believed the major effort would be directed against the Pas de Calais. In April 1944, Allied strategic bombing attacks on long-range batteries along the assault beaches of Normandy supported Operation Fortitude by bombing two targets elsewhere for every one battery attacked in the future main assault area. After the actual D-day landing on June 6, the deception continued in order to perpetuate the German anxiety over a main assault in the Pas de Calais.

Operation Fortitude was an important facet of the Allied success at Normandy. As a result of the continuing deception, the German buildup of forces there was slower and smaller than expected.[35] The entire operation would have failed if the Germans had suspected that their agents had been turned or their codes broken. The broader counterintelligence effort rested on the back of sound security and effective counterespionage. In the context of the overall scheme, counterintelligence was as critical to the success of D-day as the tons of explosives dropped on France in anticipation of the invasion. Both softened the Wehrmacht's formidable defenses.

Covert Action

As with counterintelligence, history is replete with examples of the advantages that accrue to states that blend an effective covert action capability into their overall policies, and of the problems besetting those that do not.

The Soviets' massive political covert action infrastructure in Europe played an important part in their efforts to overturn NATO's decision to modernize its tactical nuclear forces with the neutron bomb in the late 1970s. It did not, in and of itself, determine the outcome. In the context of NATO's relatively weak leadership at the time, uncertainty about the need for the modernization, and overt Soviet military and diplomatic pressure, the clandestinely supported network of front groups, publicists, and activists was a key supplement to the Soviet policy goal of stopping deployment of the new weaponry.

The history of covert action—the practice of trying to influence events, decisions, and opinions covertly in other states with a measure of plausible deniability—is by no means confined to the West's struggle with the Soviet Union. Although the Soviet Union in some respects, through intelligence and secret support for Communist internationals, may have employed this particular tool of statecraft more thoroughly and more successfully than any state in history, covert action is nothing new.

Well known to historians is the covert aid provided by the French monarchs Louis XV and Louis XVI to England's rebellious colonies in North America.[36] The kings' advisers argued that French assistance to the rebels not only would diminish the power of Britain while augmenting French power and trade, but might also lead to the restoration of certain French colonies in the New World that had been lost to England and Spain after France's 1763 defeat in the French and Indian Wars.[37] An unintended consequence of the defeat was the abatement of anti-French sentiment in the colonies, with growing anti-English fervor to fill the vacuum. Now France sought to exploit that fervor.

The French, at first, secretly supported anti-British propaganda in the colonies.[38] When the American Revolution formally began in 1776, the French government had to decide if it would escalate its assistance to the rebels. The risks were considerable, including possible war with Britain. However, Louis XVI's foreign minister, Constantin Gravier, Comte de Vergennes, argued that war between Britain and France was likely whatever France did, and that it would be better to weaken Britain as the opportunity presented itself by possibly denying her the men and resources of North America. Vergennes, along with other advisers to Louis, argued for a program in which France would overtly reassure England about its nonintervention in North America, meanwhile providing "the insurgents secret help in munitions, in money, etc. . . . veiled and hidden aid to appear to come from [normal and legitimate] . . . Commerce."[39]

Others cautioned the French monarch against siding with the Americans. The argument was closely fought. As a monarch, Louis XVI could hardly be sympathetic to the liberal and antimonarchist rhetoric of the Americans. But in the end, he sided with Vergennes, agreeing that the enemy of his enemy should be supported even if the French had no control over the war, nor over exactly how the rebels would use the aid. In early May 1776, Louis authorized one million livres for his adviser Pierre Augustin Caron de Beaumarchais to purchase supplies for transfer to the Americans. In August, Beaumarchais opened the firm of Roderigue Hortalez et Cie. as a cover to hide the government's direct hand in the affair. Within a year the firm had sent the Americans eight shiploads of military equipment and supplies, drawn in large part from France's own royal arsenals.[40] Meanwhile, Spain, too, was providing assistance.[41]

Prior to the formal outbreak of hostilities, the Second Continental Congress had accredited a Secret Committee of Correspondence in September 1775. The committee was given large sums to obtain military supplies secretly, and while in Philadelphia, its members met with a French secret agent traveling as a Flemish merchant.[42] The Congress then sent Silas Deane to Europe in 1776 to act as its agent to arrange for supplies.[43] In September, the Congress elected two additional commissioners to the Court of France, Benjamin Franklin and Arthur Lee, resolving that "secrecy shall be observed until further Order of Congress."[44] Franklin arrived in France in November and openly served as a diplomatic representative of the rebellious colonies. At the same time, his chambers also became the coordination point for the secret aid of men and material from Europe to America.

It is difficult to know what would have happened if this aid had not been delivered. But many at the time, as well as later scholars of the Revolution, argued that the initial secret assistance from France (and Spain) was decisive in the early stages of the Revolution.[45] By the fall of 1777, following the British capture of Philadelphia, American prospects for victory were in doubt. But the news of rebel victories at Saratoga and George Washington's stand at Germantown convinced the French that the rebels could win and played a significant role in the formal French-American alliance in February 1778.[46]

Later, France, though not her monarchy, directly benefited from this aid. For example, when war broke out between Britain and France in 1803, Napoleon did not have to contend with an enemy backed by the resources and strategic depth that might have been provided by its former colonies in North America.[47] The German failure to prevent and delay American participation in World War I arose, in part, because of poor security and counterintelligence. The failure was reinforced by Germany's largely ineffective and counterproductive attempts at covert action.

At the beginning of World War I, German leaders believed the United States would enter the war on their side.[48] This illusion was soon dispelled, and Germany's goal shifted. Now the Kaiser's government would try to prevent American arms from reaching Allied forces in

Europe, as well as keeping America neutral—as Woodrow Wilson had promised before his narrow reelection victory in 1916.

One advantage the Germans had going into the war was the animosity toward Great Britain that still existed in the United States. The Germans secretly used Irish- and German-American propaganda and political fronts to fan this. In addition, the German ambassador to the United States and his military and naval attachés masterminded and financed sabotage operations to delay and prevent American arms shipments to Europe. Munitions plants were blown up and ships disabled.[49] In its boldest move, Germany secretly sought to provoke Mexico into war with the United States; this, the Kaiser hoped, would distract the United States from the conflict in Europe.

But Germany's actions were contradictory and often awkwardly blatant. To keep U.S. arms from the Allies, the Germans not only conducted clandestine sabotage but also engaged in unrestricted submarine warfare that resulted in a substantial loss of American lives and property. Moreover, German support for covert campaigns aimed at undercutting Britain among U.S. political and business leaders was so transparent that it ultimately produced an anti-German backlash among the general public. Exacerbating this, and largely due to operational security lapses, was the exposure of German sabotage missions,[50] which seemed to give credence to British-inspired stories of German atrocities committed in Europe.[51] By the time the Zimmermann telegram appeared, Germany's own clandestine efforts in the United States had already whipped up American suspicion of the Kaiser's government. German covert action not only failed to prevent the United States from joining the Allies, it actually encouraged that move.

In contrast, the British, availing themselves of better opportunities and a more sympathetic American leadership, were able to conduct a more subtle, sophisticated, and ultimately successful covert program in the United States. The British effort, of course, was not the only reason the United States sided with the Allies in 1917. But it did help shape Wilson's decision, and it enhanced his ability to mobilize the country quickly for a war that the American people had initially not been eager to join.

What was the key to British success? First and foremost, it was placing the head of British intelligence in the United States, William Wiseman, close to President Wilson. This young, not very successful businessman and playwright became one of this century's more important agents of influence. According to Sir Arthur Willert, a well-placed observer, Wiseman became for all intents and purposes the private secretary to Colonel House, Wilson's closest adviser.[52] In fact, in Willert's judgment, the relationship between House and Wiseman was virtually that of father and son, even though House and a few other senior American officials knew Wiseman was a British emissary. House went so far as to coach the Englishman on the best way to handle Wilson. Eventually Wiseman overshadowed the formal liaison role of the British ambassador in Washington and the American ambassador in London, becoming the chief point of contact between the White House and the British government.

Even after Wilson made his decision to enter the war, the British Foreign Office used Wiseman to influence how quickly the United States would actually join in the war effort. In addition, Wiseman was able to use his position of trust to orchestrate greater cooperation between the Allies and the new member than might otherwise have existed.[53] For example, given details of Wilson's War Address in advance—even before Wilson's cabinet—Wiseman arranged favorable coverage by the British press, which was relayed by the media back into the United States to enhance Wilson's prestige. Evidence also suggests that Wiseman wrote policy memoranda that went through Colonel House directly to President Wilson. So trusting was the president of Wiseman that when the war was over, he wanted Wiseman to serve as his personal adviser at the Versailles Peace Conference.[54] As one former senior British intelligence official has argued, Wiseman may have been "the most successful British 'agent of influence' we know about."[55]

British covert action largely succeeded in the United States for a number of reasons. First, the decision whether the United States should enter the war was a closely fought political battle, that is, an instance where secret political and propaganda programs could make a small but critical difference. British intelligence was not starting from scratch; there were substantial pockets of pro-British and anti-German sentiment in the United States, especially in elite media, business, and government circles. In general, it was easier for British than for German operatives to function in the Anglophile environment of the U.S. East Coast. In addition, the British were often able to penetrate and neutralize German operations and, in turn, exploit German incompetence for the purposes of British propaganda.

Why was London and Berlin's covert struggle in the United States significant? For this reason: as a result, the United States entered the war, mobilized quickly, and tipped the balance of power—narrowly—in favor of the Allies.

Although evidence is still murky, it appears that the British also used covert action with some effect to secure their supply lines in the United States and to influence U.S. public opinion and government behavior in 1940 and 1941. Senior officials of the U.S. government apparently colluded with these publicly unacknowledged activities. According to Desmond Morton, Churchill's personal assistant throughout the war (and probably the source of the leaks of secret British intelligence on German war production to Churchill before the war), ". . . another most secret fact of which the Prime Minister is aware but not the other persons concerned is that to all intents and purposes U.S. security is being run for them, at the President's request, by the British. A British officer sits in Washington with Mr. Edgar Hoover and General Bill Donovan and reports regularly to the President. It is of course essential that this fact should not be known in view of the furious uproar it would cause if known to the isolationists."[56]

Morton was referring to another major agent of influence, William Stephenson, and his organization in the United States, the British Security Coordination (BSC). Under the cover of the UK's Passport Control Office in New York, Stephenson played a role somewhat similar to Wiseman's in World War I. Stephenson's affiliation was known to many senior U.S. government officials, but not acknowledged publicly. They worked with him. He was shown copies of Roosevelt's speeches in advance, presumably so he could not only give advice, but also help evoke a favorable reaction in the United States, Britain, and elsewhere.[57] He assisted American counterintelligence in uncovering Nazi operations in the United States. (The FBI arrested forty-two German agents between 1941 and 1942, thirty-six of them with British help.)[58] He helped William Donovan organize America's first centralized intelligence bureaucracy, the Office of the Coordinator of Information (COI) and later the Office of Strategic Services (OSS).[59] In addition to working closely with top officials inside the government, Stephenson and his BSC built up a large secret network within the United States. At its peak, BSC had employed two thousand in America, including perhaps as many as one thousand operatives in the field. It generated its own coded transmissions, and at one point the FBI was sending three hundred coded messages a week to British intelligence in London on behalf of the BSC.[60]

What is not clear is whether top U.S. officials were aware of or encouraged BSC's clandestine efforts to use propaganda, political action, and paramilitary action to shift American public opinion away from neutrality toward European war and to counter German plans to prevent or stall American supplies from reaching Britain before 1942. According to accounts by David Ignatius and Mary Lovell—both based on a still-classified history of BSC operations in the United States, to which they were given access—the BSC sponsored enormous and successful media operations in America,[61] with the collaboration of major newspaper publishers, editors, and journalists. They subsidized press agencies, radio stations, and Hollywood filmmakers. In addition to infiltrating groups like America First, an isolationist lobby to keep the United States out of the war, they also created their own competing front groups. They worked closely with other major nongovernmental groups like the American Federation of Labor (AFL) and ethnic fraternal organizations. They fed rumor mills to support people and issues they favored and to discredit those they did not. They used a variety of devices, including what would clearly be called "dirty tricks" today, to neutralize their opponents.

Given the character of the Nazi regime and its demonstrably imperialist behavior toward its European neighbors, it would not have seemed especially difficult for the BSC to influence American opinion in a favorable direction. But at the time the American public was reluctant to become embroiled in another European war. The BSC believed that its activities at a minimum helped keep that isolationist sentiment from cutting off what U.S. assistance was finding its way to Britain, and ultimately prepared the ground for America's quick entry into the war in Europe after the attack on Pearl Harbor.[62]

An equally striking demonstration of the value of covert action took place in Europe during the early and dangerous years of the cold war. At the end of World War II, the fate of much of Europe hung in the balance. As the Nazi armies were being rolled back from their occupation of the western USSR, the Baltic region, and Eastern Europe, the Red Army and Soviet security forces jumped to control these "liberated" states. Moscow busied itself defeating anti-Soviet partisans in the Ukraine and in the Baltic republics, as well as consolidating political control over Eastern Europe. In Greece, the Soviets backed the effort of the Communist Party to take control. Elsewhere, Communist parties that Moscow had secretly financed and politically controlled for decades became key political players, particularly in France and Italy. In Eastern Germany, the Party was backed by Soviet military power; in the occupied zones of Western Germany controlled by the United States, France, and Britain, the Party was revived.[63] In addition, the Communists had infiltrated a number of important nongovernmental organizations, including many of the labor unions of Western Europe.[64]

In fact, by the late 1940s, Moscow had established in Europe the largest and probably the most skilled collection of covert operatives that the world had ever seen. A major coordination point was the Communist Information Bureau, the Cominform. The Cominform had its own secret staff, funds, communication networks, couriers, and agents throughout the world. Taking advantage of the economic and political turmoil of the interwar years and the struggle to defeat the fascist powers during the war, the Soviets had built up a formidable overt and covert apparatus throughout Europe.[65]

In the fall of 1947, as the United States prepared to implement the Marshall Plan to help restore the European economies and, in turn, stabilize the democratic regimes of Western Europe, Stalin ordered the Communist parties of Western Europe to take the offensive. The parties and the labor organizations they controlled tried to destroy the Marshall Plan and demonstrate that no government could effectively govern without the consent of the Communists.

Without access to Soviet documents, it is impossible to know whether Stalin hoped to subvert and overturn the democratic states of Western Europe or whether he merely intended to cause as much turmoil as possible, believing this would divert U.S. and Allied attention and energy from Moscow's efforts to consolidate control of Eastern Europe. If his objective was diversion, Stalin was successful. The United States devoted itself primarily to containing Soviet influence in Western Europe for the first year or two after the war, maintaining only a small military presence there.[66]

Beginning in late 1947, with elections in Italy, the United States and the democracies of Western Europe moved aggressively to prevent Moscow from using its covert and overt assets to wreck the governments of the region. Washington was playing with a strong hand: the United States was the most powerful nation in the world, and most Europeans after the war were not interested in trading totalitarian rule from the right for totalitarian rule from the left. Under these favorable circumstances, U.S. operations in Western Europe became a virtual model of the successful, regular use of covert action.

To start with, the overall direction of U.S. foreign policy was fairly clear, and it was conveyed unequivocally to subordinates and maintained with remarkable consistency throughout changes in U.S. political and military leadership.[67] The State Department, the Department of Defense, and the intelligence community largely marched to the same tune, and both the majority and minority parties in Congress were supportive. Such consensus cleared the way for the United States to provide massive secret political and propaganda assistance to Europe through economic assistance (the Marshall Plan), promises of military support (NATO), and public diplomacy. This cohesive U.S. policy demonstrated to Western Europeans that Washington was serious in its support of resistance to Soviet expansionism; it provided both the incentive and the means to defeat Soviet overt and covert activity aimed at destabilizing Western Europe.[68]

Of course, covert action was not the only factor that prevented the Soviets from undermining U.S. efforts to rebuild a democratic Western Europe. But like the Marshall Plan, it was a key element in supporting American policy goals for that vital region. This conclusion is at odds with the view that covert action—even when successful—is of only marginal significance. As argued by one of the most influential studies of the subject, "seen in the long light of history most successes of covert action look small, ambiguous and transitory."[69] True, if one focuses on a few spectacular historic events—the efforts to overthrow governments in Iran (1953), Guatemala (1954), Cuba (1961), and Chile (1970). In reality, however, the historic record is far more complex. At a minimum, U.S. covert programs in Western Europe after World War II seriously challenged the notion that covert action is of little value, as do U.S. covert action operations in places like the Philippines in the 1950s and, more recently, in Afghanistan and Poland.[70] At worst, covert action has fared no worse than other instruments of statecraft such as public diplomacy, economic assistance, and even military force. Although rarely a magic bullet, covert action is neither as marginal nor as ineffectual a policy tool as it is often portrayed.

Both covert action and counterintelligence have at times made significant contributions to protecting a state's national security interests. Conversely, a lack of capability in these areas has left states at a significant disadvantage with respect to their adversaries. Are counterintelligence and covert action essential to the security of a democratic regime? Usually not. But, neglect of these elements makes it riskier and more costly for such a state to fulfill its foreign and defense goals.

2

STEPS AND MISSTEPS:
COVERT ACTION
SINCE 1945

THE HISTORY OF U.S. INTELLIGENCE suggests a prejudice against covert action except in exceptional circumstances, the price of which is starkly evident in the story that follows.

Until World War II, there was no organization in the U.S. government devoted solely to the covert influence of events abroad. The executive branch and the Congress took it upon themselves to perform this function when necessary, sometimes quite effectively. Indeed, the story of territorial growth of the United States is rife with examples of official complicity in private plots of one sort or another. The construction of the Panama Canal was a notorious case. The importance of the canal for U.S. strategic control of the region had been demonstrated in 1898 during the Spanish-American War when the U.S. battleship *Oregon* had raced around South America. In 1902, Colombia, which controlled the Panamanian isthmus, refused to ratify a treaty giving the United States canal rights in Panama. The problem then became how to ensure U.S. rights of control over the canal. This challenge was farmed out to the New York law firm of Sullivan and Cromwell.[1] The lawyers' political maneuvers were supplemented by those of U.S. warships, which prevented Colombian troops from squelching the Panamanian revolution. And so the Republic of Panama came into being. Though covert action was not a regular instrument of U.S. policy in those days, the perpetrators apparently felt no embarrassment about what they had done. Later, the United States did pay an indemnity to Colombia.[2]

Movement to remedy the lack of covert action capability was minimal during World War I and its aftermath. The United States also delayed entering World War II. But once the United States became involved after Pearl Harbor, a covert action capability was established in 1942 in the Office of Strategic Services (OSS), known initially as the Coordinator of Information.

Under the influence of British intelligence, the OSS developed two types of covert action. One was "morale operations" (alternatively known as psychological warfare) to encourage resistance to the Nazis and demoralize enemy personnel. This strategy consisted of dropping propaganda leaflets to enemy soldiers, helping the resistance movements operate printing presses (in occupied territories), and broadcasting clandestine radio programs. Material and intelligence support was also provided covertly to resistance movements in occupied Europe and parts of Asia.[3]

At that point, the OSS did not have political action programs. The bumbling footwork by which the United States sought to maintain a stance of neutrality was not so much a story of unsuccessful choreography; rather, it was choreographically impossible, with countries such as France torn by internal dissension among Communists, Socialists, and Gaullists. The dominant U.S. position that internal differences must await the end of hostilities for resolution ignored the facts of wartime. Most participants in World War II accepted the Clausewitzian dictum that war "is the continuation of politics by other means," but the United States, the military in particular, persisted in separating the two. General Omar Bradley later summed up the American viewpoint: "As soldiers we looked naively on [the] British inclination to complicate the war with political foresight and nonmilitary objectives."[4] Although the wartime OSS might have been expected to benefit from greater flexibility, it did not.

Even before the war's end, General William Donovan, head of the OSS, argued for retaining a similar type of postwar intelligence agency with capabilities for psychological operations. But President Truman ordered the OSS entirely disbanded on October 1, 1945. Almost all those involved in its morale and paramilitary activities returned to civilian life. A few stayed to work with the OSS's small successor, the Strategic Services Unit (SSU); the research function was put in the State Department, the others in the War Department. Under the auspices of the latter, the SSU was almost exclusively concerned with intelligence collection. Thus, by 1946 the United States had returned to its prewar position of lacking the means to exert covert influence, or even to conduct overt propaganda, abroad.

This development was an expression of the basic prejudice against the clandestine arts so deeply ingrained in America's democratic psyche. Basically, Truman adhered to the traditional view that secret influence operations abroad were contrary to democratic tenets. He was also an heir of Sam Adams rather than John Adams in his instinctive concern that secret tools might be used against American citizens. In any case, the war was over. The Third Reich had been reduced to ashes, the perceived threat removed. What would be the purpose of institutionalizing clandestine capabilities?

During the next two years the United States followed its traditional practice of unattributed, ad hoc assistance to political forces abroad. Typical was a project by Secretary of the Navy James Forrestal in 1946–47 to help French trade unionists resist Communist Party control—a project operating on private funds that Forrestal himself helped to raise.[5] Meanwhile, a promising nucleus for covert action existed in the State Department, but it did not exactly flourish. In the 1930s a small group known as EUR-X had been created under the direction of Ray Murphy. It specialized in the international Communist movement and encouraged sophisticated Foreign Service officers to do all they could to help anti-Stalinist elements. But EUR-X had a limited budget and practically no influence outside the State Department. What little influence it had was overshadowed by Stalin's wartime abolition of the Comintern. For all intents and purposes, then, there was no official organization to identify needs or opportunities for covert action, much less to take advantage of them.[6]

By the beginning of 1946 the Truman administration, having disposed of the OSS, was already concerned about the apparent disarray and divergent views in the intelligence reports reaching the president. The result was the creation in 1946 of the Central Intelligence Group (CIG), with Admiral Sidney B. Souers, at the time deputy director of naval intelligence, appointed as Director of Central Intelligence (DCI). The CIG was responsible to the National Intelligence Authority, composed of the Secretaries of State, War, and Navy and the president's Chief of Staff. The CIG was almost exclusively concerned with collection and analysis; covert action was not part of its mandate.

By late 1946, however, with presidential authorization, the Secretaries of State, War, and Navy, concerned about Soviet intentions in Europe and increasing Soviet and Communist influence in Western

Europe, began to formulate guidelines for the conduct of psychological warfare. In June 1947, while the authority and responsibilities of the Central Intelligence Agency—destined to replace the CIG with the passage later that year of the National Security Act—were still being debated in the bureaucracy and the Congress, they formed the inter-agency Special Studies and Evaluation Subcommittee. There was no clear-cut mandate, only an agreement that some unattributed propaganda activities were needed to counter Soviet influence.

If it was difficult to work without clear guidelines, it was even more difficult to find an agency willing to shoulder the responsibility for covert activity, at least in peacetime. In November, Truman assigned responsibility to the Department of State, but Secretary George Marshall feared that any exposure of covert activity would damage the department's reputation. Many citizens, even without the press's eager lead, looked upon such activity negatively. Marshall favored some type of secret assistance program, and he wanted it to be subject to the guidance of the State Department while remaining outside its official umbrella.

The military, for their part, took the view that covert activity was not part of their mandate in peacetime. Unless war broke out they did not want this responsibility, but nor did they want anyone else to acquire it. The military were particularly uncomfortable with giving the mandate to the newly formed CIA.

Admiral Roscoe Hillenkoetter, the third DCI and the first to head the CIA, was himself unenthusiastic about covert operations. According to official CIA historians, Hillenkoetter, as opposed to Donovan, did not believe covert action had made a difference during World War II. Further, he was convinced that covert action missions would adversely affect the CIA's collection and analysis of data. After considerable wrangling in the newly created National Security Council (NSC), which had just come into being in the National Security Act of 1947, Truman sided with Marshall. On December 14, 1947, the NSC adopted NSC Directive 4/A, giving the CIA responsibility for covert psychological operations under the political guidance of the State Department. Although the State Department now appeared to have the upper hand in the management of covert action, that was not destined to last. Within a few years, the CIA would become the dominant intelligence bureaucracy, with covert action one of its major missions.[7]

The spur that brought about the December 1947 decision was the Italian election set for April 1948. A Communist victory was possible, notwithstanding the Italian government's tough stance against Communist agitation. Several NSC directives from November 1947 to March 1948 were aimed at organizing support for non-Communist Italian political leaders and parties. Most of the actions in support of democracy were overt: shipment of wheat and other essential commodities to Italy, port calls by American warships, and supplies for the Italian armed forces, which faced an experienced Communist military force of approximately seventy thousand. NSC Directive 1/3 called for speeches by "government officials and private individuals, including labor leaders, and a letter-writing campaign by private citizens regarding the political issues in Italy."[8] (The American public's response to this suggestion was positive.) The only truly covert action consisted of essential financial assistance to Italy's Christian Democrats, the anti-Communist Social Democrats, the more conservative Liberal and Radical parties, and individual left-wing Socialists, plus some useful propaganda and counterpropaganda initiatives. The mandate for such activity was sketched in the vaguest terms by the NSC directives.[9]

U.S. policy was in tune with the sentiments of many Italian centrists, so it is hard to measure the influence of American overt and covert assistance with the elections. The Christian Democrats, under Alcide de Gasperi, won the support of almost half the electorate and an absolute majority in the Chamber of Deputies. De Gasperi then brought into his government a smattering of Social Democrats, Liberals, and Republicans. This prevented the Communists, who had received about a third of the votes, from posing as the non-Catholic alternative.

From a professional viewpoint, the hasty patchwork of overt and covert activity to help Italian democratic forces was a violation of diplomatic norms. No Soviet ambassador in either Eastern or Western Europe—in fact, few ambassadors anywhere—ever entered so publicly and vigorously into a local election campaign as did U.S. ambassador to Italy James Dunn, whose speeches up and down the peninsula were a notable and effective feature of the campaign. In carrying out his instructions, counselor of embassy Edward Page, a U.S. Foreign Service officer with long experience of the Soviet Union, gained a certain notoriety as the source of American contributions to Italian party campaign funds. Diplomatic norms aside, the U.S. government was persuaded at the time that its overt and covert orchestrations had worked. The result was a surge in American enthusiasm for "combined operations," reflecting a perceived threat of Communist domination of Western Europe as well as the fear that war with the USSR would erupt.

Meanwhile, in addition to countering Moscow in Italy and elsewhere in Western Europe, the CIA, using its secret intelligence collection organization, the Office of Special Operations (OSO), had initiated psychological operations in Central and Eastern Europe. The OSO's activities were reportedly quite limited, carried out with a radio transmitter for broadcasting into Soviet-controlled territory, a secret printing plant in Germany, and a fleet of balloons that could fly propaganda over the Iron Curtain.[10]

The first months of 1948 brought matters to a head in Washington. The Communist coup in Czechoslovakia in February, the narrow victory in Italy in April, and the Soviet blockade of Berlin that same month sharply reinforced the perception of threat in the West. There was a growing perceived need for a mechanism for more effective defense and response than psychological operations could offer.

In May 1948, George Kennan, head of policy planning at the State Department, proposed the creation of a more permanent covert action capability under State Department control, but again not formally associated with it. On June 18, the president approved NSC Directive 10/2, which replaced NSC 4/A and authorized a sweeping "expansion" of "political warfare" against the Soviet Union under a new agency, the Office of Special Projects.[11] The idea was to make covert action an integral part of U.S. policy in response to the growing crisis in Eastern and Western Europe. The earlier problem resurfaced: if not under State's, then under whose auspices would this function be carried out? The military did not want to handle it, nor did they want to see the power of the DCI enhanced. The CIA chiefs were reluctant to establish a "dirty tricks" department, as one CIA historian, echoing the popular phrase, dubbed it. The initial solution to all these conflicting urges and positions, the CIA's Office of Special Projects, kept everyone's nose clean.

Halcyon Days

Possibly to avoid any confusion with OSO, the Office of Special Projects, even before its establishment in the autumn of 1948, was renamed the Office of Policy Coordination (OPC).[12] The solution to the problem of where to rest this hot potato was a bureaucratic master stroke, though it was not destined to survive bureaucratic storms. OPC was lodged in the CIA, but as a completely separate entity. It drew on the personnel and support of all federal departments and agencies. The DCI provided OPC with quarters and "rations" (logistical support), but kept it separate from the OSO. The OPC operated under the authority of National Security Council directives. Policy guidance came from the State Department, on a daily basis via the Policy Planning Staff, and as occasion required from the Defense Department (usually the Joint Chiefs of Staff). The head of the organization was not an appointee of the Director of Central Intelligence, nor did he have to report to the DCI.

In the fall of 1948, Frank G. Wisner was placed in charge of "policy coordination."[13] Wisner, a Mississippian who had studied at the University of Virginia, was a well-connected, well-to-do former Wall Street lawyer who had served in several OSS assignments—most notably as head of the OSS mission to Romania when the Romanians turned against the Germans. He was energetic and, according to colleagues, brilliant. Wisner brought in about ten people and held his first staff meeting on September 8, 1948, among other things to begin drawing up a policy paper organizing covert action in Italy. Wisner's chief lieutenants were former OSS colleagues and several officers lured from other CIA departments. He sought to attract promising officers from the armed forces and energetic Foreign Service officers with European experience.[14]

OPC was divided into a headquarters staff stationed in Washington and undercover personnel working in U.S. embassies and U.S. military installations abroad. Headquarters personnel were split into four functional staffs—political warfare, psychological warfare, paramilitary operations, and economic warfare—and six geographic divisions, which in turn controlled OPC officers abroad. OPC did use the OSO central registry, which assigned pseudonyms and operational names and served as a repository for documents.

Over the next few years, OPC took off. Wisner recruited heavily, and the organization rapidly acquired personnel, money, projects, and geographic responsibility. The NSC wanted it involved in Western Europe, Eastern Europe, and the USSR. With the Communist victory in China in 1949 and the outbreak of the Korean War the next year, OPC rushed into Asia as well. In 1949, the office had 302 personnel operating on a budget of $4.7 million. By 1952, it had 2,812 personnel and a budget of $82 million. In the same period, it expanded from seven to forty-seven overseas stations.[15]

In creating OPC, the U.S. government papered over certain irreconcilable conflicts in the organization and administration of intelligence, most notably that between clandestine collection and covert action. There are inevitably tensions between the two. Clandestine collectors frequently work with sources who have political goals, the same kinds of people who would also be targeted by covert action officers. Covert action officers' connections, meanwhile, are almost by definition good sources for collectors. How to foster cooperation between the collectors and the covert action officers without compromising their separate aims? Collectors are most reluctant to share sources or risk exposing them through covert action, while covert action practitioners see little point in gathering information that is not used. That the OPC did not attempt to address such differences is surprising, because during World War II Americans had witnessed the unrewarding struggles between two competing wartime secret organizations in Britain: the collectors in MI6 and the resistance personnel in the Special Operations Executive (SOE). It was a classic case of bureaucracy outweighing the influence of wartime experience abroad.[16]

Not surprisingly, by the early 1950s a rivalry had developed between OPC and OSO. The OSO view was expressed by one former SSU and OSO veteran: "Over the years, the stations which have distinguished themselves in covert action have generally been those which were well regarded as collectors of intelligence. In both instances, the key to success has been access to the movers and shakers of a country."[17] His conclusion: separating the two functions deprived the collectors of the benefits of covert action, and the covert action specialists of the benefits of collection. Covert action officers, on the other hand, found collectors naive about political ends and insufficiently skilled in achieving them. An example was OSO operative James Angleton's insistence— successfully rebuffed by both embassy counselor Edward Page in 1947–48 and his OPC successors thereafter—on secretly photographing Italian politicians receiving U.S. funds.[18]

There was also the practical problem of collectors and covert action practitioners not answering to the same authority. Case officers in two different agencies recruited the same people as agents, enabling the latter to play one agency against the other. In Bangkok in 1952, competition even led to violence between OSO and OPC officers.[19] Still another problem was that OPC lacked the means for counterintelligence and operational security. The OSO, with its counterintelligence group and its Office of Security, had both capabilities. But OPC director Wisner could and did ignore or override OSO and the Office of Security. OPC came in due course to recognize, as the British SOE had in World War II, that covert action backed by too little counterintelligence and operational security can spell disaster.[20]

Other aspects of organizational rivalry included differences in salary and mission. The 1976 Church Committee report noted that at the time of its creation in 1948, OPC received considerable funding to attract personnel quickly. The burgeoning bureaucracy also enabled people, once hired, to rise rapidly in salary, rank, and status. As a result, not only did OPC have a larger proportion of the CIA's total civil service supergrades, but its personnel at almost all levels held better-paid, higher-ranking positions than their OSO counterparts.[21]

The catalyst for the resolution of these differences was President Truman's appointment of General Walter Bedell Smith to replace Admiral Hillenkoetter as DCI. General Smith was not one to tolerate an independent entity under his command. Preliminary steps to merge OPC and OSO, that is, the management of clandestine collection and covert action, began in 1951, were almost complete by June 1952, and were made effective in August. The result was the CIA's Directorate for Plans (DP). Initially Allen Dulles was named Deputy Director for Plans (DDP). Shortly thereafter OPC's Wisner, was named deputy director for plans and the merger became effective. Mergers took place in the DP's geographic divisions in Washington and in stations abroad. OPC's Washington headquarters staff also became the DP covert action staff that assisted geographic divisions and coordinated covert action programs that crossed geographic divisions.

Consensus: Stopping Communism

The decisions to create OPC and to implement the first covert action programs in Italy in 1947–48 were taken with little thought for the future. The United States urgently needed a covert action annex[22] to its public policy on Italy, and eventually for its general Western European policy. Initially there was no global plan, or even a European plan, for folding covert action into U.S. policy. Instead, the State and Defense departments lurched forward with defensive responses to perceived Soviet pressure, first in Greece in 1946 and 1947, then in Italy in 1947 and 1948, and in many other European countries soon thereafter. Truman approved the departments' initial proposals and later approved the general decision to use covert techniques. Given the consensus on basic policy, congressional or public approval of specific covert action techniques was not thought necessary. The executive branch, with the approval of senior congressional figures, saw covert action as its prerogative, institutionalizing its use in the CIA bureaucracy without agonizing over political considerations.[23]

In the 1940s, U.S. leaders saw themselves primarily as helping Europeans resist Communist takeover, then in the 1950s as helping Asians, Latin Americans, and others do the same. In the American view, there was a power vacuum in the world that the Soviets would fill unless they were stopped. Who else but the United States could stand up to Moscow militarily? Who else could stand up to the well-organized and well-financed Communist parties and the media-driven labor, intellectual, and youth fronts Moscow operated on almost every continent? The United States sought to use covert action to stop the "fire" of Soviet-controlled Communism from spreading. The perception of threat had weighed in to alter the American definition and practice of intelligence.

The original idea of containment, which implied constant defensive action around the periphery of the Soviet Union, prevailed in U.S. diplomacy. The policy rested on the contention that in due course Soviet expansionism, if constantly and solidly resisted, would run its course and be obliged to accept limitations. As the years wore on and what appeared to be Soviet aggression continued unabated, many American conservatives denounced containment as a form of appeasement, leading to a policy rift that would be reflected in the nature and extent of future U.S. covert action.

U.S. policy and covert action programs were not intended to overthrow Communist regimes—at least not in the short term—unless war broke out.[24] Deterrence, at costs far exceeding all CIA operations, was the prescribed antidote to war. The expense of military deterrence and of foreign aid met with few objections, for the American public was not prepared to go to war over most of the areas subject to Soviet aggression, especially after the ramifications of nuclear conflict became clear. But in authorizing and planning covert action, American leaders displayed a certain schizophrenia. In public and in private they vowed to promote democracy throughout the world, meanwhile failing to design the means to achieve this result in the foreseeable future. Covert action programs were not set up to promote democracy per se. In the absence of a positive goal or strategy, they ended up simply as mechanisms to "stop Communism."

From the late 1940s to the late 1960s, this defensive policy remained fairly consistent. The NSC authorized double-edged covert action programs designed to meet two goals: one, containing the spread of Communism in the non-Communist world by supporting governments threatened by takeover, strengthening other non-Communist political and military forces, and countering Soviet propaganda; and two, weakening Communist regimes on their own terrain by supporting internal resistance movements and eroding patriotism with radio broadcasts, leaflets, and Western literature.

This was not "dirty tricks." The United States was not manipulating people to do what they did not want to do. On the contrary, in the intelligence community the covert action staff were seen as helping foreigners whose hands would be tied without U.S. aid. The United States mainly provided unacknowledged moral, political, and material support to those leaders of democratic political parties and nongovernmental forces who wanted to remain outside the Communist orbit, and to those within it who wanted to make trouble for Communist parties.

In democratic countries, the CIA's activities were designed to maintain the democratic process. Occasionally it gave a hand to conservatives. But most covert action officials believed the Communists were seeking to capture the democratic left and the center. Therefore, the United States would get the best return on its efforts by strengthening socialists, social democrats, trade unionists, and intellectuals as well as the center right, particularly liberal Christian democrats. Hence covert action in democracies meant giving support and money to the leaders of the non-Communist left and the center.[25]

There were differences among CIA personnel about the wisdom of this emphasis on the left, particularly about support to socialists, trade unionists, and intellectuals who condemned the faults of American society with as much vigor as they condemned Stalinism. Some believed that anti-Americanism made the recipients of U.S. aid more credible anti-Communists and hence more useful to the United States. Others took the view that anti-American leftists were undependable allies, indeed that they would make common cause with Communists and use the assistance to defeat their pro-American, anti-Communist rivals.

This rift affected, among others, the international labor movement. Within the movement itself, a battle royal raged for decades. On the one hand were anti-Communists who wanted to exclude Communists from coalitions and international labor activities as well as condemn the Soviet Union—the "workers' state" that oppressed workers! On the other were non-Communist trade unionists who wanted joint action with the Communists, and who therefore downplayed their differences with the USSR. The prevailing inclination at the CIA was to support "the political process"—in effect, both sides—but to put most of its money on the left rather than deciding which factions were most deserving of support in any given situation.[26]

Among authoritarian states battling the Communist threat, especially in Asia and the Middle East, the CIA usually chose allies who were the strongest military, ethnic, or political leaders available. Some U.S.-backed leaders, for instance, Ramon Magsaysay in the Philippines, were democratic. Others, such as the shah of Iran, were far less so. Whether or not the CIA's managers were fostering democracy in these states, the U.S. government's main concern was preventing the success of pro-Soviet elements. U.S. policy, which the CIA carried out, was to help those who would be effective. The CIA itself often played a lead role in determining who that might be.

At the same time, some senior Clandestine Service officials and station chiefs nudged their authoritarian allies to be less repressive and more tolerant of anti-Communist agitation. This varied from place to place and time to time. Personal beliefs aside, the rationale was that harsh repression would drive people into the hands of the Communists, and that Westernization and development would help eliminate poverty and the causes of extremism. Not all CIA leaders believed in this doctrine, but it was American policy in much of the Third World.

Beginning in the days of OPC and continuing through the OPC-OSO merger, a set of operational procedures developed that produced varying results. NSC policy directives gave the Directorate for Plans' planners and executives only general authority, not detailed guidelines. Thus DP planners and operators had the flexibility to "do their own thing" how and when they judged best. No committees, either in the executive branch or in the Congress, provided detailed review of covert action programs. Thus, there was no mechanism to ensure that programs contributed to the overall success of U.S. government policy.

Formal approval of programs came through a series of NSC subcommittees that had different names in different administrations: the Psychological Strategy Board, set up in 1951, the Operations Coordinating Board, in 1953; the 5412 Group, in 1955; the Special Group, in 1961 (after the Bay of Pigs); and the Forty Committee during the Nixon administration. While these subcommittees had different emphases, their procedures were similar. Participants consisted of a small number of second- and third-level officials from State, Defense, and the NSC. They usually met every few weeks, for only a few hours, and sometimes in lieu of meeting they conferred by telephone. The committees had minimal staffing; perhaps one person at the NSC handled the paperwork. State and Defense proposed many programs. Most often State and Defense approved the plans prepared for them by the DP, now in charge of covert action. At times they went so far as to quibble or even to say no to DP proposals. At other times, they overrode DCI and DP objections to specific programs proposed by State or Defense, usually on the grounds that the programs would be ineffective and simply waste time and money.

But nobody took responsibility for making a program pay off. Although that responsibility, and the job of coordinating with State and Defense, ostensibly rested with the DP, DP had neither the breadth of view nor the authority to fulfill it.[27]

This was not apparent in the 1950s, because John Foster Dulles headed the State Department and his brother Allen was the action-oriented DCI. The actual coordination and leadership was left to Frank Wisner, energetic and well connected in Washington, and later to the able Richard Bissell, who became DP in 1958 and then to Richard Helms (1962–65) and Desmond FitzGerald (1965–67).

A Sometime Instrument of Policy

Over a twenty-year period, from the Truman through the Johnson administration, the concept and role of covert action expanded. In the beginning, covert action was considered an ad hoc adjunct to economic and military measures, somewhere between doing nothing and "sending in the Marines." But gradually over this period, the top policymakers in the executive branch and Congress developed the conviction that covert action should be implemented as a matter of everyday policy. It was no longer viewed as a magic bullet expected to carry the full burden of U.S. policy, or to substitute for a whole panoply of diplomatic, military, and economic techniques. Rather, the White House, the State and Defense departments, and the CIA came to regard covert action as one of a number of complementary instruments to be employed in the struggle against Communism and Soviet power.

Covert action, however, did not receive as much institutional support as diplomacy, aid, and overt information programs. Most U.S. government bureaucracies gave only lukewarm support, tolerating it but sometimes venting their frustration by leaking details of specific programs. Outside of the cold war, the prevailing sentiment went, covert action did not have much to offer in support of America's interests. Nor were the various bureaucracies happy about the DP, over which they wielded so little control, having the power and resources to influence foreigners. Those with reservations were acting, in most cases, under the influence of the traditional view of American democracy that covert action was an expedient to be restricted to extreme circumstances, while the CIA's stewardship of the responsibility granted by NSC 10/2 and subsequent specific authorizations were initially the result of its role as the dominant bureaucracy.

As the years went on, that authority became entrenched and covert action was viewed as the special preserve of the CIA. State, Defense, CIA, and the White House did approve and sometimes plan combined operations involving covert action, but on the whole, planning and implementation were left to the DP's specialists. The DP was no rogue elephant. Exhaustive investigations designed to prove such a charge have shown that the CIA acted well within the general guidelines established by the president and the NSC, even with regard to assassination plots.[28] The truth is less sensational: over the decades, the rest of the U.S. government made covert action the CIA's exclusive business by gradually withdrawing from it. The Defense Department, except during wartime and for logistical and cover arrangements, kept its distance. Although initially the State Department helped design covert action programs, it gradually became less and less involved in their planning and implementation. Senior State (as well as military) officials almost always participated in the NSC's approval process for covert action, sometimes even initiated programs, and provided some logistical and cover arrangements. But planning and execution lay outside their preserve—that was something the Agency did.

Most Foreign Service officers, even ambassadors, knew nothing of American covert action. There were no training sessions or briefings on covert action in the Department of State. On occasion, some ambassadors and deputy chiefs of mission were apprised of CIA activities, which they sometimes supported, as in the Philippines in the early 1950s, and sometimes opposed.[29] But almost never were Foreign Service officers asked to coordinate closely with local stations to develop and implement covert action plans, for example, by "working" local officials, journalists, and union leaders after consulting with DP case officers. And over the years, the Department of State's role in influencing internal politics in other countries diminished, while that of the CIA increased.

Foreign Service officers rarely capitalized on covert action directly. Although indirectly they benefited from the weakening of Soviet power and the strengthening of some non-Communists, in negotiations with local politicians, military, and nongovernmental leaders they were basically "out of the loop." Throughout the 1950s and 1960s, a whole generation of Foreign Service officers who would rise in the ranks in the 1970s and 1980s remained in the dark about most covert action programs, and many came to dislike the instrument that deprived them of influence. The good political brains in the Foreign Service were gradually frozen out of covert action. As James McCargar, a foreign service officer detailed to the OPC pointed out, there was no love lost between those two parts of the executive.[30]

Nor was covert action well integrated within the CIA. Many collectors, and counterintelligence specialists in particular, made distinctions among the various clandestine activities. Everyone believed espionage should be top-secret, even after the fact, so as to protect the agents and methods. Covert action, however, needed to be only partly secret, because much of it, and almost all of its results, would be visible. Only the sponsor of the action and some of the techniques were to remain veiled, and then often thinly. As one former counterintelligence specialist suggested, perhaps with the wisdom of hindsight, covert action was like flying a kite—everyone could see the kite and follow the string down to its source.[31] Because of this visibility, many collectors and counterintelligence specialists wanted nothing to do with covert action.

Now and again, these same specialists also objected on political or ideological grounds to covert action by their colleagues in support of anti-American elements abroad. An illustration of this more general problem is a reported dispute in the 1950s concerning covert action plans in Italy involving James Angleton. Angleton objected to OPC and later the DP patronizing the left-wing Socialist Party led by Pietro Nenni. On the basis of his extensive OSS and OSO Italian experience, Angleton (who became head of the DP's counterintelligence staff in 1954) felt that the Socialists and their trade union allies, the CGIL, were too close to the Communists, and that the Communists had the means to prevent any Socialist defection from their alliance for the foreseeable future.[32] This kind of direct intervention in covert action policy by the CIA's counterintelligence staff was tolerated, though sometimes just barely.

Then there were the CIA analysts. Many doubted both the efficacy and the ethical foundation of covert action. Perhaps above all, they believed that covert action distorted the CIA's mission and priorities and took precedence over analysis. Furthermore, it was argued, covert action gave the agency as a whole a bureaucratic interest in a particular policy. Analysis might be skewed to support covert action and the policy it represented. This development, they believed, was compromising the CIA's role as a collection-analysis agency that made judgments more or less objectively and allowed the chips to fall where they may.[33]

Successes

In the halcyon days of U.S. covert action, many operations were characterized by clear-cut, consistent policy coordination and leadership at the top that seized opportunities for the United States to use its prestige, reputation, and resources. Creative planners knowledgeable about their regions identified allies who shared specific American objectives. Case officers in turn developed effective projects, providing moral and material encouragement and advice to local allies who were able to realize their objectives.

One of the best examples of this pattern is American assistance to European democracies recovering from World War II. Many OPC operatives who worked on Western Europe were products of American colleges that focused on European history and civilization. They had lived in Europe and often spoke at least one European language. Many had served in Europe for the OSS. Most were liberals driven by a sense of mission who naturally sought out liberal allies, which from the late 1940s through the mid-1960s meant anti-Communists. OPC looked for effective European allies; so long as they were anti-Soviet it didn't even matter if they were Marxists. Indeed, some of the most effective anti-Stalinists were former Communists who now ranged the ideological spectrum from Trotskyist to socialist to conservative. Case officers could identify the political orientation of a potential ally with an unusually high degree of precision, not least because these Americans were intimately familiar with Europeans from prewar, wartime, or early postwar experience.

Consider, for example, assistance to anti-Stalinist European trade union leaders. American labor's aid to democratic political groups in Europe went back to the prewar era.[34] During the 1930s, AFL leaders—notably AFL president William Green, secretary-treasurer George Meany, typographical chief Matthew Woll, Railway Clerks leader George Harrison, and Ladies' Garment Workers leader David Dubinsky—raised union funds to help exiles from fascist and Soviet oppression maintain contact with their homelands before the United States entered the war. After it entered, the AFL cooperated with the OSS labor division, headed by CIO labor lawyer (and later Supreme Court justice) Arthur Goldberg, to use labor's underground network for sabotaging the Nazis and collecting information useful for the war effort. Well before 1945, AFL leaders anticipated a struggle with the Communists for control of Eastern and Western Europe. American labor leaders and exiled Europeans planned campaigns and organized drives to oppose the Communists as soon as the Nazis were driven out.

In 1944 the AFL started raising hundreds of thousands of dollars from its members to implement these plans through its Free Trade Union Committee. It provided money, typewriters, mimeograph machines, printing presses, and other equipment in short supply to democratic labor groups in Italy, France, and the Western zones of occupied Germany and Austria. It also interceded with U.S. occupation forces to protect democratic groups often treated unsympathetically by the U.S. military.

Although some U.S. officials such as Secretary of the Navy James Forrestal also helped raise private funds, the U.S. government as a whole did little to prevent Moscow from gaining control of much of the recovering labor and socialist movements until the fall of 1947. Then, in 1948, the government became heavily involved. One of the key OPC operatives, Tom Braden, wrote an account of these and other CIA activities in 1967 in the *Saturday Evening Post*.[35] Braden pointed out that American labor had been helping the anti-Stalinists in the European labor movement resist Moscow for years. He went on to describe how, to promote this effort, the U.S. government after 1947 made millions of dollars available to American labor leaders. The article caused enormous damage to a number of individuals and destroyed some operations still functioning successfully. (The Intelligence Identities Protection Act of 1982 would likely prevent publication of similar information today if it were part of a "pattern" of such stories.) Braden also neglected to write in his flamboyant exposé that the people with whom he was dealing were not usually the ultimate recipients of the funds. The money was used by democratic European unions to prevent the Communists from blocking the Marshall Plan and the NATO buildup through their influence over organized labor, particularly in the transportation industry. Had the Communist Party, using psychological and physical threats against workers who unloaded American ships in European ports, been successful in blocking the docks, railroads, and barges in France and Italy and Germany, the Marshall Plan could not have gone forward. The AFL, together with anti-Stalinist European labor leaders—some of them Marxists, anarchosyndicalists, and Trotskyists who did not want to follow Soviet orders—even organized protection for those who wanted to work.

In the Mediterranean, this effort was spearheaded by Pierre Ferri-Pisani, a Corsican maritime leader who had been deported by the Nazis to Germany during the war and who returned to find the Communists nearly in control of Marseilles and other ports. Pisani used his connections with the Corsican Mafia to organize strong-arm squads that protected non-Communist dockers. At one point in the early 1950s, he led a demonstration to Communist Party headquarters and warned that if any harm came to the dockers, Communist leaders, not their minions, would become targets.[36] Pisani, Braden boasted, had CIA funding to back up this threat and to help with other activities in support of the Marshall Plan and NATO.[37]

Such secret U.S. government assistance was small compared with the funding Moscow lavished on European Communist parties and the trade unions and fronts they controlled, but in combination with the efforts of private American and European anti-Stalinists, it helped prevent Moscow from using its political operators to dominate major ports of the continent.[38]

One of the reasons for the success of many of the CIA's European operations was that on the Continent, OPC and CIA case officers did not have to be meticulous about hiding from local security services. In fact, they often got extra mileage by intimating that the United States supported certain causes. Most West European security services, though perhaps at times suspicious of American involvement, welcomed U.S. efforts to help fight local Communist adversaries. As long as the United States did not bring its influence to bear on domestic political forces in ways they did not approve, the local security services usually went along.[39]

It also helped CIA operations that in postwar Europe, American case officers were hard for outsiders to identify. The European continent was swarming with U.S. occupation (later NATO) forces, Marshall Plan employees, American journalists, businessmen, students, and labor leaders, and American money was flowing in from the Marshall Plan itself, business interests, private foundations, allies, and nongovernmental organizations. Try as they might to expose secret assistance from the United States, on the whole the KGB and the Communist parties found it difficult to produce smoking guns. Party and front publications were vociferous in their denunciations of CIA aid, but this was written off as simple Communist propaganda. At the time, this secret American assistance drew little fire. At home, those few people outside the DP who were aware of U.S. covert action projects in Europe remained sympathetic. Inside the executive branch there was little pressure to leak information, and those in the Congress and the media who got wind of such projects kept silent. Until the mid-1960s, U.S. covert action was not so much covert as it was unacknowledged and accepted.[40]

Another region where OPC, and later the CIA, helped anti-Stalinist forces was Latin America. The United States provided political, propaganda, and sometimes paramilitary assistance to local forces in many democratic or quasi-democratic countries struggling against Soviet-supported Communist parties. Again, most of this aid went to the reformist democratic left, in the form of financial assistance to nongovernmental organizations such as trade unions, cooperatives, the media, and intellectual groups, and to candidates in local and national elections.

A good example is Chile. There in the 1950s and 1960s the United States spent millions to discredit Communists and Socialists who favored political and trade union alliances with Moscow. Extensive use was made of the press, radio, films, pamphlets, posters, graffiti, and direct mailings, and support was given to the Conservatives and later to the centrist Christian Democratic Party. From 1962 to 1964, for example, the NSC authorized over $3 million in projects that ranged from organizing slum dwellers to funding political parties in the hopes of blocking the election of a Socialist or Communist president. The CIA as well as many outside observers believe this aid was important in staving off the Communists and Socialists until 1970. In that year, President Nixon decided not to back any candidate for president, depending instead on covert propaganda for a "spoiling campaign" that failed to prevent the veteran Socialist Salvador Allende from winning the presidency.

In other countries where authoritarian leaders or regimes were being challenged directly by elements believed to be sympathetic or open to Soviet pressure—for example, the Philippines in the 1950s,[41] Iran in 1953,[42] Guatemala in 1954,[43] and Laos in the 1960s and early 1970s[44]—U.S. political, propaganda, and paramilitary operations proved equally important, at least for a time. The United States, which projected a powerful profile abroad and capitalized on favorable local conditions, found local leaders willing to cooperate with the United States in its efforts to influence local events, and on terms set by the Americans—whether open or secret. Again, U.S. operatives did not have to excel in secret tradecraft—DP planners were knowledgeable enough about local conditions, who was who, and how politics worked. Foreign intelligence services like Britain's were willing to lend them a hand, and hostile local security services were too weak to prove much of an obstacle. Thus U.S. operatives managed to get the job done, even if at times they bumbled.

Missteps

The story of U.S. postwar covert action, however, is not all success. There were also mistakes and failures, and responsibility for them started at the top. Presidents from Truman through Kennedy were known at times to waffle about what they wanted to do in the face of conflicting objectives, or about the means or instruments for accomplishing objectives. Presidents had a tendency to commit a little to all sides of the policy ledger. Covert action became a weight to be thrown on one side of a power balance in a given country, counteracted by other U.S. government activities supporting the other side—not a policy tool, but a policy hedge.[45]

The greatest ambiguity arose about ruling Communist parties in the Baltic states and Eastern Europe. American presidents certainly wanted to weaken these regimes so that they would pose less of a danger to their neighbors and to the United States in case of war. But presidents often strayed beyond this prudent aim. In hopes of eliminating Communist, especially Soviet, domination, they encouraged the CIA to work with forces trying to overthrow governments—while simultaneously maintaining diplomatic relations with them. The United States made little effort to enforce secondary trade boycotts or other overt policy measures that would help bring about the demise of Communist governments. Without such overt measures, it was unlikely that CIA covert action alone could bring down these regimes in the foreseeable future. And if the CIA could not do that, who could? The U.S. leadership never really made up its mind. It rested foreign policy on countervailing axes and considered it "balanced." This happened in the Baltic republics in the late 1940s and in Poland, the Ukraine, and Albania in the late 1940s and early 1950s.[46]

Albania is a good example of the resulting dilemma. As we have seen, from the late 1940s until 1953, the United States flirted with the idea of overthrowing the ruling Communist Party. In 1949, a joint Anglo-American operation was launched to probe whether there was enough local resistance to overthrow Enver Hoxha and his regime. Assisted by the British, the OPC brought together Albanian exiles to create a political front, training, equipping, and landing a guerrilla force to gauge the opposition.

The Americans and the British, it turned out, were woefully ignorant of the degree to which Hoxha had fastened his grip on Albania. Neither Britain nor the United States had an embassy in Tirana. Only a handful of British SOE and OSS veterans had been inside Albania during the war, and next to none had gone there after the Communists took power. The OPC planners were equally removed. Try as they might to master their subject, none had ever set foot in Albania, and none were experts on the terrain or the people.

Moreover, the KGB and the Albanian security service, the Sigurimi, penetrated and ran much of the opposition apparatus, much as Moscow had run the Trust operations in the USSR in the 1920s. For over three years the CIA and British intelligence coordinated, financed, and trained hundreds of men and sent them into Albania—and to their deaths. After many of the guerrilla fighters were publicly tried in Tirana in 1953, the United States and Britain finally gave up. In view of the fact that the Albanian operation was a probe and not a full-scale effort to overthrow a government, the question remains why it dragged on for so long. A similar pattern can be found in OPC operations in Lithuania and Poland from the late 1940s through the early 1950s.[47]

Another good example is Cuba. From 1961 to 1964, the United States engaged in a variety of covert paramilitary activities there. The biggest and best-documented operation was, of course, the Bay of Pigs in 1961[48]—the attempt to overthrow the Cuban government. There was no ambiguity in the White House about ousting Fidel Castro, but because no single-minded purpose was communicated to the bureaucracy, it followed an uncertain trumpet.

Earlier, near the end of his term, President Eisenhower told the CIA to prepare a plan for exiles to invade Cuba and overthrow Castro. The CIA was to carry out the mission. The plan, fleshed out in the early weeks of the Kennedy administration, was flawed in many ways, specifically that part calling for the use of American air cover to protect the exiles when they landed at the Bay of Pigs. When the invasion was underway, President Kennedy refused to provide air cover, apparently believing that this would show too much American involvement in the operation; later, changing his mind, he allowed only a third of the strikes originally planned. It was a case of too little, too late, and a major reason why the invasion force never even got off the beach, much less to a position where it could form the nucleus of an uprising against Castro. One commentator summed up Kennedy's thinking succinctly: "He was more alarmed . . . by the possibility of noisy success than he was by the prospect of quiet failure, failing to see that failure itself is the noisiest thing of all."[49]

The American reluctance to use overt force in this instance cannot be easily explained. Castro was believed to be a serious threat to the United States, and Congress and the American public were hostile to his regime. The United States had used force in Korea in the early

1950s and in Lebanon in 1958. In 1961 it was prepared to use force in Berlin if the city was blockaded, even though the military situation there was unfavorable. But in Cuba, where the situation was favorable, the president balked. Covert action, neither for the first time nor for the last, was a substitute for well-thought-out policy, that is, clearly defined objectives, and resources and techniques calculated to achieve those objectives. Instead, covert action was viewed as a magic bullet that in a single round could achieve a desirable objective without committing the United States militarily.

Indecision at the top was compounded by serious flaws inside the CIA itself. Perhaps the most glaring was the dearth of good positive collection, analysis, and counterintelligence at the disposal of covert action practitioners. In almost every case from the late 1940s to the mid-1960s, the CIA, indeed the intelligence community as a whole, was woefully uninformed about countries for which it had grandiose plans. The CIA also failed to develop realistic paramilitary plans and to develop and protect the operations of the agents and allies slated to implement them. In no case did the U.S. and the foreign intelligence services that were asked to collaborate on plans come up with a strategy that had a realistic chance of overthrowing a newly established or, in the case of Ukraine and Lithuania, reestablished Communist regime. Covert action planners knew so little about resistance forces and the security apparatuses of various targeted regimes that their plans, even if they had been well implemented, stood little chance of success.

In retrospect, at least, this should not be surprising. Though the top covert action managers and most of their case officers had some wartime experience with OSS in the European theater, only a few knew anything about Eastern Europe, the USSR, or the People's Republic of China, and consultation with analysts inside or outside the agency was rare.[50]

The DP staff doubted that agency analysts, or many others for that matter, knew much about trends inside the Communist world. Moreover, they suspected that analysts were at best lukewarm about covert action. So instead the DP relied on underground organizations inside the Soviet bloc, exile movements, and allied intelligence services for much of its information and analysis. Unlike analysts in the Directorate for Intelligence (DI), these sources were very much in favor of action. But they were hardly objective about their own chances of success, by definition being disposed to accept whatever aid was given, no matter how inadequate.

The DP, however, completely underestimated the ability of various Communist regimes to manipulate CIA perceptions and operations. Although covert action managers could get by with poor operational security and avoid manipulation by Communist intelligence services in Western Europe and areas outside Soviet bloc control, that was almost impossible inside the Communist world. As far as can be determined, every single major U.S. paramilitary operation to overthrow a regime inside the bloc was known to the ruling elements well in advance. The Albanian operation, it will be recalled, was penetrated both by the Soviet agent Kim Philby from inside British intelligence and by Soviet double agents in the exile community. The same was true of British and American operations in the Baltic states, American operations against the Chinese, and the operations against Castro.

Bloc intelligence services not only neutralized most CIA operations, they also helped regimes maintain their power by demonstrating that outside forces were to blame for indigenous problems such as crop failure, flagging economic performance, and social unrest. All these ills were laid at the door of the "imperialists," perfect scapegoats whose agents and clandestine equipment, when caught, were put on public display as visible proof.[51]

In their heyday, many covert action planners regarded counterintelligence specialists, uneasy about so much CIA contact and interaction with underground forces in territory controlled by bloc security services, as naysayers. If counterintelligence officers were anti-Communists, they were also professional skeptics. They knew about the Soviet operations that had fooled the British and others in the 1920s, and they themselves had helped dupe the Germans in 1944. Unlike counterintelligence agents, however, CIA covert action managers could not conceive of themselves, professional manipulators, being the object of manipulation. To be fair, it is not clear that counterintelligence staffers skillfully pressed their concerns on covert action managers. In fact, the counterintelligence staff hardly ever explained to the DP or to station chiefs why and how their operations were flawed. DP managers interviewed on the subject have complained that the CIA's counterintelligence staff chief, James Angleton, rarely gave reasons or evidence for his skepticism, and they were reluctant to take on faith his ambiguous warnings about security risks and Communist deception. These were not the only covert action embarrassments stemming from CIA incompetence.[52]

Exposé

The extent to which even the many successful CIA operations rested on a consensus among the policy elite in Washington became obvious when that consensus began to crack. The first big scandal was the exposé in the New Left magazine *Ramparts* in February 1967. Several articles with information supplied by former employees of the National Students Association (NSA), a liberal organization of some one hundred student governments, alleged that the NSA had been run and financed by the CIA for years to gain access and channel assistance to foreign student leaders.[53] *Ramparts* speculated about the connection between the American "foundations" that had contributed to NSA and grants that these same foundations had given to labor, intellectual, and media organizations.[54] The magazine article initiated a collapse of many major pillars of the covert action structure. According to Cord Meyer, the CIA officer then responsible for these programs, the media outdid itself uncovering heretofore secret funding relationships.[55] This was not difficult, because the facts were not well concealed. The incident produced many "smoking guns" that Moscow had not been able to come up with for years. More important, it was a sign of the long-term, deep-seated distrust of covert action in American culture, a distrust that did not originate with the *Ramparts* affair.

Given the consensus in Washington in the 1950s, one can understand why covert action officers paid little attention to tradecraft. Had they diversified their secret funding channels, however, the 1967 *Ramparts* exposé would not have destroyed in a single stroke so many of the secret funding mechanisms in place for labor, youth, and intellectual groups in Europe and elsewhere. But that would only have drawn out the agony, for when the exposé appeared, White House officials who had once been proud of these activities decided that they should be discontinued.[56]

The CIA also might have sought, over two decades, to turn the groups it had helped to start, such as the International Congress for Cultural Freedom, into self-sustaining parts of the body politic. This would have made them much less vulnerable to penetration or to the leaks of 1967, as well as forcing them to compete in the world of ideas and politics. Secret U.S. government funding started in 1948. For the first five or ten years it might have been necessary to subsidize such groups secretly, but afterward they became part of the government's secret "welfare state." Organizations started as stopgap measures quickly established themselves as a bureaucracy with hundreds of employees.[57] Labor, youth, intellectual, and broadcast operations became fixtures of the CIA's secret budget, from one decade to the next supporting a small army of bureaucrats who created and ran businesses, foundations, and other "proprietaries." Some of these were indispensable. For example, the CIA had to have its own aircraft to transport men and material for paramilitary operations in Southeast Asia, particularly Laos in the 1960s. Other proprietaries became large, cash-hungry bureaucracies whose management by the CIA ate up more than $1 billion in the United States and abroad. This development took the organization far afield of its original mandate.[58]

The question remains why the United States kept its funding secret for so long. If, in the late 1950s, the executive branch had taken advantage of the consensus in the United States on the need to bolster anti-Communist nongovernmental organizations and had gone to Congress and the country for support, it seems unlikely that many would have opposed assistance to anti-Communists abroad, so long as the entire democratic spectrum from right to left was included. Indeed, the executive did just that with radio propaganda in 1971; the debate in Congress ended two years later in an overwhelming victory for continuing Radio Free Europe and Radio Liberty.

That single victory did relatively little to help anti-Communist youth, labor, and intellectual groups after CIA funding nearly stopped in the 1970s.[59] A vacuum developed that was filled in part by Soviet, Cuban, Libyan, and other antidemocratic forces. By this time, exacerbated by the Vietnam War, the foreign policy consensus in Washington had begun to unravel. The halcyon days of U.S. covert action were drawing to a close. The perception of threat had altered, and would be replaced by the idea of a long-term struggle between nuclear-armed superpowers. Military deterrence would diminish, but not eliminate, the urgency of the Communist threat. There were domestic political changes taking place as well. The constant rivalry between Congress and the executive was turning, after some three decades of executive superiority, toward congressional dominance, with all that meant for the bureaucracies involved.

The Wind Shifts

Beginning in the late 1960s, a whole series of events dramatically changed the balance of forces in Washington. Administrations from Johnson through Carter considered containment as increasingly less vital to American interests. It was not so much that Soviet leaders had changed their spots, the reasoning went, as that Stalin's heirs were more realistic, no longer bent on world domination. According to the Washington elite, the desire for détente, the Sino-Soviet split, the rise of Euro-Communism, the increasingly neutral stance of Western Europe, the threat of mutual assured destruction, and the split between developing and developed nations all changed the nature of international politics.

Most important, during the 1960s anti-Communism lost its allure. Many came to believe this position had led the United States into a protracted war and ultimate defeat in Vietnam. Why had the United States become involved in the first place? Answer: anti-Communism and containment. Remedy: anti-anti-Communism and less containment. Though both Nixon and Ford continued aiding anti-Communists and supporting containment overtly in Vietnam and covertly in places such as Chile and Angola, they did so with ever-diminishing vigor and conviction.[60]

By the time of the Carter administration, both the White House and Congress were disillusioned with the anti-Communist ethos. Not surprisingly, support for covert action fell off dramatically. In congressional testimony just before he became Secretary of State, Cyrus Vance introduced the "threshold doctrine," according to which covert action should be not outlawed but only undertaken in extreme circumstances, when "absolutely necessary."[61] Carter's DCI, Stansfield Turner, shared Vance's view. He conceded that "once or twice during an administration" covert action might be useful, but only if it did not stir up controversy.[62] And so the traditional prewar U.S. position on covert action as the exception rather than the rule reemerged.

Carter began his administration disaffected with the policy of containment, and with a few exceptions, National Security Adviser Zbigniew Brzezinski being one, his political appointments reflected this bent. But after a year or two in office, the president's view of Soviet power began to change. First he worried about the modernization of weapons in the USSR and its growing nuclear war capability. Then, after the fall of the shah of Iran, the rise to power of the Ayatollah Khomeini, and the Soviet invasion of Afghanistan in December 1979, Carter grew concerned over the increasingly antidemocratic direction of the Sandinistas in Nicaragua. As a result, shifts took place in national security policy as well as in the administration's attitude toward the intelligence community. Instead of believing the United States was practicing too much covert action and counterintelligence in the United States, the White House and some members of the Democratic-controlled intelligence committees began to fear it was doing too little.[63]

With the success of conservative Republicans in both the presidential and Senate races in 1980, containment came back in vogue. Some in the administration even talked about rolling back recent Communist victories in Nicaragua, Afghanistan, and Angola and intensifying opposition inside the Soviet empire. But the Reagan administration did not define its objectives clearly or build a solid constituency for them, not even inside the executive branch. The White House staff, particularly the president and his most powerful aides, James Baker and Michael Deaver, were preoccupied with managing domestic affairs. Although some of Reagan's high-level political appointees fit the activist anti-Communist mold—for example, DCI William Casey and security advisers Richard Allen and William Clark—many lower-level appointees did not.[64]

There was little agreement in the executive branch or in Congress on whether and how to oppose Moscow-oriented Communists trying to take over in Central America, Mexico, southern Africa, and the Middle East. Nor was there consensus about what to do in areas where the Communists had already taken power. What should American objectives be in Nicaragua and Afghanistan? Should the United States bloody up and weaken those and other Communist regimes so that they posed less of a threat to their neighbors? Or should the U.S. objective be to overthrow them? The Reagan administration and Congress waffled.

Some hard-liners in the administration, such as William Clark and Undersecretary of Defense Fred Iklé, argued strongly that the Soviet army in Afghanistan should be turned back, and that this objective was more important than the overthrow of the puppet regime in Kabul. Ultimately, after years of debate in the White House and Congress, and over vehement objections shared by many senior officials in the CIA's new Directorate of Operations (DO),* this position prevailed.[65]

Congressional Assertiveness

The 1960s and 1970s also saw a shift in the balance of power between the executive and legislative branches. The power of Congress increased dramatically. No longer was foreign policy, and covert action in particular, primarily the preserve of the executive branch. Starting quietly in the late 1960s and then more aggressively in the mid-1970s, Congress took on the job of overseeing U.S. intelligence, specifically

---

* The Clandestine Service of the CIA has had several names. For convenience, it will be referred to here as the Directorate of Operations, or DO.

covert action. After the attacks on covert action and counterintelligence during the Church Committee and Pike Committee hearings in 1975 and 1976, Congress set up two permanent select committees to oversee intelligence. Congressional involvement in this area had been virtually nonexistent in the 1940s and 1950s; the pendulum had now swung the other way.

In the fall of 1974, Congress, with no hearings and little debate, passed the Hughes-Ryan Amendment to the 1961 Foreign Assistance Act. This required the president to come up with a "finding" for each covert action stating that it was "important to the national security of the United States." Findings were to be reported to eight committees of Congress "in a timely fashion."[66]

The amendment prohibited nothing, but it did raise the stakes within the executive branch regarding covert action. From then on, even when a covert action was considered useful at every level of the intelligence community and on up to the president himself, the executive branch often "folded." It would not fight for the use of covert action if there was a reasonable chance of a failure for which it would be held responsible. Even when there *was* policy consensus and little involvement on the part of Congress, covert action as exemplified in the Bay of Pigs had been a means of avoiding decisions that might discredit the White House. Now that decisions in favor of action were riskier than before, they would be much harder to come by.

Thus when, in 1980, the Congress passed a law reducing the reporting requirements of Hughes-Ryan, it did not seem to make much difference. By and large the system established in the mid-1970s—consisting less of regulations than of attitudes—is in force today.[67]

Before the passage of Hughes-Ryan, the CIA worked under general NSC authorizations. Afterward, it could not avail itself of any opportunity without specific, usually written, authorization from the president himself. Findings were translated into directives to DO divisions and stations, and CIA station chiefs or case officers were forbidden to encourage foreign politicians, journalists, students, or anyone else to act in furtherance of U.S. interests without a specific finding. This was a far cry from the day in 1948 when the suggestion that OPC be lodged in the Executive Office Building was rejected on the grounds that it would put intelligence activities too close to the person of the president—and endanger the possibility of "plausible denial."

Although the president could sign findings authorizing such generic actions as preventing Communists from coming to power, Congress would want to know what the nature, scope, and purpose of a particular action was, and how long it would last. The CIA would have to prepare a scope paper to tell the president precisely what he was authorizing and the Congress what it was approving.

Theoretically, this was a healthy exercise in intellectual and political responsibility. In the hands of a strong president, the finding mechanism could have forced the executive branch to think through its goals and coordinate the means of achieving them. It also would have forced the Congress either to accept actions and the reasons behind them or to oppose them. But the finding mechanism reinforced the reluctance of uncertain presidents and of senior staff in different parts of the executive branch who were unaccustomed to explaining their actions even to one another, let alone to Capitol Hill.

The Central American Drama

U.S. policy in Central America in the late Carter and early Reagan years illustrates the difficulties imposed on policy formulation and implementation by the finding process. Both Carter and Reagan wanted to take action on the Sandinistas, who had overthrown Samoza in Nicaragua in 1979. Many in Congress shared their concern. But there was no consensus about what sort of action to take. Neither president was prepared to develop a clear-cut policy and force the issue. Instead, both chose to authorize small-scale covert action rather than do nothing. Neither administration thought through how covert action was supposed to carry, more or less on its own, the weight of American policy.

Consider, for example, the findings concerning U.S. aid to the Nicaraguan resistance.[68] Within weeks of the Sandinistas' takeover of Managua, President Carter's DCI presented a finding to Congress recommending that the United States encourage democratic elements in Nicaragua rather than risk the emergence of a new totalitarian regime allied with Moscow in Central America. While the United States was providing overt financial assistance to the new Sandinista-dominated government of Nicaragua, Jimmy Carter signed a finding that authorized secret support to democratic elements in Central America.[69] This reflected the administration's concern about the effect on democratic institutions in the Central American region of the Sandinista takeover. It authorized, not "lethal" aid, but covert action to strengthen democratic elements. Some in Congress questioned the means by which this goal was to be reached. They doubted covert action would be sufficient to bolster democracy. But few chose to argue against the diagnosis of the illness and the prescription for the cure.

Some have claimed that President Reagan had a coherent doctrine to roll back Soviet expansion. Certainly a variety of instruments, including covert action, were used toward this general end, but there were no clear-cut objectives, and ultimately the necessary means were not made available to accomplish the mission.

In the fall of 1981, the Reagan administration submitted its first finding on Nicaragua. It was more emphatic than the Carter administration's in its description of the dangers of a Communist beachhead on the North American continent. It specifically authorized U.S. covert aid to the "Contras," the paramilitary forces already operating against the Sandinistas.[70] But why? To accomplish what? The administration, like its predecessor, was vague. There was talk about compromising the Sandinistas' ability to spread revolution and keeping pressure on the regime, but there was no specific objective.[71]

Official Washington perceived a lack of unity and resolve within the administration, and attacks from Capitol Hill were not long in coming. Congressional committees asked difficult questions. How would military pressure on the Sandinistas in Nicaragua prevent them from covertly fueling the Communist-backed FMLN insurgency in El Salvador? Indeed, many in Washington even doubted the FMLN was supported from Nicaragua, despite the fact that it was heavily influenced by Communists. Moreover, others asked, what if the Sandinistas responded to covert pressure by becoming not more but less democratic? Would the U.S. government pursue its program to the point of overthrowing the Sandinistas? Throughout 1982 the administration avoided direct answers to questions such as these. Senior officials merely maintained that pressure applied by the Contras would make it harder for the Sandinistas to fuel the war in El Salvador.

Several in Congress, among them Senator Christopher Dodd and Representative Tom Harkin, offered amendments to the defense appropriations bill for fiscal year 1983 that would have prohibited the CIA from using any funds "for the purpose of assisting [any] group or individual in carrying out military activities in or against Nicaragua."[72] These amendments were voted down. Subsequently, the administration worked out a deal with Representative Edward Boland, chairman of the House Permanent Select Committee on Intelligence, to support an amendment prohibiting CIA spending "for the purpose of *overthrowing* the Government of Nicaragua" (emphasis added).[73] Thus a precarious line was drawn between assisting the insurgents, which was allowed, and working to overthrow the government, which was prohibited. The administration's strategists, whose intelligence finding did not explicitly envisage a coup, saw the Boland Amendment as a way to finesse congressional endorsement of its program.

That is not how the amendment was interpreted in the Congress and the press. Many complained that the administration violated "the intent of the law" by supporting Nicaraguans *whose intent* was to overthrow the Sandinistas. Throughout 1983 and 1984, the administration tried to prove to the Congress and the media that it was not trying to oust the Sandinistas, and that its aid would be inadequate to that end.[74] The administration tried to find other rationales for the program, such as "interdicting supplies to El Salvador," but succeeded only, said Undersecretary Fred Iklé, in being "ratcheted down."[75]

Meanwhile, the CIA's William Casey had his own plan. By keeping pressure on the Sandinistas, Casey and Duane Clarridge, the DO's chief of Latin America operations, believed, the momentum of the resistance would pick up and eventually sweep the Sandinistas from power.

In 1984, President Reagan decided that he would not make an issue of Nicaraguan covert action in the upcoming election.[76] Nor would he contest the latest, most restrictive version of the Boland Amendment, which denied CIA funds to the Contras. Thus the administration was caught in a trap of its own making. It had chosen to treat Nicaragua covertly, even though much of the U.S. activity there was public knowledge, largely because it refused to choose between two alternatives: committing itself to the demise of the Sandinistas, or accepting their rule and all the consequences that would flow from that. Only after the Iran-Contra affair became news did the administration assert that Congress lacked the authority to restrict the president's options in Nicaragua.[77]

So it was that in 1984, President Reagan decided to continue the program of using the Contras by getting the money, not from the U.S. Treasury, but from foreign governments and private individuals. At the same time, under the pressure of a delayed budget agreement that had already forced a furlough of federal workers, he would sign the appropriations bill containing a new, revised Boland Amendment that now prohibited the use of CIA funds for "supporting, directly or indirectly, military or paramilitary operations in Nicaragua by any nation, group, organization, movement or individual."[78]

Only when Iranian factions in Lebanon made public the trading of arms for hostages between the White House and Iran, and thus made clear that the already controversial program of Contra aid was being funded with the profits from that arms activity, did many of those who opposed aid to the Contras accuse the Reagan-Bush team of having violated the law. The Iran-Contra scandal would dog the administration until the end of its tenure.

Widespread knowledge of the administration's covert help to the Contras is not what almost killed the official U.S. covert program of aid. That happened because of publicity about the several different "tracks" the president was following in pursuit of his goal, and by the fact that, when faced with the need to reconcile the contradictions between them, he would not fight. He never demanded an up-or-down vote in Congress.

The example of covert support to the Contras helps explain much of what is wrong with American covert action. It is weak not primarily because of excess information in the public domain (leaks), or excessive executive and legislative branch procedures, or bumbling operators. It is weak in large part because of the president's inability to formulate policy and his reluctance to challenge opponents on the merits of that policy. Many a president has chosen covert action as a half measure when he was unwilling to force an issue. Half measures enable a president to do *something*, even when, as with covert action inside the Sino-Soviet bloc in the late 1940s and 1950s, it is not enough to achieve much, let alone ensure victory.[79]

Covert Action in the 1990s

No wonder the bureaucracies within the executive branch have reflected the contradictions that presidents have been unwilling to resolve at the highest levels. No wonder, either, that congressional opposition has so often influenced the battle within given administrations. The CIA has come to believe it is "equidistant" between Congress and the Oval Office. This was not the view of William Casey, but it has been the view of many senior managers of the intelligence community since the late 1970s.[80] Hence, if the president supports a certain operation without putting his own reputation on the line, and Congress opposes it, the CIA is understandably reluctant to risk its own relations with Congress for the sake of the program.

Beginning in the 1960s, the CIA's capability to mount covert action—known in the trade as the infrastructure—began to atrophy. By the late 1970s, there were few specialists and covert action advocates left in the Agency, a consequence of the Carter administration's philosophy, implemented by Stansfield Turner, that covert action was an inappropriate instrument of statecraft in most instances. Few CIA officers believed that covert action was rewarding for the United States politically or for themselves personally. Thus the mere hint that Congress was opposed to a given action was usually enough to dissuade the CIA from devoting resources to developing a plan for the president.

From the late 1940s until the late 1960s, the White House and the CIA had been able to draw on the American private sector to support covert action. Usually, the CIA would recruit and fund citizens from different walks of life to work with anti-Communist activists abroad. American student leaders or businessmen would recruit or assist foreigners in their efforts, and occasionally American case officers posed as members of the private sector so as to pass and move more easily among foreigners. The private sector was willing, even anxious to help—as long as the government provided it with confidentiality.

Through the media exposés in the 1960s and the congressional investigations in the 1970s, a whole generation of skilled political action specialists, as well as Americans and foreigners affiliated with U.S. organizations whom the Soviet apparatus had previously claimed, without proof, to be CIA-controlled, were now *shown* to have substantial CIA ties. Others, who had nothing whatsoever to do with the CIA, were "identified" as controlled CIA agents. With Moscow's active measures effort, lists of alleged CIA operatives—some genuine and some not—found their way into books and newspapers from Washington, D.C., to Wellington, New Zealand.[81] Exposure, false or real, eroded the political effectiveness of anti-Communist organizations, as well as that of specific individuals who had relied on American assurances of confidentiality. Some went so far as to commit suicide.[82] The CIA lost organizations, agents, and supporters, who would no longer run the risk of exposure that working secretly for the United States now involved.

During congressional investigations into intelligence abuses in the mid-1970s, the CIA volunteered not to draw on certain professions either for cover or as a recruitment pool for agents. The full list of such professions has never been made public, but according to reports it included journalists, educators, religious leaders, and certain categories of government employees such as Peace Corps workers. Thus, just as American influence abroad was waning, the United States was deprived of the opportunity to avail itself of much of the cover, potential allies, operatives, and agents that the private sector could provide.

In South Africa, for example, blacks and whites who opposed apartheid and who also opposed Marxist-Leninist domination of the ANC could not receive covert U.S. government support through labor, student, and church groups in America. In this environment, Communist elements in the ANC, with massive Soviet backing, made great strides in consolidating their position. In the Middle East, Arabs, Iranians, Palestinians, and others opposed to Islamic and Marxist extremism also lost a potential patron. The United States did not bolster pro-Western elements in the region to the extent that the USSR, Libya, Iraq, and others aided extremists. So when, in the 1980s, the United States needed political operatives to help in the struggle against Islamic terrorism and extremism, it was usually without assistance from local political operatives.

At the CIA itself, the covert action muscle deteriorated from lack of exercise. Covert action managers, case officers, specialists, and allied agents and assets had to find other outlets for their time and talent, and other means of making a living. In its report, the Church Committee viewed the development from another perspective: over the years, it claimed, the covert action infrastructure drove the CIA to do things the CIA and the United States otherwise would not have done; if the apparatus was kept in place, it would inevitably find a rationale for itself.[83] From either perspective, the practical result was the same: the infrastructure almost faded out of existence.

The most serious loss was in the ability to carry out secret political operations. Deep-cover officers versed in political operations were phased out. There were few of them to begin with, as the government generally preferred to use official cover for case officers. But there had been contract agents, people who worked, sometimes for years, as part-time or full-time CIA operatives. Most contract agents were let go, and the proprietaries (businesses and foundations) that had been used to fund many of them and their operations were dismantled. It became difficult, if not impossible, to explain to an unwitting foreigner where a million dollars for a political operation came from without arousing suspicion.

The United States did retain a covert paramilitary capability. It maintained warehouses with arms and ammunition from different countries to prevent them from being traced to the United States. This capability was kept on the shelf, however, reserved primarily for wartime scenarios that envisioned the arming of indigenous forces in the event of a Soviet invasion of an allied country. The CIA continued to hire Americans and others with military experience, and when the United States increased its support for the Afghans, Angolans, Nicaraguans, and others in the late 1970s and 1980s, the infrastructure was in place to support various resistance movements without American markings.

But many of the experienced officers retired or were let go. Those who remained did not especially want the few covert action slots left in the DO. On the contrary, chiefs of station that had covert action programs usually assigned such work not to their most skilled and experienced case officers but to junior officers.[84] Did experienced CIA operatives pass on their knowledge and skills? Would the new generation of case officers hired in the 1970s and 1980s promise to be as competent in the conduct of covert action, or even as interested in it? Did management ensure that the United States had the human resources for adequate intelligence in the late 1980s and 1990s? On the whole, the answer is no.

With rare exception, the new breed of case officer was not chosen with political action work, overt or covert, in mind. Most of the DO case officers who started in the 1970s and 1980s were hired because it was thought they would make well-rounded generalists.[85] The major job of the DO being clandestine collection, they were to perform that task along with some counterintelligence and covert action. But they were not supposed to be specialists, particularly not covert action specialists (with the possible exception of those who had military experience). Few were versed in the business of influencing politics or working with labor, business, ethnic and religious movements, the media, youth, and intellectual leaders to reinforce American goals abroad.

For the most part these case officers, now middle managers and soon to be senior staff, are white middle-class males who grew up in the United States and during tours abroad have, in effect, lived the lives of American diplomats. They have worked out of U.S. embassies, under diplomatic cover, in various parts of the world. Few are regional specialists. In the 1950s the chief of the DP's western hemisphere division, J. C. King, insisted that his managers and case officers know the predominant language of the region in which they worked. That is no longer the case. There is a pay incentive to learn languages, but in other ways the system discourages such study, which can take several years of full-time application. The ambitious case officer can try to pick up a language after work and on weekends, but that is no easy task. A young officer can take a year or two off, even at government expense, but that means losing experience in the field as well as valuable time that might be used to recruit an agent—an accomplishment that advances a career farther than language acquisition does. Moreover, ambitious officers have to demonstrate the ability to perform a variety of assignments in several different regions. It is a rare case officer or manager who can conduct business in the language of the region where he or she happens to be working at the time, much less who has a feel for the nuances of the local culture that language reflects.

Most of the newer case officers—unlike many of their predecessors who grew up in foreign countries, or worked or fought in them, or held various jobs before joining a bureaucracy—have spent the lion's share of their professional time in the CIA bureaucracy. What does this mean for the effectiveness of covert action?

It is no secret that bureaucrats are most comfortable with routine and are not inclined to be risk-takers. Even if they were so inclined—and somehow managed to survive the system—they might share the fate of others who since the 1970s have run into trouble with Congress and the media. Many CIA leaders have been publicly criticized and chastised. Practicing covert action in this atmosphere means protecting yourself by waiting until all the managers from the top to the bottom of the chain of command, along with a host of lawyers in the CIA and elsewhere, have signed off on your program. Obtaining approval can take months, even years, and by then new forces at work in the world may well have killed the original rationale. The situation today is far different from that which prevailed in the 1940s and 1950s, when drive and flexibility characterized the practice of covert action.

In addition to this new wariness, recruits have learned that one way to get ahead is by devising covert action projects that can be measured and quantified. The CIA has always shown a tendency toward "projec-titis,"[86] evaluating officers by the number of programs they originate, run, or complete rather than by the long-term effectiveness of any particular one. But the tendency became more pronounced as the years went by. It is much easier to recruit a journalist and plant articles in a local newspaper than to build a group of local leaders—political, business, ethnic, or union—in a region where the United States needs moderate allies, say, in the drug-ridden parts of the Andes or in the West Bank of the Jordan and Gaza where Muslim extremists are significant. But it is through such strenuous effort to shore up support from local moderates that the United States may find political solutions in unstable regions.[87] It takes five to ten years or more, as well as patience, money, and political skill, to winnow out opportunists, hostile agents, and prevaricators and build political support. Over the long term, helping to nurture leaders can pay off—as American experience three decades ago in Europe showed.

Nor has the new generation entering the DO received much covert action training, apart from clandestine tradecraft. Covert action is the least-studied field. The KGB of old used to teach successful cases, representing decades of covert action experience, to newcomers so that they could learn the do's and don'ts, at least in the classroom.[88] In contrast, the CIA's recruits of the 1980s and 1990s have learned the doctrine and ethos of collectors. They have been taught classic recruitment, control of sources, and tradecraft. But by the late 1970s there were few experienced personnel left to teach neophytes that as a rule, covert action assets should not be recruited and controlled in the same way collection sources are. The dwindling number of senior officers also limited the effectiveness of "on-the-job training." Even when some case officers and new managers did begin to develop expertise, they would be reassigned to other jobs. Few managers learned the covert action business, few station chiefs became proficient in it, and only the rare case officer developed into a specialist in the field. To some extent this was deliberate, reflecting DO's desire for generalists, but it was partly accidental. DO's top leadership and personnel managers failed to see the effects of not having a professional core of covert action practitioners.

Thus as the number of competent covert action specialists dwindled, there were few replacements, role models, substantive training programs, or incentives for covert action operatives. During the late 1970s and 1980s, when senior managers needed covert action personnel quickly, their solution was to hire retired specialists on full- or part-time contracts. This filled some short-term needs—for example, enabling the United States to build up its cadre of paramilitary specialists who trained the Contras in the 1980s.

But expedience had its costs. For one thing, the annuitants were rusty. Many did not know about the changes that had occurred on their old stomping grounds—the younger leaders who had emerged, and the history of their relations with U.S. officials and case officers. Nor did they understand the nuances that had developed in American politics. As a result, many launched projects and engaged in activities that stirred up controversy when they were leaked to the Washington press. For instance, a retired military specialist from the Special Forces who had taught at Fort Bragg and was brought in to train the Contras wrote a manual that indirectly advocated assassination. In the 1960s, this would have caused no more than a ripple. By the early 1980s it was political dynamite, undermining the cause of the Contras, weakening advocates of U.S. aid to that group, and compromising the case officers who hired him.

This sort of experience, instead of refurbishing and improving the stock of covert action managers and specialists, only further depleted it. The DO initiated a closed cycle: incompetence generated contempt for covert action, which led to decreased investment in personnel. It is one area of deficit spending for which the United States will have to pay in the future.

The history of U.S. covert action during the early part of the cold war was unusual. The perception of danger and the bureaucratic struggles that made possible the accomplishments of the 1940s and early 1950s evaporated, leading to several projects in the 1970s and 1980s whose most pronounced effect was to whip up public controversy. Those projects that were successful synchronized policy, means, and other elements of intelligence—but their accomplishments do not make it any more likely that we will see a revival of U.S. covert action capability in the near future.[89]

The Current Ethos

Over two decades, the practice of covert action in the United States has been transformed. The acceptance of covert action in the 1940s and 1950s, based on the perception of external threat, gave way, beginning in the 1960s and continuing on into the 1980s, to a quite different ethos. That new ethos, "exceptionalism," has over the course of its development wreaked havoc on American covert action capabilities. Dominant today, exceptionalism holds that covert action should not be engaged in unless there are grave and unusual circumstances—the definition of which varies from one exceptionalist to another.

The exceptionalists are schismatic. For many, covert action is synonymous with secret government, dirty tricks, dirty wars, and other activities generally viewed as incompatible with the foreign policy of an open and democratic society. Proponents of this view generally believe covert action should be banned altogether, or used only as a tool of last resort. This came to be the dominant view in the American foreign policy establishment in the mid-1970s. Although some policymakers and members of Congress believe most forms of covert action are compatible with American values and are sometimes a useful tool of foreign policy, the conclusions embodied in the Church Committee's final report (1976) are still prevalent.[90]

Another school of exceptionalists tends to regard covert action as a substitute for policy: doing what you can when diplomacy will not work and military action is too dangerous; doing something when everything has failed; or doing *something* rather than doing (or being accused of doing) nothing.[91]

Lurking unspoken beneath exceptionalism is an unbridged gap between the attitudes of two American Founding Fathers, John Adams and Sam Adams, toward power and the state. John Adams and most of the other Founders had confidence in each other's basic aims and instincts, which would have inclined them to be more favorable toward any use of covert action by the new federal government. Sam Adams, on the other hand, feared that power such as that embodied in covert action could all too easily be turned by rulers against the populace. This view would have led him to an outright rejection of the use of covert action.

There are those, however, who base their exceptionalism on a genuine problem. It has nothing to do with the assertions of the Church Committee's final report or the report of the Twentieth Century Task Force,[92] both of which, in effect, dismissed covert action as contrary to the American form of government. The real problem has been most notably espoused by historian Ernest May.[93] While he does not go so far as to contend that covert action is incompatible with democracy, he views it as not easily accommodated by the American democratic system. He maintains that the United States is not constituted to meet several of the major requirements for covert action. For example, the U.S. Constitution was intended to make it difficult to define national interests, and hence to specify goals for coherent, well-coordinated policies. In May's view, the Founding Fathers designed a political system making wide consultation and consensus-building preconditions for designating any interests as of overriding common concern. The American political system is designed on the premise not only that delineation of a national interest ought to be hard, but also that no such interest should be deemed permanent.

These are impediments, even obstacles, that the executive branch and Congress face in meeting the challenges of a dangerous world. But as the relatively successful use of covert action to support U.S. interests in the early decades of the cold war illustrates, these obstacles need not rule out covert action. Therefore, they should not be used to prevent the maintenance of effective covert action capabilities, if only as a matter of prudence in today's world.

3

BUILDING AND REBUILDING: COUNTERINTELLIGENCE SINCE WORLD WAR II

IF, IN RECENT DECADES, Americans have become suspicious of covert action almost to the point of paralysis, they have always been ambivalent about the most secret element of intelligence, counterintelligence. They believe in major limitations on the government's power, especially the power to intrude on privacy. Yet ever since the Revolution they have been alert to the possibility that foreigners might undermine their liberty with spies and saboteurs. Historically, when the United States perceives a threat, it develops a counterintelligence response; when the threat is thought to have subsided, the counterintelligence capability diminishes. The pendulum swings from one extreme to the other depending on political circumstance. Rarely has there been an articulated government-wide strategy or policy with regard to counterintelligence, and debate on the subject has been limited.

Only one government entity has taken upon itself the task of considering overall counterintelligence policy, and that only recently and sporadically: the White House. In the mid-1970s the White House began to show some interest, but not until the mid-1980s did a single member of the president's staff acquire full-time responsibility in this area. Prior to the mid-1970s, Congress occasionally passed legislation relevant to counterintelligence or dabbled in it some other way.

Who, then, had authority for counterintelligence in the twentieth century? Three parts of the executive branch shared it: the Department of Justice and its principal investigatory branch, the FBI; the U.S. military, where responsibilities were divided up among the services and the Department of Defense; and the principal foreign intelligence service of the United States—the OSS, its postwar successors, and later the CIA. None of the specific programs, modi operandi, or organizational arrangements of these agencies was managed by a single government entity.

Building the Cold War Consensus

Deep-rooted ambivalence resulted in little or no counterintelligence unless senior policymakers in Washington believed there was a specific threat. Threats came and went. In the first half of the twentieth century, attention focused on European immigrants and aliens on American soil who, it was feared, might be sympathetic to foreign powers and ideologies. During World War I these suspects were primarily Germans and other Europeans, some of whom Germany did try to recruit for paramilitary covert action (sabotage) and propaganda.[1]

During and after that war, some in the Washington establishment turned their attention to European immigrants who were socialists or Bolshevik sympathizers. Until the rise of antifascist popular fronts in the 1930s, many Communist sympathizers were first- and second-generation immigrants from Eastern Europe and Russia.[2] Then in the mid-1930s a small number of German-Americans entered into contact with Hitler's Nazis, prompting concern in both Congress and the White House. The House Un-American Activities Committee was created and the Foreign Agents Registration Act passed. President Roosevelt went so far as to circumvent his Attorney General, asking J. Edgar Hoover at the FBI to keep him informed on Nazi and Communist activities in the United States even if the information was not gathered for law enforcement purposes. The president also made little distinction between foreign and American elements involved.[3]

When, in the late 1930s, Roosevelt sought to push American opinion behind support for Britain and France in their struggle with Germany, he welcomed information about those Americans who opposed his policy, whether they were isolationists or Nazi sympathizers. Needless to say, after Germany and Japan became allies in 1935 and U.S. policy clashed with Japanese expansion in Asia, the president, along with the War and the Navy departments, began to consider as well the potential for Japanese- and German-sponsored sabotage, subversion, and espionage on American soil.[4] The unconditional surrender of Germany and Japan and the overwhelming loyalty of Japanese- and German-Americans reduced worry about immigrants from these countries.

After World War II, FBI attention focused on the substantial number of Americans who had become sympathetic to Communism. In 1945 and 1946, even though the prevailing public perception was that Russia was not hostile to U.S. interests, the most senior FBI officials suspected there were significant links between American Communists and the Soviet Union. Revelations about Soviet spying in the United States from GRU code clerk Igor Gouzenko, who defected to Canada in late 1945, and from American KGB courier Elizabeth Bently further alarmed official Washington.[5] Additional warnings were sounded by small, isolated government entities such as the State Department's EUR-X and some high-profile nongovernmental groups like the American Federation of Labor. On the whole, however, civilian Washington was not much interested in intelligence threats emanating from the Soviet Union or elsewhere.

In the early days after World War II, the American military abroad had its hands full with denazification and the protection of American fighting men and bases abroad. The Army, particularly its Counter Intelligence Corps (CIC), was busy establishing postwar governments in Germany, Austria, and Japan. But as the months passed, American military commanders became increasingly aware of German communists and their connections across Russian lines.[6]

As for those American foreign intelligence operatives who remained after the disbanding of OSS in October 1945, they disagreed about the extent of the threat posed by Soviet intelligence and Communism. Some were concerned, others less so. The counterintelligence capability built up in OSS from 1943 to 1945 did not evaporate, but only a handful of operatives were assigned to counterintelligence in the small successor to the SSU and the CIG.

As the perception of the Soviet threat intensified in Washington and among U.S. military forces in Europe, American counterintelligence mobilized. There was rising fear of both hot and cold war, and a growing sense that Moscow was using secret intelligence to recruit sympathizers throughout the world in an effort to shift the global balance in its favor. From 1947 till the mid-1960s, most senior officials of the executive and legislative branches, Republican and Democrat alike, believed that thwarting Soviet bloc espionage, subversion, and sabotage should be one of the U.S. government's key priorities.[7]

However, unless an American ally or a neutral was suspected of being penetrated or manipulated by Moscow, almost no one consid-

ered the use of counterintelligence against other countries and movements. This explains why the military lost interest in denazification.
This was to remain the cardinal policy orientation even after the
breakup of the cold war consensus in the 1970s and the rebuilding of a
counterintelligence consensus in the 1980s.

The U.S. perception of Soviet intelligence, along with perceived
Soviet intentions to acquire converts throughout the world, fueled
Washington's fear and helped shape postwar American counterintelligence. Intelligence, particularly counterintelligence, played a major
role in the Soviet Union, which some have characterized as a "counterintelligence state."[8] Others have suggested the KGB and the military
were the pillars that sustained party power.[9] Whatever its precise role
in Soviet politics, the KGB was believed to be integrated with the Party
and highly centralized. Unlike Western intelligence systems, whose
managers did not usually number among the most senior government
leaders and whose authority, when it existed, was divided among
numerous agencies, the KGB was seen as run primarily by members of
the Politburo who controlled both foreign and domestic intelligence
and security. Note the contrast with the U.S. intelligence community, a
system marked by major limitations on intelligence and by multiple
organizations. In law, and in practice, many activities are proscribed to
U.S. intelligence. Its functions are also divided into multiple bureaucracies that largely ensure that intelligence cannot play a major role in
domestic affairs, and that it is under the control of both the executive
and legislative branches. The Central Intelligence Agency, the Federal
Bureau of Investigation, the Secret Service, the National Security
Agency, the various military intelligence services, and even the Coast
Guard report to different commanders and members of the cabinet.
The U.S. system is fashioned in such a way that there is no concentration of power, authority, and capabilities in any single body. The KGB,
American intelligence believed, had responsibility for most collection,
covert action, and counterintelligence, and there were few effective
checks on its power.

By the late 1940s, Soviet hegemony had swallowed up Eastern
Europe. American specialists were convinced that Moscow had either
helped in or insisted upon the creation of similarly integrated, centralized intelligence systems for its satellites in that region, and that
Moscow used them for its own ends.

This was evidently achieved in a variety of ways. One was to assert
Moscow's political, military, and economic influence over other ruling
Communist parties. Another was to assign advisers to allied services.

Sometimes native-born officers were recruited inside allied services. U.S. officials believed they were confronted with a highly centralized, elite intelligence net cast by Moscow over all the ruling Communist parties in Eastern Europe, and later extended with varying degrees of cooperation to China, North Korea, Vietnam, and Cuba.[10] The network, built on solid lines of communication and able to pool resources and knowledge, was difficult to penetrate. When it did penetrate the spokes of the wheel, however, Washington could gain more insight into the workings of its enemy than the latter could gain by penetrating an American ally, whose intelligence was relatively less well integrated into that of its superpower ally.

The close-knit relationship between the Communist Party and bloc intelligence systems appeared to prevail not only in countries where there was a ruling party, but also where the party was not in power. For many decades the Communist Party of the Soviet Union and the KGB exploited this nexus, using ruling and nonruling parties alike for espionage, covert action, and counterintelligence purposes against its self-defined main enemy: Britain before World War II and the United States after that war. Moscow was able to recruit espionage agents from the Communist Party USA (CPUSA) cadre and contacts. It could also draw on the CPUSA and its allies to exert political influence on or conduct covert action in the United States. On occasion, the CPUSA even assisted the KGB in counterintelligence.[11]

This pattern of activity, not unique to KGB operations in the United States, had gone unnoticed in the 1930s. Later in the 1940s, Western counterintelligence agencies began to catch on. In the 1950s the American public was outraged when the KGB's tactics became widely known—a reaction exploited by demagogues such as Senator Joseph McCarthy.

The origins of these tactics that so inflamed America can be traced back to the conspiratorial ranks of the czarist underground. Unlike Western intelligence chiefs, Soviet leaders were not raised as part of the establishment. Even after the Bolshevik Revolution put the Communists in power, operatives of "the organs," as the intelligence and security services were known in Soviet parlance, could not work abroad as their British, American, and French counterparts did. In the 1920s, very few Soviet operatives abroad functioned as diplomats or under diplomatic cover for the simple reason that Western governments did not recognize the Soviet regime, and at home few worked as policemen or law enforcement officers. Instead their modus operandi reflected their Bolshevik underground experience: they were expert at penetrating their own government as well as antigovernment movements. They were used to running, and to protecting themselves against, double agents, and they were proficient at various kinds of complicated deception.[12]

For more than a decade after the Bolshevik seizure of power, many governments refused to recognize the Soviet Union. Unable to rely on official cover in embassies and other diplomatic establishments, the KGB and GRU became as comfortable running illegal operations as the West did running legal establishments.[13] Even after the Soviet regime became widely recognized in the 1930s, Moscow continued to apply the offensive and defensive techniques that had been honed during the prerevolutionary Bolshevik conspiracy and in the days when Soviet operatives abroad learned to operate without the benefit of diplomatic establishments.[14]

The Soviet bloc alliance against the West, the Soviet habit of pitting Communist parties throughout the world against the United States, and the KGB's underhanded modus operandi gradually kindled an American reaction. Washington sought to build up an intelligence alliance of Western states to counter the Soviet threat. In the early postwar era until the 1950s, its major allies were Western European and British Commonwealth countries. The United States supplemented these relationships by establishing friendships in Latin America and other decolonized areas. To be sure, it had favorite partners, and there were strains with even the closest allies, for example, Britain. Nevertheless, American counterintelligence was able to benefit greatly from the counterintelligence resources of scores of governments around the world.[15]

Thus, with the exception of areas where the U.S. military was present in force, such as Germany or Korea, the United States relied heavily on foreign services for information about the identities and activities of Soviet bloc services and Communist parties. There was little pressure for the United States to build up a unilateral counterintelligence capability abroad to protect itself from the Soviet bloc outside of the bloc, and allied services posed little threat to positive American intelligence operations on their soil. Some U.S. allies sought to protect their own governments from U.S. penetration and took steps to identify and neutralize U.S. intelligence operations against them.

Soon after the war, Western counterintelligence began to take advantage of technologies that would identify and neutralize Soviet bloc activity. Moscow had supplemented human couriers with clandestine radios to communicate with illegal agents in the West. It had also begun to rely on coded communications with the KGB in legal and diplomatic establishments. Before long, Western counterintelligence was intercepting and decrypting this message traffic,[16] and by the 1950s the technological balance had swung further in favor of counterspies. The application of technology to the surveillance of spies on Western soil, especially those operating out of diplomatic establishments, gradually increased.

During this time, the first two postwar decades, Washington considered counterintelligence almost wholly a matter for the executive branch. This suited the Congress. The White House was not much concerned with overall counterintelligence priorities, strategy, or policy, not even with regard to the Soviet bloc after the onset of the cold war. It divided counterintelligence into foreign and domestic. Foreign counterintelligence was guided principally by NSC Intelligence Directive No. 5: U.S. Espionage and Counterintelligence Activities Abroad (1947). This secret document, which was amended from time to time and which defined espionage and counterintelligence, gave the DCI authority to coordinate all clandestine activities abroad. He would consult with other agencies and resolve interagency disputes. The CIA was to have primary responsibility for all U.S. clandestine activities abroad, which included counterintelligence. It would maintain central files and provide other common services, but outside agencies and military commanders could conduct espionage and counterintelligence abroad, including liaison with foreign services, under the overall direction of the DCI. The NSC directive spelled out how and when the DCI was to coordinate with military commanders and the Secretaries of Defense and State. Domestic counterintelligence would not be the domain of the CIA.[17]

Another presidential directive concerned counterintelligence at home. Its origin can be found in a classified directive Roosevelt issued in June of 1939, just before the outbreak of war in Europe.[18] It gave investigative jurisdiction over all espionage, counterespionage, and sabotage to the FBI, military intelligence, and naval intelligence. It instructed the directors of these three entities to function as a committee, later called the Interdepartmental Intelligence Conference (IIC), under the chairmanship of FBI Director Hoover. Later, the FBI and military intelligence outlined their respective areas of responsibility in three Delimitation Agreements, signed in 1940, 1942, and 1949.[19]

This directive was followed by one made public on September 6, 1939, that called for all law enforcement officers in the country "to turn over to the nearest representative of the FBI any information obtained by them relating to espionage, counterespionage, sabotage, subversive activities and violations of the neutrality laws."[20] Three public presidential directives restated and reaffirmed these instructions. They were issued on January 8, 1943 (by Roosevelt), July 24, 1950 (by Truman), and December 15, 1953 (by Eisenhower). In 1962, President Kennedy designated his brother, the Attorney General, as the official who would oversee IIC operations.[21]

In sum, the president delegated to the DCI and the Director of the FBI primary responsibility for the formulation and implementation of counterintelligence policy. Although the National Security Act of 1947 named the NSC in the White House as the sole organ for coordinating domestic and foreign policy, no single agency or person had overall responsibility for American counterintelligence. Nor did anyone on the NSC or White House political staffs specialize in it. There was no center for bringing the different bureaucracies together, and although agency chiefs were supposed to work together, without anyone authorized to oversee their cooperation, that was not assured.

Coordination was not made easier by the overlapping functions and geographic jurisdictions designated in the directives. It was left to the intelligence chiefs to sort this all out through bargaining. While the CIA was primarily responsible for counterintelligence abroad, the military had some responsibility both abroad and at home. The FBI was supposed to pursue counterintelligence at home only. As for law enforcement, it was to be practiced at home, but there was no mention of enforcement for crimes committed abroad. The military had some such responsibility with regard to personnel and installations abroad and at home. The FBI had enforcement authority at home only, the CIA none at home or abroad.

One reason Congress was little interested in the subject of counterintelligence in the 1950s and early 1960s was that bipartisan consensus prevailed on the major goals and means of policy.[22] Everyone was anti-Communist and anti-Soviet, some more militant than others. The legislative branch was content to allow the executive almost exclusive control of national security policy formulation and implementation. Congress gave its general approval after being apprised of developments and only rarely inquired into details or sought to micromanage intelligence agencies. From the perspective of the 1990s, this attitude may be hard to imagine. At any rate, the agencies working in counterintelligence had great flexibility. Adhering to overall U.S. policy and the consensus on containment, the FBI, CIA, and military services each independently defined their mission and the means necessary to achieve it with varying degrees of interagency coordination.

The FBI

The FBI, or rather a section of it, became the premier American counterintelligence service during the cold war. This is the role that it came to see itself playing, and it had the lion's share of the resources and personnel the country devoted to counterintelligence. A dominant bureaucratic ethos gradually emerged in the agency, in part because of consistent leadership. This, of course, was provided by J. Edgar Hoover, who managed the Bureau from its creation in 1924 until his death in 1972. Hoover's associate director for most of the postwar period was his close friend Clyde Tolson.

The part of the Bureau that concentrated on counterintelligence was the Intelligence Division.[23] In effect, it had only three directors from the mid-1940s till the early 1970s (the title was actually assistant director, Intelligence Division). Three were FBI agents who had worked on counterintelligence and pleased Hoover: D. M. Mickey Ladd, Alan Belmont, and William C. Sullivan. All three in turn were promoted from chief of the Intelligence Division to assistant to the director for investigations, in effect the number-three spot in the Bureau hierarchy. When Sullivan was promoted in 1970 he even persuaded Hoover to appoint one of his longtime colleagues, C. D. Brennan, as assistant director of the Intelligence Division.[24] At Washington headquarters there was a great deal of continuity.

On the whole, counterintelligence operations took place in field offices scattered throughout the country, including a Washington field office housed separately from national headquarters after the 1950s. Headquarters personnel, veterans of field office operations, supervised field officers and performed some analysis. A few headquarters personnel, especially in the early postwar years, were veterans of criminal investigation as well as counterintelligence. But over the years, counterintelligence specialists, both at headquarters and in field offices, evolved into a breed apart from criminal and law enforcement officers. The change had something to do with these agents' physical distance from the Justice Department. More important, counterintelligence differed in many ways from pure criminal and law enforcement work. Many counterintelligence personnel became specialists in their subject matter. Headquarters personnel did not expect to return to field offices for rotational assignments or to work on criminal cases in addition to counterintelligence.

What was the difference between the Intelligence Division and the rest of the Bureau? As part of the Justice Department and primarily a law enforcement agency, the FBI sought to investigate violations of the law and then prosecute. The counterintelligence division regarded its activity as something assisted by, but not synonymous with, prosecution and law enforcement.

Hoover was interested in all of these subjects—intelligence and counterintelligence on the one hand, and criminal prosecution and law enforcement on the other.[25] To shore up his power and to take advantage of their overlapping functions, he kept intelligence and law enforcement together. He did not follow the British model and create a non-law-enforcement domestic security service. It was not long, however, before he realized that counterintelligence was distinct enough to require a specialized structure and somewhat different methods from those employed by the Bureau's traditional law enforcement division.

Hoover and his senior lieutenants came to believe that criminal work was much more cut-and-dried than counterintelligence. In criminal work there were bad guys and good guys. The bad guys could be investigated and prosecuted under the rule of law. They were not backed by secret organizations and the powers and resources of foreign governments. Counterintelligence was different. As William Sullivan put it, "The man who excels at criminal investigation would be lost in intelligence. Instead of . . . clear cut black and white issues intelligence is full of gray areas. In intelligence a man can investigate for years without getting any real results. A man who enjoys solving tantalizing and complex problems, who likes to experiment, could be bored stiff catching bank robbers and belongs in intelligence."[26] Hence although not everyone in the FBI agreed, Hoover saw the need for counterintelligence's separate organization, distinct tools, and specialized knowledge.

The Intelligence Division consisted of internal security, counterespionage, and central research sections. Internal security was the largest, reflecting the traditional fear that any threat to undermine the Constitution would emanate from American soil, with or without foreign involvement. The counterespionage section was a response to wartime experience with Nazi, Japanese, and Soviet intelligence.

The internal security section eventually split into IS-1 (extremism), which targeted potential terrorist groups, and IS-2, responsible for Communist groups. Most notable of these was the CPUSA, subservient to the Soviet Communist Party. IS-2 also covered opposition Communist groups such as the Trotskyite Socialist Workers Party.[27] Each of these sections was staffed by five to ten supervisors who oversaw the management of counterintelligence matters in FBI field offices.

The counterespionage branch supervised field office investigations and operations against Soviet bloc services. Its espionage section concentrated on the KGB and GRU, its nationalities section on the bloc services and their ties to American ethnic communities. Each section included five to ten supervisors. There was also a liaison section that coordinated with the CIA, the military, and FBI legal attachés, that is, liaison personnel stationed at U.S. embassies abroad.

The central research section grew to approximately ten to fifteen FBI agents, although much of the analytical work was in effect done by managers at FBI headquarters. In the 1950s, research was headed by William Sullivan, who even after he became assistant director of the Intelligence Division in 1961 continued to take special interest in central research. Research was focused on internal security but also studied counterespionage matters.

The headquarters staff supervised FBI agents who were organized into squads in field offices. Unlike internal security squads, which worked out of smaller cities as well as major metropolitan areas, squads working on Soviet counterespionage were clustered in a few cities with a solid legal/diplomatic infrastructure: Washington, New York, and Chicago. In the early 1950s, not much was known about the post–World War II KGB, and so these squads opened cases on suspected KGB officers and their American contacts with little thought to the KGB's organization or mission. During this period the squads in each field office amounted to twenty-five or thirty special agents plus support staff for physical and technical surveillance.

Collection

During the early cold war, counterintelligence, though distinct from criminal work, was conducted similarly with regard to collection or investigation. Rarely did the Intelligence or the Criminal Division sit down and plan a top-driven strategy. In other words, neither tried to figure out which U.S. secrets needed special protection, or where targets of the KGB were likely to be located, or what sort of activity the KGB might be engaged in. Although in the late 1950s and 1960s there was some planning, FBI work was primarily driven by specific cases. There were general guidelines, and annual conferences attended by headquarters and field counterintelligence agents, but in the main, agents opened cases when individuals or groups were caught or suspected of violating espionage or internal security laws. This essentially bottom-driven strategy, which developed out of experience in criminal investigation, carried over into the Bureau's prewar and wartime investigations of U.S. Communists, Nazi sympathizers, and those with ties to foreign intelligence, though these cases were not necessarily intended to lead to criminal prosecution.

During World War II, virtually every suspicion that an American might be a spy or a saboteur was investigated by the FBI. Mark Felt, a young supervisor at the wartime headquarters espionage section who in the 1960s would become a senior FBI official, commented about the Bureau's zeal during this period: "My responsibility was to review as many cases as possible—fifty or more files a day—of the thousands of cases that poured in for scrutiny by our four man team. New to the work, we were overly cautious and we tended to resolve doubts by continuing the investigations. In time we realized that ninety-eight percent of the cases could have been closed immediately and we made substantial reductions in the case load."[28]

After the war, and a brief period of optimism that an espionage section would no longer be needed, Hoover re-created the section under the direction of the Intelligence Division. Cases were opened when the FBI had reason to believe any foreigner was a spy or any American a subversive. As in wartime, the FBI was juggling many thousands of cases at any given time. There were general guidelines about when cases should be opened and closed, but there was no legal threshold of evidence to ascertain when a person should be investigated. The Bureau ethos, and that of much of the country at the time, was that the United States was in the midst of a cold war that could turn hot at any time. Almost anyone connected with an organization believed to be subversive was a potential suspect, and, potentially, so were any of his or her associates. A veil of suspicion also hung over people in contact with a suspected spy or foreign intelligence officer. The idea was to smother the enemy, even if the coverage was sometimes too broad.

In the mid-1940s, membership in the CPUSA peaked around 75,000 to 85,000 members. Ten years later it had dropped to about 25,000, and from there it tapered off to a few thousand in the 1970s. The FBI opened cases on virtually all these people and many suspected Communists as well. It identified and sought out the location of most of them, as required under various executive branch guidelines and laws. And Communists were not the only people under investigation. When, for example, President Truman's Loyalty and Security Program set up boards checking the patriotism of federal employees, the Bureau had to make inquiries about both job holders and applicants.[29]

The Emergency Detention Act of 1950 gave the FBI authority to investigate anyone who might be detained in the event of war or national emergency, and so the FBI opened files on thousands more. In 1950, over President Truman's veto, Congress passed the McCarran Act, which established the Subversive Activities Control Board and required both Communist and Communist-front groups to register with the government. In 1956, the Supreme Court reduced the power of the government to investigate and prosecute those it deemed subversive under the 1940 Smith Act, which had made it a crime to advocate the overthrow of the government by violence. But the new interpretation still required the Justice Department to keep track of those who might reasonably be expected to use violence (as opposed to those who merely advocated it) toward this end.

With so many laws on the books and the executive branch's loyalty program, the caseload was staggering. By 1960, the FBI had opened 432,000 files at headquarters on individuals and groups. Between 1960 and 1963 an additional nine thousand files were opened. And an even greater caseload was maintained in FBI field offices.[30]

The counterespionage section tried to identify and keep track of the activities of foreigners suspected or known to be intelligence officers. It would open cases on these individuals and decide whether to open cases on Americans who came into contact with them. By the mid-1950s, there were about ten thousand active counterintelligence cases.

In deciding to open a case and conduct an investigation, the FBI used a variety of techniques and sources.[31] One type was open sources. For example, the Bureau examined visa requests from foreigners. It also maintained more or less overt contacts with administrators at universities that had foreign students or activists, and with ethnic organizations in countries ruled by a Communist Party.

In addition, the Bureau developed clandestine human collection programs based largely on its pre–World War II and wartime experience. It conducted surveillance on Soviet bloc installations and embassies that covered among other things mail, physical premises, phones, and personnel. Though official/legal installations were located in only a few cities, keeping track of them and the Americans who came into contact with them was manpower-intensive, and so most field office agents were called upon to assist.

The FBI also had more sophisticated, ambitious methods for deciding which cases to pursue. One was to use double agents. The Bureau had employed them alone and in cooperation with the British before and during World War II. The counterespionage squad had only twenty to thirty full-fledged double agents at any given time. By posing as sympathetic to the Soviet camp or to a subversive organization, they were supposed to elicit information on its mission, programs, or modus operandi. Almost all double agents were average Americans, not Bureau personnel, who "walked into" Communist Party offices or Soviet bloc installations and volunteered, ostensibly for ideological or financial reasons. The internal security squads in FBI field offices, on the other hand, had hundreds of double agents at any one time. Precise personnel figures are unavailable, but based on the Church Committee hearings and the writings and interviews of former senior FBI officials, about half of the Bureau's Intelligence Division personnel were assigned to internal security work. It appears that in the 1950s about one-third of the Bureau's *total* of 4,800 special agents were working on internal security, and the FBI had about 5,000 informants on its payroll.[32] The number of FBI agents peaked in 1973, at 8,500.[33]

Another Bureau technique was recruiting foreign intelligence officers or the leaders of U.S. organizations suspected of being subversive. This was attempted with a variety of standard carrots and sticks such as sex, money, and appeals to ego. But recruiting was difficult unless the target wanted to defect or change sides. Until the early 1960s, in fact, the FBI was not at all successful in recruiting foreign intelligence officers, because up to that time few of them had abandoned their cause. Even after that, it was not always easy to persuade a potential defector to stay in place so that the Bureau could take advantage of his or her continued access to an organization's secrets.

In the early postwar period, the FBI did not use its own officers as deep-cover access agents (people who could get close to the target, or who had access to the target, but who did not appear to be U.S. government officials). Hoover distrusted long-term undercover operations (there was too little accountability), and it took a long time to approve of this specific technique. Nonetheless, after 1960 the Bureau successfully recruited as agents in place a number of Soviet bloc personnel. Though the precise number has not been revealed, it was probably fewer than a hundred. The FBI strove to keep their recruits assigned to posts inside the United States. If a recruit was reassigned abroad, the Bureau either turned him over to the CIA for handling or broke off contact until he was reassigned to the United States at some later date.

It was much more difficult to keep track of Soviet bloc illegals operating in the United States. Little is known about Soviet and American successes and failures in the illegal war in the United States, for neither side has shown all its cards. It is likely that the Soviet bloc was operating more than a few and at one time as many as a hundred illegals on American shores. Some disappeared when the FBI caught their scent.[34] Indeed, one longtime Bureau counterintelligence specialist maintained, perhaps with a little hyperbole, that there may have been as many illegals in the 1950s as there were Bureau agents assigned to counterintelligence. Others were found out,[35] either through luck[36] or skillful counterintelligence.[37] Overall, evidence indicates that while Moscow's legal operatives had a hard time outwitting American counterintelligence on U.S. soil, its illegals did not. With its relatively open borders, the United States was easily penetrated by illegal immigrants, and after they entered there was almost no control over their movements, financial transactions, or communications abroad.

Almost all the intrusive human and technical sources and techniques that the FBI employed during the cold war—the extent of Soviet knowledge of which is unclear—had been used in World War II. Now, however, they were put to more creative use. Electronic intercepts kept tabs on both Soviet bloc and Communist facilities as well as individuals. As in World War II, this technique was not applied indiscriminately, for it was expensive to transcribe, translate, and make sense of the information from wiretaps and bugs. At the height of the cold war there were only seventy-eight wiretaps in operation. (It is not clear whether a "wiretap" covered all the offices, residences, or other property of an individual.) In 1965, apparently, Hoover decided arbitrarily that he wanted the number cut in half.[38] This was opposed by Alan Belmont and William Sullivan, but Mark Felt, on Hoover's orders, imposed it.

Another technique was the break-in or "black bag" job, in which the FBI would surreptitiously search an office, home, or hotel room and copy any interesting documents. In addition to successful break-ins at foreign embassies and other official installations,[39] the Bureau conducted 238 entries from 1942 to 1968 at fourteen "domestic subversive targets."[40]

The FBI opened the mail of selected targets in the 1950s and 1960s. It benefited from CIA work that secretly examined communications between the United States and the Soviet Union,[41] as well as from the Department of Defense's receipt of private international cable traffic.[42]

Thus the Bureau helped and was helped by other parts of the intelligence community. The liaison section of its Intelligence Division, which had a staff of ten to twelve, coordinated with other agencies, often enjoying close cooperation in specific cases. Sometimes, for example, the Bureau answered other agencies' requests to surveil Soviet intelligence officers visiting the United States, or to produce codes and ciphers that could be obtained from break-ins or recruited agents.

The Bureau received enormously valuable help from signals intelligence (sigint) specialists at the Army Security Agency (ASA) in Arlington, Virginia (which in 1952 became the NSA). The story of how the ASA broke some of the KGB's wartime codes was sketched by Robert Lamphere, one of the few Bureau counterintelligence specialists to write his memoirs. According to Lamphere, after 1948 the FBI, the ASA, the British MI5 and MI6, and to some extent the CIA collaborated in directing their field agents to explore possibilities and connections in the information divulged in KGB messages.[43]

Among the famous spies directly uncovered by this collaboration were Judith Coplon (then working in internal security for the Justice Department) and her Soviet handler Valentin Gubetchev, and Klaus Fuchs and his American handler Harry Gold. These cases alone generated forty-nine new cases. Out of the investigations, eight people were convicted of serving as agents or couriers of the KGB. Others were Soviet nationals who had to leave the United States or Americans who were neutralized, that is, removed from access to classified information but not convicted of a crime.[44]

At times, however, relations were frosty between the agencies, particularly at the top. Hoover did not take much personal interest in close collaboration with other agencies, and apparently meetings between him and the DCI were rare.[45] For many reasons, including concern for security, and perhaps partly because of decades-long turf battles, Hoover remained suspicious of the CIA. In 1970, precipitated by the CIA's refusal to divulge which of his special agents in Denver had told the CIA about an FBI case, he went so far as to break off all official liaison. Nevertheless, liaison continued at the working level. Counterespionage supervisors from headquarters and some field offices collaborated with the CIA's counterintelligence staff.[46]

Analysis

Collecting information is one thing. Making sense of it and using it to frustrate and exploit foreign services is another. In the first few decades of the cold war, analysis was left to field operators and headquarters supervisors. They gathered scraps of information from overt and secret sources in a case file, then, on a daily or weekly basis, decided what to do next.

They received some help from those working on internal security, which was the focus of what became a small central research unit created by the Intelligence Division in the 1950s and headed by William Sullivan. Sullivan, not the physical ideal of a G-man, was a short, craggy, rumpled New Englander, a reflective person who relished books and the company of liberal intellectuals. Sullivan had strategic vision. He believed in interagency cooperation, and he saw that counterintelligence could be an effective instrument of policy, not merely defensive. To his mind, liberal democracy was locked in combat with enemies on the left and the right who were out to destroy it. His job, and the job of the FBI, was to use counterintelligence to weaken if not destroy the enemies of free society. For most of his career, Sullivan kowtowed to Hoover. When they disagreed, Sullivan backed down. Hoover liked and steadily promoted him until they had a falling-out in 1970. (In the late 1960s, Sullivan, either for personal reasons or because he believed that Hoover's megalomania was harming U.S. security, turned on his master.)

The ten-to-fifteen-member research staff focused on internal security, producing overview monographs for Hoover and senior Bureau officials. Copies were sent to field offices, where they were usually locked in the safe of the most senior official responsible for counterintelligence, either the special agent in charge or his deputy. In the late 1950s, the research group began producing shorter memos on current topics, but again the subjects were internal security and the audience was primarily the headquarters staff. Occasionally, analysis of Soviet bloc subjects was conducted, but apparently Sullivan believed that the FBI could do very little to assist the CIA in this area.

The research staff also wrote material on general security awareness. Almost all of it dissected Communist ideology and operational tactics. Some of it, for instance, *Masters of Deceit* and *A Study of Communism*, appeared in popular books that listed Hoover as the author.[47] Some turned up in public speeches given by Hoover, Sullivan, and other top Bureau officials.[48]

Exploitation

Given the way it defined its mission, the FBI could take pride in the use it made of information collected and analyzed in the 1950s and early 1960s. Among its most outstanding accomplishments was education of the public and the government about security. To a variety of educational organizations such as the American Bar Association, the Bureau provided a stream of both factual and lightly fictionalized accounts of Soviet techniques used to exploit the CPUSA and its fronts. To be sure, there was great public receptivity to this campaign, and Hoover and the others took advantage of it. However, they did not seek to whip up hysteria. Although they maintained friendly relations with congressional investigators, their goal was to provide balanced evidence and avoid excesses such as those of Senator McCarthy. This is not to say that they always succeeded. Many mistakes were made. But overall the public education program made it harder for Soviet legals and the CPUSA to recruit American agents. Meanwhile, the Bureau's work was made easier by publicity about Soviet repression at home and imperialism abroad.

Despite the vigilance implied by the Bureau's education program, Hoover and his lieutenants could be surprisingly lax about some aspects of Bureau security. For example, while Hoover's puritanical standards for the recruitment and behavior of FBI agents probably helped prevent Soviet bloc penetration of the Bureau itself, communications devices, such as car radios and telephones, were often not secure. Undoubtedly the KGB listened in. There was little compartmentation inside Bureau field offices and among headquarters supervisors. Special agents and their support personnel could learn about people and operations they had no need to know about—a violation of a cardinal principle of security.[49] Moreover, once they were hired, few credit or financial checks were run on Bureau personnel to disclose any unexplained cash. Security in the cold war years concentrated on neutralizing the ideological subversive threat. The Bureau, while sophisticated and effective in many ways, did not seem attuned to some of the techniques used by sophisticated hostile services, or to the danger of American government volunteers to the USSR who might not be driven by ideology and hence would have little contact with the CPUSA or its fronts.[50]

The cipher break of the CPUSA and of official Soviet installations in the United States enabled the Bureau to decrypt a number of wartime Soviet bloc operations being conducted on American soil. As a result, the FBI went on the defensive. It caught, prosecuted, or otherwise neutralized many Americans involved in espionage. The FBI's physical and technical surveillance hindered the bloc's attempts to use several hundred case officers it had deployed in the United States to recruit and run others.[51] Moreover, the Bureau, in cooperation with other agencies, was able to identify some of the illegals working in the United States.

The FBI ran some offensive operations as well, most of them against the CPUSA. Apparently Sullivan noted that the Trotskyite Socialist Workers Party (SWP) was recruiting its own ranks from inside the CPUSA, which the Bureau believed to be a major source of support for Soviet espionage. The FBI was looking for an excuse to "foster factionalism" between groups such as these, as well as to stir up "dissatisfaction among rank and file members of the CP."[52] And so after Hoover briefed the president and the NSC in March 1956, the FBI began a program known as COINTELPRO to disrupt and disorganize the CPUSA and other groups. Approximately half of all COINTELPRO operations would be mounted against the CPUSA. In the 1960s, the FBI's internal security section would also mount COINTELPRO operations against suspected white or black extremist groups and a mélange of groups and individuals such as the Ku Klux Klan, the Nation of Islam, and Martin Luther King. The COINTELPRO strategy was not simpleminded: there was to be a two-pronged attack, from the left and the right. The vehicle from the left would be another Communist organization, the SWP. The SWP did not need encouragement to attack the CPUSA, but well-informed and well-coordinated Bureau agents in the SWP could make any attacks more effective. The attack from the right would come from conservatives and the liberal establishment, drawing on FBI information about party secrets and the Bureau's sophisticated counterintelligence techniques.[53]

Twelve field offices participated in COINTELPRO. Ideas submitted from the field were selected for implementation and coordination by headquarters supervisors. One key activity was neutralizing CPUSA efforts to infiltrate mainstream organizations such as the National Association for the Advancement of Colored People (NAACP) and the nascent United Farm Workers union. The Bureau, for example, might inform the head of a local organization that a known Communist had joined or was about to join. This did not always work. Attorney General Robert Kennedy had Thurgood Marshall inform Martin Luther King that several of his key advisers were either Communists or part of the secret Soviet funding operation in the United States. An exasperated President Kennedy even raised the issue with King himself. King said he would act, but he refused to distance himself from the associates in question. It was as a result of this that the Bureau, with Robert Kennedy's approval, intensified its surveillance of the civil rights leader. Later, after concluding that he had become a danger to the country, the FBI sought to weaken his influence through a variety of genuinely dirty tricks.[54]

Another technique for sowing disruption was to frame leaders of the CPUSA. When someone was framed as an FBI informant, it discredited the person and kindled suspicion among other CPUSA leaders, who could not be certain who in their midst was working for the Bureau.[55] Then there was the use of anonymous, acrimonious telephone calls and letters to prevent an alliance between the SWP and the CPUSA. Over a fourteen-year period, 1,850 separate action proposals were submitted by field offices, of which 1,388 were approved, with "known results" achieved in 222 situations.[56]

During the 1950s and 1960s more than half of the FBI's manpower, analytical resources, and leadership focused on disrupting and weakening the threat to internal security. Less attention and fewer resources were devoted to penetrating and manipulating Soviet bloc services, although the Bureau did continue prewar and wartime information-gathering in the course of counterintelligence to accumulate positive intelligence. For example, double agents and high-level informants in the CPUSA obtained information about Soviet bloc internal affairs and foreign policy direction. This information was "scrubbed" to protect the source, then usually disseminated to a few policymakers in the State Department and the White House or to selected CIA analysts. It was not, however, compared with other positive sources before being passed on, or carefully vetted to ensure that it was not disinformation.

Moreover, only a few of the FBI agents in contact with these sources were aware of the significance or subtleties of the positive information they were receiving. After all, the agents were counterintelligence investigators or case officers, not positive collectors or specialists in foreign affairs. Policymakers and positive collectors from other agencies rarely briefed Bureau agents on their needs. Hence, although the FBI agents were in a position to obtain positive intelligence and did pass it on from time to time, they were not as helpful in this area as they could have been.

The CIA

The CIA's counterintelligence was heavily influenced by the experience of World War II—tutorials and techniques learned from the British, and work conducted against Nazi and fascist intelligence organizations. But postwar counterintelligence specialists in the CIA for the most part were not as fortunate in matching the sources of information that their wartime predecessor, the X-2 branch of OSS, had enjoyed, nor in conducting the same level of defensive and offensive exploitation. Furthermore, they were not generally regarded by their colleagues in the CIA as a major instrument of U.S. intelligence.

In the postwar CIA, counterintelligence was conceived of as a staff function, to service or assist the major frontline activities—collection and covert action.[57] It was regarded primarily as a defensive aid to protect intelligence collectors and covert action programs from penetration. The job of counterintelligence was twofold: to help prevent enemy services from planting false double agents or defectors on CIA case officers and to ensure that CIA professionals were not working for hostile powers. As most CIA espionage and covert actions were conducted by the geographic divisions of the DO, the divisions at headquarters assigned one or more of their officers to counterintelligence work. For these DO case officers counterintelligence was a rotation assignment, not a specialty. They worked with stations and case officers in the field to determine whether potential recruits or defectors were bona fide. Most stations outside of the Soviet bloc maintained contact with local security services to obtain information about bloc intelligence activities and personnel in the country where the stations were located.

By far the most important DO division was the one working against the Soviet Union and Eastern Europe. In addition to the operations run out of Washington and Germany, the DO maintained a small legal presence in U.S. embassies in most Soviet bloc countries. But the Soviet bloc division operated worldwide, trying to gain access to and recruit personnel at Soviet missions wherever they existed.

The small group of counterintelligence referents—those responsible for counterintelligence—in the Soviet bloc division received help from two other parts of the CIA. One was the Office of Security, which reported to the deputy director for administration. This body was designed to physically protect CIA installations and personnel in the United States and around the world. It vetted most of the professional personnel that the CIA hired and investigated allegations that CIA personnel or installations had been compromised or recruited by foreign services.

The other group that assisted was the counterintelligence staff. In the early days of the CIA, only a few people, ten to fifteen, worked fulltime on counterintelligence in Staff C (counterintelligence) of the OSO. A full-blown counterintelligence staff was created in 1954 after a variety of scandals indicated that the geographic divisions and the Office of Security alone were unable to protect U.S. intelligence operations from infiltration by the Soviet bloc. Among the most egregious scandals were the failures of OPC to protect its operations from Soviet bloc penetration, for example, in Albania, Thailand, and Poland. OPC had meager counterintelligence protection. OPC case officers did submit the names of assets (potential recruits) for counterintelligence review. The small OSO counterintelligence staff would check a name against central files to see if the person had a Communist or fascist background. If so, he was often turned down for employment. On the other hand, a variety of subterfuges were developed by OPC chief Frank Wisner to get around the counterintelligence screen if it was believed a particular individual was important. Moreover, the OSO was largely segregated from the OPC bureaucratically and culturally. OPC operators were activists and less inhibited about strict clandestine tradecraft. They had to draw on the people available, and almost all OPC operations, especially paramilitary operations inside the Soviet bloc itself, came to be penetrated and compromised by bloc intelligence.

The veteran X-2 officer who worked for SSU and OSO, James Angleton, was appointed head of the new counterintelligence staff in 1954 and remained in that position until he was forced to retire twenty years later. He divided the staff, recruited from among X-2 veterans and others in the DO who shared his concerns, into several branches. Among the most significant was the operations branch, which worked with other CIA divisions, the FBI, and the military on suspected counterintelligence cases. The research and analysis branch prepared studies on foreign service operations and current order of battle descriptions. The international Communist division sought to penetrate nonruling Communist parties around the world in an effort to identify and recruit Communists and their Soviet handlers.

During the first two decades of the cold war, the counterintelligence staff had fairly consistent leadership. Almost all its senior staff were DO operators, even in the analytical branch. And over time most of the counterintelligence staff became, in effect, professional counterintelligence officers, despite a system of rotation and the fact that counterintelligence was not officially recognized in the DO as a career specialty, as were collection and covert action. Many in the staff did not rotate out of counterintelligence; most remained in headquarters with occasional assignments abroad.

Unlike the X-2 in World War II, the counterintelligence staff did not have its own communication system from the field to headquarters that bypassed station chiefs. Nor did it have permanent field representatives working on an equal footing with other DO case officers in areas such as collection and covert action. With some exceptions, counterintelligence staffers were supposed to assist collectors and covert action operatives within geographic divisions. They were not on par with them, although for a variety of reasons Angleton was a powerful leader who, like other staff and division chiefs, always had access to the head of the CIA Clandestine Services.

The counterintelligence staff had two main sources: reports from DO agents that were passed to the division (in those days, not all such information was passed on), and information resulting from liaison with "friendly services." Station and division chiefs maintained direct relations with local intelligence services, but the counterintelligence staff was supposed to coordinate them, keeping track of the terms and progress of liaison relationships and seeing to it that those relationships were not manipulated by foreign intelligence services for the purposes of penetrating the CIA. Angleton personally managed the Israeli account.

There were numerous other sources of intelligence, for instance, people recruited by the international Communist division.[58] Such recruiting was more extensive in some geographic regions, such as Latin America, and often it was resisted by division chiefs who did not welcome counterintelligence staff on their turf. The counterintelligence people also drew on open sources. More than other operators, they kept track of books and articles on foreign intelligence activities, and they sought out former operatives of foreign services in the hopes of exploiting their historical knowledge for current operations. Information from technical sources could be helpful, too, for example, data collected from the cipher breaks of foreign services. Then there were intelligence defectors. Although the divisions were responsible for handling and exploiting defectors, the counterintelligence staff sometimes milked them for research purposes long after the divisions had got the information of more immediate significance that they needed.

The counterintelligence staff also profited from mail going between the United States and countries ruled by Communist parties. Although this was later considered by some a violation of the CIA prohibition against operations in the United States, from 1954 to 1973 the CIA opened more than 215,820 letters and photographed more than two million envelopes. Two to four analysts, sometimes more, would review the contents and disseminate the "product" to various components of the CIA and the FBI. Unlike FBI agents, counterintelligence analysts employed no specific criteria for determining which mail to open, although they had a watch list of about seven hundred people. It was left up to the analysts to decide if an item was useful for counterintelligence or positive intelligence.[59]

These sources enabled the staff to perform various kinds of analysis. During his X-2 days in Italy and later when he was chief of the counterintelligence staff, Angleton had his staff dissect foreign operating techniques and prepare reports to protect non-counterintelligence

intelligence practitioners. Ray Rocca, who had done this in Italy during the war, stayed on with the SSU and OSO. He returned to the United States in 1953, joined the counterintelligence staff, and went on to become chief of the newly formed research and analysis (R&A) branch, a post he would hold for more than a decade before being promoted to deputy chief of the counterintelligence staff.

The R&A branch produced book-length historical studies on Soviet methods in such work as the Trust operations of the 1920s and the Rote Kapelle, the GRU espionage rings operating against the Nazis before and during World War II.[60] It also compiled regular overview reports on the major tasks, methods, and organization of many foreign intelligence services with which the United States was dealing worldwide. These studies and reports were made available to divisions, station chiefs, and case officers going abroad.[61] Some of the reports were read; most of the long studies were not.

It was not the R&A group's function to provide major assistance in specific operations. For example, Angleton did not seek R&A's help in important cases to ascertain the bona fides of key agents or defectors. R&A did not monitor reports from two of the most important of the CIA's agents inside the GRU. At some point in the 1950s the KGB caught Pytor Popov, and in the early 1960s it caught Oleg Penkovsky. How and exactly when did it catch these American moles? The R&A was not called on to answer. Nor did it provide a study of the bona fides of the most controversial Soviet defector, Yuri Nosenko, whose case went on for years. This sort of assessment was done by the operators in the Soviet division, the counterintelligence staff's operation group, and others, but not R&A.

The combined efforts of the division counterintelligence operatives, the Office of Security, and the counterintelligence staff appear to have yielded mixed results. There were significant achievements, for instance, only a few penetrations of the CIA's professional staff. Only one long-term dispatched agent is now known to have infiltrated CIA security over a long period of time, the Chinese Larry Wu Tai Chin. He became a CIA translator in the 1950s and was given considerable access to materials from Chinese sources for several decades. Shortly after being caught and jailed in the mid-1980s, he committed suicide.[62] To be sure, others were "caught" but not prosecuted, people either never hired, or fired after a relatively short time.[63] And some people were unjustly fired or made to resign when they fell under suspicion. Indeed, in the 1980s the CIA paid indemnities to a few officers who had been mistakenly identified as working for foreign intelligence.[64]

Many potentially able people were not hired because they could not meet the stringent requirements of the Office of Security. Aware of Soviet penetration of the OSS in World War II as well as of other parts of the U.S. government, the CIA had its guard up, sometimes too high.[65] But on the whole, based on the available evidence, the system was reasonable. In the 1950s, the CIA was a haven for liberals who had earlier had Communist associations. A number of them who came under suspicion during that era were suspended, and then after investigations were able to resume their duties.[66] If the "office cops" at the Office of Security were being too zealous, they could always be overruled by DO managers.[67]

The combined efforts of the three units also seem to have protected many CIA operations. There were spectacular successes, most notably the recruitment of Popov, who worked for the CIA for over six years (Penkovsky was run for only fifteen months). Soviet communications were variously penetrated, for example, in Vienna. Much was obtained from liaison. Some friendly liaison services were penetrated by Soviet bloc agents, but relatively few CIA officials appear to have succumbed to friendly foreign blandishments. Soviet defectors, screened and exploited, yielded a lot of beneficial information, and they were usually well protected from their former masters, even if they did not always happily adjust to American life.

It is difficult, to be sure, but on the whole, during the first two decades of the cold war, U.S. collectors (as opposed to covert action practitioners) do not appear to have been deceived in a major, systematic way by people working for foreign intelligence services. (This is not to say that the United States was never fooled by double agents or freelancers.) And in the mid-1960s, the counterintelligence staff got the DCI's support for an education program to expose and neutralize Soviet disinformation and active measures operations.[68]

Moreover, the counterintelligence staff as a whole, and Angleton in particular, had some notable successes in obtaining positive intelligence, for example, when they got hold of Khrushchev's secret speech to the CPSU's 20th Party Congress denouncing Stalin.[69] The U.S. government disseminated the speech through various avenues, which eventually weakened the Communist cause in many parts of the world.[70]

But counterintelligence in the CIA had its failures. It is not easy to assign blame or credit. Perhaps Soviet bloc successes were due to first-rate operations rather than U.S. weaknesses. The fact remains, though, that many operations were not well protected. The OPC failures, already discussed, can be explained in part by lack of counterintelligence protection, in part also as a result of the rapid acquisition of staff and assets and the quality of people hired to do covert action.[71] And even when OPC and OSO merged, most OPC officers had little interest in or knowledge about counterintelligence.

Though some OSO officers were more sympathetic to counterintelligence, notably those who had served in X-2, many underestimated the skill of their adversaries and resented attempts to divert energy and resources to counterintelligence within their own divisions. Even more, they resented the skepticism of the counterintelligence staff. Particularly after the search for Soviet penetration of CIA staff—the "mole hunt"—began in earnest in the mid-1960s, division and station chiefs believed they knew much more than the counterintelligence staff about their local terrain and adversary services.[72] After all, with so little rotation in and out of the counterintelligence staff, it was a world unto itself.[73]

Moreover, the counterintelligence staff chief was, by DO standards and perhaps by anyone's, rather idiosyncratic. Angleton had his strengths. He was clever, creative, knowledgeable, and dedicated. And most unusually in the operational world, he had a relatively explicit doctrine of counterintelligence.[74] Based on the experience of X-2 in World War II, he regarded counterintelligence as the queen on the intelligence chessboard.

Because counterintelligence would know the secrets of other intelligence services, it could not only protect its own service from their machinations but also manipulate adversary services. And because of its unique window into the security services of authoritarian regimes, it was in a position to understand the strengths and weaknesses of foreign governments. Angleton's doctrine derived from the penetration that was accomplished through Ultra and the Double-Cross system, which had enabled the British to read most German intelligence secrets and hence control and manipulate German agents, ultimately using the penetration for positive collection. Angleton sought to replicate this wartime ideal as best he could in the absence of a major cipher break and without the control of double agents that the Allies enjoyed in World War II.

Angleton also took advantage of good connections abroad and at home. He had a private network of former OSS colleagues in the DO and foreign intelligence services. He spent a lot of time with senior colleagues at the FBI and the Office of Security. Most DCIs and DDOs of the day were his personal friends and social acquaintances, even if they did not always see eye to eye with him on specific cases. He was trusted by the most senior managers of the DO, if not by every division chief. And yet in many ways Angleton was a recluse. He came to work in midmorning, had long lunches, and worked late into the night—an unusual pattern in bureaucratic Washington. He managed important cases instead of his staff. Often one deputy did not know what another was doing. Angleton compartmentalized his work, so that full information was withheld even from senior counterintelligence staff managers who could make major contributions to cases (an example of this is the failure to use R&A personnel to analyze the Yuri Nosenko case). It was difficult for others in the DO to know if Angleton had the full picture in a given case, or only thought he did, or whether he was bluffing when he claimed to have superior knowledge.

Even in the best circumstances, tension exists between those whose job is primarily collection and covert action and those whose job is counterintelligence. Symbiosis is not easy to achieve. But when the counterintelligence chief regards his area as the most significant in intelligence, it aggravates tensions considerably. Indeed, the head of X-2, James Murphy, ran into this problem in World War II and was subsequently fired from SSU for trying to implement what many of his colleagues viewed as too grand a role for counterintelligence.[75] Angleton probably would have run afoul of the dominant DO culture on this account even if he had not been idiosyncratic. It was the combination of his idiosyncrasies with his desire to replicate the X-2 role without X-2's capabilities that made for great tension. And that tension tended to discredit the counterintelligence staff as well as the counterintelligence function in the DO.

The result was that the divisions did their own thing, and the station chiefs had a great deal of leeway to do likewise. There was minimal liaison with the counterintelligence staff, and because the counterintelligence staff was the main link to the FBI, there was not a great deal of contact with or benefit from the FBI's espionage section. The problem should not be overstated. Joint operations were conducted among the three entities—the counterintelligence staff, the division, and the FBI—and they assisted one another from time to time. But the coordination was far from ideal.

Usually, but not always, a DO division checked with counterintelligence staff central files to see if anything derogatory was known about a potential recruit. The counterintelligence staff did have the opportunity to veto a potential recruit—if they were informed of the matter. Sometimes they were, and sometimes they did. The division could then appeal to the DO. Sometimes it won. At other times the DO sided with the counterintelligence staff. However, there were operations where the counterintelligence staff was effectively cut out and the division did its own counterintelligence. Examples include the Popov case, the Bay of Pigs in 1960 and 1961, and many cases during the Vietnam War.

The tension also impeded programmatic use of double agents targeted at foreign services and intelligence officers. The divisions were not primarily interested in foreign intelligence services; they wanted Soviet bloc recruits for positive intelligence. They ran walk-ins, such as GRU officers Popov and Penkovsky, and many others from Eastern Europe. But Soviet bloc intelligence officers were hard targets. Inside the bloc it was almost impossible to recruit them; outside, they could be studied and assessed, particularly in small cities far from the bloc where foreigners congregated in enclaves, for instance, in certain African towns. Station chiefs had the discretion to choose their targets, and there was an incentive to go after easier targets.

This did not leave DO stations with much time and energy to use double agents as a major offensive or defensive counterintelligence technique. Little effort was made to turn Soviet bloc agents back against their recruiters, or to dangle U.S. agents in front of the Soviet bloc so as to learn its modus operandi and control its operations. Granted, there were a few U.S. double agents at work, but the divisions considered double agent operations to be time-consuming and not a top priority.[76] As for the counterintelligence staff, it lacked the authority or capability in the field to mount programmatic operations of this sort.

Meanwhile, the revolution in technical collection capabilities taking place in the United States was not being protected or exploited for counterintelligence purposes. Particularly in the field of imagery in the 1950s, massive new capabilities were being developed by CIA research teams that in the 1960s became the Directorate for Science and Technology (DS&T). On the whole, neither the geographic divisions of the DO nor the counterintelligence staff were involved.[77] The Office of Security was to provide some degree of security to private-sector contractors such as Lockheed and TRW, which were producing many of the new capabilities, but this didn't usually concern the counterintelligence staff or the division's counterintelligence operatives. Few of them were cleared for the new techniques, or even for the "take"—the product of the imagery. Thus it was not their role to prevent the new collection technologies or their products from being compromised. Nor did counterintelligence personnel (nor many others in the DO) avail themselves of the new capabilities in their work, for example, in validating an agent's photograph or ascertaining what kind of technical intelligence capability the Soviet bloc was developing. Counterintelligence generally ignored technical advances until the 1960s and 1970s, even as the United States was becoming more and more dependent on technical sources.

It is clear, then, that in the so-called golden age of intelligence, U.S. counterintelligence practices fell short of perfection. Two loose-knit groups of former CIA officials have sought to set the historical record straight with claims that counterintelligence was either ideal on the one hand or all-powerful on the other. The idealists, pointing to the behemoth Soviet intelligence threat, maintain that they successfully resisted it until they were undermined both from within the DO and from without, especially by Congress.[78]

The proponents of the all-powerful image assisted several journalists in writing accounts that provided considerable detail of specific cases about James Angleton and the counterintelligence staff.[79] Their thesis that Angleton and his staff dominated the division chiefs and the heads of DO, even the DCIs of the day, is not supported by the facts. As was pointed out, Angleton might have wanted to replicate the powerful role that X-2's Murphy had sought and failed to achieve, but he certainly could not overrule his superiors in the DO, let alone the DCI. Moreover, the counterintelligence staff was not well enough represented in the divisions to wield that sort of power. Angleton might have used his salesmanship and intellect to achieve more influence than he had on paper, or than many of his colleagues in the DO thought he should have. But it is incorrect to claim that he alone, or the counterintelligence staff alone, was responsible for what the division chiefs, the DO, and the DCI achieved during the cold war. It is equally erroneous to argue that Angleton was "responsible" for counterintelligence, or "unhindered by the normal chain of command," so that "if he chose [he] could easily bypass the DO."[80] The dynamics of a whole set of institutions were at work. The counterintelligence staff could not have generated success—or, for that matter, failure—on its own.

Finally, there are those who make counterclaims—that the CIA's counterintelligence was woefully incapable of frustrating foreign intelligence services.[81] This too is an exaggeration. While far from ideal, the counterintelligence system was able to protect the CIA itself, if not all its operations, from serious penetration. This was no mean achievement. The CIA was operating against the largest and probably most sophisticated centrally coordinated intelligence alliance in world history. The CIA's counterintelligence capability was adequate to permit the DO to take advantage of U.S. power and influence, to run some collection and covert action operations successfully, and to frustrate many of those of its main enemy.

Military Counterintelligence

The U.S. military has never regarded intelligence as a function equal in importance to combat command. Nor are those who specialize in and become proficient in intelligence considered the equals of the top commanders. Not surprisingly, counterintelligence is thought of as even less significant, the "stepchild" of intelligence, necessary, but with no claim to priority. The only service in the postwar period that considered counterintelligence as at all significant was the U.S. Army—in the aftermath of World War II and again in the 1980s. On the whole, the Navy and the Air Force relegated counterintelligence to the status of an adjunct to criminal investigation and law enforcement. Indeed, the small counterintelligence staffs were attached not to the intelligence branches of the services but rather to their law enforcement arms. And this, as will be seen, was to have unintended but unfortunate consequences.

In the decades after World War II, Army counterintelligence played a unique role by filling a major gap in the U.S. intelligence system abroad. The FBI was limited to operating at home, OSS-X2 was disbanded, and the SSU and OSO staffs of the CIA had a limited counterintelligence capability—all this at a time when the United States was responsible for building democracies on the ruins of defeated enemy regimes. Soon enough, the United States began to see that it faced a determined, sophisticated Soviet empire that was flexing its intelligence muscle in an effort to dominate world politics.

The main instrument of power in the occupied areas, especially in Austria, Japan, and the Western zones of Germany, was the U.S. Army. It also had to protect the frontline states and those in their rear against major intelligence and military threats. With a dearth of positive intelligence on Soviet and Communist-ruled areas of Europe and Asia, Army counterintelligence was charged in part with obtaining that as well.

The Counter Intelligence Corps (CIC) had become part of Army intelligence in 1917. It protected the U.S. military and sometimes the U.S. government from espionage, sabotage, and subversion both at home and abroad. Effective implementation was subject to the fluctuating fortunes of the U.S. Army as a whole. The CIC was nearly disbanded after World War I, and apparently in 1920 only six men and a dog remained on the rolls.[82] Even after the outbreak of hostilities in Europe and Asia in the late 1930s, only a skeletal staff of about fifty people was maintained until early 1941, when a tenfold increase in personnel and a training school were authorized.

During World War II, the CIC operated in the field in collaboration with both OSS-X2 and the military and civilian counterintelligence of U.S. allies. There was even a period during which the Allies coordinated counterintelligence field operations centrally out of the London counterintelligence War Room. But after the war, Allied cooperation and joint operations in this area were curtailed. Now the CIC, with several thousand personnel in its employ, was on its own, reporting to Army intelligence brass in Washington and to Army intelligence and combat commanders in Europe and Asia. Gradually the CIC developed cooperative relations with newly emerging OSO and OPC operators, with the DO, and to some extent with the FBI's intelligence division. Most of CIC's several thousand personnel were located abroad, and many spoke or learned German. Eventually they were divided into four desks: countersubversion, counterespionage, security, and positive intelligence.

The strong suit of Army counterintelligence was collection. The CIC had almost limitless opportunities to recruit informants and agents in devastated Germany and Japan, to whose citizens the U.S. Army was providing essential services and the basic necessities of life. These defeated populations might not have welcomed the U.S. military as liberators, but considering the alternatives they readily collaborated with the United States. But there were complications. After the war many hedged their bets. It was not clear who would emerge as the dominant power in Europe. Not even Allied unity could be taken for granted. The United States had its eye on France, afraid that the government there was riddled with Communists who had participated in the French Resistance against the Nazis. This suspicion was heightened by French occupation of one of the four Allied zones in Germany. Another complication was implementing denazification while trying to prevent the Communists from filling the political vacuum left by that policy.

In this environment, then, the CIC's bountiful opportunities were challenging. The CIC used and sometimes recruited former Nazis to identify Communists, and it used former Communists to penetrate and report on the Nazis. It collaborated with the French at the same time that it was trying to penetrate French operations and fend off attempted French penetration of the American occupation zones.

Right after the war, denazification was the priority. But within a year or two the priority switched to preventing Communists from the Eastern and Western zones of Germany as well as Austria from building local power bases to assist Soviet political or military operations. This meant penetrating the West German Communist Party and its front organizations.

The counterespionage and security sections had their work cut out for them. The KGB, and later its Eastern European partners, flooded the Western zones with operatives and agents who used the cover of Soviet military liaison and reparation offices. In this capacity, they were free to enter most parts of the Western zones of Austria and Germany. Some agents were dispatched by the KGB as refugees. Others were genuine refugees or locals recruited by the KGB. The KGB's attitude was that while many of its agents would be identified, enough would slip through and join the Western services to eventually become useful for collection, covert action, and even counterintelligence.

The CIC's positive intelligence section was first tasked to obtain political, economic, scientific, and military information from refugees, defectors, and antifascist activists who had been helped by the United States during and after the war, and who still had contacts in the East. Later, the CIC headquarters in Frankfurt received orders from the European Command's director of intelligence to break new ground and embark on positive intelligence across the Iron Curtain. One such operation, "Devotion," which ran from 1949 to 1954, monitored the Soviet order of battle just across the border. Gradually it became so difficult to operate across the curtain that Berlin was one of the few places that could be used as a base for this purpose. Counterintelligence information coming into Berlin was passed to Army intelligence, which then determined where it would be distributed.

In the first decade of the cold war, various components of the CIC probably contained within them more knowledge of Soviet bloc intelligence than any other U.S. government entity, expertise that largely remained in their main operational center, Germany. Some of the case officers and interrogators transferred to other agencies, such as the CIA. Others stayed on in Europe as civilians in the Army and became experts in counterintelligence, performing their own analysis in support of their operations. They did not try to understand global politics, but rather concentrated on identifying and frustrating Soviet bloc operations in their respective areas. Few CIC operatives felt constrained by NSC Directive No. 5, which gave the DCI and the CIA primary responsibility for counterintelligence abroad.

The results were mixed. The U.S. Army, primarily through its large-scale human intelligence (humint) counterintelligence operations, was able to take advantage of its dominant position in the defeated Axis countries to enhance U.S. security. Communist attempts to gain electoral power and influence in political parties, trade unions, and the media, like Communist attempts to recruit Americans and Europeans, were often frustrated, in part by CIC operatives. But the bloc had its coups, managing to penetrate both the U.S. occupation government and the reviving German, Austrian, and Japanese governments.

The CIC had some other successes. A great deal of positive information was obtained at a time when few positive sources existed across the Iron Curtain, and the Army's positive intelligence managers learned to integrate it into their overall assessment and operational planning. In 1955, CIC's positive intelligence was transferred to the new discipline of field operations intelligence. In 1957, some counterintelligence specialists joined positive intelligence collectors in multidisciplinary intelligence units to support field commanders. In 1961, the CIC formally merged with field operations intelligence units to form the U.S. Army Intelligence Corps. For this reason the Army was well positioned during Vietnam to utilize counterintelligence information in its combat operations.

To its credit, the Army realized that obtaining a wealth of information on adversary services could be useful for recruitment and penetration. Particularly helpful to Army counterintelligence specialists were double agents, who could get close to hostile operators. But the Army did not have authority to recruit foreign intelligence operators; that responsibility was formally given to the CIA abroad and to the FBI at home. Nor were Army counterintelligence specialists given responsibility for deception. That was assigned to another part of the service.

What about the U.S. Navy's involvement with intelligence and counterintelligence? The Office of Naval Intelligence (ONI), created in 1882, had long been concerned with the security of naval installations and personnel. In World War I and the interwar period, it devoted considerable resources to security. This interest in intelligence expanded during World War II when ONI conducted psychological warfare against the Axis and became involved in other forms of covert action as well. After the war, the Navy's interest in intelligence in general dwindled, being confined almost exclusively to maritime matters. Because the Navy bore little responsibility for the occupation, it did not conduct countersubversion or use counterintelligence for positive intelligence purposes. Rather, the service returned to its historically more restricted concern, the security of its personnel and equipment.

In this context, counterintelligence was a defensive activity, one that the Navy did not believe required great knowledge or skill—even when, at various times, its ships and personnel were sent into hostile areas to acquire positive intelligence for the Navy or the United States as a whole. Naval counterintelligence had only a small headquarters staff and a hundred or so representatives in various ports, naval installations, and ships around the world. These people ran background checks on naval personnel and contractors for security clearances and investigated alleged security violations. For the first few decades of the postwar period, few, if any, counterintelligence analysts took on the more daunting task of examining the Navy's vulnerabilities. The Navy believed that the purpose of its counterintelligence was defensive security, and that it was the responsibility of the CIA abroad and the FBI at home to study, penetrate, and exploit foreign services.

As for U.S. Air Force counterintelligence, its origins go back to a potential arms procurement scandal shortly after the service's creation in 1947. Apparently, top Air Force officials consulted J. Edgar Hoover about the impending scandal and Hoover recommended that one of his supervisors with criminal investigation experience be brought in to assist the service. Hence the Air Force adopted the FBI model of fusing criminal with counterintelligence matters, but without specialization in counterintelligence. The Air Force Office of Special Investigation (AFOSI) was placed in the Office of the Inspector General and headed by the FBI's Joe Carroll, commissioned a colonel and later a general. Like the postwar Navy, the Air Force regarded counterintelligence as a defensive security function, not as a part of Air Force intelligence. Its job was to assist in the investigation of security clearances or suspected violations of security at Air Force facilities in the United States and abroad. There was a small headquarters staff in Washington, and generalist AFOSI agents at various installations in the United States and abroad dealt with both criminal and security investigations.

In short, the Air Force had no significant analytical capability. Like the Navy, it left to others the job of exploiting counterintelligence information for positive purposes and of disrupting and exploiting foreign services for national purposes. The Air Force as a whole was gradually to become more interested in exploiting foreign intelligence for the purposes of deception, but deception planning was not the mission of the AFOSI.

Breaking the Mold

As we have seen, in the 1960s America's early postwar consensus about counterintelligence gradually eroded, and by the mid-1970s it had almost disappeared. Ironically, it was not a diminished perception of threat that initially weakened the consensus, but rather increased domestic disturbances and their possible connection to subversive and hostile foreign intelligence operations.

Both the FBI and the Army were ordered, first by the Eisenhower administration and subsequently by the Kennedy, Johnson, and Nixon administrations, to step up their monitoring of civil rights, racial, and later antiwar activists. As Vietnam War protests heated up, the CIA and the NSA were called in to monitor contacts between protesters and Soviet bloc operatives. The White House tended to believe there was a significant connection. The White House wanted to know to what extent social unrest in the United States and specific attacks on U.S. policy and institutions were being supported, manipulated, or financed by the Soviet bloc.

During the Johnson administration, this gradually led to a massive increase in Army counterintelligence clandestine collection and analysis on the activities of American civilians, FBI collection and disruption against U.S. organizations, and CIA clandestine collection against substantial numbers of Americans at home and abroad.

When this counterintelligence buildup was well under way, the direction of U.S. policy changed. The Nixon administration, fearing that the postwar policy of containment could no longer command the support of the American people, devised a Machiavellian strategy, under the auspices of Secretary of State Henry Kissinger, to curb Soviet expansionism. It called for détente, negotiation, and friendly relations with Communist rulers, particularly in Moscow and Peking, with the aim of playing these rulers off one against the other. The Ford and early Carter administrations, while not adhering precisely to the script of that strategy, continued the détente approach.

With this new policy, the political leadership sent a signal, intentional or not, to American intelligence managers: counterintelligence concerns were no longer the priority they had been during the height of the cold war. Furthermore, the actions intelligence and counterintelligence managers had taken for over ten years in response to White House requests to monitor and disrupt political groups were now repudiated by the nation's political leadership.

Meanwhile another basic element of the Washington consensus had changed: Congress was no longer the passive supporter of national security policy that it once had been. As pointed out earlier, Congress became much more involved in covert action when the Hughes-Ryan Amendment was passed in 1974. Then, in late December 1974, a *New York Times* story claiming that the CIA had been monitoring the behavior of Americans triggered the initiation of the Church Committee in 1975, the most extensive congressional investigation in U.S. intelligence history. The result was massive exposure and criticism of many of the FBI's counterintelligence collection and exploitation techniques, especially those directed at Americans, as well as condemnation of CIA, NSA, and Army "domestic spying." The episode prompted Congress in 1976 and 1977 to create permanent select committees in the Senate and House to oversee intelligence in general and covert action and counterintelligence in particular.

To the outside observer, the disclosures emanating from these hearings were shocking. The major intelligence agencies, it seemed, had abused the trust the government and the people had placed in them. Lost in the swirl of accusations was the fact that the agencies had been following White House instructions, and that Congress had been aware of the overall program if not the details. In this environment, any objective assessment of the accomplishments of counterintelligence, or its failures, was impossible.

Inside the intelligence and counterintelligence professional world, the FBI and CIA especially, some people welcomed the turmoil and change of the mid-1970s. Undoubtedly chagrined by the public chastisement of their agencies and profession, they were nonetheless dissatisfied with the way American intelligence and counterintelligence had been defined and practiced in the early postwar decades.

In the FBI, a small number of younger supervisors who specialized in counterintelligence at headquarters and in field offices agreed with much of the criticism that was launched at the countersubversive element of the Intelligence Division. Apart from qualms about civil liberties, they believed too much effort had been devoted to this and not enough to understanding and mastering the KGB and its sister services. Now, with the death of Hoover and the departure of Sullivan and most of his top lieutenants, they looked forward to changing the direction of the Bureau's counterintelligence. The Congress and new Attorneys General with their freshly promulgated counterintelligence guidelines did not strike them as major impediments to their work.

Indeed, some at the FBI welcomed the cumbersome new rules as insurance against another period of turmoil; if necessary, they could be invoked to demonstrate that the agencies were carrying out the mandate of the executive and legislative branches.

At about the same time, in the mid-1970s, James Angleton and his senior staff at the CIA's counterintelligence staff retired. The counterintelligence staff was reorganized, which met with approval in most of the CIA. Negative rumors about Angleton that had been circulating inside the CIA for years had been publicly aired by now. The search for Soviet moles inside the Agency was blamed on Angleton and a KGB defector, Anatoliy Golitsyn, who was believed to have had too much influence on Angleton. Many senior collectors, covert action specialists, and analysts felt that the counterintelligence staff was inefficient and sometimes exercised undue influence. Whatever turmoil the investigation of the 1970s had caused, they believed, at least it had opened the door to reform of the counterintelligence staff and other elements at the CIA. But while many welcomed this opportunity, few CIA officers—unlike their counterparts in the Bureau—could offer an alternative view of how to manage, collect, or exploit counterintelligence.

As for the Army, it had started to cut back on domestic collection in the early 1970s because its chiefs of intelligence thought the program was not a good use of Army resources. They wanted the Justice Department to handle nonmilitary counterintelligence matters. Another reason for the Army's change of heart was congressional criticism. In January 1970, a young Army intelligence officer had published an article on real and alleged Army surveillance of civilian dissent. The ACLU filed a class-action suit to stop this practice, and Senator Sam Ervin, Jr., chairman of the Senate Subcommittee on Constitutional Rights, complained about it to Congress. Although ultimately the Supreme Court, in *Laird v. Tatum* (1972), decided that it was legal for the Department of Defense to conduct domestic surveillance in various circumstances, the Army curtailed the practice, concentrating its counterintelligence effort on foreign intelligence services and supporting operational security for Army units.

Rebuilding

During the latter half of the 1970s and into the 1980s, then, a new consensus about counterintelligence evolved in Washington. Democracy's constraints tightened. Counterintelligence would target only demonstrable threats—and these were almost exclusively perceived to be foreign. There was some debate about where to draw the line. At what point should Americans, foreigners resident in the United States, and foreigners visiting the United States who were sympathetic to hostile foreign governments be subject to counterintelligence scrutiny? But the center of gravity established during and after World War II had shifted. Unless some concrete evidence linking an American and a foreign intelligence service could be produced, a person's behavior should not be monitored. That became the general position of Congress, the executive branch, and the counterintelligence agencies. No longer would ethnic background or verbal support for foreign governments or domestic extremism be enough to stir up counterintelligence interest. A series of guidelines in every intelligence agency prescribed rules for when American citizens and foreign residents in the United States could be subject to counterintelligence scrutiny. Even then, the agencies had to jump a series of hurdles if they wanted to use intrusive techniques to investigate further.

Most of the rules were classified, with the congressional intelligence and judiciary committees receiving briefings and their staff experts being consulted on proposed changes. Occasional criticism was voiced about the rules and how they were implemented. In the late 1970s, some in and out of government believed they were too restrictive, while in the early 1980s others felt they were too lax. A new and different consensus about counterintelligence was emerging.

Meanwhile, in the minds of some government officials, notably intelligence managers and congressional overseers, the perceived threat posed by services controlled by ruling Communist parties intensified, if not to the extent experienced in the 1950s. While appreciation of the military threat from the People's Republic of China (PRC) diminished, consensus grew about the need for a response to foreign intelligence activities, especially those of the Chinese. Even when Congress and the administration crossed swords over major budgetary and foreign policy questions in the late 1970s and 1980s, there was little disagreement about counterintelligence.

In the early 1980s, Congress was inclined to accept the intelligence agencies' assessment of the overall threat, approving the Reagan administration's increases for counterintelligence personnel and operatives. However, as the decade wore on and more than two dozen sensational arrests took place for espionage and other apparent counterintelligence lapses, congressional hackles rose. The Soviet bloc, the People's Republic of China, and others had evidently been able to penetrate or take advantage of every major U.S. national security department, including the CIA, FBI, and NSA. The government and the public concluded that for decades U.S. secrets—military, technological, and intelligence—had been hemorrhaging. Evidence also accumulated that Moscow and others had been taking active measures, crude as well as sophisticated, to discredit the United States abroad and influence the political debate at home. The so-called Year of the Spy, as 1985 became known, grew into the decade of the spy as more and more cases came to public attention. With the public as well as Congress demanding action, the cycle was complete: in 1975–76 people had felt there was too much counterintelligence; now in 1985–86 they felt there was too little.

The Reagan NSC staff and the revivified President's Foreign Intelligence Advisory Board (PFIAB) were much more concerned with counterintelligence than the Carter NSC had been,[83] criticizing both what they believed had been overly skeptical congressional investigations in the 1970s and the intelligence agencies' failure to examine their own weaknesses. However, with most Reagan appointees in the White House and the departments of State and Defense distracted by other tumultuous policy matters, the president left counterintelligence to the DCI.

Intelligence managers who had risen to the top at the FBI and CIA remained cautious, having seen their agencies and senior colleagues "burned" when Washington turned on them in the early 1970s. But some believed that they needed to reform the interagency system and their own agencies' modi operandi. They realized that Soviet bloc services had taken advantage of détente to increase their presence in the United States and throughout the world. In the late 1970s and early 1980s, it dawned on them that the bloc was using these regions to operate against the United States. America's early cold war approach to counterintelligence and the mechanisms established for it were now perceived to be out of date. For example, the mandated division between counterintelligence abroad and counterintelligence at home, established in NSC Directive No. 5 back in the late 1940s, was an open invitation to foreign intelligence services to conduct hostile intelligence operations against the continental United States from abroad. This could mean that foreign intelligence services would meet their agents living in America in foreign capitals where there was no FBI surveillance.

Some FBI and CIA managers also began to see the utility of counterintelligence analysis. It became apparent to them that the United States could not compete against the manpower and resources being poured into intelligence by foreign services, whether abroad or at home. U.S. agencies would be outmanned and outclassed. Analysis might help. If the United States could determine enemy patterns and methods, then surveillance capabilities could be concentrated on high-priority targets rather than widely dispersed. Some American counterintelligence managers had also learned that they did not have to be purely defensive to neutralize the enemy—they could throw adversaries off balance with provocative counterintelligence operations, thereby relieving pressure on American counterintelligence defense.

But even the most innovative counterintelligence managers were still caught up in the cold war containment paradigm. Almost all planning in the 1980s focused on defending against Soviet bloc and Chinese operatives and operations. Little thought was given to U.S. secrets or institutions that needed special extra protection; American managers tried to protect everything from the Soviet bloc, without assigning priority. Also, scant attention was paid to nontraditional adversaries other than terrorist states, and none was paid to states or to nongovernmental groups, such as Colombian drug traffickers, that were emerging as key players in the early 1980s.

Counterintelligence managers did begin to focus on intelligence collection technology, which had given U.S. intelligence such a boost in the 1960s and 1970s. They woke up to the counterintelligence implications of state-of-the-art collection technology and its use by the Soviet bloc, even if the technology was still foreign to many of them.

All of these developments gradually remapped American counterintelligence—its relative importance, the way it was managed from the top, and the way individual agencies went about performing it. These were small changes, too dramatic for some and not radical enough for others.

They began in 1978 with President Carter's Executive Order 12036 on intelligence.[84] It called for the creation of a central counterintelligence mechanism in the NSC, the Special Coordination Committee (SCC). The SCC's job was to develop national counterintelligence policy, issue a yearly report to the president about the counterintelligence threat, set standards and promulgate doctrine, and, finally, evaluate the effectiveness of counterintelligence programs.

President Reagan's Executive Order 12333 of December 1981 placed even greater emphasis on counterintelligence performance, even though counterintelligence management shifted out of the White House. Reagan's early national security advisers, Richard Allen and William Clark, were interested in the subject (Clark had been an Army counterintelligence operator in postwar Europe). The administration created a senior-level interagency intelligence committee, the SIG-I, chaired by DCI William Casey, a cabinet member, the president's former campaign manager, and in the early 1970s a member of the PFIAB. The SIG-I in turn had subcommittees, for example, the Interagency Group for Counterintelligence (IG-CI) and the Interagency Group for Countermeasures and Security (IG-CM and Security). Casey arranged for the IG-CI to be chaired by the most senior FBI counterintelligence official (the assistant director for counterintelligence) and the IG-CM and Security by a senior DoD official with responsibility for counterintelligence.

A small interagency staff was to coordinate national counterintelligence policymaking and implementation. One player would fill a new position in the small NSC intelligence directorate, the director of counterintelligence. (Although not mandated as an FBI slot, this position from the mid-1980s on was held by FBI counterintelligence specialists.) Another participant would be the special assistant to the DCI for counterintelligence, a position created in the later Carter years by DCI Stansfield Turner. A veteran OPC and DO operator, George Kalaris, originally brought in to head the first post-Angleton CIA counterintelligence staff, was selected for this position. He in turn brought to the staff Admiral Donald "Mac" Showers, who had NSA experience, and one or two others to assist him. Their primary responsibility was preparing the annual threat assessment and coordinating some interagency counterintelligence operations. In the Reagan years, William Casey shifted this group to the intelligence community staff, which he managed. Kalaris retired, and Showers became chief.

In the DoD, too, there were attempts to bring together the diverse elements concerned with counterintelligence in the services and in the Office of the Secretary of Defense. But until the so-called decade of the spy, few DoD senior officials had much interest in the subject.

In addition to formal policy directives that called for coordinated, national consideration of counterintelligence, there was a less tangible development: more interest in interagency cooperation. The new generation at or near the top of counterintelligence management in the late 1970s and early 1980s—among them Richard Krieger, James Nolan, and Jim Geer at the FBI, George Kalaris, Hugh Tovar, and Gus Hathaway at the CIA, Dan Grimes, Merrill Kelly, and Noel Jones in the Army, and Charles Torpy in the Air Force—wanted to overcome the obstacles presented by entrenched jurisdictional disputes and parochial jealousies.

The development was significant but not pronounced enough to eradicate major legal and bureaucratic obstacles to full cooperation. These persisted. The National Security Act's division of the world into foreign versus domestic, military versus civilian, law enforcement versus pure counterintelligence still shaped the way counterintelligence managers conducted their business. The individual agencies remained the principal players. They helped prepare the threat assessment, for example, but they were not bound to follow its findings individually or collectively. Overall, American counterintelligence usually was the sum total of what individual agencies did or did not do.

The FBI

After the death of Hoover, the turmoil of Watergate, and the congressional investigations, the FBI regained stability. President Carter replaced the transitional head with federal judge William Webster. Webster ran the Bureau for nearly ten years, after which President Reagan moved him to DCI in 1988 and appointed another federal judge, William Sessions, as FBI Director. The other top Bureau positions were held by experienced FBI generalists who had devoted their careers primarily to criminal matters. Becoming a counterintelligence specialist and manager at headquarters was not the way to the top of the Bureau as it had been during Hoover's tenure. However, the Bureau's upper echelon did not change the balance between law enforcement and counterintelligence that had developed in that era. Rather, they oversaw a new generation of counterintelligence managers who gradually reformed the organization and its operational ethos.

The new counterintelligence managers still focused on the intelligence services of the Soviet bloc. They saw themselves as continuing the containment mission, but almost all their resources were directed at foreign collectors operating in the United States. Their mission was not to discover the specific priorities or targets of foreign services or the secrets they were collecting. It was definitely not to take a close interest in the four to six million Americans with access to classified information, or in U.S. citizens hostile to the Constitution. Instead, their mission was to identify Communist bloc services and frustrate them in whatever they were doing on American soil. A subsidiary mission continued as before: to apply information from counterintelligence operations for positive intelligence purposes, and to educate the American people about the foreign espionage threat as well as Soviet active measures.

To address these new priorities, counterintelligence managers turned their attention more systematically to hostile services and their organizations rather than, as before, focusing on individual hostile operators and their cases. They sought more information about the overall operations of their adversaries, then disseminated it to field offices. Operators were the principal players conducting this mission, but as the years went by, managers grew more interested in the role that analysts could play in support of operations. Gradually the number and caliber of analysts increased.

The FBI's basic organizational structure remained intact. The relatively small number of Washington supervisors and analysts now joined the rest of the Bureau in the large new headquarters building on Pennsylvania Avenue. A much larger group of operators and support staff, but few analysts, worked out of field offices.

Counterintelligence headquarters was divided into three main branches: one for operations against the Soviet Union; the second for operations against the Warsaw Pact and other governments ruled by Communist parties; the third for support of the first two operational branches. The support branch conducted analysis, training, and liaison with the NSA.

The two principal operating branches were in turn divided into sections dealing with individual bloc services—in the case of the USSR, the KGB and GRU. The sections reflected organizational components in a given service, for instance, the KGB's Line PR, which specialized in political intelligence and active measures, and Line X, which specialized in scientific and technical information.

The main field offices with counterintelligence manpower were in cities that had a concentrated legal foreign intelligence presence—Washington, New York, and San Francisco. Now, in addition to the mushrooming foreign presence in embassies, consulates, and UN headquarters, the United States hosted many thousands of foreign visitors, students, businessmen, tourists, and journalists from the Soviet bloc and China. To identify and neutralize the hundreds of intelligence operatives among them, field offices continued to operate in squads. Each squad, with a supervisor and up to thirty agents, specialized in one service or, as in New York or Washington, one line element of a service. To assist the vastly outnumbered operators, there were also support staffs. These were manned by more junior FBI personnel skilled at technical tasks such as bugging and wiretapping, translating recorded conversations, and physical surveillance—tasks that had occupied a lot of time for operators during Hoover's heyday.

There was a great deal of continuity in Bureau collection and investigation. The field offices still employed a panoply of defensive surveillance techniques to keep track of the movements and contacts of hostile establishments and operatives. But they were much more aggressive than their predecessors in using double agents and recruiting hostile operatives.

The Bureau ran its own double agents, working with the military to widen the pool of available talent. The services did not always see eye to eye with the Bureau on the purpose of double agents. To the FBI, the agent had a temporary assignment to identify hostile officers, learn their methods of operation, and help with recruitment of his foreign handlers. The Army wanted more permanent double agents, to uncover not only hostile methods but also enemy priorities and intentions, especially in wartime. The Navy was less interested in temporary or permanent agents. Its view of counterintelligence was to educate and deter naval personnel from espionage or sabotage. Naval personnel approached by hostiles or caught in the act of spying or sabotage were not to be made into double agents. As for the Air Force, it wanted to use double agents primarily in deception, passing false or misleading information to manipulate hostile governments.

The Bureau was not opposed to the objectives of the services or the other agencies. In fact, many joint operations of unprecedented scale and intensity took place. But the FBI did have its own priorities and ethos, and because it was the principal agency responsible for coordinating counterintelligence inside the United States, this could and did create tension.

Like joint operations, Bureau penetration and recruitment of hostile intelligence officers picked up. The vastly expanded number of potential targets was studied not just from a distance but up close as well. For example, Bureau personnel, even operators, would disguise themselves and enter into personal relationships—much more personal than had been the case in Hoover's day—with foreign intelligence operatives in an effort to recruit them. Sometimes the FBI shared recruitment, or information about potential recruits, with the CIA. Other times, fearing the recruit might be compromised and reveal Bureau techniques, the FBI preferred to wait for a recruit or potential recruit to return to the United States after a posting back in Moscow.

The Bureau's counterintelligence education and training also intensified. Specialists attended courses at the FBI training facility in Quantico and elsewhere. They held more specialized Bureau-wide conferences on subjects such as trends in the KGB's Line PR, and to hone their skills they role-played and practiced investigatory techniques.

Gradually analysis became more important, especially at headquarters, where the counterintelligence staff grew to several dozen. If most field operators remained skeptical of this more intellectual side of counterintelligence, some in effect became analysts. They studied the history and modi operandi of their adversaries in order to improve their own and their colleagues' performance. Their efforts, which required creativity and innovation, were not always welcomed or rewarded.

As before, the Bureau used the information it gathered to improve security and countermeasures. Some of the techniques were refined carryovers from the Hoover years. William Webster did not, like Hoover, have books published in his name, but selected journalists and authors were invited to briefings or given access to defectors or former double agents. The FBI succeeded in getting the Attorney General to prosecute some spies and publicly expel diplomats caught *in flagrante delicto*. This educated the public about the activities of some foreign services and the danger they posed, at a time when many believed, prematurely, that the cold war was over and that China's intentions toward the United States were benign. After learning about extensive efforts by the Soviet and Chinese to acquire U.S. secrets from the American private sector, the Bureau also launched a briefing program for hundreds of thousands of citizens, government contractors among them, who worked on classified projects. In Hoover's day, the FBI concentrated on the danger of Communism; now it focused on the vulnerability of people and installations to hostile services.

In response to the realization that its opponents had become very sophisticated, the FBI tried to address flaws in its own security. For example, communications were made less vulnerable to penetration. Despite its efforts, security loopholes remained. This became clear when several cases broke, notably that of Special Agent Richard Miller, who entered into a sexual relationship with a Russian émigrée in California and gave her Bureau counterintelligence manuals. These ended up in the hands of the Soviets.

No doubt partly through bureaucratic self-interest, the FBI also stepped up its support of countermeasures in other government agencies. For example, it pushed the State Department to create the Office of Foreign Missions to monitor the movement of hostile establishments and operatives, and it assigned senior counterintelligence personnel to the NSC and to the State Department's Bureau of Diplomatic Security.

In a cultural milieu rather adverse to counterintelligence concerns, such efforts were not always welcomed. However, after the Year of the Spy, the Bureau's strenuous efforts to assist the government and the public at large in thwarting hostile intelligence were better received by Congress, the media, and the academic and scientific communities.

Another of the FBI's main concerns was shifting to more offensive tactics to frustrate foreign services. In addition to cutting back the absolute number of foreign intelligence operatives in the United States, it attempted to lower the caliber of foreign operatives coming here. Based on data from offensive counterintelligence collection, the Bureau put together profiles of hostile service personnel. Thus, when the opportunity came along, it was able to recommend which diplomats, students, and journalists should be denied visas or allowed to travel. When President Reagan decided to expel a number of Soviet diplomats in the mid-1980s, the Bureau went for key choke points in enemy ranks, seeking to curtail the effectiveness of the best foreign operatives and allowing the worst recruiters or active measures specialists to stay.

The FBI started to work closely with other parts of the government on more than security awareness. By the mid-1980s it became clear that hostile services were taking advantage of the geographic and bureaucratic seams in the counterintelligence system. For example, Americans who had volunteered their services to the KGB in the United States might be handled by the KGB from abroad, particularly from Vienna and Mexico City. The Bureau sought to work more closely on joint counterintelligence operations in the United States and abroad to overcome this dangerous fragmentation of the U.S. system. Finally, it continued to provide policymakers with substantial positive information gleaned from its counterintelligence operations, a practice still little appreciated by positive collectors and analysts, right through the end of the cold war.

The CIA

The CIA's basic counterintelligence mission and the way that mission was carried out did not shift much after the purge of the counterintelligence staff in the mid-1970s. This may seem surprising, given the controversy about James Angleton as represented in anecdotal accounts by former senior CIA officials. To be sure, the general atmosphere changed along with personnel, and techniques and bureaucratic arrangements evolved. But counterintelligence remained a staff function devoted to protecting CIA operations, particularly human intelligence. DO managers wanted counterintelligence to protect, but not to interfere with, CIA operations. The DCIs of the 1970s and 1980s—William Colby, Stansfield Turner, William Casey, and William Webster—did their best to bring this about, and for the most part, counterintelligence remained the prerogative of the DO. Few spoke out for major change.

Contrary to popular myth, the counterintelligence staff actually grew slightly after Angleton's departure to approximately one hundred. The divisions still had their counterintelligence referents. The Office of Security continued to perform much as it had before. But some major organizational shifts did take place.

In 1978, after President Carter issued his executive order calling for an annual counterintelligence threat analysis and national management, Stansfield Turner realized that neither the counterintelligence staff in the DO nor the DO divisions could address the whole of the hostile intelligence threat, especially that posed by foreign technical capabilities. George Kalaris, after he became a special assistant to the DCI for counterintelligence, had a small staff in the early 1980s that blossomed into the first *national* counterintelligence staff.

In the late 1980s, after evidence pointed to far-reaching counterintelligence weaknesses inside the CIA, DCI William Webster decided to pull disparate elements in the DO and other parts of the CIA together. Toward this end, he created the Counterintelligence Center in the DO as well as the position of associate deputy director for operations for counterintelligence. Thus Webster hoped to weld together various elements in the CIA, as well as to integrate counterintelligence work being done by the CIA with that of other agencies. However, this new position and the Counterintelligence Center, with its management for the most part staffed by senior DO officers, were in effect governed by the DO ethos: counterintelligence should be a staff function performed in support of DO collection operations. Moreover, much more importance was attached to counterintelligence operations than to high-level intellectual analysis. And finally, there was still the hangover from the myths that developed in the Angleton period—that too much counterintelligence was bad for collection and the CIA. Thus counterintelligence, in the CIA, was still not viewed as a strategic instrument of government-wide policy.

But there were other developments. Although Angleton's managers, like Angleton himself, had originally come from the DO, over time they were regarded by their DO colleagues less and less as regular DO operators. There had been minimal rotation in and out of the top levels of the counterintelligence staff. Little counterintelligence staff work was done by the geographic divisions or DO officers in the field. Under George Kalaris and his successors, this changed to some extent. Now senior counterintelligence staff operators arrived fresh from the collection operations abroad. There were regular turnovers in the counterintelligence staff and among counterintelligence referents in the DO divisions. When the Counterintelligence Center was created, personnel from the Directorate for Intelligence (DI), the Office of Security, and the Directorate for Science and Technology (DS&T) also rotated in and out. This had decided advantages.

The DO divisions to some extent grew more conscious, and accepting, of counterintelligence—especially in the late 1980s, when it became clear that a significant percentage of their operations around the world had been compromised by weak counterintelligence. Some DO officers, now exposed to the operations and concerns of the Counterintelligence Center, carried the experience into work for their respective divisions. A few in the DO began to realize that some analysts could be trusted and that analysts could be valuable in helping protect operations. The same attitude began to develop, if slowly, among personnel from the Office of Security, the DS&T, and other agencies such as NSA who were being rotated in and out of the Counterintelligence Center. The new arrangements also succeeded in creating better, but far from ideal, symbiosis among counterintelligence elements and other parts of the CIA.

But there were disadvantages, one being a reduction in the number of operators and analysts with extensive historical knowledge of foreign services. Few of the best DO officers wanted to make their career in counterintelligence. Instead, many DO officers who were considered unpromising or problematic, such as Aldrich Ames, were parked in counterintelligence work.[85] Most DI and DS&T personnel who devoted a lot of time to counterintelligence were not really welcomed into the DO culture and in turn were vulnerable to accusations from their home bases in the DI and DS&T of neglecting their regular CIA work.

The top DO counterintelligence priorities had changed little from the early cold war years—recruitment of foreign intelligence personnel from hostile regimes, particularly the Soviet Union and its minions, and liaison with foreign services, especially internal services that monitored the Communist bloc. These activities, in addition to interviews with defectors, it was believed, would provide the basic information needed to indicate which American intelligence officers, officials, or agents had been compromised. Some of the DO's information was shared with DI analysts assigned to the Counterintelligence Center, who added it to data from technical collection sources. The analysts, concentrating more than before on current counterintelligence threats and less on historical work, issued warnings about Soviet bloc technical as well as humint attacks on U.S. interests and helped assess the validity of some DO agent recruits.

Within the Agency overall, the Counterintelligence Center staff was taken more seriously than the counterintelligence staff before them. Personnel from the Center gave counterintelligence briefings to various elements of the CIA, conducted surveys of counterintelligence vulnerabilities and the counterintelligence threat posed by Soviet bloc services to CIA stations abroad, and worked more closely with other agencies in the United States and abroad to catch spies and help shield CIA operations as well as other agencies from manipulation by hostile services. This did yield results. There were successes: identifying as spies State Department diplomat Felix Bloch; James Hall, an Army sergeant with access to sensitive communication sources; and Steven Lalas, a State Department communicator in Athens. Nevertheless, as the Ames case revealed, the reformed process was not perfect. Moreover, the CIA made little attempt to use counterintelligence information for positive purposes. Neither counterintelligence managers nor positive intelligence managers at the DO saw much purpose in this, and the managers of analysis at the DI did not pursue it. On the whole, foreign collection took precedence over covert action and counterintelligence at the CIA, even in the DO.

This orientation resulted in DO, DI, and DS&T officers receiving little counterintelligence training. Few became well versed in the subject. As former DO operator George Kalaris noted after he retired in the mid-1980s, even with reforms that he had helped institute, serious weaknesses still plagued the CIA's (and the country's) counterintelligence system as a whole. One of the key failures, he believed, was that the CIA personnel abroad did not undertake effective counterintelligence; the CIA was not as attentive as it should have been to protecting other governments' secrets in addition to its own, and counterintelligence training for positive DO operators was inadequate. "Counterintelligence," Kalaris said, "must be raised to a level of authority that gives it command and operational responsibility across the entire intelligence community as well as throughout the CIA itself."[86] On hearing Kalaris's remarks, Kenneth deGraffenreid, who had served as the senior director of intelligence at the NSC from 1981 to 1987, commented in the late 1980s, "I am dismayed . . . that virtually all of these recommendations have been made before, most certainly at the beginning of this decade. . . . It is indeed remarkable that they have to be made again, in view of the frightening events that have occurred during the past decade to confirm the need for these reforms."[87] The shocking failure of the CIA to protect nearly all its human sources in the USSR in the 1980s from betrayal by Ames, and to identify and neutralize Ames for nearly a decade, tend to substantiate the conclusions of Kalaris, deGraffenreid, and others who warned of counterintelligence weakness in the 1980s.

The Military

In both the DoD and individual services, changes took place in the counterintelligence bureaucracy. Carter's executive order required DoD representation on the NSC's Special Coordinating Committee (SCC) concerned with national counterintelligence. And it was increasingly recognized inside the DoD that counterintelligence should not be left exclusively to the individual services—that there were threats to many DoD functions, for example, civilian research, engineering, and procurement, that did not fit neatly under an individual service's jurisdictional umbrella. Each service, too, oversaw defensive security matters that were of common concern, matters that might be handled more efficiently if the task was centralized. Indeed, in the early 1970s the armed services were freed from the burden of providing security clearances for their several million personnel. In 1973, the Defense Investigative Service was created to perform this job for individual services and their contractors, for personnel and contractors in the Office of the Secretary of Defense (OSD).

In the late 1970s and throughout the 1980s, many other security and countermeasure matters were brought under the auspices of two undersecretaries of defense—for policy and for research and engineering. Though the undersecretaries themselves rarely got involved in counterintelligence matters, they now had staffs to handle the multibillion-dollar security program that the DoD was running worldwide to protect defense information, personnel, equipment, and combat forces.

Individual services remained primarily responsible for their counterintelligence portfolios: no group of DoD counterintelligence operators identified or frustrated foreign intelligence services, though there was some systematic counterintelligence analysis conducted by the more positive-oriented Defense Intelligence Agency.

Despite its reduced mission, the Army still had the most expansive view of counterintelligence. Even if its counterintelligence components no longer had a positive intelligence mission, the Army remained sensitive to the use of counterintelligence for positive purposes, encouraging the dissemination of relevant counterintelligence information to serve the Army's positive intelligence needs. No longer concerned with either civilian subversion or security clearances, counterintelligence concentrated on protecting Army operations by frustrating Soviet bloc intelligence services. Its role was not merely to play defense to Soviet bloc offense; it would develop an offense as well. Some enthusiasts in Army counterintelligence believed that this capability could be applied to broader national purposes, but most general officers disagreed. To play this dual role, the Army developed counterintelligence specialists, some of them former officers who directed regular Army personnel assigned to counterintelligence duties. The Army studied foreign service methods and expanded its training programs. Its specialists and active-duty personnel were drilled in tradecraft: assessing, recruiting, and running agents as well as implementing defensive security.

Collection was supported by multidisciplinary counterintelligence analysis, a technique pioneered by the Navy which the Army quickly adopted. Analysts at Washington headquarters as well as in various European and Asian commands compiled information on various hostile intelligence threats—those posed by foreign sigint, humint, and imagery. This, it was hoped, would enable the Army to warn combat commands of the sort of intelligence threats they faced, thereby enhancing countermeasures and security.

Apart from using such information for defense, some Army counterintelligence managers saw the potential for applying extensive collection and analysis to offensive operations aimed at disrupting hostile intelligence. Perhaps the most important aspect of this program was the development of extensive double-agent operations. Starting with just a couple of double agents in the 1970s, the Army was running more than one hundred a year by the mid-1980s. This stable of handlers and operatives uncovered a great deal about the Soviet bloc's methods, tied up Soviet bloc manpower in U.S.-controlled operations, and misled the Soviet military with disinformation about U.S. operations.

The double-agent program served more than the Army's interests. The FBI was happy to take advantage of it, and the CIA found information obtained on the enemy's intelligence order of battle valuable. Still, the Army was basically running a single-service show. Its program was not integrated into an overall national strategic counterintelligence plan; in effect, there wasn't one.

The Navy and Air Force continued to see their counterintelligence mission in much more defensive and parochial terms than did the Army. Counterintelligence personnel would protect service operations by advising various service components on the hostile threat and investigating cases of suspected espionage. Both services built up a core of five to ten civilian managers in their Washington headquarters and relied on several hundred generalist civilians to cover criminal and counterintelligence matters, advising and conducting investigations at their bases throughout the United States and abroad. Gradually, these investigators received more counterintelligence training. However, the Navy and the Air Force did not develop the specialists and the capability with which the Army eventually equipped itself.

Both services also became interested in multidisciplinary counterintelligence analysis. Their defensive counterintelligence units passed on information from the FBI and to a lesser extent from the CIA to a central group of Army analysts. Most of the analysis was done in service intelligence units rather than in counterintelligence components. Small double-agent programs were set up by the Navy for education and deterrence and by the Air Force for deception. Neither service encouraged its counterintelligence components to assist with positive intelligence. Unlike their counterparts in the Army, the counterintelligence components in the Navy and Air Force were far removed from their service's active-duty positive collectors, strategists, and combat command planning units.

The evolution of American counterintelligence in the twentieth century can be explained in large part by fluctuations in the perception of threat. During the last decade of the cold war, a new counterintelligence architecture developed in response to a general consensus within the government about the need for more effective counterintelligence and how best to accomplish this mission.

Policymakers in both the executive and the legislative branches, as well as the country at large, continued to believe counterintelligence was important to American interests. Despite a degree of ambivalence on the subject, natural in a democratic country, counterintelligence was for a time officially elevated to the status of a national issue. Directives were issued and staffs expanded to integrate counterintelligence into the development and implementation of national security policy. The Congress, well aware of these arrangements, not only supported them but called for more national counterintelligence strategic planning and better-coordinated implementation.

Despite these efforts, by the late 1980s there was still little central counterintelligence strategy that set out national priorities and the means for accomplishing them. Some in the counterintelligence agencies and on the NSC staff wanted to move in this direction. But most counterintelligence managers were content to improve interagency coordination rather than to develop a national strategy.

The CIA, for example, was interested in beefing up protection for its humint collection operations, but devoted little attention to using counterintelligence to enhance the Agency's multifaceted technical collection and analytic capabilities, much less all the diplomatic and military operations of the U.S. government. The FBI, while more broadly concerned with protecting and enhancing U.S. policy and institutions, was focused on institutions in the United States. The Bureau's mandate and the division of positive intelligence responsibilities with the CIA and the military precluded it from filling the vacuum created by hostile foreign intelligence services operating simultaneously in the United States and abroad, even if the Bureau leadership had wanted to. The DoD and the military services, for the most part, devoted their counterintelligence resources to huge security and countermeasures programs in installations at home and abroad. As a result of these separate priorities there were few national strategic planning initiatives in the 1980s, a fact duly noted in the Senate Intelligence Committee.[88]

The need to improve American counterintelligence collection, analysis, and exploitation was increasingly felt, though just how deficient individual agencies were was hard to determine. Clearly, the agencies themselves recognized certain of their weaknesses and undertook a number of initiatives to improve performance. It is ironic that some of the apparent counterintelligence "failures" became known in the 1980s as a result of improvements in U.S. counterintelligence. For example, many arrests and convictions of Americans in the decade of the spy would probably not have been possible without the bolstered resources and better-quality counterintelligence personnel that had been introduced in the preceding years. Consider the Walker spy ring, one of the most effective clandestine networks of all time. It provided the Soviets with top-secret U.S. codes from the late 1960s until the early 1980s. The identification, arrest, and conviction of its members was accomplished not just through luck (Barbara Walker denounced her ex-husband, John) but also through good FBI follow-up made possible by improvements in the late 1970s in counterintelligence analysis and collection.

It is also hard to know how much more successful hostile foreign services would have been if U.S. agencies had not honed their counterintelligence resources in the 1970s and 1980s. The reforms, however, could not avert major failures. In addition to Soviet bloc moles such as Aldrich Ames, some intelligence services managed to penetrate the U.S. defenses repeatedly. Among others, the Cubans and East Germans for many years almost completely frustrated U.S. positive humint collection. Although American counterintelligence managers began to develop respect for analysis, analysts remained in many respects second-class citizens who took a backseat to operations. And although the United States strengthened its ability to frustrate some foreign intelligence operations (as was seen, for example, in the Gulf War in 1991), it was still unable to disrupt or manipulate many foreign operations in a significant way, or to utilize counterintelligence fully and regularly for positive intelligence.

4

HANDMAIDEN OF POLICY: PRINCIPLES OF COVERT ACTION

FOR MANY AMERICANS, covert action, in the absence of clear and present danger, is a controversial proposition at best. It smacks of dirty tricks or clandestine wars, and is generally incompatible with a democratic foreign policy. Partisans of this view, which came to dominate the American foreign policy establishment in the mid-1970s and remains popular in some circles today, believe covert action should be banned or used only in exceptional circumstances.[1] At the other end of the spectrum, there are those who regard covert action as a substitute for policy—doing what you can when diplomacy alone will not work, or when overt military action is too dangerous; doing something when everything else has failed; or doing something rather than doing nothing.

What can happen when these two perspectives clash was amply demonstrated in the late 1970s and early 1980s when the United States became concerned about events in Central America. The problem, particularly as it evolved during the Reagan administration, ultimately came down to a lack of clearly defined goals. Was the United States interdicting arms to the Salvadoran rebels or overthrowing the Sandinistas? Few outside the NSC and the CIA (and not many in those two places) really understood what was going on. With policy unclear both inside and outside the government, covert action, rather than being a useful instrument of policy, became itself the subject of public controversy. Eventually the Congress cut off funds to the Contras and the White House resorted to irregular maneuvers to fund them—a strategy that ended in the so-called Iran-Contra scandal of the mid-1980s. Results of this kind are not inevitable. As was demonstrated after World War II, it *is* possible to conduct effective covert action in the service of the national interest.

First Principles

The essential principle of covert action is this: to be effective, it must be a part of a well-coordinated policy. Ends should be thought through, and the means to achieve those ends reasonably calculated. This cannot be emphasized too strongly. Covert action is a policy tool, not a substitute for policy or an excuse for foreign adventures. To succeed, covert action should usually be conceived as a very long-term proposition. Such was the thinking behind Elizabeth I's plans to weaken Spain and the Catholics in the sixteenth century, and behind France's support of the American Revolution against Britain in the eighteenth.[2]

Because covert action is not a substitute for policy, it is generally counterproductive when used by a government that has not decided what it wants to do—a government that acts simply to do something while it refuses to commit resources in a sustained, coordinated manner. Examples of such government wavering are Britain and the United States in their dealings with ruling Communist parties, first after the Russian Revolution and into the 1920s, then from the late 1940s on. While unwilling to sit idly by, the two Western powers could not decide exactly what to do in response to the growing tide of Communism. In this state of indecision, halfhearted covert action seemed a reasonably risk-free option.

Nor is covert action a magic bullet to be used alone when almost everything else has failed. It must be coordinated with and supported usually by diplomatic, military, and/or economic measures. There may be an occasional situation in which a one-shot covert operation serves a clear purpose, for example, an assassination (or prevention of an assassination) that could change the internal or external balance of power in a targeted state. The death of Hitler might have achieved that. But history indicates that such circumstances rarely present themselves, and that acting on them to bring about a desired end may not be as easy as hindsight would suggest. More properly, covert action is viewed as one of a number of instruments to achieve policy objectives when they cannot be achieved exclusively, or as effectively, by overt policy means. In this case, too, it is best to weigh carefully the risks and difficulties of covert action.

To enunciate these principles is to plead for neither more nor less covert action. It is to exhort the government to develop clear policy that it would be willing to defend with covert action, if necessary, in conjunction with a whole spectrum of other measures both covert and overt. A democratic government should not, as a rule, embark on foreign initiatives unless there is a reasonable chance of gaining support for its policy, and unless it is willing to mount a sustained public campaign toward that end. In a democracy, goals and the overall means reasonably calculated to achieve them must be laid out in public. That is not to say the government should spell out the specifics of covert action programs, merely that its programs should dovetail with its policy. This is insurance against opposition—leaked details will not have the power to incur public wrath as they did in what was widely perceived as an arms-for-hostages swap by the United States during the 1980s.[3]

Policy, Opportunity, and People

For covert action to fulfill its role, there must be an opportunity to influence events abroad—and people who can transform that opportunity into a program. Moreover, a government contemplating covert action must have the power and authority to make effective use of it. This is especially the case when, as it so often does, covert action requires that foreigners be enlisted in a joint effort. For example, it would be useless for Iceland to try secretly to mobilize Americans to support its claim to fishing rights in the Arctic against Great Britain; Iceland has no clout in the United States, and furthermore the issue would be of no strategic interest to the United States. Of course, there may be opportunities to achieve specific objectives of which a small country without much authority can avail itself. Even a small, weak state can spot an opening and seize the opportunity—as Israel did in a covert program to extricate Jews from Iraq and Iran in the late 1940s.[4] To achieve its goal, Israel won secret cooperation from senior officials in those hostile governments. Israel spotted and exploited the opportunity to persuade Iraqi and Iranian officials to turn a blind eye to Israeli covert presence in their countries.

Timing is important in seizing opportunity—anticipating the flow of events, and acting while there is still time. Launching a covert program too early can be disastrous, while doing so after a crisis has developed—and after the adversary has prepared its defenses—can be equally futile. Covert action is far more effective as a preemptive measure, something the United States learned as a matter of course in dealing with Communists in the 1950s and 1960s but forgot in the mid-1970s, when it did little to neutralize Soviet active measures campaigns.

At the top there must be sustained leadership interested in hiring commanders or managers who can exploit opportunities preemptively and who are capable of orchestrating overt and covert action programs. These covert action specialists tend not to exhibit the ideal military virtues of discipline, straightforwardness, and obedience so much as creativity and imagination. They develop ideas, transform them into covert action, and coordinate that action with overt measures—a task that requires considerable intellect. In the sixteenth century Elizabeth I surrounded herself with such men.[5] In fact, it was no accident that she encouraged her commanders to pick the brains of leading creative spirits of the day such as William Shakespeare and Christopher Marlowe; that Louis XVI sided with the playwright Pierre-Augustin de Beaumarchais against the advice of his foreign minister; that Roosevelt relied on playwright Robert Sherwood and oddball soldier-lawyers such as Bill Donovan.

It also helps if policymakers and their senior commanders are strong enough occasionally to critique their own performance and the performance of their covert action system. This does not mean merely firing commanders or subordinates who fail; it means evaluating the system to learn what went wrong and then trying to fix it. (The bureaucracy itself, with its vested interests, usually cannot be expected to carry out this sort of self-examination.) For a brief period after World War II, U.S. administrations conducted such reviews, but they have not done so regularly since then. Honest self-evaluation is the fruit of strong leadership from within and without, and like strong leadership, it is rare.

Creative leadership, coordination, and self-evaluation at the top are still not enough to bring about effective covert action. There must be skilled operators who can translate general policy directives into specifics—helping faction X and weakening faction Y in Ruritania. These skilled operators need to be committed, motivated individuals. Covert political operations, even when they involve little personal risk, require men and women who care about the outcome. Many of the best operatives over the years have been those wedded to a cause—whether of the right or the left, whether of the monarch, the empire, the religion, or the clan. Needless to say, overcommitment or fanaticism can invite disaster by inhibiting accurate analysis of the situation. Those who try to lead uprisings when circumstances are not ripe, like

Che Guevara in Bolivia in the 1960s, learn this harsh truth to their everlasting chagrin.

Operators must also be committed to the instrument of covert action itself. They must know that it can and has worked. It is no good sending people into battle who do not believe in the power of their weapons.

Operators, like their managers, need to be creative, able to spot opportunities and develop programs to exploit them. Precise instructions for dealing with complex circumstances and unpredictable personalities on the scene will not come from the top. Covert action often requires a highly creative person to take advantage of the grand opportunity and exploit it, to identify the issues and the people that can be brought together to achieve results—T. E. Lawrence in the Arabian desert persuading the Hejaz Arabs to rise against the Turks in 1917; businessman Gustav Parvus arranging for Lenin and other Bolsheviks to be transported across Germany and deposited on the Russian border during World War I, after the overthrow of the czar. Parvus saw an opportunity that would help take Russia out of the war, and surmised that the Bolsheviks would help weaken the provisional post-czarist government of Aleksandr Kerensky.[6]

This kind of creativity, the ability to judge on the spot, to improvise, to act on that intangible blend of knowledge, conviction, and instinct, is not the stuff of modern bureaucratic organizational doctrine in authoritarian or democratic regimes. Today's lightning communication technology has not greatly altered the challenges. Covert action operators need the capacity to decide and to act as Admiral Nelson did in 1801 at Aboukir, where he destroyed the French fleet and crippled Napolean's Egyptian expedition, though the voice of the Admiralty was weeks away.

Creativity most certainly does not rule out craft, or knowledge of the causes and cultures an operator is working for and against. There is little substitute for knowledge. Enthusiastic new recruits just out of university who have never lived or worked in an alien culture are not likely to make the best covert operators. Competence in their particular specialty—be it paramilitary operations or propaganda—is a *sine qua non* for operators. More broadly, they need to develop a sixth sense for what works and what doesn't, like Rudyard Kipling's fictional Kim, or the German "Lawrence" Wassmus, who rallied tribesmen to fight the British in Persia during World War II.

Consider the directive "Mobilize Ruritanian public opinion in support of X and in opposition to Y." That can be meaningful only to the person who knows what themes are likely to appeal to Ruritanians and how those themes might be brought to their attention. The specialist should know whether an overt appeal from abroad, combined with diplomatically prearranged statements of support from Ruritanian leaders, will be enough, or whether it is first necessary to build support in Ruritanian society at large. If so, the covert action specialist needs to know which Ruritanians can be counted on to help initiate the rhetoric of support. If, for example, the subject is trade or agriculture, the specialist (assuming, of course, that this person has the authority and that the policy has been well planned) should call on his own government's commercial and agricultural agencies to garner support with timely overt acts and by quietly lobbying Ruritanian commercial and agriculture circles. The head of British intelligence in the United States, William Wiseman, did this when he won operatives' support for rapid U.S. involvement in World War I after the U.S. declaration of war in 1917.

What about the directive "Use covert methods to complement overt techniques to reverse the growth of the Ruritanian Symbolist Party"? This requires more complex translation. Savvy operators will give certain themes currency in public discourse and remove others from the public eye. In every major sector of society where it is active, they will strengthen opposition to the party and sow dissent from within. They will apply ideas, techniques, and resources to shore up the leadership and effectiveness of opposition political groups—all without giving the Ruritanian Symbolists a single opportunity to prove that their opponents are tools of a foreign power.

A covert action specialist looking at the resources available for this task may well conclude that there is simply too little to work with in Ruritania, that such an ambitious operation would end in embarrassing disclosures, and that current efforts there should be aimed merely at building "assets"—that is, relationships on which one can draw with reasonable confidence at a later date. If the specialist is courageous, he or she will say just that. This is what one CIA specialist did in 1970 when Nixon ordered the CIA to prevent the election of Salvador Allende in Chile, overriding CIA objections that the United States did not have the assets to do the job.

Of course, higher authorities, lacking any viable policy toward Ruritania, may see even half-baked covert action as better than nothing. But the consequences of a decision to go ahead with it will be theirs, not the covert action managers' or specialists'. Once staff specialists translate the covert action directive into specific terms, individual case officers, whether under official or unofficial cover, will go into the field and try to enlist designated players to perform the roles assigned to them. Unless these players are close to being what the covert action planners had envisioned, new players will have to be recruited quickly—a delicate, little-understood, and complex aspect of covert action. Effectiveness depends in large part on an infrastructure that is in place before it is needed.

The Infrastructure

Without people and material support in place, policymakers cannot influence events abroad through covert action—especially in modern, complex societies. An infrastructure can be enlarged or improved after a program has been initiated, but usually, to operate covertly and effectively, there must be some existing infrastructure. Not all components have to be covert—some can be overt or semiovert—but they do have to be coordinated with covert components.

The infrastructure always consists of two parts: people and material arrangements.

Personnel

Apart from professional case officers and managers, two other types of specialists are needed for effective covert action: deep-cover officers or assets, and technical specialists. The first should be nonofficial or "illegal" intelligence officers, or foreigners already in place, willing and able to serve on the front line. They are either deep-cover officers, illegal full-time professionals, or part-time recruits who have the skill, knowledge, and access or authority to influence foreigners or events abroad. They can be journalists, politicians, student leaders, retired military officers, trade union leaders, businessmen, academics, or public relations specialists. Their colleagues do not generally believe they are collaborating with foreign intelligence services. The role of the deep-cover officer in the infrastructure is to assist regular case officers and work with either recruited foreign agents or collaborators on specific missions in a covert action plan.

The case officers and their networks need to be maintained, even in skeletal form, more or less permanently, letting covert action planners know on very short notice who is influential in a foreign society, who is reliable, and who is an opportunist. Only then can the covert action instrument be successfully activated when the order is given. The British maintained such an infrastructure in post–World War II Iran. In 1953, when the Americans and British decided to overthrow the Mussadegh government, the British had the networks in place. For decades, Moscow maintained an infrastructure in many parts of the world. For example, in the 1974 Portuguese revolution, Soviet leaders were positioned to make a major play for that country—and very nearly took it over. The United States built up such a capability to contain Communism in Western Europe, Latin America, and to some extent elsewhere after World War II. But it was allowed to atrophy. When the United States needed a human infrastructure to exert its influence in Iran in the mid-1980s, the resources were not there. The White House and CIA had to rely on the Israelis, who had their own agents in place in Iran, and on private citizens who were not experts on Iran and lacked a range of reliable connections there.

Covert action capability depends on a network of trusted contacts and people with the know-how to influence events in a region. Those who would build an infrastructure must seek out those who can and will help, for a variety of reasons ranging from ideological conviction to financial remuneration. Ideally, these assets will be adept at conceptualizing how to influence events, and willing to spot and recruit other collaborators.

There is no need to *control* foreign assets—whether politicians or journalists, ethnic leaders or activists—as bureaucracies rooted in the Anglo-American tradition, favoring precision and efficiency, are tempted to do. Many foreigners willing to collaborate on specific missions do not want to be viewed as paid, controlled agents. The best covert action campaigns help people do what they want to do more effectively than they could do without such assistance. This means providing advice, guidance, moral, material, and technical support, and possible safe haven. It does not require manipulating an asset's every move.

Traditionally the United States (and perhaps Britain) has sought to control foreign collaborators by turning them into recruited agents. The Soviet Union often was much more subtle. It provided guidance and material support to a whole range of types from controlled agents, who responded to specific tasks and received money for carrying them out, to trusted contacts who received only general guidance on the direction of Soviet policy and how to help implement it. As Hugh Tovar, a former senior U.S. practitioner, put it in discussing weaknesses in postwar U.S. covert action:

> I have already expressed uneasiness about the term *agent* as such. The word has a connotation that I consider unrealistic and unnecessarily pejorative. More often than not, the so-

called agent is a collaborator rather than a person doing someone else's bidding. The relationship with the agent, if it is to be effective, will usually be reciprocal, predicated upon a mutually compatible agenda and objectives. . . . The agent or collaborator must not be totally dependent on his or her covert partner. In many, if not most instances, the agent will have some organizational affiliation that is of operational interest or value, and the support given should be limited to that needed to attain marginal advantage, perhaps only to achieve a catalytic effect.[7]

It is the job of the case officer to identify the interests of suitable foreign assets and to help ensure that their interests continue to overlap with those of the United States. Case officers must keep assuring assets that their role is important, that the covert relationship will make a difference. Their assets must be persuaded that they can be helpful for an extended period of time, and that even in the event of failure they will not be abandoned. At crucial times, nothing helps so much as a record of success and fidelity. Case officers may have to train their assets in the use of new equipment or in the workings of a new operation. Often circumstances require a new team to be put together composed of people who may be unfamiliar with or even dislike one another. The case officer has to determine what glue, if any, will hold the network together: the mission itself, hatred of the enemy, camaraderie? If a foreigner is unable to play his part in an operation, should the foreigner be cut off? Such decisions require not only good judgment but courage as well: the case officer may have to admit that his initial judgment of an individual was wrong.

Also critical to the human infrastructure are technical personnel, for example those who can produce false documents to enable assets to travel, live, or work in areas where they could not otherwise. In the late 1970s the U.S. government furnished the Canadian government with false documents to help American diplomats hidden in Iran to escape. Other valuable technical specialists are those with paramilitary skills who can train foreigners in offensive and defensive tactics, and those versed in political techniques—how to build support for candidates, to use modern polling techniques, to get out the vote. Maintaining a list of such specialists is the job of the infrastructure. If the list is not maintained, covert action managers will have to scramble to find the appropriate expertise when the "balloon goes up."

Material Support

The other half of the covert action infrastructure consists of material support. Among the most important aspects of material support are the means to transfer money, communicate, and travel covertly, and the facilities for meeting, safe haven, and training.

It is not very difficult to transfer money covertly. A bank account may be set up in Switzerland (or Luxembourg, or the Cayman Islands or other Caribbean haven), then the money transferred to a numbered account in another bank in the same country. Then, when needed, it is sent to an account in a different country. Occasionally states get caught in these transactions, but not often. Another technique is for a government to set up an otherwise legitimate bank in a foreign country. The recipient opens an account in that bank. Money is then transferred from the government account to the recipient's. Moscow used this sleight for decades.

In the 1970s, Moscow financed activities in Italy, Greece, and elsewhere by having legitimate trading companies already doing business with the USSR pay a commission to a company controlled by the intended recipient of the funds. The collapse of the Soviet Union has, of course, brought to light other, simpler conduits, such as the delivery of large cash payments to Communist parties in the United States and elsewhere in the West.

Communications are a linchpin of successful covert action that link headquarters with the field operation. This is not difficult either, if there is an embassy close by. Coded messages can be sent by managers at headquarters to the embassy for clandestine dissemination to local agents and assets. Elsewhere, as the Israelis have often found, clandestine radios and couriers from headquarters directly to field agents are useful. If couriers are employed, then arrangements have to be made to infiltrate and exfiltrate agents from the contested area. Meetings between couriers or case officers and their agents and assets take place in safe houses or safe havens.

Agents can purchase and transport supplies—logistics—by buying medical or military goods on the open market, then hiring a shipping company to send them to a target or neighboring country. Sometimes supplies are so specialized or are required in such quantity that they cannot be purchased on the open market or transported overtly without attracting unwelcome attention. In the 1950s, the United States ran into this problem and had to establish commercial airlines or acquire commercial air carriers to transport goods to various parts of the world. Air America, for example, was secretly owned and controlled by the U.S. government. It sold some of its services on the open market while routes, pilots, and cargo-handling were controlled by covert CIA managers. This airline played a particularly important role in U.S. paramilitary operations in Asia in the 1950s and 1960s.

Supply routes for weapons and other military equipment can be ironically sinuous. The Soviet Union, for example, was able to make use of vast stocks of U.S. weapons left behind in Vietnam in the 1970s; eventually they found their way to Cuba and Marxist-Leninist insurgents in Central America. The United States and other countries in turn provided the Afghan resistance movement with Soviet weapons, many of which Brezhnev had sold to Egypt prior to Sadat's break with Moscow in 1976.

A dramatic example of good infrastructure is the hasty preparation in 1979 for the rescue of U.S. embassy hostages in Iran. The United States sent professional operatives and agents into Iran on third-country passports. They set up services for the anticipated rescue force largely through a network of hurriedly created companies that they owned and staffed. Meanwhile, two other Americans flew clandestinely to selected airstrips in the Iranian countryside to preposition equipment for the rescue force. The United States also used a variety of radio transmitters outside Iran to communicate with its operatives and their agents inside. The operational plan made full use of an exemplary covert material infrastructure. This is not to say that the actual rescue attempt, when it came, was well planned and executed—quite the contrary. These operations serve as an object lesson: even an exemplary infrastructure will not compensate for defects in operational planning and execution.[8]

Question of Values

Another guiding maxim for a democratic government practicing covert action is that the circumstances under which actions are taken and the secret means of bringing them about should be consistent with its society's values. There is a good chance that sooner or later the action will be uncovered by the target's counterintelligence service or leaked from within. To minimize disruption if an operation is blown, it is much better to use covert means consistent with a society's sense of justice and proportion. There is also less likely to be a leak if the means are consistent with the society's values.

It is not always easy to determine what means are consistent with a society's dominant values. Generally, the test in a democratic society is how the people and the legislature would react if they were informed directly about specific techniques. For example, most Americans in the 1990s would regard many of the covert actions discussed in the following pages—advising foreign leaders, giving material support to promising young leaders, supporting pro-liberty forces—as perfectly compatible with democratic values, even if they disagreed about which specific leaders or causes to support. Americans, however, have traditionally been very uncomfortable with techniques such as targeting foreign leaders for assassination, at least in peacetime. They would also disapprove, in peacetime, of disseminating disinformation—intentionally false information—intended to influence public opinion abroad. This is in part because Americans would like to hold their government to an ethical standard of truth in its dealings, but also because they believe that ultimately truth is more effective, and that the habit of using disinformation might pollute America's own internal political debate. Americans would probably not be opposed to manipulating adversaries by passing false information through double agents or other channels outside the media.

The United States, along with most democratic cultures, would also approve in principle of covertly helping secure the safety of its own citizens, or even that of foreigners facing the massive abuse of civil rights, forced starvation, violent assault, or genocide. Assistance to the antifascist undergrounds and targeted minorities in Europe prior to World War II would have been consistent with democratic culture—though the United States and Britain did less then than in Croatia and Bosnia-Herzegovina at the beginning of the 1990s.

Likewise, providing covert support to democratic elements in countries threatened by antidemocratic forces would be compatible with democratic norms, as would covert involvement in the politics of foreign societies subject to outside intervention by outlaw regimes such as Libya, Iraq, and Iran in the early 1990s. A more difficult question arises in cases where the extent of foreign intervention is unknown, or known to be slight, while antidemocratic forces are close to taking power through a combination of democratic and nondemocratic means—as the Nazi Party did in Germany in the 1930s.

It would not be inconsistent with a democratic culture for a government to use covert action to save the lives of its citizens threatened by terrorists, drug smugglers, guerrillas, or a combination of all three. The problem is knowing exactly when covert action in general, and specific techniques in particular, dovetail with values. There is a hazy middle ground that shifts in response to perceived threats, other international developments, and so forth. But the two poles of approval and disapproval—if the public knew the truth—are usually quite visible.

Symbiosis

If covert action is to be effective, it should be integrated not only with policy and cultural values but also, as we have pointed out, with the other elements of intelligence—collection, analysis, and counterintelligence. Granted, covert operators are usually reluctant to share their operational secrets with counterintelligence specialists and even analysts, for fear that they will be criticized by skeptical, ultracautious colleagues, and in part for security reasons. But if all the elements of the equation are properly balanced, counterintelligence and analysis can be of great value to covert action planners and operators.

Collectors benefit from and have much to contribute to covert action. Collection is obviously useful to covert action planners. Many foreign agents who are willing to share information discreetly do so for political rather than financial reasons. They want the foreign government to support them and their causes. A cabinet minister in the Indian government, say, is unlikely to furnish information for money or excitement, of which he already has both. But he may provide detailed reports on the cabinet meeting if he thinks a foreign government will aid him, his party, or his cause. He is potentially a natural covert ally. Former practitioners have pointed out that some of the best collection operations have benefited from covert action.

Similarly, covert action benefits from good analysis, especially opportunity analysis. Analysts who spot opportunities and weaknesses in the foreign society—who know who is who, who wants what, who is vulnerable to what political, economic, and military pressure—are invaluable to operators; analysts who merely crank out reports describing empirical trends in a society—say, the growth of military forces in a given region—often will not be as useful to covert action, even if they are accurate.

To illustrate the value of opportunity-oriented analysis, assume that analysts could identify which specific factions or leaders in Colombia's ruling party are beholden to drug traffickers and reluctant to stop the flow of narcotics. A U.S. president in possession of this information would better understand the negative pressure on a friendly Colombian president, and might be positioned to help the latter overcome some of the pressure by overtly or covertly assisting factions not so beholden to drug lords, and by weakening those that were.

Take the position of policymakers and covert action managers faced with ethnic groups in, say, the Caucasus, Central Asia, or the Balkans, who are seeking assistance to secure their independence or to prevent their citizens from being slaughtered by neighboring ethnic, nationalist, or religious groups. Analysts and collectors who really know their subject will be able to identify the crooks and the opportunists, to say who can be relied on to make good use of aid and in whose hands aid will simply dissipate. Again, acknowledging the existence of ethnic and religious tensions is not enough. Operators need to know the strengths and weaknesses of the key players in a foreign society, what motivates them, and what opportunities there might be to influence them.

Another, albeit lesser advantage of close collaboration between analysts and covert action practitioners is that analysis can be used in actual operations. An analyst's description of an adversary politician's corruption and machinations, for instance, can be used in an operation to discredit him or her. And analysis—in a sanitized form—can be passed to a foreign leader to shape his or her perception of the world. This was the British tactic when it set out to influence Roosevelt and bring the United States into World War II. This is not to say that the marriage between analysts and covert action operators should be a close one, for that invites the danger that either will become too involved or committed and hence lose the advantage of objectivity. Covert action managers need to harness the skills of analysts while keeping them at arm's length.

Covert operators also lean heavily on good counterintelligence. Are their foreign allies genuinely loyal to the causes that they espouse, or are they puppets being manipulated by foreign governments and their intelligence services? The success of covert action may turn on the correct answer to these questions.

The use of double, even triple, agents is as old as history. Most notable in the twentieth century, and perhaps of all time, was the Soviet bloc creation and manipulation of false "opposition" movements in Soviet bloc countries, movements that one generation after another of Western covert operators was drawn into supporting. The United States and other governments apparently also were fooled and manipulated repeatedly by an ostensibly "moderate" faction in Iran in the 1980s.

There are pros and cons to placing responsibility for covert action in the same bureaucracy with other elements of intelligence. In fact, they do not have to be lumped together, but there can be important advantages if they are, and most democracies in the twentieth century have housed the functions together. For a period in the 1940s, both the United States and Britain vacillated between establishing a separate agency for covert action and maintaining a more centralized intelligence service. Eventually, the United States settled on a centralized system, the British on a less centralized one. The British believed that paramilitary covert action, because it is so "noisy," should be housed separately rather than within the military or the British foreign intelligence service, MI6.

Ends, Means, and Historical Lessons

Although covert action, in some respects, may be regarded as an art, it should not be conducted for its own sake. There are three broad purposes for using covert action: (1) to influence the internal balance of power in a country or in a transstate group, such as an ethnic alliance or an international criminal cartel; (2) to influence the climate of opinion in them; and (3) to induce *specific* actions unrelated to the internal power balance or climate of opinion.

Influencing the composition of a government, a key decision-making group in a country, or a transstate organization is the major objective of most covert action. The aim is to ensure that the key forces in the government or group are favorably disposed to one's own government or its policies. This may mean simply changing key personnel, or it may entail a complete overhaul of the government or group. Sometimes factions are supported in the ruling group, or in the opposition, to pressure the government or group to act in a certain way.

Influencing the climate of opinion in a target country, or the character of its body politic, is a subtle, less openly tendentious form of covert action. The purpose is not to affect any given decisions, or the near-term specific balance of forces within the government or group. Rather, it is to press key decision-makers to act in desired directions by shaping the conditions and the pressures that exert influence on them.

Inducing specific actions in a government, an international organization, or a nongovernmental organization is a common goal of covert action. The Israelis, for example, influenced key Iraqi leaders in order to extricate Iraqi Jews in the late 1940s and early 1950s. The United States has sought by various means to influence specific votes at the United Nations, for instance, to expel foreign intelligence officers from a third country where they were undermining U.S. interests. In the

1970s, the United States also tried to induce specific actions on the part of nongovernmental organizations such as the PLO.

To achieve these objectives a variety of techniques can be used, alone or in combination, overtly or covertly or both. These techniques fall into the general categories of *political action, propaganda programs, paramilitary activities*, and *intelligence support*. The dividing lines among these various categories often may be blurred.

Political Action

Governments have an advantage when they use a variety of political techniques to complement their diplomatic, economic, and military capabilities (assuming, of course, that they also have coordinated policy, imaginative and sustained leadership, skilled operatives, and strong intelligence structures). To influence foreign targets a government can formally and openly try to exercise its influence within the framework of traditional diplomatic relations. This is the stuff of normal diplomacy. But official representatives also may have opportunities to become much more influential as secret or confidential advisers to foreign governments or nongovernmental groups. Alternatively, circumstances may be such that special operatives can be secretly dispatched and stationed more or less permanently to influence the head of state or head of government and his ministers, or the leaders of important nongovernmental groups. The target government or group will be well aware that the foreign government is using confidential advisers. Sometimes it will not recognize the foreign government and its ambassadors but will accept the presence of secret envoys. In the nineteenth century the United States, seeking influence with foreign governments with which it did not maintain diplomatic relations, occasionally relied on such secret inroads. In more recent times Israel found it necessary to establish Mossad (Israel's foreign intelligence service) stations, usually under commercial cover, in countries that refused to recognize the State of Israel, and Israeli operatives have been able to achieve a great deal through discreet, unacknowledged action.

Where there is diplomatic recognition, ambassadors, in addition to their regular diplomatic role, sometimes become influential confidential advisers—especially when they have excellent intelligence collection and analysis to rely on. An especially astute practitioner of this sort was Diego Sarmiento de Acuña, Count of Gondomar, representing Philip II of Spain in England in the early 1600s. The so-called Super Spy of London, Gondomar collected intelligence through networks ranging from royal councillors to dock workers, but relied mainly on a small circle of court and official informers. His signal success was his relationship and influence with James I. Through this influence he played a major role in keeping Protestant England neutral in the war that Catholic Spain was waging against the Protestant Netherlands.

Ambassadors cannot always be as discreet as circumstances might require. In the sixteenth century, ambassadors from Italian city-states, their arrival the object of ceremony, speculation, and interpretation by the receiving country, were often unable to act covertly. "Such circumstances furthered the adoption of a variety of diplomatic agents, ranging from the *mandatario*, usually a man of lesser social status than an ambassador with either a limited or full mandate, to a friend at court (*amico*), or merchants who would be merely spies. All of these men could be employed with greater secrecy than an ambassador and with less risk of offense to a susceptible ally."[9]

In the late seventeenth century, the French spotted an opportunity outside ambassadorial channels to take their cause to the court of England's George I. Disguised as a Dutch gentleman, Cardinal Dubois, the French regent's adviser, joined King George's retinue and fostered an alliance between France and England through the British secretary of state, James Stanhope. During state dinners Dubois, eavesdropping on the indiscreet table talk, gathered valuable intelligence that was eventually parlayed into an alliance signed by England and France in January 1717. He went on to lead an espionage system in England and conduct various secret negotiations with Spain, Russia, and Sweden.

With the turn of the twentieth century, covert techniques to influence key foreigners became more and more the preserve of professionals working out of intelligence bureaucracies. The very able British intelligence operative William Wiseman became a close adviser to President Wilson and his aide Colonel House. Wiseman's influence helped to bring the United States into World War I, and then to deliver rapid American help to stop the Germans in the crucial battles of the spring of 1918. The British campaign to exert similar influence on President Roosevelt and his advisers in the late 1930s operated through the MI6 chief in New York, William Stephenson. Both Wiseman and Stephenson, British intelligence officers whose identity was known to the Americans with whom they dealt but not to the public, helped alter the internal political balance and the climate of public opinion in the United States and thus opened the path to specific U.S. decisions to aid Britain. After World War II, many CIA chiefs of station in Arab, Latin American, and Asian countries became trusted advisers to foreign leaders and were able to supplement the activities of other branches of the government. William Colby writes in his book *Lost Victory* that he, a CIA officer, and not the U.S. ambassador, was called in to mediate deadly factional struggles in South Vietnam in the 1950s and 1960s. Another CIA officer, Ted Shackley, did the same in Laos in the 1960s.[10]

Why, in our time, is an intelligence officer rather than a diplomat often the best person for the job? There are a variety of reasons. Ambassadors, especially those from powerful countries, lead highly visible lives. Their actions, meetings, travel, and statements are subject to constant scrutiny by the media, opposition leaders, and other embassies. As a practical matter it is extremely difficult for them to become the close confidant of the chief of state or key ministers, or potentially important nongovernmental leaders such as muftis or imams, without this quickly becoming public knowledge. An intelligence officer can operate with a much lower profile. Often he or she is an expert on the assigned country, having served there once or twice before, and is a specialist in the language. The intelligence officer has the time and opportunity to develop close personal contacts. He may earlier have worked confidentially with the head of government or key ministers, or befriended religious leaders when they were more junior. The intelligence officer also has impressive resources at his disposal, working with overt sections of the embassy and frequently with a covert apparatus as well. He can call on the worldwide assets of his service for confidential support, and he may find additional advantage in providing such personal inducements as financial assistance, special medical care, or physical protection to a foreign leader and his family, especially in the event of a coup or revolution.

An intelligence station chief also can play good cop to the ambassador's bad cop, or vice versa, though this game has its disadvantages. A foreign leader can easily become confused about the priorities of another government if he is receiving contradictory messages from its ambassador and its chief of station—a risk underlining the need for coordinated policy and action among the different agencies of government.

In general, it can be said that personal, confidential relationships give a government an added voice at the highest levels of foreign society, if that government is flexible enough and has operatives who are skilled enough to take advantage of opportunities. This general proposition is particularly relevant to the United States' relationships with nondemocratic governments, where the second or third most important figure is almost always the minister of the interior or the chief of the security service (often two roles combined in one). The head of state relies on his security chiefs to keep track of and neutralize opponents believed to be dangerous. Furthermore, because nondemocratic regimes often depend on conspiracy and secret channels of influence for longevity, they tend to believe other governments work this way as well and therefore that an ambassador and a ministry of foreign affairs have less influence than an intelligence service in the domestic politics of a Western government. This bias is a useful opening for influential relationships in many governments throughout Asia, Africa, the Middle East, and Latin America.

The chief of station is a logical clandestine contact point between one country and another. From a collection and counterintelligence standpoint, the chief wants to maintain liaison with local security chiefs. They can provide him with useful information, particularly on local operations being conducted by hostile services of special interest to his government, and they can offer him a unique opportunity to influence key figures. But there are risks. The local service will have its own priorities. It may try, for example, to discourage foreign involvement or contact with opponents of the regime in order to encourage its own more intimate relations with the station chief. This appears to have happened in the 1960s and early 1970s in Iran, when the United States in effect became a prisoner of SAVAK, the shah's security service. The CIA and the American embassy as a whole were dissuaded from maintaining contact with the Islamic revolutionary forces that eventually took over Iran until very late in the game. Another risk is that the station chief's intelligence service and his government may be outfoxed by the local security service, becoming a transmission belt for the latter's priorities. Evidence suggests that this was the case when the CIA was involved with Manuel Noriega in the 1970s and 1980s. As Panama's military intelligence chief in the 1970s, Noriega collaborated closely with the United States, which used Panama for various collection and covert action programs in Central America and the Caribbean. But when Noriega became Panama's head of state in the early 1980s and subsequently became embroiled with Cuban and Latin American drug dealers, U.S. officials were reluctant to denounce him and assist his political opposition, lest this jeopardize America's base of operations in Panama.

· Usually, however, there are opportunities for *skilled* covert action practitioners, alone or together with diplomatic personnel, to influence local leaders by providing advice and counsel on common enemies. Foreign-source information on the plans of terrorist groups targeting local leaders, for example, will ingratiate anyone with the leadership of the local security service, paying a direct dividend in access to the top leaders of the local government.

Agents of Influence

Another political technique is to supplement overt channels of influence in a foreign government by secretly befriending and assisting private individuals or leaders so they will influence the government now, or later when they rise to important positions. This is known as recruiting agents of influence. Individuals formally recruited for this purpose can become paid, witting, and controlled agents working in their own society on behalf of a foreign intelligence service. It is often easier and more effective, however, to find allies who are willing, even anxious, to collaborate with foreign intelligence officers or their agents *without* being paid and controlled. On occasion, it is possible to find useful connections who are not even aware that they are collaborating with a foreign intelligence service—people willing to work with outsiders because they believe in a common cause and see it as an advantageous, even righteous, thing to do.

Some governments and services are particularly good at a technique known as seeding, that is, identifying potential agents of influence at an early stage and then acting to advance their careers. Seeding is obviously a long-term, delicate project. Identifying an individual of promise and competence who will remain a collaborator for decades is no easy task. Even when such a person is found, it may well take years before he achieves a position of significant influence. Moreover, if he does most of the work of advancing himself inside the system single-handedly, he will not ultimately be beholden to the foreign power that originally launched him on his upward journey.

Developing agents of influence is by no means a recent technique. The ancient Greeks employed *proxenoi*, respected citizens of foreign states who looked after the interests of a particular city-state in their own countries. In addition to intelligence-gathering, some *proxenoi* were involved in subversion, sabotage, political disruption, and assassination, and some acted as commercial agents and negotiators. The Catholic Church believed in seeding techniques. The Society of Jesus, founded by Saint Ignatius Loyola in 1534, was originally devoted to the mission of wresting control of Jerusalem from the Turks. The Jesuits later switched their focus to fighting the Reformation in Europe. Among their weapons of choice in this holy war were special seminaries for training priests. Loyola and his successors placed the Jesuits, following a long and rigorous training, in European courts where they could influence rulers, not just on spiritual matters but also on matters of war and peace. English Catholics employed the same strategy. Under the patronage of the pope and Philip II, they set up seminaries in France to train missionaries to go back to Protestant England and propagate the faith. Recruits from fourteen to twenty-five years old were put through a seven-year program of study under severe bodily and mental discipline. The novice swore "to Almighty God that I am ready and shall always be ready, to receive holy orders, in His own good time, and I shall return to England for the salvation of souls, whenever it shall seem good to the superior of this college to order me to do so."[11] The English government, aware of what was going on, grew alarmed at the numbers seeking entrance to the seminaries and instituted heavy penalties to combat recruitment. The English word "seminarist" came to mean conspirator.

The Poles have historically used a form of seeding that employs impostors, including a failed attempt to take over the Russian throne in the early 1600s. In 1605, a dispute flared up over the succession to the Russian throne. Ever anxious to bring Roman Catholicism to Eastern Orthodox Russia, the Polish Jesuits took a hand in this dispute, as did Poland's King Sigismund, who hoped to realize Polish territorial aspirations for Livonia and Byeloruss, lands long fought over with the Russians. They supported an Eastern Orthodox monk, Demetrius, as the true heir to the Russian throne, falsely claiming that he was the younger son of Ivan IV. Demetrius in return vowed allegiance to the Roman Catholic Church. The Poles invaded Russia in hopes of realizing their goal at last, but their high-stakes operation failed when Demetrius was murdered.

In more recent times, the Poles developed seeding operations to infiltrate the Soviet government. Moscow never acknowledged it officially, but apparently the Polish intelligence service took advantage of the chaos after World War I to slip an impostor into the Soviet government in the 1920s. The man, whose real name was Poleschuk, took on the identity of a Ukrainian Communist named Konar who had been killed in the war between Russia and Poland. He rose through the ranks of the Ukrainian Party and then was transferred to Moscow. As deputy commissar of agriculture, he attended meetings of the highest political bodies, submitting memoranda to Stalin and other senior Bolsheviks. It seems that Konar wanted to stop working for the Poles, but they would not let him go, and eventually he was caught by the Soviets.[12]

Seeding with impostors is extremely difficult, requiring not only an unusual opportunity to plant an impostor but also a tightly disciplined intelligence infrastructure to maintain the deception. Identifying and supporting native agents of influence early in their careers is a more manageable covert activity. But it still requires skilled case officers to identify and run such agents. Since World War II, the Israelis and the Soviets have developed occasional long-term agents of influence who could also be used for intelligence collection, and sometimes these have been successful. Eli Cohen, an Egyptian Jew who emigrated to Israel, is a case in point. In 1959 the Israelis gave him a false identity or "legend" as an Argentine-Syrian Muslim. Cohen went to Syria and over a three-year period rose high in Baathist circles there, reporting sensitive information to the Israelis. But in 1965, when he was about to be named to a position in the Syrian government, he was caught and executed.

But it is the Soviet intelligence service that has been the preeminent service for this type of covert action in the twentieth century. How was it done? The most obvious and most easily documented cases involve Communist Party leaders. The section of CPSU that came to be known as the International Department, often in collaboration with the KGB and its predecessors, worked hard to spot and assess likely candidates. These individuals were sent for training to the USSR, where they were assessed by informants in training school. Upon their return home, Moscow sometimes continued to subsidize individual leaders secretly. Some of those employed by local Communist parties and their labor and media fronts rose to key positions. Others were directly recruited and paid KGB agents. Thus, Moscow—"the Center"—set up reliable channels of influence in local Communist parties outside of normal interparty channels, and was often able to dominate the institutions. Moscow also developed promising military and political leaders, who received scholarships or training in the USSR, either overtly under their own name or covertly under assumed names. Some of these individuals sought out Soviet officials and volunteered their services to the KGB. Others were spotted, assessed, and recruited in the same manner as espionage agents.

Whether an agent is a recruit or a volunteer, the essence of seeding is the same—helping the agent assume ever more important positions of influence in his society, and at each step cementing the relationship with him. Usually this involves financial subsidies—for training, for his family, and later to help defray personal expenses while the individual climbs the ladder of power. In the background there is almost always the promise of physical protection if things go wrong. Some individuals may not want or need money, preferring instead information that helps them advance their careers.

Developing and using an unpaid collaborator requires special skills and flexibility. This individual does not want to be a "paid agent" or puppet, but at the same time it is in the interest of the intelligence service to make him as pliant as possible. Obviously, the case officer must know his subject well enough to overcome this implicit conflict. The officer's service must also be flexible enough to allow for cooperation with individuals not under direct control. For example, to gain hard-sought information from a journalist, the case officer has to persuade or bargain with his superiors as well as the journalist-collaborator to ensure that everyone's interests are protected. Both balance and the reconciliation of disparate aims are involved: in the short term, the case officer may (or may not) want certain stories to appear in the media; in the long term, the case officer's service wants to have a highly placed journalist or editor in its infrastructure. There are potential recruits who want nothing for themselves, but seek instead to advance the fortunes or influence of their family, clan, or tribe. This may be the case in the developing world, where family or clan often takes precedence over state or ideology, and any requests for military protection, financial assistance, or information about the machinations of clan enemies are made in behalf of these smaller, more intimate groups. The most effective case officers and covert action managers are prepared to bargain and exchange favors rather than to demand obedience in exchange for cash.

This question of control over an individual or group that a foreign intelligence service has chosen to aid is a thorny one. Clearly, the service would like to maintain as much control as possible. The chosen individual will have his own ideas about what he wants to accomplish and how best to do it. American policy and operations after World War II offer an example of this dilemma. In the late 1940s, American leaders determined that it was in the national interest to rebuild the European continent along democratic lines. To that end, they identified and supported individuals in politics and institutions who believed in democracy and who had leadership ability. By the 1950s, with U.S. aid, some of them had reached positions of power. In the 1950s and 1960s, similar support was provided to youth leaders who would rise to prominence in Africa and Latin America. Some of them remained friendly to the United States, while others became critical of American foreign policy. Many developed a liking and appreciation for the United

States, its people, and its institutions, even as they sought to distance themselves from the country itself. In other words, the United States bet the field, a not very discriminating policy that led to mixed results. The program was not as successful as it could have been had more stringent guidelines been used to limit help to the most reliably pro-American individuals.

This program of long-term support came to an end, for the most part, in the 1970s. The United States no longer took advantage of the opportunity to spot, assess, and help potentially friendly—or at least moderate, reasonably pro-Western—future leaders. The areas neglected included many that were to be in the world spotlight in the 1980s and 1990s, such as Iran, the West Bank and adjacent Arab countries, South Africa, and Mexico. Meanwhile Libya, Iran, North Korea, and the former Soviet bloc continued to select young leaders for training and support in various regions of the world. The Iranians, who are still training and supporting Muslim groups from Asia to South America, do have such a long-term infrastructure in place. Covert techniques like seeding can be very successful over the long term, but covert action can also be used effectively for short-term gains.

During the Ming Dynasty, a renegade Chinese named Hsü Hai led a group of Japanese and Chinese bandits on a plundering foray through Chekiang Province, defeating the government and accumulating booty and captives. In 1556, a clever civilian named Hu Tsung-hsien, following the teachings of classical writing and folklore, defeated these marauders not by military means, but by turning them against one another and baiting them with bribes and promises. In one of his most interesting ploys, Hu provoked fighting by sending agents with beautiful trinkets to influence Hsü Hai's favorite mistresses, who then urged Hsü Hai to turn on one of his key allies, Ch'en Tung. At the same time, Hu used a former ally of Hsü Hai, who had been taken prisoner by Hu, to write to Ch'en suggesting that Hsü was betraying him. Then in a triple cross, Hu had his agents show the letter to Hsü. This killed two birds with one stone, kindling hostility between Hsü and Ch'en and showing that Hu was not antagonistic to Hsü. The result was a war between the former allies that weakened them and benefited Hu—all without the use of force by the latter.[13]

Only a few decades ago, in the Chinese warlord period, similar devices and agents were brought into play to break up enemy coalitions. In 1921 the Japanese, seeking to control northern China, wanted to unseat the anti-Japanese warlord in control of Peking. The way to do this, they judged, was by persuading one of the warlord's allies, Feng Yü-hsiang, to revolt against his ally. As intermediary they selected a man they felt was reliable, a Chinese named Huang Fu. Huang had studied in Japan, had worked with pro-Japanese Chinese, and had access to Feng and his entourage. He used a variety of appeals, including money and doctored documents, to show Feng that some of his former allies were American agents. Later, after Feng did the Japanese bidding and the anti-Japanese elements were eliminated, Japanese advisers served directly in his entourage.[14]

Western history, too, offers numerous examples of agents of influence accomplishing significant short-term objectives. The seductress has long been a favorite ploy. In an unoriginal but effective move, Louis XIV dispatched Louise de Kerouaille to become a mistress of Charles II when he was negotiating for the secret alliance that became the Treaty of Dover (1670).[15] A few decades later, his successor, Louis XV, was more creative. He designed a plan and secured the services of an unusual and talented agent, a female impersonator, to prevent the Russians from aiding Britain against France. Previous French attempts to influence the czarist court had been neutralized by the pro-British Russian chancellor Bestuchev, Russia's internal security service (spy-conscious then as now), and British gold, which had been well distributed among the czarina's entourage. The French sought access to Empress Elizabeth of Russia through a French nobleman accompanied by his "niece," the lady "Lia de Beaumont." The plan was to obtain an audience with the empress, gain her confidence, and influence her. Lia, born the Chevalier d'Eon in 1728, was described as small and slight, with a pink-and-white complexion, a pleasing, gentle expression, and a melodious voice used to advantage. Her portrait was admired in a French men's club.[16]

Lia had little difficulty in gaining the confidence of the empress. She became a reader to Elizabeth, and even, so it is said, attended the ritual bathing of the empress. The immediate effect of Lia's attendance on Elizabeth appeared to have had much to do with the British ambassador's report to London that the Russian chancellor was finding it impossible to sign the treaty which His British Majesty King George "so earnestly required."[17] Eventually Lia was found out. Still, the Chevalier d'Eon continued to be influential, the empress playing along with the disguise to oppose the ideas of Bestuchev, with whom she disagreed, and offering d'Eon a high-ranking post in the Russian army. D'Eon was later sent by Louis XV on a number of other intelligence missions, sometimes as himself, sometimes as the irresistible Madame de Beaumont.

In the twentieth century, the Soviet Union supplemented its overt machinations to influence Western policy by secretly securing the support of high-ranking officials such as Harry Dexter White and Alger Hiss in the U.S. Treasury and State departments, and Guy Burgess and Donald Maclean in the British Foreign Office. Moscow was also able to recruit British members of Parliament, both Labour and Conservative. In 1961, the Soviet defector Anatoliy Golitsyn identified major Soviet agents of influence in French president de Gaulle's entourage— a story described in the memoirs of the French intelligence chief in Washington, Philippe de Vosjoli, and fictionalized in Leon Uris's *Topaz*.[18] Among those convicted during the 1970s of working secretly for Moscow were the journalist Pierre Pathé in France, senior Norwegian Foreign Office official Arne Treholt, and Sidek Ahouse, political secretary to Malaysia's deputy prime minister. KGB defector Stanislav Levchenko revealed in the late 1970s that Hirohide Ishida, a former Liberal-Democratic minister in Japan, was a Soviet agent, and that leaders in the Japanese Socialist Party worked directly for the KGB.

Potential agents of influence may have different motivations. To avail itself of the benefits derived from such agents, an intelligence service must skillfully ascertain the interests of politically minded people in the target society. Some, for one reason or another, will be friendly to the service's country. Others will be sympathetic to the specific policies the service is seeking to promote, if not to the country as a whole. Still others, while they may not be sympathetic to the service's country or a specific policy, will be opposed to the service's *enemy* and thus willing to collaborate. This is often the case with terrorist groups, which develop bitter and sometimes deadly rivalries. Though typically they are unwilling to be recruited by Western agents, terrorists may provide information or otherwise compromise their rivals in exchange for money or information.

Helping Organizations

Another covert political tool is to influence institutions that affect either the balance of power in a given region or the key political decisions of local actors. The idea is not new, but it became much more effective in the twentieth century when pluralistic society widely replaced the monarch, the court, and the monarch's chief rivals. Now political parties and nongovernmental organizations—the media, labor, business, and religious, ethnic, criminal, and professional groups—shape the outcome of power struggles as well as specific policy decisions. In a pluralistic society such entities can help or block the implementation of government policy through protest, strike, negative publicity, and obstructionism. If foreign powers persuade them, they can also influence conditions or events in target countries. In addition to homegrown organizations, there are numerous transstate entities that in recent years have developed the ability to influence conditions and events across state boundaries—among them religious and ethnic groups and criminal cartels.

There is ample historic precedence for influence-peddling from afar. For thousands of years, rulers have sought the power to pull strings by supporting religious and ethnic organizations outside their borders. The ancient Hittites used subversion to win Asiatic vassal states away from their rivals, the Egyptians. Aziru of Amor, a vassal, was recruited by the Hittites to weaken the loyalty of the faithful Egyptian vassal Rib-Addi of Byblos. Historic records show that Rib-Addi issued constant warnings to the Egyptian pharaoh Amenhotep III of Aziru's defection, but these were ignored.[19]

Napoleon, perceiving in nationalism a potentially powerful strategic weapon, supported nationalist movements to weaken the multinational empires of his major rivals. To incite Latin America against Spain and her ally Britain, he mobilized a whole team of operatives inside the United States and Central America. Their plan was audacious. They would fan the flames of local dissatisfaction with Spain and encourage and assist local elites to revolt. The French team, which arrived around 1809, skillfully shaped negative propaganda themes capitalizing on the Indian hatred of Spanish exploitation in Latin America, and positive themes appealing to democratic yearnings similar to those that had led to the French and American revolutions. For better cover, some of the French agents actually took U.S. citizenship. They built up a clandestine network of about 150 people who traveled as merchants, sailors, and cooks, and established an infrastructure in the areas now known as California, Mexico, and New Orleans that disseminated propaganda and financed local figures willing to challenge Spanish rule. The Spanish, who were on their guard, identified many of the French agents, but their efforts were not sufficient to snuff out the nationalist revolutions that started in Mexico and spread throughout Spanish America. Though the Mexican priest Hidalgo acted independently, his revolutionary forces appear to have been financed in part by French money.[20]

In the nineteenth century, Russia sought to undermine both the Turkish and Austro-Hungarian empires through covert assistance to pan-Slavic groups in Bulgaria, Macedonia, and Serbia. And in the twentieth century the Nazis, stirring German irredentism, supported German nationalist organizations in much of Eastern Europe—with notable success in the Sudeten area of Czechoslovakia. In addition to support for religious and nationalist organizations, states have made good use not only of ideological allies abroad but also of ideological enemies of their chief enemies. A clear example is Germany's significant covert support for the Bolsheviks in 1917, by which they hoped to bring down the czarist government.

Movement of Money and Support

There are various avenues for channeling financial support for covert activity. Assistance may be in the form of cash, which can enter a country legally—through the diplomatic pouch—or be smuggled in by couriers.[21] Suitcases or bags of money are given to a trusted contact inside the country for delivery to a subsidized organization. A trusted individual deposits it in the organization's bank account or makes it available when necessary. With modern technology, this technique has become more sophisticated and less complicated. Money can be sent electronically and anonymously from the national bank in the donor country to the organization's numbered account in the recipient country or to a numbered account in a third country.

The foreign government may purchase products of an enterprise owned by the subsidized organization—as Moscow did for years with the produce from the Italian Communist agricultural cooperative. The cooperative simply charged Soviet bloc governments more for its oranges than the market price and relayed the profits to the Italian Communist Party. Similarly, anyone who wanted to do business in the USSR found it beneficial to pay a commission to particular import-export companies to arrange the transaction. These companies were owned by or transferred their commission to the Communist Party. Similar setups have helped finance Communist and other parties throughout the world for most of the twentieth century.

Material assistance need not be confined to funding, of course. Helping a subsidized organization gain influence through technical proficiency can be highly effective. For example, organization members might be trained in computers and the latest media and "get-out-the-vote" techniques in a third country, or at home, in the targeted country, with trainers who have been sent in from outside. The organization adopts the ruse that it is hiring a foreign public relations firm to help it keep abreast of media innovations. This sort of assistance is relatively easy to administer.

Providing political support to an organization is more complex. Here the external power might have to give the internal group covert support without revealing its source. Sometimes the internal group will be aware of a particular effort and collaborate in it. On other occasions, to protect the local organization from "contamination" by a foreign government, that government will keep it in the dark about specific political maneuvers designed to aid it. At least, the organization will feign ignorance. An example of the latter situation came in the Italian elections of 1948, when the U.S. government made it clear that if the Communists were victorious against the Christian Democrats and Social Democrats, U.S. economic aid would be cut. But the anti-Communist parties did not publicly trumpet this. It would have been counterproductive—politically—if these parties had been seen as collaborating with a foreign government at the expense of their domestic rivals.

There are examples of intelligence services actually using covert support to sell out their friends abroad when they thought it useful. Moscow was known to do this, as a classic case from the 1970s illustrates. At the expense of the then strong French Communist and Socialist parties, the Soviets helped Giscard d'Estaing win the French presidency by receiving him in Moscow before the election of 1974, suggesting that he was a perfectly acceptable negotiating partner, and, probably unknown to him, providing him with secret propaganda support. Apparently Moscow feared that a victory by its close ideological allies, Communist or even Socialist, would not be as useful to disrupting NATO and weakening the U.S.-European relationship.

Democratic leaders are often torn between their desire to help friendly foreign political parties and their concern about interfering in democratic elections outside their own borders. Covert material and technical support can be useful. But sometimes, covert assistance alone accomplishes little and runs the risk, should it be exposed, of damaging the party or faction requiring aid. Even if the faction has the know-how and ability to hide covert support, unless covert action is coordinated in an overall plan sufficiently buttressed by long-term domestic support to achieve results, success is very unlikely.

Influence-peddling is not necessarily restricted to open societies. There are totalitarian regimes where powerful nongovernmental entities such as religious or labor organizations operate legally or semi-legally and, with financial aid or access to communications equipment, can be sustained in the face of suppression. These groups are unlikely to become the government or make the decisions that affect society as a whole. They may, however, be able to sway the regime or influence its calculations during wartime or a crisis.

All governments have to take into consideration the loyalty of the population in case of war. Will railroads and communications be sabotaged? Are there those who will cash in on a crisis by attempting to overthrow the government? Support for nongovernmental opposition groups, even in a situation where they are not able to affect the government decisively in the short term, may be a powerful tool for long-term or critical short-term influence.

Tensions frequently exist between an external sponsor and an organization. The sponsor already has ideas of what would be most effective, money or some other resource, and how that resource should be expended, and will try to persuade the internal client. The client, subject to pressures from its own constituency, may want to do things differently. Typically, very few members or even leaders of a group, whether a trade union, church, or professional association, know about the secret relationship with a foreign sponsor. The conflicting demands of the external sponsor and the internal constituency put the leadership cognizant of foreign sponsorship in a difficult position that may lead to termination of the relationship. As we have seen, covert action practitioners must be steeped in the politics and culture of their clients in order to smooth out the rough spots and achieve desired ends.

What creates friction between an intelligence service and the leaders of client organizations? One source may be the different operational styles of the case officer, who works for a government bureaucracy, and the recipient, who is likely to be a much more freewheeling individual. To be successful, case officers cannot be rigid bureaucrats. They have to be able and willing to adapt to the peculiarities of their clients. While the clients, ideally, should take into account the peculiarities of government bureaucracies, many are by nature independent, freewheeling, individual leaders who resist pressure from their own governments. They will thus not easily accept instructions from a foreign one, and this makes for some stormy relationships. For example, with secret financing, sponsors have to see that they are getting a fair return for funds and other assistance provided, but they must also know when to be flexible and whom specifically to support, and to what end.

Another source of friction derives from the nature of nongovernmental organizations, which are often affiliated with similar organizations in other countries. In our century many peace, labor, environmental, business, and professional organizations have operated across national boundaries. This has numerous benefits for covert action practitioners. Trusted contacts in a nongovernmental organization become involved in the politics of foreign countries and travel freely back and forth. Organizational leaders in one country can be met clandestinely in a third country without arousing suspicion. These conditions—an international orientation and the mobility it generates—are almost ideal for a government that wants to use nongovernmental organizations for political influence.

But using a nongovernmental organization in one country to influence events in another can complicate matters. The leader of an international nongovernmental organization who is working with an intelligence service—let's call him Pierre—has to persuade all or most of the national affiliates to follow his policy preferences. For operational security, none of the national organization's leaders, even those who may have been secretly recruited by the same intelligence service, can be told of Pierre's relationship with the intelligence service. (Few, if any, intelligence services would want to tell one of their agents about the recruitment of another in case one or both were double agents or were careless with the information.) Hence, Pierre has to rely on persuasion without reference to the external sponsor. In doing so, he inevitably acts without explaining all his calculations, even if he is not actually deceptive. He must establish the position he takes as his own, lest it become clear that he is working with the intelligence service. If Pierre is identified with this particular view, and the intelligence service subsequently tasks its assets elsewhere to support the same position, the role of the intelligence service tends to be obscured. But if the service takes a position before anyone else has put forth that view and then requests its agents and connections to support it, it will become clear who is working for whom.

Again, the case officer and manager must be bold enough to identify or to recognize opportunities to use their collaborators in nongovernmental organizations. Because these organizations cross national boundaries, some even working worldwide, the case officer and manager must be knowledgeable about regional conditions in, say, the labor movement, or the church, or in the diaspora of a particular ethnic group in order to achieve results. They must also grasp the politics of the international nongovernmental organization in a detailed enough way to be able to coordinate and integrate its activities with their own national policy. This requires either hiring people native to the target region or training generalist case officers to handle the job. Whichever path is chosen, the case officer and manager have to transcend the geographic and cultural boundaries of their own bureaucracy, adapting to the peculiarities of the "horses" they have decided to back.

In this field, the Soviets were ostensibly handicapped by the weaknesses of Communism, the abuses of Stalinism, and a mammoth bureaucracy. Nevertheless, for decades the leadership of the CPSU established a superb mechanism for both overt and covert coordination, training, and influence of foreign groups of both Communists and non-Communists all over the world.

In the future, political institutions and nongovernmental forces covering the political spectrum in Eurasia and other geostrategic areas will offer opportunities to many governments willing to assist them, including the U.S. government. Some Western officials will oppose aid to groups and organizations they do not control, and to those who are not recruited agents. Some Western conservatives will oppose aid to labor and socialist groups, while more liberal politicians and their staffs will oppose aid to conservative intellectual, media, and business groups. These are political obstacles that potential sponsors will have to overcome if they are looking for geostrategic advantages. The antidote to bias is knowledge of the politics of client organizations and skill in managing relationships with them—still primary requirements for covert influence in support of policy objectives.

Covert Propaganda

Many states seek to influence the climate of opinion abroad through overt propaganda, that is, official government pronouncements, books, magazines, radio and television broadcasts, cultural and athletic exchanges, and foreign-based information centers, all of which require considerable effort and resources. In the United States, overt propaganda, the domain of the United States Information Agency (USIA), is referred to as "information and education." Overt propaganda identifies the sponsor, and it is usually truthful. If it is not, that fact will eventually come to light, to the discredit of the sponsor.

Covert propaganda refers to information, ideas, and symbolic actions whose sponsor remains unknown. The sponsor may judge that anonymous propaganda is more effective, or that at worst it can be disowned. Covert propaganda can be black (well hidden) or gray (disseminated with a thin veil of cover). The propaganda itself may be truthful or intentionally false. The current term for the latter is "disinformation."

Gray propaganda hides its source from the uninitiated public, but not from sophisticated observers. One common channel for gray propaganda is clandestine radio broadcasting. This began in the 1930s when radio receivers first became widely available. As Hitler silenced his opponents in Germany and then in Austria and Czechoslovakia, some took to the air, claiming to be more powerful than they were. Later during World War II, clandestine radio broadcasting became routine. While some broadcasts clearly originated with the enemy, sponsorship could be so well hidden as to sow confusion among friendly elements unaware of a covert project.

According to an official OSS report, for example, in 1944 a covert Allied radio broadcast known as Volksender Drei claimed to be an internal movement opposed to Hitler. Broadcasting from liberated France and directed at German civilians, it was believed to be genuine not only by German POWs in France and French journalists but also by American commanders. During the first broadcast, U.S. officers, unaware of the station's true sponsorship, awakened General Omar Bradley to report on the outbreak of internal revolts in Germany. The Nazis, of course, knew that these broadcasts were not what they purported to be. Through direction-finding equipment they located the transmitter in France, but because it could easily be moved or started up again there was little sense in wasting resources to bomb it. Instead, the Nazis focused on jamming the broadcasts.

Britain, the United States, the Soviet Union, Germany, and Italy all operated radios and were themselves the targets of gray radio broadcasting. Sophisticated methods were developed to increase the effectiveness of this sort of communication. One was called "ghosting"— secretly interrupting another broadcast and overlaying one's own broadcast on the "legitimate" broadcast signal. The British, with varying degrees of subtlety, interrupted Hitler's radio speeches with derisive comments and laughter. Before it was legalized in 1989, Poland's Solidarity organization perfected and updated ghosting techniques, interrupting official television broadcasts with its own messages and visuals.

A related technique is "snuggling." This is a gray broadcast made on a frequency immediately adjacent to a regular broadcast so that listeners inadvertently tune in to the wrong station. During World War II, the Nazis used to run a station close to an American station, but substitute their version of the news on an otherwise straightforward Allied music station. Since then this technique has been used periodically. During the Vietnam War, American operators would broadcast over frequencies adjacent to the North Vietnamese and the National Liberation Front frequencies, substituting American versions of key portions of an otherwise bona fide program.

Covert radios can be used for specific tactical purposes in support of the military. At the end of World War II, the Americans ran a station code-named Operation Frolic to discourage Nazi leaders from mounting final resistance to the Allies in the mountains of Bavaria and Austria. But most covert radio operations are designed for more broad-range objectives.

In the less developed world, where literacy rates are low and communication and transportation difficult, radio broadcasting is a major means of mass communication. In countries whose governments restrict freedom of the press, covert radio programs are commonly broadcast by the internal opposition as well as by foreign adversaries and even the government itself.

China is a prime example. Since coming to power in 1949, the regime has sponsored Radio Free Japan, the Voice of the Malayan Revolution, the Voice of the People of Burma, and more recently the Voice of Democratic Kampuchea. Meanwhile China was the target of Soviet, Vietnamese, and Taiwanese gray radio broadcasts. One of the most sophisticated, Radio Ba Yi, came on the air in 1979 purporting to speak for a leftist dissident faction in the Chinese People's Liberation Army. It lambasted the United States and reformist leaders in China and supported a Sino-Soviet reconciliation. The broadcast in fact originated in Vladivostok, and it was cut off in 1988 when Gorbachev sought to heal the Sino-Soviet rift. The Chinese leaders were aware of the Soviet sponsorship, but many Chinese dissidents had no way of knowing. Soviet Moscow had used a similar technique in earlier disputes with the ruling Communist parties of Yugoslavia, Hungary, and Czechoslovakia.

Other major examples of gray propaganda are the CPSU's international fronts, ostensibly nongovernmental organizations created by Moscow that mushroomed after World War II. Western governments and some outside specialists were aware that Moscow created, funded, and controlled the key officers and the propaganda output of these organizations. But as with the gray radio stations, the average worker or peace activist remained in the dark even though the front's cover was relatively thin.

The fronts have worked well at different times. Soviet and European Communist organizations did a good job of identifying issues and sentiments with which non-Communists would identify, notably antiwar opinion and anticolonialism. From the 1930s on, the fronts attracted many in the United States, Europe, and newly decolonized countries to causes controlled secretly by Moscow. In the 1950s, Western intelligence services exposed the fronts and many members dropped out. Then in the 1970s they regained influence, capitalizing on growing antiwar and antinuclear sentiment. Once again the pendulum swung: in the 1980s Western governments helped uncover Soviet involvement, and the fronts' appeal diminished. This happened before the advent of *glasnost* and *perestroika*.

As mentioned, gray propaganda can be true, false, or a combination of both. During World War II, British and American gray outlets exaggerated or even lied about internal opposition to the Nazis. Such broadcasts would have undermined the credibility of a "white" Allied radio like the BBC. To make the falsehoods more credible and effective, these same outlets disseminated a great deal of true information such as casualties and bombing raids on the home front, subjects the Nazis did not allow their own media to cover. In this way, clandestine radio networks prepared the way for the false information that helped Allied troops in April 1945.

Propaganda is black when the source is false and well concealed, or when the information itself is false. Disinformation belongs in this category. To discredit an adversary the disinformer intentionally disseminates falsehoods, say through forgery or rumor, going to great trouble to hide his involvement in creating and/or releasing the information. He may disseminate true information—for instance, genuine documents stolen from a government that incriminates an individual or group—while seeking to hide his role in disseminating it. This can be done by sending the information anonymously to a foreign newspaper, or using a secretly controlled journalist to write about it. The black propagandist, unlike the gray, takes extreme care to cover his tracks, making it difficult for any foreign intelligence service to identify him with a particular project.

Black propaganda is probably as old and widespread as civilization. The ancient kingdoms of Mesopotamia circulated false rumors to influence enemy troops. Shamshi-Adad, ruler of Shubat Enlil, used fifth columnists to help capture the city of Zalmaqum by encouraging its citizens to revolt against their rulers as he advanced into the region. He often used such "men of rumors" to spread tales of an advancing Assyrian army, persuading the enemy to abandon its positions without a fight.[22] Millennia later, the founder of China's Ming Dynasty used deep-cover agents to spread false rumors that led to the disbanding of a large army set to oppose him. The thirteenth-century Mongol conqueror Genghis Khan used the same technique. Inside societies where there is little freedom of information, it is next to impossible to check on rumors, and so it is not surprising that both opponents and proponents of the regimes employ black propaganda.

Forgery is a classic form of black propaganda. The forger either attributes statements to people who did not make them or he manufactures false information. For example, in the later sixteenth century in India, opponents of the Mogul emperor Akbar, seeking to destroy his lieutenant, framed that unfortunate with false documents to make the emperor believe he was disloyal and corrupt. In Elizabethan England, to weaken the opponents of Protestant religious reform, one of the queen's councillors authored a "report" from an English Catholic to the Spanish court that intentionally exaggerated English military strength and English Catholic antipathy to the pope. The ostensible author, an English Catholic who had been executed, was not in a position to deny its authenticity. The letter found its way into the hands of numerous influential people across Europe and tended to reduce their interest in opposing Elizabeth.

Perhaps the most famous forgery is the "Protocols of the Learned Elders of Zion," fabricated by Czar Nicholas II's secret police at the beginning of the twentieth century to suggest that there was a Jewish conspiracy to dominate the world. It has been used by various anti-Semitic governments and groups ever since, despite the fact that the document was exposed as a forgery in 1921. Written forgeries can usually, like this one, be exposed for what they are, but exposure may never offset damage already done, particularly if it is cited and recycled by the media or by politicians who had nothing to do with the original forgery.

The effectiveness of disinformation often depends more on the predisposition of the intended recipients than on the quality of the disinformation or the vehicles used to disseminate it. People will believe what they want to. Disinformation is unlikely to have much impact on targets not predisposed to a certain belief. Therefore, the primary consideration of the forger is to identify and play to predispositions; worrying about the quality or plausibility of the disinformation comes second.

States practice black propaganda to influence friends and enemies. Even after the French openly allied themselves with the American Revolution in 1778, they secretly hired Americans to maintain the alliance and to guide American politics in a direction that favored

France. Publishers of the day printed precious little about America's revolutionary ally. To ensure that any articles that did appear contained the right slant, the French secretly paid such talented Americans as Samuel Cooper, Hugh Brackenridge, and the most widely read author of the Revolution, Thomas Paine, to write and plant stories under their own and assumed names.

In the twentieth century, allied countries have employed black propaganda to "strengthen" and "guarantee" alliances. During World War I, as part of their concerted effort to lure the United States into the hostilities, the British sent unattributed propaganda pamphlets and letters to influential Americans and put out the Bryce Report alleging German atrocities in Belgium. The latter was published in U.S. newspapers, though its allegations were for the most part refuted after the war.

Most covert propaganda now is aimed at the mass media, formerly the print media but increasingly the electronic media as well. Sometimes governments set up newspapers or acquire controlling interests in them—an expensive and usually transparent mechanism. A more common tactic is to persuade journalists to carry gray or black propaganda by providing them with information or money. The case officer may actually deliver the text of the message to the journalist. However, most journalists, often better writers than intelligence service operatives, resist such crude manipulation and prefer to write up their own stories using an outline or some specific facts provided by the case officer.

Other types of covert propaganda include petition drives, public demonstrations to influence public opinion, and payments of other "assistance" to academics so that they will shape the intellectual climate in a certain way, in turn—it is hoped—influencing journalists and politicians. Governments also use agents to circulate rumors by word of mouth, discrediting individuals or organizations. Soviet bloc intelligence services did this often against opponents at home and abroad. If an official Soviet source were to openly circulate derogatory information about an opponent, it would be discounted even if it was true. But if the rumor was circulated without being attributed to a source, it would be more credible to the intended audience and stand more of a chance of fostering dissension among opponents of a regime.

Take the case of the classic Soviet agent of influence Arne Treholt. A senior Norwegian Foreign Office official, Treholt was found guilty of spying for the Soviet Union and Iraq and sentenced to twenty years' imprisonment in June 1985. Treholt had served as Norway's counselor of embassy at the UN, and in the Norwegian Foreign Office as under-secretary for the law of the sea (vital to the Norwegians), and as assistant permanent secretary and head of the press division, the post he held when arrested. Thus he had been strategically positioned to advance the standing of political figures, government officials, and journalists sympathetic to Soviet interests, to discredit others, and to promote Soviet views in influential Norwegian circles.

To be effective, covert propaganda must be coordinated with overall policy. It serves little purpose to dabble in the trade unless there are important strategic goals to be achieved and tactical plans for carrying them out. The OSS black radio broadcasts that encouraged Germans to revolt against Hitler flew in the face of American and British policy, as well as other propaganda proclaiming unconditional surrender. Furthermore, they proposed no vision of the kind of Germany that might rise from the ashes of war, and no motives for Germans to risk their lives against the Gestapo. By contrast, as we have seen, British overt and covert propaganda in the United States on the eve of both world wars was precisely geared to the policy of enlisting United States help, which it succeeded in doing.

Effective covert propaganda also carefully considers the target audience—whether it consists of allies, enemies, or both. One of this century's propaganda master strokes was the British effort aimed at enemy territory in World War I. The British had scholars, such as R. W. Seton Watson, who knew that the multiethnic Austro-Hungarian Empire was vulnerable to nationalist appeals. To undermine the Austrian war effort, the British used propaganda to stir up various ethnic groups under Austrian rule. And then there is the example of the Americans' black Radio 1212 during World War II. It demonstrably reduced the effectiveness of German troops facing U.S. forces in the spring of 1945.[23]

But good research is not enough; good tradecraft is essential. Black radio broadcasts, leaflets, and forgeries need to disguise their sponsor or the fact that the information they are conveying is false. In the 1980s the Soviets, neglecting their tradecraft, often made stupid mistakes in forgeries, so that the United States could easily prove to target governments that they were forgeries perpetrated by Moscow. By contrast, in World War II the Western Allies took pains to ensure that black broadcasters had the right regional accents and that the German they used reflected the class and personality of internal leaders likely to oppose the Nazis. In this work the Allies benefited from good intelligence collection. Radio programmers would gather all the latest intelligence reports on bombing raids, battles, and even local football results (scooping the German press in the process) so that their broadcasts would be interesting, credible—and listened to.

Another condition that makes covert propaganda more effective is interpretation and amplification by credible people—two-step communication. Simply delivering information, even if the target audience is predisposed to the theme and message, is unlikely to have the same degree of impact as inducing someone to discuss it. Some revolutionary organizations have realized this. In the 1980s, for example, the Salvadoran Farabundo Martí para la Liberación Nacional (FMLN) reinforced its radio broadcasts from Nicaragua with formal group listening and discussion in Salvador. Aiming to instruct their FMLN cadres, the leadership understood that propaganda alone would not accomplish much without human follow-up to shape interpretation.

Similarly, there is little point for the United States—no matter what its convictions and how earnestly they are held—only to disseminate propaganda in, say, Colombia that drug cartels are bad for that country. It would be much more effective if the statement were to be picked up, recycled, and reinforced by local committees of respected citizens from all walks of life, if international conferences on the subject were to take place in the region, and if there were sermons from the pulpit and by sports heroes and schoolteachers.

But developing this sort of two-step communication is not a short-term proposition. It requires a human infrastructure that includes creative, knowledgeable people who can operate covertly in diverse cultures.[24]

Paramilitary Operations

Covert paramilitary action is unacknowledged use of force, or assistance to those perpetrating or resisting the use of force. Though the actions and the means vary widely, the same overall principles for effective covert action apply to all. The government has to decide on its strategy, its long-term goals, the covert and overt resources needed to achieve these goals, and the means available for doing so.

Elizabeth I of England was not very astute when it came to helping the Protestant forces fighting Catholic Spain in the Netherlands. Her regime had little strategy. Covert paramilitary aid, turned on and off, never did much to weaken King Philip. By contrast, during the American Revolution Louis XVI made a keen calculation when he decided to risk war with Britain and aid the colonists—and he stuck to his decision.

There is not always an opportunity to exploit. Although the British were mistaken in the belief that they could get the Arabs to revolt against the Turks in Mesopotamia in 1915, when the tide of war turned in 1917, they correctly judged an opening for just such a revolt in the Hejaz. During World War II, the power vacuums in Central and Eastern Europe were so effectively exploited by the Soviet Union that in the end the entire region was under either direct Soviet or subordinate Communist control. Paramilitary activity helped achieve this result. For the Western Allies, opportunities in the same area were more limited, in part by geography but also because Moscow had begun preparations to exploit the region years before the Nazi attack. Decades later, many in Washington saw little opportunity to push the Soviet army out of Afghanistan by paramilitary means; others maintained there was an opening. It took several years for Washington to resolve the dispute and act.

However, opportunities may not present themselves all that often, yet they cannot be seized without sustained, committed, creative leadership.[25] The Soviet Union, despite Stalin's purges, turned out skilled people who after the defeat of the Nazis provided paramilitary support to future leaders of subservient governments throughout Eastern Europe. Moscow's long-term spotting, assessing, recruiting, and support system, engineered by Comintern leaders such as Otto Kuusinen, was put in place in the 1920s. It paid off two decades later in a full stable of skilled operatives, leaders, intelligence sources, and opportunities to acquire what the Soviet Union and the West had just denied to Hitler. By way of contrast, the Allied governments before and during World War II failed to develop a policy for the use of paramilitary forces other than to help defeat the Axis powers. Little thought was given to postwar political objectives or how paramilitary forces might advance them during and after the war.

Assassination

Assassination, common practice in some areas of the world such as the Middle East, whence comes our word for the act, is paramilitary action at its most elemental. Effective assassination requires, first, technical skill to carry out the deed, and second, a well-thought-out policy to exploit it for political purposes. The initial key is access to the intended victim, best gained by penetrating the victim's guards with agents. In the Middle Ages the Shiite assassins[26] became adept at closing in on their targets. For two centuries, from about 1090 to 1275, they penetrated the security system of Westerners in the Levant and of the

Seljuk Turks in Persia, Iraq, and Syria to get close to their victims, usually Sunni Muslims or Christian Crusade leaders. The Shiite assassins organized extensive networks in sympathetic urban centers, securing direct access to their victims through bribery, intimidation, and conversion. Not uncommonly, a Shiite youth would infiltrate the service of a high official and, after years of service, plunge a dagger into his master.[27]

In the twentieth century, Stalin's intelligence service honed the technique of political assassination. Leon Trotsky was a victim of one of the more notorious Soviet "liquidations." In 1940, after several unsuccessful attempts by others, the Soviets used a trusted aide to plunge an ax into Trotsky's head when he was living in exile in Mexico. Lack of access kept American agents from similar "success" with Castro, though they tried repeatedly to assassinate him in the early 1960s.

There are other ways of assassinating a leader than penetrating his entourage, for example, using mercenaries or commandos hired or trained for this purpose. The British helped a resistance team to kill Reinhard Heydrich, the Nazi ruler of Bohemia, in 1943.[28] Both penetrating an entourage and recruiting those without direct access require special operatives, usually one or more secret teams backed by an intelligence service or some other organizational infrastructure. Though the Israelis have demonstrated such a capability, they have also committed embarrassing blunders, for example, when they targeted a PLO leader but killed a completely innocent man in Norway in 1975. As it turned out, the operatives included young recruits with almost no training who were unable to withstand even minimal interrogation under arrest. Their infrastructure was weak, they were not compartmentalized, and they chose a very difficult place for such a sensitive operation—an isolated town where foreigners were readily identifiable.

The most important element of assassination—not to mention other techniques of paramilitary covert action—is not technical but political. How does the assassination advance policy? What are the risks and benefits of using this instrument? Assassination may not benefit the perpetrator. The assassinations of Leon Trotsky and Anwar Sadat seem to have done little for those who ordered them. There were consequences, to be sure, but it is hard to see that the murders themselves made much significant, long-term difference to the institutions that the victims represented. Other assassinations have had broad historical repercussions. The killing by the Shiite assassins of Conrad of Montferrat (1192), the Crusader who opposed Saladin, "was a blow from which the Christian forces never recovered, and as a result of his murder a perfect chance to recapture Jerusalem was lost."[29] Had Hitler been assassinated—a proposal made at various times in the 1930s and 1940s but which the British and Americans refused to act on—no doubt the act would have had worldwide impact.

Providing protection to foreign leaders *against* assassination can be a complex and difficult task. Occasionally the United States does this. If the foreign leader is powerful, if his or her policy is of strategic significance, and if the regime and government policy would be seriously disrupted by assassination, then it would be folly not to provide that leader with protection. Good protection requires not only physical security specialists—experts in bombproofing, crowd control, and physical screening, as well as counterintelligence advisers—but also penetration of the leader's bodyguards by one's own service. A coordinated protection program ranges from nuts-and-bolts technical matters, to assessments of the threats to and vulnerabilities of the leader, to testing the loyalty of bodyguards. One way to test guards is to see if they are vulnerable to recruitment by outsiders. A foreign service that, for example, wants to protect a foreign leader can also seek to penetrate the leader's own service to keep an eye on his guards.

In the postwar period, governments as diverse as those of the United States and East Germany have foiled assassination attempts of foreign leaders. At other times, they failed to provide an integrated program and individuals they supported were overthrown, often with significant consequences.

Terrorism

Terrorism is an elemental political tool with a long history. When it is not part of a well-thought-out policy, or when there are few opportunities to exploit, terrorism achieves little politically. One such case is that of the Thugs (more properly, *phansigars*, "stranglers") in India. The Thugs were members of a clandestine organization that took root in the seventh century, grew powerful in the thirteenth, and was destroyed by the British in the nineteenth. Expert stranglers, they probably murdered around one million people—mostly travelers—to please Kali, the Hindu goddess of terror and destruction. Although their impact on commercial exchange in the region was considerable, and presumably their spiritual welfare was served by their actions, they made only a small dent on the political development of the Mogul Empire and the Indian rajahs.[30]

There are examples of religious fundamentalist groups that constructed a policy, identified an opportunity, and developed the capability to achieve both short- and long-term results to exploit that opportunity, sometimes without a state sponsor. One of the most successful groups was the Jewish Sicarii, who wanted to erase Roman influence in Palestine before the birth of Christ. The Sicarii (named for the daggers they used) employed three main tactics: symbolic assassination, arbitrary killing, and kidnapping. Their primary targets were fellow Jews suspected of collaborating, or known to collaborate, with the Romans. They also took hostages to gain the release of Sicariis taken prisoner. The Sicarii strategy was to frustrate all attempts to reconcile Jews and Romans and to make Roman repression so intolerable that a revolt was inevitable.[31] In twenty-five years, they managed to stir up enough resistance to touch off the Jewish revolt that ended in a mass suicide at Masada in A.D. 70. Although Rome was able to restore order, the revolt considerably weakened Roman power throughout the empire. From the same region, the Middle East, also come examples of modern-day fundamentalist terrorists. Iranian-sponsored groups practice violence throughout the Middle East and elsewhere to support their political objective of Muslim political hegemony.

States can use covert action to counter terrorism as well as to counter assassination. This type of covert action focuses on states that sponsor terrorism, terrorists themselves, or terrorist support groups. In democratic countries these might be legal political groups that aid terrorists but whose members do not actually pull triggers, plant bombs, or rob banks. Once sponsors, terrorists, and support groups are identified, a variety of overt and covert techniques may be used to neutralize them. One is deterrence—creating a climate that severely diminishes their willingness to become or stay involved in terrorism.[32] Thus the British isolated and punished Syria for a few years in the mid-1980s after it was proved in court that the Syrian embassy in London was partially responsible for terrorists planting bombs on aircraft.[33] Other deterrent actions take place behind the scenes: warning the perpetrators, gathering international support through covert propaganda and political action in allied states, working with foreign intelligence services to harass the terrorists, and even killing them—either by aerial attack or by selective assassination, as the Israelis have done. Another option is to go after terrorists' families. This does not have to be violent. Simply warning a family that its sons and daughters, brothers and sisters are working with a terrorist ring is likely to ratchet up the psychological and emotional pressure on terrorists. Needless to say, the subtler forms of pressure can give way to more direct sanctions and punishments.

When deterrence fails, covert action practitioners can create dissension within the ranks of terrorists and their supporters. For instance, by planting evidence that faction A is in contact with the police, covert practitioners may convince faction B that faction A is plotting its demise. The technique of pitting one group against another is similar to that used by the Chinese leader Hu Tsung-hsien in the Ming Dynasty or by the people who framed the Mogul emperor Akbar, as mentioned earlier. And French special forces were apparently able to use the technique to cause infighting within the Algerian National Liberation Front (FLN) in the 1950s.[34]

One of the most successful of French operations was carried out by a clever Arabic-speaking officer, Captain Léger, who led a special unit based in Algiers. Léger thought that one of the FLN prisoners being interrogated, eighteen-year-old Tadjer Zohra, or as she was known to her friends, Roza, would be a useful addition to the ranks of terrorists he had already "turned." But after her interrogation he realized that she could not be won over. He therefore decided to alter his recruitment plan by convincing her that a number of known terrorists were in fact French agents. So that the FLN would believe that she was a French informer with access to information about FLN turncoats, he made a point of being seen in her company all over Algiers. Upon her release, Roza fled to her friends in the FLN. Mazour, the local commander, had her arrested and tortured. Convinced that the terrorists whose names she revealed were genuine French agents, he arrested and tortured them in turn. Then Léger dispatched a real double agent, Kadour, to the FLN. Under torture, Kadour provided false details about French special operations that only confirmed Mazour's suspicions of certain Arabs who had been entrusted to his command. The result was the most severe campaign of purges the FLN had ever undergone. Henceforth the FLN was in constant danger, not only from French bullets but from the knives that its own comrades-in-arms were wielding against one another.

Another covert technique for combating terrorism is to exploit existing fissures in a group, whether they are caused by jealousy, money, or rivalry. Counterterrorists need to know a great deal about the group they are up against, for instance, the peculiarities of its key leaders, its various factions, and the political culture of its targets. Only then can they develop what is usually a fairly long-term plan to disrupt the group, and only with skilled officers and an infrastructure for implementation.

In the nineteenth century this technique helped the British break up the Hindu Thugs. British collectors and operators, spotting an opportunity to exploit corruption among the Thug brotherhood, persuaded older members that their patron goddess Kali would destroy the brotherhood because younger leaders were more interested in money than in serving her. Hence they were able to turn the older members into informants against the younger adherents.[35]

More recently, in the summer of 1989, Western intelligence agencies joined the PLO in an effort to exploit a fissure in one of the most dangerous Palestinian groups, the Fatah Revolutionary Council, led by PLO renegade Sabri Al-Banna (Abu Nidal). Disputes arose, particularly over money, and several key Abu Nidal leaders suspected—correctly—that among other things Sabri Al-Banna was siphoning off the group's funds for personal reasons. He in turn accused them of plotting against him and collaborating with Yassir Arafat and Jordan's intelligence service, and they were shot to death. Libya and other state sponsors of Fatah became concerned and clamped down on Sabri Al-Banna.[36] Subsequently the PLO and the intelligence services of several states took the Abu Nidal dissidents under their protective wing and further widened the breach in the Fatah Revolutionary Council.[37]

Another method of disrupting terrorists is to sabotage their equipment and operations. Bombs, for example, may be fixed so that they will malfunction during a terrorist attack. Reportedly, in the early 1980s the United States purchased antiaircraft missiles in Poland for shipment to the Mujahideen, the force resisting the Soviet puppet government in Afghanistan, and these proved to be defective. It was widely believed that the Soviets knew of the purchase and skillfully arranged for someone to tamper with the missiles. Yet another way to neutralize a terrorist group is to penetrate it by human or technical means so that its operations can be stopped after plans have matured. This is what caused the Popular Front for the Liberation of Palestine–General Command's (PFLP-GC) four-plane bombing spree to go awry in October 1988. Jordan, West Germany, and possibly Israel had penetrated the PFLP-GC, but the key information about its spectacular plan came from Jordanian Marwan Kreesat, who had been seeded in the organization years before by Jordanian intelligence and was serving as one of its bomb-makers.

Guerrillas and Resistance Movements

Another paramilitary option is support for guerrilla and other resistance movements. The English term *guerrilla* (from the Spanish *guerra*, or "war") originally referred to those who took up arms and fought in an unconventional manner against Napoleon's forces in Spain at the beginning of the nineteenth century. Since then, many guerrilla movements have sprung up to resist occupation forces, and many foreign countries have supported them.[38] One of the most notable such foreign-assisted movements was the loose network of Muslim groups known as Mujahideen in Afghanistan. With aid from the United States, Egypt, Pakistan, and others, the Mujahideen resisted the Soviet invasion of their country for almost ten years throughout the 1980s. As part of a well-conceived and well-coordinated policy, even loose-knit guerrillas can be extremely helpful in weakening a foe and denying him unchallenged or relatively cost-free control of foreign territory. But while useful in the short term, it is also necessary to consider long-term objectives. Just as the United States and the British helped the resistance during World War II, they helped the Mujahideen without figuring out how to transform the Mujahideen's wartime effort into postwar results.

Another recent example comes from Nicaragua in 1981. The United States started backing the Contra forces created out of the remnants of the Samozista National Guard with covert help from the Argentine military, without carefully planning how these forces could actually integrate anti-Samozistas and anti-Sandinistas politically, or how they could achieve victory. For the first half of the 1980s, too little care was given to relating the means to the end.

The same limitations hold for support of insurgencies and counterinsurgencies. Insurgencies are internal revolutions whose aim is to introduce social, economic, and political change by means of an armed, clandestine organization. The success of an insurgency depends not so much on military prowess as on the ability of the insurgents to build a network of secret political cells that takes effective advantage of guerrilla tactics. And the success of a counterinsurgency depends less on defeating the terrorist, guerrilla, or military tactics of the insurgents than on uncovering and undermining the secret network and neutralizing its violent tactics.

The pivotal elements of counterinsurgency are intelligence and counterintelligence. The Communist regimes in Vietnam, China, and Cuba, which came to power in large part through insurgency, learned this lesson well—and they infiltrated and destroyed every group that attempted to build a guerrilla or insurgent base to overthrow them. For the United States, France, and Britain in the post–World War II period, the lesson took longer to sink in. Gradually, the security services of these countries developed policies and collection and analytical techniques that allowed them to identify the cadres in Third World insurgent cell structures and to use the information to arrest, penetrate, and sometimes neutralize them. One of the most effective techniques was getting former insurgents to identify their old comrades. The British, after early failures in some of their colonies—Malaya and Kenya, for example—made good use of their counterinsurgency intelligence capability. The French began to develop theirs against the Vietminh in Indochina in the early 1950s, and later applied it to undermining the cell structure of the FLN in Algeria, until France tired of the Algerian war. Likewise, in Vietnam, the United States had started developing good information on the enemy's domestic cell structure and neutralizing it. In the end it was not the insurgents' cell structure that won the war, but North Vietnamese troops.[39]

Other paramilitary operations include support for conventional forces. Usually such support is given overtly, because it is difficult to provide the necessary amount of aid without its source being revealed. But support can often be officially unacknowledged. This has been the case at various times in the past. The United States enabled the Laotian Meo military leader Vang Pao to prevent the North Vietnamese from taking over much of Laos in the 1960s. The United States being officially neutral (as was the Soviet Union, although supporting North Vietnamese forces in Laos at the same time), this aid was unacknowledged.

Sometimes leaders of conventional military forces are assisted in their efforts to stage a coup, or are prevailed upon to resist foreigners or fellow officers seeking to mount a coup. Time and again in this century, the United States and other states have come to the aid of those who plot and those who resist coups.

There are various forms of covert assistance that can be provided to paramilitary and conventional forces: political and moral support and encouragement at one end of the spectrum, material support and sanctuary at the other. One of the most effective forms of covert assistance to foreigners involved in paramilitary operations is to give them political support in third countries and in international forums with the aim of influencing perceptions and political decisions. For decades, Arab governments provided this kind of support to favored Palestinian groups, including factions of the PLO as well as the PLO itself. The Soviet Union, Cuba, and Romania for years lent covert political and moral support to selected guerrilla terrorists and insurgents such as the South West Africa People's Organization and the Vietcong.[40] Soviet political leaders and intelligence chiefs met secretly with the leaders of sponsored groups, arranging covert propaganda and political influence operations in foreign countries and in the UN to gain political support for their causes. And as we have seen, the United States did the same for the Contras in Nicaragua in the 1980s.

This type of support relies heavily on covert propaganda and political action. The supporting state applies its own covert propaganda and political infrastructure to strengthen its friends and weaken their enemies. One of the best examples is U.S. and British support to the Mujahideen in Afghanistan in the 1980s. The enemy's atrocities are given worldwide publicity, eroding external support and financial aid, while at the same time an image of just victory is projected for the friend. This in turn leads to added external support for the friend, enhances morale, and discourages the enemy. The friend receives assistance to set up offices in major capitals. Press and translation services are provided when the friend holds conferences and seminars, tours are arranged for journalists, academics, and clergymen. Television coverage is increased, and documentaries, films, and books are rolled out.

Effective covert assistance may also include direct help to the perpetrators of violence. One important technique is to provide training, particularly by third parties so as to maintain plausible denial. During the early stages of the American Revolution, the French were not eager to have their countrymen found training and assisting the revolutionaries; it was more expedient to encourage and assist skilled European officers to join the American side. Vergennes and Beaumarchais worked secretly with the American emissary Silas Deane in Paris to lure Prussians such as Baron Friedrich von Steuben and Baron Johann de Kalb to the American side, and these Europeans went on to play a significant role in training Washington's army. (The French leaders actually sought to discourage the young French aristocrat the Marquis de Lafayette from joining the Americans because he was French, but he outwitted them and ended up fighting at Washington's side.)[41]

After they seized power in Russia, the Bolshevik leaders began more than seventy consecutive years of training foreigners in how to overthrow "bourgeois" governments. In the decades preceding 1991, many thousands—probably no Westerner knows the precise number—of Communists and non-Communists whom Moscow believed useful traveled to camps in the Soviet Union, Eastern Europe, and Cuba for training. Moscow developed an elaborate, sophisticated system for conveying trainees from one place to another. Some entered the Soviet Union under their own name. Others flew from their homeland to a third country where they were met by Soviet agents and given false documents and passports before entering the Soviet bloc. This protected them when they returned home, not only from domestic opponents but also from fellow students or instructors who might defect at some later point and reveal the trainees' identity. Instruction lasted from a few months to a year. Some trainees made several trips over the course of a decade or so for more advanced training. In this way Moscow built up a friendly paramilitary cadre.

The Soviet bloc also sent paramilitary instructors abroad. In the 1980s, Cuban, Soviet, and East German officers ran courses in Angola for the Popular Movement for the Liberation of Angola (MPLA), and in Nicaragua both for Nicaraguans and Salvadorans. And during that time, Soviet bloc leaders trained thousands of young recruits—some of whom, at least, it can reasonably be assumed, will be operating for one cause or another for decades to come.

Over the years—ever since their extensive experience in World War II training Nazi resistance movements—the British too have delivered covert paramilitary training. As they withdrew from their global empire, they gave many of the governments of their former colonies the skills to resist violent takeover. Thus, in the 1960s, the British apparently provided a great deal of training and advice to Oman (at the strategic Straits of Hormuz) to resist the Dhofar rebels aided by South Yemen and the Soviet bloc. A limited amount of training helped keep this small, strategically important nation in the Western camp for decades.

Covert paramilitary assistance can also come in the form of political and technical advice, operational planning, and even coordination of military operations. Advisers must be skilled military technicians on the one hand, and on the other leaders capable of identifying opportunities and working in a foreign culture to support political objectives. They are unconventional warriors in the true sense. They cannot be model military officers who expect disciplined troops to carry out their orders. They cannot act as diplomats formally negotiating treaties or agreements on behalf of their government. Instead, they must possess a peculiar mix of military and diplomatic qualities to bring about a desired military end in an alien culture. The political component of covert military action cannot be overemphasized. Action is only a means to a political end, and it depends on blending local allies, tribes, clans, the greedy, the opportunists, and the ideological into a fighting force and getting them to exploit the vulnerabilities of the enemy.

T. E. Lawrence, known as Lawrence of Arabia, provides an example of how decisive the role of a covert military adviser can be. The real history of Lawrence is more interesting than the fictionalized accounts and films have made it out to be. Lawrence was a young British scholar who had studied the history of the Middle East and participated in archaeological digs there before World War I. He joined British military intelligence at the beginning of the war and was posted to Cairo, where he ran agents in Turkish-controlled Palestine. In 1915 he was sent to bribe a Turkish military leader who had surrounded British troops at Kut, in what is now Iraq. He failed. After considerable effort, Lawrence convinced his superiors that the Bedouin tribes could be persuaded to revolt, assisting the British in ridding the region of the Turks and ensuring that the French did not replace them. Lawrence was sent to train the Bedouins on the Arabian peninsula, where he quickly became the chief coordinator and military adviser to chieftains whose internal feuding had been encouraged by the Turks.

On August 20, 1917, in a long, detailed dispatch in the "Arab Bulletin" (a classified British internal publication circulated to those working in the Middle East), Lawrence listed twenty-seven "commandments." They were meant "to apply to the Bedouin"; "townspeople or Syrians," he wrote, required "totally different treatment." Lawrence's commandments were reportedly studied for decades by British special forces officers working in the region. They are brilliant examples of the kind of cross-cultural understanding essential to covert military assistance. Among them were the following:[42]

1. Be easy for the first few weeks. A bad start is difficult to atone for, and the Arabs form their judgement on externals we ignore. . . .
2. Learn all you can about your Ashraf and Bedu. Get to know their families, clans, and tribes, friends and enemies, wells, hills, and roads. Do all this by listening and indirect inquiry. Do not ask direct questions. . . .
3. In matters of business deal only with the commander of the army, column, or party in which you serve. Never give orders to anyone at all, and reserve your directions or advice for the C.O. however great the temptation (for efficiency's sake) of dealing directly with his underlings. Your place is advisory and your advice is due to the commander alone. . . .
5. Remain in touch with your leader as constantly and unobtrusively as you can. Live with him so that at meal times and at audiences

you may be naturally within his tent. Formal visits to give advice are not so good as are the constant dropping of ideas in casual talk. When stranger sheiks come in for the first time to swear allegiance and offer service, clear out of the tent. If their first impression is of foreigners in the confidence of the Sheriff it will do the Arab cause much harm. . . .

11. The foreigner and Christian is not a popular person in Arabia. However friendly and informal the treatment of yourself may be, remember always that your foundations are very sandy ones. . . .

13. Never lay hands on an Arab. . . .

17. Wear an Arab headcloth when with a tribe. Bedu have a malignant prejudice against the hat, and believe our persistence in wearing it . . . is founded on some immoral or irreligious principle.

18. Do not trade on what you know about fighting. Learn the Bedu principles of war. . . . If there is plunder in prospect and the odds are equal you will win. Do not waste Bedu attacking trenches (they will not stand casualties) or in trying to defend a position, for they cannot sit still without slacking. . . .

25. In spite of ordinary Arab example, avoid too free talk about women. It is as difficult a subject as religion. . . .

Covert practitioners who follow this or similar such keen insight have not always been as successful as Lawrence. Opportunity may be lacking. Many sometimes inscrutable factors make for the success or failure of covert military action. But practitioners who combine political with technical military skills are more likely to be successful. The purpose, after all, is to achieve political results.

Safe Haven

Governments can also help guerrillas, insurgents, or terrorists by providing safe haven. A safe haven is not always a necessary, and probably is not a sufficient, condition for victory, but it appears to be an important factor. In the 1980s, Pakistan, and to some extent Iran, offered safe haven to Mujahideen in Afghanistan. Without it, they probably would not have won. In Central America, the Contras could not have grown to a force of ten to fifteen thousand in the mid-1980s if they had not been able to operate out of Honduras and Costa Rica. Palestinian and Shiite terrorists would have posed much less of a threat to Israel and the United States during the 1980s if they had not had safe havens in various Eastern European states and throughout much of the Middle East, including countries such as Lebanon, Syria, Iraq, Iran, Libya, and Algeria.

Major powers rarely provide safe haven themselves, but they do often help negotiate such arrangements for insurgents or guerrillas. They also provide economic assistance to alleviate the burden that covert paramilitary forces place on the host sanctuary state, as the United States did for the Afghans and the Contras. Occasionally, major powers may also extend military aid to states harboring insurgents so as to protect them against retaliation by either target states or their powerful allies. The United States provided such aid for Honduras and Pakistan in the 1980s.

Materiel Support for Paramilitary Operations

Materiel support, another important element of paramilitary assistance, ranges all the way from pack mules to food and medical supplies, updated communications equipment, and weapons and ammunition. As we have seen, American Revolutionary forces benefited enormously not only from European officers who trained raw recruits but also from external material aid sent by the French and Spanish, among others.

Materiel support can be expensive, especially for nongovernmental groups. The following chart is an example of the estimated cost (in 1990 prices) of equipping a single guerrilla fighter for a few weeks in the field:

Item	Estimated Cost ($)
Automatic rifle	175
Seven magazines for rifle	105
Two grenades	40
Two fatigue shirts	40
Two fatigue pants	40
Three ammunition pouches	21
210 rounds of ammunition	21
Jungle boots	30
Field pack	30
Lightweight poncho	10
Lightweight hammock	20
Lightweight blanket	10
Canteen, clip, cover	20
Utility knife with sheath	10

Item	Estimated Cost ($)
Jungle hat	5
First-aid kit with pouch	5
Small cooking pot	5
Soup spoon	1
Compass	5
Toothbrush	1
Small can of oil	1
TOTAL	595

This does not include salary and the cost of base camp support between deployments in the field, or communications in the field.

The other logistics of war are expensive as well. Guerrillas or resistance fighters can live off the land and steal their weapons and ammunition, but this is not always feasible. To be effective, guerrillas or resistance fighters need patrons to free them from having to play farmer, bandit, and manufacturer. Even when there is money, equipment is not always readily available.

A graphic example of the significance of—and the sort of logistics problems attendant on—materiel support is the story of the Stinger antiaircraft missile and the Mujahideen resistance against Soviet domination. Until the Afghans had the weapon and the training to use it in the mid-1980s, they were being decimated by Soviet airpower. The Mujahideen could not afford to buy the weapon on their own, and in any case the only place they could get hold of it and train with it was outside Afghanistan. For some months debate raged in Washington about whether to supply the Stinger. Finally Congress and the weapon's proponents inside the administration won out. The Afghans were trained in the use of the weapon, a major factor in driving Soviet forces, who could no longer count on victory, to withdraw.

Materiel support was also critical to the growth of the Contras. When it was flowing in, the Contras were able to increase their number from a few hundred to ten or fifteen thousand, and this in a country of just a few million. (The Sandinistas had taken power in 1979 with just a few thousand, but then built up an army of sixty thousand.) When the U.S. Congress cut off aid in 1987 and 1988, the Contras withered to some seven thousand men. As this case suggests, materiel support can be particularly useful for forces on the offensive against an entrenched government. This is not to say that such support, any more than the previous kinds discussed, is by itself a sufficient condition for victory, whether it be for the offense or the defense.

Most types of prolonged covert paramilitary support pose difficulties for democracies. On the whole, the British and French have been much more successful than the United States in maintaining plausible denial about the support they give friends, though this was not always the case. In the late 1940s and early 1950s, the United States supplied Ukrainian, Polish, and Albanian resistance organizations opposed to Moscow with materiel support that remained unacknowledged and largely unknown for many years. Then, in the late 1960s, the U.S. foreign policy consensus broke up and the era of congressional oversight commenced. By the mid-1970s and 1980s, it became increasingly difficult to provide such assistance without it being publicly aired.

As opposed to intelligence support, training, or advice to high-level leaders, materiel support involves a large cast of international characters and goods that have to be purchased, transported to faraway places, distributed, and used. With so many individuals participating, it can be almost impossible to disguise the source of large-scale support or sophisticated equipment. Nevertheless, as the Afghan case indicates, covert action that comes to the public's attention doesn't have to be acknowledged; the "fig-leaf approach" can still be effective.

Under such circumstances, continuation of this type of covert action should be considered if the support is necessary to a venture's success. For instance, if overt passage of men and material from one government to support friendly paramilitary forces in another state is refused by a third, neighboring government, the covert route could be used effectively. If, on the one hand, the situation allows a government to covertly assist rebels in another state without provoking war, the fig-leaf approach makes sense. This, of course, is what the French did in the 1770s before they openly acknowledged their assistance to the American Revolutionaries. If, however, it is simply a way of avoiding hardheaded calculation and commitment, and of rallying public support for the policy, as the United States did several times in the 1980s, then this approach is not worth the potentially high cost.

Special Forces

A government may decide to go beyond intelligence or materiel support alone and commit its own forces covertly. This has not been common practice except when states are already overtly involved in military operations, mainly because a government is hard pressed to maintain plausible denial if its citizens are found dead in a foreign country or are taken prisoner and forced to confess meddling in the country's affairs. There is also the danger of political fallout at home. As we have seen, these problems were on the mind of Louis XVI and his ministers before the French-American alliance in 1778. To avoid provoking the British unnecessarily, the French discouraged their military officers from joining the American patriots, while at the same time secretly encouraging Prussians and other Europeans to bolster the American effort.

Since World War II, governments have only rarely committed their own forces secretly to combat, though many maintain the capacity to do so. The most widely known contemporary use of covert forces is for antiterrorism and hostage rescue. Examples include the Israelis at Entebbe (1978), the West Germans in Mogadishu (1977), French forces at Mecca (1987), and the U.S. Delta Forces in Iran (1979). Although on balance governments do not want to commit their own forces to covert combat, they will on occasion take the risk when there is no other choice and the commitment seems a necessary condition for success of the operation. Moscow, for example, sent special covert forces into Afghanistan before the 1979 Soviet invasion.

The success of special forces depends on excellent intelligence and a good covert infrastructure, preferably in place before the operation occurs. Forces should know exactly what they have to do, when, where, and how. Men, materiel, and communications gear have to be ready. The United States has sometimes had excellent logistic support, but been weak in the type of operational intelligence to complete the mission. In recent decades, there have been two examples: the Son Tay raid, the attempt to free American prisoners of the North Vietnamese in the early 1970s who had been moved prior to the U.S. attack; and the mission to rescue American embassy hostages in Iran in 1980, which failed in part because special forces planners did not have basic information about, for example, the desert terrain in the relevant part of Iran. The Israelis have demonstrated, as in their raid on Entebbe, that special covert forces can be put to good use.

Some countries have forces capable of operating secretly behind enemy lines—either to help prepare for the outbreak of war, or to pave the way for an invasion, or to operate as a stay-behind force collecting intelligence and organizing resistance and sabotaging enemy information gathering and communications during wartime. The United States and Britain did this during World War II, but most such forces were dispersed afterward. When the Allies found themselves facing a similar problem on the continent in the late 1940s, the United States helped create stay-behind nets in case of a Soviet invasion of Western Europe, and special forces were organized to drop behind Soviet lines in Eastern Europe in the event of war.

In the 1970s and 1980s, Moscow created KGB and GRU forces specifically to operate in the West in support of a Soviet surprise attack. Some were sent on training exercises in Europe—perhaps even in the United States—to familiarize themselves with the terrain and cultures in which they would be operating. The Swedish government distributed films on the techniques in which these "Spetznaz" forces had been trained; their purpose was to paralyze Sweden so that the Soviets could cross that country and go on to neutralize NATO bases in Norway. If war had broken out, the Spetznaz could have been an important tool in overcoming Western defenses.

Apart from the need for antiterrorist resources and for wartime capabilities to hinder invaders, some countries also benefit from some sort of force that can operate covertly to protect or attack key installations of governments abroad. For example, should there be a coup in a strategically important neighbor, such as Mexico, that brought hostile forces to power, it might be preferable for the United States to send in a few Americans covertly to help Mexicans replace the plotters, rather than to send in conventional forces, or to try to cope with a hostile neighbor. The U.S. force, in all likelihood, would be ineffective unless it existed before "the balloon went up."

Coups d'Etat

Potentially, one of the most important covert operations is facilitating or preventing a coup d'état. The French phrase *coup d'état*, literally "blow to the state," has been adopted in many languages to signify a violent change of government at the highest levels. Staging a coup is a completely or largely covert activity, as is protecting a regime from a coup. There are several ways to mount an effective coup, and they require the usual combination of well-thought-out policy, identification of opportunities, skilled practitioners, and above all good intelligence and counterintelligence—in short, the hallmarks of effective covert action.

As Machiavelli pointed out centuries ago, coups generally result from a chief of state's miscalculation about the loyalties of his or her subordinates, usually after staff people or principal lieutenants have been alienated or insufficiently rewarded, or after they have been suborned by those other than the chief of state. Or a coup may originate outside the chief's immediate entourage, if he or she is weak and strong people are allowed to approach the palace or other seat of government. An outstanding example of such a coup is the Bolshevik seizure of power in 1917 from the provisional revolutionary government of Aleksandr Kerensky, who had helped overthrow the czar the preceding spring. The relatively small but tough Bolshevik Party overpowered the Duma and Prime Minister Kerensky's guard, and in the succeeding months used black-leather-coated toughs, the Cheka, to prevent British and Russian opponents from doing the same thing to them.[43] The sheep allowed the wolves to approach the palace. Sometimes the wolves storm the palace, kill its occupants, and occupy the throne, as when Ibn Saud's forces recaptured his family's old seat of power in central Arabia in the early part of the twentieth century.

To assist or neutralize a coup, there must be a clear-cut calculation that the new leadership will not merely replace one set of leaders with another, even worse group. As William Colby points out, this was not the case when the United States supported the overthrow of Diem in South Vietnam in 1963.[44] It would be interesting to know what calculations the United States made in subsequent similar cases, for example, in helping arrange the overthrow of "Baby Doc" Duvalier in Haiti in the mid-1980s.

After the policy calculation has been made, opportunities must be identified to exploit discontented palace guards and trusted lieutenants, or to identify strong men who can take advantage of weak leadership. Collection, analysis, and counterintelligence performed to ascertain the practical opportunities for mounting a coup should be opportunity-oriented. Opportunity may or may not exist. Fidel Castro and Saddam Hussein have surrounded themselves with loyal aides whom they replace, sometimes by execution, if any doubt arises as to their fidelity; they have consistently removed the opportunity to resist.

Case officers need an infrastructure in place to assist a coup. The outcome of a palace coup leans heavily on the securing of assets close to the leadership, most importantly in the military and security services. The military may be induced to run a coup by case officers, recruited agents of influence, recruited family members, collaborators,[45] even organizations outside the circle of power that persuasively demonstrate their support. Civilian support groups, the media, trade unions, religious organizations, or even mobs in the street can let it be known that they would support the plotters and not oppose the government's overthrow. To reach and encourage such groups initially, a political and propaganda infrastructure is useful. The United States effectively took advantage of the British infrastructure in Iran in 1953 to create such momentum and restore the exiled shah to power.[46]

To prevent a coup, intelligence is needed to determine if discontent permeates the palace or if leadership has become so weak that it cannot stand up to its opponents. The palace guard and the infrastructure in the streets are encouraged to let it be known through demonstrations, the media, and so forth that a coup by particular leaders or factions will not be tolerated. Case officers and their managers must have the authority, resources, and imagination to maneuver quickly to mobilize the infrastructure. For example, they have to have the money and contacts to "rent a crowd," as the United States did in Iran in 1953, or to buy a black radio station, as the United States did in Guatemala in 1954.

A weak leadership or one that has alienated its key supporters is hard to protect. Effort must then be devoted to providing guidance to rulers either directly through confidential advisers or indirectly through agents of influence. But as further insurance, covert action managers may actually clandestinely recruit within the leader's personal security forces, as well as in the ranks of potential coup plotters,

Intelligence Support

One effective way to enhance a state's resources is to provide secret intelligence support to another state and thereby profit from its improved capabilities. As with other forms of support, success depends on long- and short-term policy calculations, identifying and exploiting opportunities, leadership, skilled practitioners, and good intelligence, particularly counterintelligence.

As part of overall policy, states can develop interdependent alliances whereby they strengthen and utilize each other's intelligence, military, and economic capabilities. But as with any alliance between states, there are risks or disadvantages that have to be factored into the policy equation. Will an intelligence service become too dependent on the services of others, so that there is a loss of independent capability? This seems to have happened to the United States in Iran in the 1970s. Before the overthrow of the shah, the United States relied on his often brutal intelligence service, SAVAK, for information about local trends. Moreover, being too closely bound to others, especially if there is not tight security, can have adverse political consequences. As history has proved, when the United States was identified as a partner of SAVAK, it hurt America's reputation in Iran and abroad.

But there is much to be gained if the alliance is well handled, as the British have demonstrated time and again. In the late 1930s they worked to bolster American intelligence, first so that the United States would step up counterintelligence against Nazi efforts to undermine British supply lines from the western hemisphere, and later so that the United States would create a full-service intelligence system to supplement British efforts. As they judged correctly, this was in their immediate as well as their long-term interest. To establish the relationship, British intelligence chiefs courted quasi-private citizen and adviser to President Roosevelt William J. Donovan on two confidential trips to England and British territories in 1940, impressing him with their intelligence organization and their techniques of political and economic warfare. It was as a result of his interaction with the British that Donovan recommended creation of the first centralized U.S. intelligence organization, the Coordinator of Information (1941), and later of the OSS (1942). The SIS chief in the United States, William Stephenson, who commanded what was known as British Security Coordination (BSC), later wrote in an official history, "The conception of coordinated operations in the field of secret activities which the BSC originally exemplified, was the basis on which the Americans built, with astonishing speed, their own highly successful wartime intelligence service."[47] Donovan himself, in a paper to President Roosevelt, credited the British with making available to the United States their "extensive experience"; without their help, "it would not have been possible to establish instrumentalities" for such purposes in this country. Donovan specifically credited Stephenson for lending him officers, obtaining billets for Americans in British intelligence and paramilitary schools, and making counterintelligence information and facilities available.[48]

Before and after World War II, Britain also helped its colonies and dominions, and later its ex-colonies, to establish their intelligence capabilities. One of Stephenson's wartime assistants, Charles Ellis, visited Canada and Australia in 1950 to urge both to set up their own foreign intelligence capabilities. The mission in Canada failed, but not the one in Australia. For two years after its founding in 1952, members of the Australian Service (ASIS) stationed abroad served in SIS offices before establishing their own independent stations.[49] In Australia, as in the United States, British intelligence effectively cloned itself.

The British also spotted and took advantage of short-term opportunities. A notable example is the SIS's daring operation on March 13, 1939, when the Germans occupied what was left of Czechoslovakia after the Munich Agreements. The SIS airlifted the leadership and files of the Czech intelligence service from Prague to London, where the service reestablished itself. The British were attentive to the Czechs and worked closely with them, but did not try to turn their service into a wholly controlled subsidiary, realizing how much more could be accomplished by giving them free rein.

When war came in September 1939, the British provided the Czechs with wireless facilities to maintain contact with their agents in and out of Czechoslovakia, funds to support the organization, and training for new recruits. The Czechs then ran their own agents, and unlike most of the intelligence and resistance organizations operating out of London in World War II, they had their own ciphers and codes. Both the Czechs and their hosts benefited from this arrangement. The British had access to key Czech agents, and they used Czechs for sabotage and political warfare during the war, as well as to help restore the European democratic system in the immediate postwar period.[50]

After World War II, as they took control of Eastern Europe, the Soviets turned the intelligence systems of various Communist regimes into subsidiaries of their own intelligence system. The United States too established intelligence alliances—sometimes on an equal footing, as with the British, and sometimes, as with the new West German organization shortly after the war, on a less than equal footing.[51] After all, the United States was the victor. It had enormous wealth and influence at the time compared to the early postwar German government, so it was able to impose U.S. priorities on the Germans.

Managing intelligence alliances to achieve their potential requires great skill. It is not a matter of one partner simply providing training and money or physical access to another. To maximize advantage and minimize friction, skilled leaders and operatives are needed who understand each other's culture and intelligence services. There is little point assigning station chiefs or case officers to this task who are not committed to both short- and long-term political goals and the personal relationships that further their realization. Operatives also have to be at least as intellectually able and professionally skilled as their foreign counterparts. Further, the managers of the intelligence alliance relationship have to see that counterintelligence is effective. Only through feedback can the relationship and the security of joint operations be protected. The donor service must take steps to protect itself in case its ally is penetrated from the outside, or passes on information, equipment, training, or anything else to adversary services. This can be done by recruiting personnel inside the foreign intelligence service or by technical means such as wiretaps. This will help ensure that the assistance and guidance will not ultimately be used against the donor by the recipient. The Soviets, for example, took advantage of the ideological, economic, and military subservience of their clients in Eastern Europe to recruit agents inside the intelligence services of these countries. This is called unilateral penetration. The KGB used unilateral penetrations to ensure the loyalty and subservience of the services it was aiding.[52] Even a more nearly equal relationship requires unilateral counterintelligence penetration or recruitment as well as analysis to serve as a feedback and protective mechanism for the manager of the relationship—in spite of the friction that may result from inept handling of this task when the ally becomes aware of it.

Counterterrorism: Synergy in Action

Terrorism is likely to remain a threat in the years ahead. Modern governments will need enhanced capabilities and, above all, clear policy to orchestrate all the available diplomatic, economic, and military means to deter and neutralize terrorists.

Policy to counter terrorism is not primarily an intelligence matter. Government must treat counterterrorism as part and parcel of its overall policy toward offending states and groups. It cannot regard terrorism as some small discrete element segregated from the total matrix of a diplomatic relationship—as the United States did in its relations with Syria in the 1980s, for example. Once a decision is made to put terrorism alongside other diplomatic concerns, then covert action has a clear role to play; it becomes part of the overall policy of deterrence and defense.

Effective counterterrorism draws on the entire gamut of covert techniques from political action to paramilitary operations to intelligence support. Covert channels can be used to expose states and groups that claim not to be practicing terrorism. For example, Palestinian groups such as the previously mentioned PFLP-GC and countries such as Syria admitted to terrorist attacks against Israel in the 1980s, but they denied any involvement in terrorism directed against the United States. This was untrue. The PFLP-GC, operating from a headquarters just outside Damascus, Syria, tried to bomb various Western airliners in the fall of 1988. The Syrians claimed that no evidence was put forward implicating Syrian intelligence or Ahmad Jibril, the head of the PFLP-GC.

Had the United States, Britain, or Germany wished to expose what they knew, they could have amplified Western media reports revealing that the Jordanian double agent Marwan Kreesat, the PFLP-GC's bomb-maker, traveled in and out of Syria in pursuit of this enterprise. Without revealing any other sources, they could have used him to document the Syrian and PFLP-GC role in attempting to bomb various airliners. If Western states want to deter state sponsors, as the British did in the mid-1980s by isolating Syria when its embassy in London was implicated in aircraft bombings, they will have to document their cases, rally international support, isolate and punish sponsors, and expose terrorist organizations. States could also step up their threats by direct military attacks such as the United States made on Libya in 1986, or by launching raids against PFLP-GC headquarters, training camps, and safe houses. The Israelis have done this, sometimes with and sometimes without attribution. True, some terrorists would be killed in these operations. The dilemma Western governments face is whether to apply retribution to terrorists and their sponsors or to risk further loss of their own citizens. As more states and non-state actors acquire access to chemical and biological agents that can be unleashed more or less anonymously and with devastating effect, this problem is likely to become more pressing.

States can still try to apprehend, prosecute, and punish individual terrorists. This reduces safe havens for terrorists and impedes their operations. But experience in the 1980s and 1990s so far has proved that the legal approach is not adequate. Too many human and material resources can be lavished on this technique with too little result.

As suggested earlier, another tactic that could prove useful as part of a well-coordinated counterterrorism program is pressure against the families of terrorists. Few Western states have availed themselves of this technique. One possible safeguard against terrorism would be to suggest to families that their children are killing and maiming innocent women and children, that these actions are inconsistent with their religion and could even precipitate revenge against the family and possible exile. This limited form of psychological pressure would be relatively benign aside from the anguish it caused. To increase the pressure, compromising photos could be distributed of respected terrorist leaders carousing in the company of women; in societies where drinking alcohol and womanizing are taboo activities, and shame is a potent weapon, this tactic could prove effective. Secret bank account numbers, and their real or fictitious balances, could be made public to stir up jealousy and rivalry within and between families. People might also be dissuaded from joining terrorist support groups or cells through overt and covert propaganda and political action.

But deterrence, even if it is well handled, is not likely on its own to eradicate the menace of terrorism. Particularly in the Middle East, some will be persuaded that terrorism is their sacred duty, a variant of Muslim holy war. Here individual Western services on their own or in alliance with the intelligence services of targeted countries will need to neutralize those who are not deterred, a task requiring specialists in the disruption and manipulation of terrorists.

What would these operatives do? The main mission would be to harass terrorist cells by tampering with their communications, sabotaging their operations, and sowing discord among members. American covert action planners operate with fewer options than some other Western counterterrorist organizations. Assassinations are banned. However, some intelligence services use manipulation programs to motivate terrorists to kill each other or other groups to kill terrorists. This, it will be recalled, is what French operations achieved in Algiers and the Western-PLO effort succeeded in doing to Sabri Al-Banna's Fatah Revolutionary Council.

A terrorist can be framed so that comrades come to believe he or she is working for rival terrorists or Middle Eastern intelligence services, Israel, or the United States. A similar ploy is to encourage political enemies to go on the offense. For example, operatives from Middle Eastern or Western services might approach the Muslim Brotherhood, through cutouts or agents of influence, using a variety of tactics, including bribery, encourage them to attack specific terrorists. If the Brotherhood adopted the idea, it would be for its own personal and political reasons, not out of the desire to support modern democracy.

What about sabotaging a terrorist operation? Western covert practitioners or their agents would have to penetrate an organization's lines of supply and communications through human sources or technical devices. The French have used this type of information warfare, such as scrambling the communications of terrorists and others in Lebanon. Sabotaging terrorist operations is neither easy nor risk-free, though sometimes it can be relatively cheap, as when the Italian police neutralized the operations of the Red Brigades in the 1970s, or when Jordanian and West German efforts foiled the PFLP-GC's grand plan to bomb several airliners in the fall of 1988. At other times sabotage may be more costly, risking the lives of agents and counterterrorist professionals.

The technical components of intelligence services that support terrorism are special targets for attack. Many terrorists, on their own, are unlikely to master all the complex technologies particularly useful to them. They need help in the form of information, training, and experimentation in order to take advantage of technologies designed to destroy computers, aircraft, and other vulnerable but highly complex structures. Penetrating and neutralizing—possibly even destroying—the organs that provide such assistance to terrorists is one way of reducing the capabilities of a cell.

As their weapons grow ever more complex, terrorists grow more dependent on a complex variety of inputs to make them work. Such dependence expands counterterrorist opportunities to penetrate supply networks and operations. This is both good news and bad: as the weaponry available to terrorists becomes more devastating, preempting their operations becomes more urgent. On the other hand, as weapons become more complex, there are more opportunities to identify and neutralize terrorist operations.

All of these techniques are capable in the next century of working to the advantage of those combating terrorism. To be effective, however, they must be based on the aforementioned first principles. Policy must be clear on the value and imperative of waging war against terrorism, and it requires a variety of instruments, including the techniques of covert action as part of the effort. Only then, and only through imaginative, sustained leadership, can opportunities be identified, programs selected, and qualified people brought to bear against terrorists and their supporters.

It takes time to train and develop case officers as specialists in prolonged struggles of this sort. Through on-the-job training, study of the culture and language of terrorists, as well as learning the lessons of the past—how, why, and when others such as the French and Israelis have been successful—new generations of managers and case officers can emerge as the cadre of a modern counterterrorist capability. They in turn would need to maintain a sophisticated infrastructure of people and technical capabilities to deter and wage covert war against terrorists. Even then, success would not be guaranteed. Covert action specialists must be backed up by opportunity analysis, collection, and counterintelligence. To be effective—to make a difference—the symbiosis basic to all intelligence operations must prevail.

5

OFFENSIVE DEFENSE: PRINCIPLES OF COUNTERINTELLIGENCE

ONE OF THE PRECONDITIONS for effective covert action is counterintelligence. What then makes for effective counterintelligence? Ideally, counterintelligence is more than the passive activity of a security backwater. It can play a valuable role in supporting overall strategy and policy—but only if it is given a seat at the tables where strategy is planned and implemented. How can counterintelligence help advance policy?

The key answer is *offensive defense*. As a passive counter to the hostile intelligence activities of foreign states and groups, counterintelligence consists of locks, safes, and genies. Passive counterintelligence waits until a wife confesses that her husband is a spy for the Soviet Union, as the American Barbara Walker did in 1982. It waits for an employee to report the suspicious behavior of a colleague, as happened before Jonathan Pollard was jailed for stealing secret U.S. documents for Israel in the 1980s. Leads given to security personnel are important and useful and help protect national secrets. But to fulfill its potential, counterintelligence needs to be more than a passive reactor; it must be part of a proactive policy of defense.

The important question is how counterintelligence fits into national strategy—how it can make a substantial difference in supporting overall policy and protecting other elements of intelligence. In answering this question, one must look at the essential components of first-class counterintelligence: counterintelligence analysis (as distinct from positive intelligence analysis), counterintelligence collection (as distinct from positive intelligence collection), and counterintelligence exploitation. Exploitation uses the products of counterintelligence collection and analysis not only to defend against and neutralize hostile intelligence but also to turn hostile forces on their heads and exploit them to advance one's own policy interests.

As we have seen, countries rarely integrate counterintelligence in more than a passive way into their strategy. They may not fully consider how counterintelligence can be used to advance overall national strategy, or decide exactly what elements of strategy need the most counterintelligence attention, or identify the largest threats to the national interest and to intelligence activities.

Central Coordination and Strategy

After deciding on the counterintelligence mission, managers must develop, mobilize, and coordinate counterintelligence elements to achieve it. This is difficult to do, more so in democratic regimes with their intentionally separated branches of power than in totalitarian regimes, and especially during peacetime. To benefit from first-class offensive defense, a government must develop unified top-driven, coordinated analytical collection and exploitation programs. The alternative is the sort of fragmented, decentralized bottom-driven counterintelligence system that was prevalent in the United States during much of the cold war. In the late 1980s, U.S. policymakers gradually became aware of the problem and began to undertake reforms to remedy management deficiencies within individual agencies and in the government as a whole.[1] But in any country, planning and pulling together the programs and resources of different agencies, especially when it involves the most sensitive intelligence matters, is a daunting task.

To identify strategic intelligence threats and opportunities and to assign priorities accordingly requires one "mind"—which may be individual or collective. George Washington was his own master of counterintelligence during the Revolutionary War. Apparently so was Francis Walsingham in Elizabethan England, Joseph Fouche in Napoleon's France, and Felix Dzerzhinsky in the Soviet Union.[2] If it is to be strategic, counterintelligence must be directed by some type of core group, made up for the most part of people who read and use counterintelligence analysis, leavened by others experienced in counterintelligence operations, and enlightened by a few who can bring in the broader perspective of statecraft.

Few who rise to senior positions in counterintelligence bureaucracies are unorthodox thinkers, and few have substantive knowledge of their state's overall military, diplomatic, and economic policy. Few counter-intelligence managers, for example, have professional opportunities to learn about the intricacies of nuclear strategy, or about emerging tech-nologies for the twenty-first century. Similarly, few creative strategists and regional policymakers know much about counterintelligence. Most non-counterintelligence professionals do not have the opportunity to go "behind the green door." Hence the need for seasoned counterin-telligence managers, with strong operational and analytical back-grounds, to work together with professional strategists and statesmen. Failing that, it is useful to provide counterintelligence managers with special training in substantive strategic and policy matters prior to undertaking a tour at the center of coordination.

Experience shows that such planning or coordinating groups often benefit by the inclusion of creative thinkers from outside government. In World War II, for example, British counterintelligence and decep-tion managers included an Oxford don, an aristocratic stockbroker, a former colonial government official who successfully influenced local politics in the colonies, a well-known British novelist, a student of crime and black magic, a financier and shipowner, a scientist, and a luminary in the tea business. A core group that included both seasoned counterintelligence managers and a few outsiders would send authori-tative directives to the bureaucracy. There the technical specialists in agent acquisition, manipulation, and analysis would refine and imple-ment their ideas.[3]

At the same time there are disadvantages to central coordination. For one, collecting so many secrets in a single place creates a huge tar-get for foreign intelligence services. But governments already concen-trate secrets under a single roof for other purposes. In the United States (and many other countries), for instance, information about the purpose, location, and budget of most "black" defense and intelligence programs in the 1970s and 1980s was gathered—literally in several cardboard boxes—in secured rooms used by the House and Senate armed services and appropriations committees. For example, during the 1980s, most of these secrets were brought together in the offices of the Intelligence Community Staff and in the Pentagon's Office of the Secretary of Defense.

Furthermore, because adversaries concentrate their attacks to get at gathered information, centralization may actually be a better way of protecting it. A variety of techniques can be used to protect the secrets.

For example, those who work in central coordination agree to subject themselves to intrusion into their personal lives, just as those with access to nuclear weapons undergo special reliability checks and lifestyle monitoring. In addition, central coordination security can be continuously scrutinized. With security resources concentrated at a single location, secrets can be better shielded than when they are scattered at various less secure locations.

Counterintelligence Analysis

Most readers of intelligence literature, and many counterintelligence practitioners, believe that the essence of counterintelligence is investigation—the collection of information needed to hunt down spies and moles who have infiltrated one's own government and society. This is a restricted view of the defensive investigative aspect of counterintelligence. Perhaps the queen of the counterintelligence chessboard is counterintelligence analysis, both offensive and defensive.

The problems start at the beginning. Where to concentrate energy and resources? Sometimes circumstances point counterintelligence in a particular direction. The defection of an officer of an adversary service, such as the KGB's Anatoliy Golitsyn in the 1960s or Oleg Gordievsky in the 1980s, provides "leads."[4] Or an agent is "turned in," as was the American spy John Walker. Counterintelligence runs down the implications of such cases and conducts a damage assessment.

Most of the time, however, determining the precise focus of counterintelligence, what resources should be deployed where to accomplish the mission, is anything but obvious. What does a counterintelligence analyst zero in on when, for example, at any one time Russia or China alone may have as many as several thousand government employees abroad? Then there is the additional problem of many thousands of émigrés from the former Soviet Union. A tiny percentage of these individuals are, despite the changes in those countries, Russian and Commonwealth of Independent States (CIS) intelligence officers seeking to enter into a clandestine relationship with U.S. citizens. But which ones?

And those are just the foreign agents. At any one time in the United States itself, several million people have access to classified information. Some are generals in the military or senior managers of intelligence agencies. Many more work in data banks, administration, and communications. Only a handful might ever be tempted to pass sensitive information to foreign intelligence services. But it takes only one

Walker-Whitworth ring or one Aldrich Ames to do a country massive damage. Even in a dictatorship, but certainly in a democracy, it is impractical to watch over millions of people, much less to secure their communications and their telephone calls from monitoring by foreign intelligence services. Moreover, each major industry, each sensitive weapons or communications system, each command and control system, each sensitive installation such as an embassy abroad, is a potential target of hostile intelligence personnel or technical collection. But which ones are targeted, and what techniques are being used to target them? U.S. satellite systems play an important role. What can foreign governments be reasonably expected to know about them—how they look, how they orbit, how and where they were built? How could they use this information for deception or to conceal their activities from collection?

Day in and day out, intelligence services receive a flood of information about foreign governments' attempts to influence events in other countries. Some of these reported activities reveal the hands of hostile intelligence. Which ones? The answers to such questions are far from obvious. If a government deploys its security agents and its counterspies without first determining the priorities of foreign intelligence operatives, it will likely miss many of the threats and opportunities it ought to be targeting. At best, and with luck, it may stumble on a few. But if a government answers these questions well—if, that is, it has good analysis—it will be well positioned to use its counterintelligence resources effectively.

Triage of Targets

Ascertaining what really needs protection is the place to begin, especially given the limited and diminishing resources available to counterintelligence. As former White House director of intelligence programs Kenneth deGraffenreid has pointed out, although democracies have far fewer secrets than authoritarian regimes (where most official actions and machinations are secret), the ones they have may be more precious. Thus in a democracy, each secret is an inviting target.[5]

What secrets need top protection in a powerful, technologically advanced country? They include strategic command and control systems, location, and characteristics of strategic weapons; the information-processing circuits that such weapons depend on; and specific plans for the use of these weapons and for the defense of leaders and retaliatory forces.

Next on the list of priorities come the details of the government's relations with scores of other regimes around the world. In the absence of an immediate common threat, relations among states can be particularly strained. Adversary governments or groups may use both overt diplomacy and propaganda and covert action to split up allies and isolate and discredit certain states.

Consider the U.S. effort to limit the flow of narcotics into America from the Andean region through Mexico. While many Mexican leaders have goals complementary to those of the United States concerning narcotics—that is, the Mexican leaders do not want their country to become another Colombia—some Mexicans also benefit from producing or exporting drugs to the United States. And some Mexican officials have benefited financially or otherwise from narcotics trafficking. Fighting local growers and traffickers and their private armies can be extremely costly to Mexican political and military officials— sometimes even deadly. In these circumstances, U.S. anger at what may appear as Mexican indifference to, or even at times cooperation with, narco-trafficking can be counterproductive. Drug traffickers could inflame U.S.-Mexican tension by, for instance, planting stories in Mexican newspapers and elsewhere on real or alleged high-level Mexican government involvement with narco-trafficking. Exposing or otherwise neutralizing those who use clandestine means to exacerbate strains between states is—or should be—a priority of counterintelligence.

Another essential element to keep under wraps is the plan one state uses in negotiations with another—for instance, where the state is prepared to make concessions, where it will draw the line. Using clandestine means to learn the negotiating position of another state is a longstanding intelligence technique. In a French example, a former French intelligence officer, LeRoy-Finville, has described how in the 1960s the French foreign intelligence service photographed documents belonging to then undersecretary of state George Ball in Ball's hotel room. This operation was conducted to assist then French finance minister Giscard d'Estaing, who was negotiating trade tariffs with the United States. When President de Gaulle was told about this intelligence coup he at first refused to believe it, and then was very grateful.[6] Apparently the French were still using this sort of technique in the late 1980s. Clearly such inside information is a great advantage in difficult negotiations.

A state's military and economic capabilities depend to some extent on technological superiority; in a democracy, this is likely to be in the more vulnerable private sector.[7] Hence, there is a need for government protection of proprietary technology, especially when it is targeted by foreign intelligence. States also need to protect their own clandestine operations—the collection of intelligence, and influencing events abroad. In the United States this is called operational security (opsec). For example, identifying hostile agents is relatively easy if dates of meetings and subject matter to be discussed are discovered, even if specific locations are not disclosed in intercepted message traffic. It was just such a cryptological break, known as Venona, that largely enabled Western services to identify Soviet networks operating in the 1940s and 1950s.[8]

Few states, especially democratic ones, centrally identify which key secrets need the most protection. Counterintelligence resources, rather than being deployed after logical consideration of what it is most important to protect, on the contrary tend to be rationed out in response to bureaucratic pressure and other less calculated factors. Counterintelligence officers on their own cannot assign priority to their country's secrets. They need to work with substantive specialists to determine what areas most need protection, what particular counterintelligence resources and interagency efforts will provide it, and whether these programs are working.

Assessing Vulnerability

Once the secrets to be protected are identified and policymakers agree, the role for counterintelligence analysis is to ascertain the peculiar vulnerabilities of those secrets. Vulnerability needs to be assessed at the beginning of a major project. A good illustration of this principle is the contrast between the U.S. and Soviet planning for new embassies in the late 1970s and 1980s.

During this time, the United States and the Soviet Union each broke ground on the sites of their respective new embassy complexes in Moscow and Washington. Gaining access to the other's building would have a decided diplomatic, intelligence, and perhaps military advantage, because embassies usually house a government's central diplomatic and intelligence secrets and sometimes key military secrets. Unlike the Soviet counterintelligence assessment, the American assessment was poor to nonexistent, and it showed in the results. Moscow picked an excellent hilltop site in Washington that had many potential benefits for Soviet intelligence activities. The United States fared less well. Moreover, the Soviets took advantage of the construction stage of the U.S. embassy to enhance their eavesdropping capabilities.[9]

Counterintelligence vulnerability should also be assessed when reviewing details of proposed treaties and other agreements. As the director of the FBI belatedly pointed out in 1989, the INF treaty and the START agreement allowed the Soviet (now Russian) intelligence service to gain routine access to numerous sensitive areas and individuals in the United States which, until then, were accessible only on a most limited basis.[10] Until 1988, Moscow had only three legal residencies or bases in the United States from which to conduct signals and human intelligence operations: Washington, New York, and San Francisco. As a result of the INF agreement and verification protocol, the Russians acquired a thirteen-year permanent site for twenty personnel in Magna, Utah—known as a "portal site." According to the FBI director, this was in a location uniquely situated for the collection of sigint and humint. Other nuclear, biological, and chemical weapons and other treaties multiply such opportunities.

Changing patterns of emigration may also pose problems. In the mid-1980s, less than one thousand Soviet immigrants entered the United States in a given year. By 1989 the number had risen to approximately twenty-four thousand.[11] Many more thousands of East Europeans, Chinese, and Middle Easterners are now entering Western Europe and Israel, and there is every indication their numbers will increase in future years. In the United States, after five years of residence, an immigrant is eligible for citizenship and a security clearance. If no compromising information turns up in a background check, the immigrant may be eligible for employment even in sensitive installations.[12] This is not to suggest that immigrants are not loyal Americans; to the contrary, those who have gained the liberties and opportunities America grants its citizens may value and protect them more vigorously. Some, however, may be subject to coercion, for example, through pressure on family members at home. And some may be moles, trained intelligence operatives masquerading as immigrants, but in fact already in the employ of a foreign intelligence service. Obviously, this immigration trend subjects the secrets of the United States and other Western countries to increased threat of exposure through the efforts of agents of foreign intelligence services. Determining the nature and degree of this and other threats is one of the first and foremost tasks of counterintelligence analysis.

Adversaries: Targets and Competence

After defining the defensive perimeter, as it were, the next job of counterintelligence is to analyze what areas foreign intelligence is targeting and assess its ability to reach those targets. On occasion, governments receive windfalls in such matters. A recruited agent or intelligence defector such as the KGB officer code-named Farewell who exposed the extensive Soviet theft of Western technology will produce internal documents evaluating the performance of his or her service. One of the clearest indication of an intelligence service's true interest is what it chooses to target, that is, what its human and technical sources are being tasked to collect or influence. For example, in the 1980s the KGB and GRU did indeed start to target Magna, Utah, as a useful spot from which to intercept U.S. telecommunications.

Counterdeception Analysis

Another matter of concern for counterintelligence analysis is identifying the clandestine means a foreign government uses to manipulate perceptions and actions. Foreign intelligence services are often used by their governments to deceive and to manage perceptions of adversaries. This may involve the intelligence service's reinforcement of accurate as well as false impressions held by adversaries. The practice and principles of manipulation have changed little throughout the ages, although modern democracy and technology have produced new opportunities as well as new roadblocks.

Deception has three requirements. First, it must be founded on a strategy or policy; deception for deception's sake serves little purpose. Second, it must answer the question: if one succeeds in convincing the adversary of something, will the adversary respond with action or not? Will it withhold its forces, for example, as the Germans did in Normandy in June 1944? Third, deception must be buttressed by an orchestrated plan.

Clever deception operations use a variety of techniques—sigint, humint, diplomacy, media, rumors, and propaganda—to prevent the enemy from learning a plan in its entirety, in other words, to keep him scrambling after pieces of the puzzle. To lead the target to draw certain conclusions, verbal or written or illustrative information may be planted on agents known to be working for the adversary, or on those technical sources known to be intercepting communications, or on imagery sources. A reliable feedback channel to gauge the adversary's reaction is helpful, if not essential, so that future messages can be constructed to reinforce any conclusions. Of course, it is critical to protect the deception plan itself *and* the real strategy being concealed, as the Allies did in planning the Normandy invasion in the spring of 1944.

If other states are seeking to control or alter perceptions by manipulating foreign collection and analysis, counterintelligence analysts can respond with counterdeception analysis. By mirroring the steps involved in foreign perception management, counterintelligence analysts protect their own government from manipulation. They may try to identify any foreign government objectives that could be furthered by a deception plan. Military operations usually (and economic and diplomatic operations often) employ a deception plan to achieve surprise and thereby to increase the chance of success. Counterintelligence analysts need to examine their own government's collection modus operandi to determine its vulnerability to foreign deception. For example, the Iraqi government in the 1980s was successful in fooling the U.S. government about its nuclear weapons program. It had a motive, and it knew a great deal about U.S. technical collection. U.S. counterdeception analysts in the CIA or DoD could have calculated that Moscow was probably teaching the Iraqis about U.S. technical collection programs so that they could manipulate U.S. intelligence collection. Indeed, post–Gulf War UN inspections indicate that this is precisely what happened.

Counterdeception analysts must identify how foreign governments perceive their target as reacting to certain information. Is the target reacting to or merely ignoring attempts at perception management? Counterdeception analysts also need to identify who is conducting the perception management. Are there deception planners in the foreign country? Where are they located? What are their objectives—what are the specific tasks of their agents, and what do they want us to "learn" about their secret military plans? Counterdeception analysts would also do well to learn the foreign country's operational security procedures, which could unlock the deception plan. If they are really good, analysts may be able to discover the information or activity that deception is trying to cover. Indeed, such information was probably ascertainable in Iraq in the 1980s.

Consider what might have happened if, during World War II, the Nazis had been able to surveil cars regularly arriving at the British War Cabinet offices and trail them back to Bletchley Park in Oxfordshire, where German communications were being decoded. This could have tipped them off that Bletchley Park was a site of significant secret activity. German counterintelligence analysts could then have searched for more clues and perhaps discovered the Allies' Ultra penetration of the German code and the manipulation of captured German agents in order to deceive the Germans, an operation known by its technical name, Double-Cross. Uncovering the Double-Cross and Ultra would have been a priceless coup for the Germans.

Or take the example of counterintelligence analysis and how it helped change American defense policy after the discovery of Soviet nuclear-war-fighting capabilities in the late 1970s and early 1980s. Moscow had directed an active measures campaign at the West, claiming that nuclear war would inevitably lead to the destruction of all life on earth. Many inside and outside the U.S. government shared this perception. On the other hand, some U.S. specialists had been warning for more than a decade that Moscow was building defense shelters designed to withstand nuclear attack. Clearly this was incompatible with the notion that nuclear war would leave no survivors. But not until the early 1980s was the United States able to pin down, with a fair degree of precision, the enormous preparations the Soviet leadership was making to ride out nuclear war. This momentous discovery was made in part because the U.S. intelligence community (forced by the Congress and the president) devoted a small effort to counterdeception analysis.

What happened? In 1983, according to the published account of a congressional staffer who specialized in the subject, analysts reviewing old satellite photography were instructed to look for suspicious activities. One noticed that a "wind tunnel" apparently used for testing aircraft near a Moscow suburb would actually damage nearby buildings if used. This led to a closer examination of pictures taken some years earlier when the tunnel was being built. They revealed a procession of trains hauling away large quantities of dirt. This activity had been routinely recorded and passed routinely unnoticed until the skeptical analysts became involved. Once the activity was recognized for what it was—deep underground tunneling rather than the deceptive research and development facility that had fooled imagery analysts for years—positive intelligence analysts were able to add up the volume of dirt removed and determine the size of the underground facilities. Further research revealed the extent of the subterranean project. It was a deep underground command bunker, built to withstand nuclear attack, for the top Soviet political and military leadership. It had redundant communication systems, a host of measures to protect against chemical and biological attack, and equipment and military stores that would enable the Soviet leadership to remain for months so far underground that no known U.S. weapon could destroy them. Secret subway lines had been constructed from the center of Moscow to the VIP Vnukova Airfield seventeen miles outside the city. From Vnukova, even more remote facilities could be reached. A fleet of planes, trains, and other transportation equipment complemented the bunker facilities, providing additional options for relocation in remote sites.[13] This extraordinary effort—a major strategic deception—was effectively concealed for more than a decade and was uncovered because counterdeception analysis afforded a new and powerful perspective not possible in the routine course of positive intelligence analysis.

Support for Operations

Counterintelligence analysis can also be used in support of counterintelligence operations. Counterintelligence analysts help both midlevel program managers and case officers in their day-to-day tactical work by culling fruitful leads from dead ends. One way is through *pattern analysis*. Rather than having individual case officers try to reinvent the wheel by surveilling each suspected intelligence officer, analysts can provide program managers working against foreign intelligence services at home and abroad with guides to the general behavior of foreign intelligence and foreign counterintelligence.

By studying the modus operandi of a foreign intelligence service, it is possible to answer certain questions. What time of day do its case officers meet their agents? What sorts of places do they pick for dead drops? When and how do they service dead drops? How does the behavior of an intelligence officer differ from that of a career diplomat? What kind of car does each drive? Where do they live? During the cold war, official diplomats, particularly those from Communist countries, usually had relatively little money to spend, while intelligence officers tended to travel, entertain, and spend money more freely. Everyone and every organization has a pattern. By collating the experience of many foreign counterintelligence operatives over a long period of time, counterintelligence personnel can detect patterns that may be of great assistance in deciding where and when to concentrate their surveillance of suspects. In the United States during the 1970s, a whole genre of literature on "how to spot the [American] spook" was developed by renegade American intelligence officers to weaken U.S. intelligence, eventually leading to the passage of the Agent Identities Act (1982). This act made it a crime to engage in a pattern of activities designed to reveal the identities of American intelligence personnel.

Often a great deal of technical and human analytical effort is expended to identify foreign intelligence officers. Peter Wright, a senior scientist with Britain's counterintelligence service (MI5) after World War II, found that by studying the history of Soviet coded radio traffic to agents in Britain who had been caught he could tell a great deal about those still operating. He divided those who were caught into "singletons" (agents working alone) and networks, and discovered that changes in the pattern of radio traffic mirrored these two different types of agent. For example, by looking at KGB and GRU call signs and by analyzing the group count and length of a message, he could identify which type of spy received it. As he explained, "the singleton sleeper received very little traffic, the GRU singleton not much more, while the KGB singleton received a . . . considerable volume. The KGB illegal resident, the most important spy of all, always took the greatest amount of traffic."[14]

By analyzing patterns of behavior it is sometimes even possible not only to identify foreign intelligence professionals, but also to specify those who are successful and in what type of operations they are succeeding, thus tipping off counterintelligence operators. Suppose counterintelligence analysts noticed an accelerated rate of promotion for Iraqi officials previously identified as intelligence officers specializing in acquiring European nuclear technology. This would suggest (not prove) that such officers were enjoying a certain measure of success in stealing nuclear secrets. Counterintelligence services could then focus their efforts on how and why they were succeeding, as well as search for spies in the nuclear technology field.[15]

This type of analysis is also useful in recruiting agents for positive collection or covert action, and in checking the bona fides of recruits or defectors. A case officer evaluating a recruit or defector will want to compare what that person says with a storehouse of knowledge about how real foreign diplomats and intelligence officers operate. The counterintelligence analyst is thus helping other elements of the intelligence community validate their sources and secure their operations against either fabrication or manipulation by foreign intelligence.

A less proven type of analytical support to counterintelligence operations is *anomalous behavior analysis*, an offensive analytical technique. Here the analyst seeks out strange or puzzling behavior pointing to a counterintelligence problem even before it is known to exist. There are various kinds of anomalous behaviors that might tip off an analyst about a foreign intelligence service's successful operations. One is strategic behavior. When a foreign government starts using the same secret technology as another government, the analyst who finds this out may hypothesize that it is because such secrets have been stolen. Certainly the former Soviet Union was adept at stealing French aircraft technology prior to World War II and U.S. technology after World War

II and using it in Soviet production. When one alliance makes changes in its war plans that neutralize the war plans of another, as the Warsaw Pact did in the late 1970s, neutralizing NATO plans, the analyst may surmise that it is more than accidental.

Another anomaly to watch out for is ostensible coincidence. For years the Soviet intelligence service seemed to know in advance of the movements of U.S. submarines, since Soviet ships trailed them. One American admiral suggested this was not just the result of loose talk by sailors in port. But most naval intelligence officers, not trained to concern themselves with counterintelligence, had little knowledge of Soviet ship movements and made no effort to locate a specific human or technical penetration. This failure to seek out alternative explanations allowed the Walker-Whitworth ring to operate undetected for more than a decade, from the late 1960s to the early 1980s, giving Moscow top-secret codes that enabled it to read not only U.S. naval traffic but traffic of intelligence agencies as well. If war had come, it would probably have been disastrous for the United States.

Aware that apparent coincidence can lead to exposure, the British in both world wars and the United States in the second went to great lengths not to act in ways that would reveal their ability to read secret enemy communications. At times, they even passed up the opportunity to exploit intelligence lest it indicate that they were too well informed.

Another type of anomaly has to do with personal behavior. What is an analyst to make of an employee with access to classified information who suddenly starts to spend well above his or her income, as have some U.S. military and diplomatic personnel over the years, and even some intelligence personnel such as Aldrich Ames in the 1980s? It may mean nothing. The big spender may just have received a bequest from a rich aunt or in-law. Or it may signify a relationship with a foreign intelligence service. An anomaly of this sort should not go unnoticed. How the case officer utilizes this type of information without infringing on an individual's civil rights is problematic—but legally manageable, especially with closer FBI and Justice Department involvement in promising cases.

Analysis of odd behavior or events can directly expose spies. Syrian counterintelligence probably caught Eli Cohen that way in 1965. Cohen, posing as Kamal Amin Taabet, apparently used a clandestine radio to provide Israel with vital political and military intelligence, including the location and description of fortifications along the Golan Heights. According to the Syrians, in 1964 they noted that Israeli radio, Kol Israel, was broadcasting secret Syrian cabinet decisions that had been revealed only to the National Revolutionary Council (of which Taabet was a member). This behavior alerted them to the possibility of a spy operating in high government circles. When they intercepted an illegal radio signal originating inside Syria, it further roused suspicion. Finally in November 1964, Israeli guns hit long-range artillery on the Syrian border with a precision that could only be attributed to secret intelligence. The Syrians hurried along tests of advanced Soviet radio-direction-finding equipment, which led them to Cohen's apartment overlooking Syrian general staff headquarters.[16]

It takes unusual counterintelligence managers to utilize anomalous behavior analysis, especially when they have limited resources. Leads may, after all, prove just to be coincidence. Managers tend to believe this type of "research" or investigation is too expensive to pursue in depth. Further, few counterintelligence managers are watching strategic developments, as the example of U.S. naval intelligence suggests. Only rarely are they likely to notice anomalous behavior outside their turf. For example, unless it is brought to their attention, they will not be aware of major improvements in foreign government airplanes, or changes in war plans. The tools are, however, available for first-class counterintelligence if the will is there to back it up.

Another major application of counterintelligence analysis—beyond collection and analysis—is in operations designed to neutralize and exploit foreign intelligence activities. Again, there are a variety of ways in which analysts can support not only their counterintelligence operational colleagues but also the larger intelligence community and indeed the entire national security apparatus.

For example, analysis can heighten the efficiency of security and countermeasures. It improves security in general, and neutralizes espionage in particular, by providing data and illustrating threats to alert personnel in sensitive positions that they are potential targets. This type of analysis, which enables employees in the CIA or NSA, for example, to recognize and avoid the major ploys of potential recruiters, is used in counterintelligence awareness training. It does not always work, but the effort is worth making.

Counterintelligence analysis also helps by painting the big picture, which few case officers have the time or inclination to study. Like most professionals, they are living off the intellectual capital of their training (which is usually limited) and their own personal experience. They become very involved in their cases, their likes and dislikes are pronounced, and their egos and careers are on the line. The effective counterintelligence analyst, armed with the benefit of detachment from operations, is in a position to tell operators what is known and what is not known. In the process, the analyst can bring information from other cases to bear on the one at hand. When the analyst is given details of an operation or case and remains detached, he complements the operators' capabilities. The analyst's broader perspective can also be of assistance when the manager and case officer have to decide how to approach an employee almost certainly involved in espionage. Should they arrest the suspect or turn him into a double agent?

Counterintelligence Analysis and Positive Intelligence

The exploitation of counterintelligence collection for positive intelligence purposes has been one of the least valued and least understood aspects of counterintelligence, at least in the United States. By regarding their sources as more than guides to the behavior of hostile services, counterintelligence managers can contribute much to the collection of positive intelligence. Indeed, often counterintelligence sources are like gold nuggets buried in layers of counterintelligence information. Extracting them for positive purposes requires savvy and determination.

J. C. Masterman, the British don who ran the Double-Cross system in World War II, learned that in 1941 the Nazis had tasked a double agent known as Tricycle to obtain details of the defenses of Pearl Harbor. At the time, the Nazis had no real interest in Pearl, but their Japanese allies did. Masterman saw the potential positive value of this information to the United States and had it passed on to J. Edgar Hoover of the FBI. Hoover in turn gave the information to the uncomprehending military, but they apparently read little significance into it. Similarly, in the weeks before the attack on Pearl Harbor, the FBI learned that a Japanese intelligence officer under diplomatic cover at the Japanese consulate in Honolulu was preparing detailed grids of the naval base and the exact location of ships in moorings. The Honolulu branch of the FBI sent this information to Washington headquarters, but again it appears not to have been considered significant positive intelligence because it was not relayed to naval intelligence and military commanders responsible for defending Pearl Harbor.

In a more recent example from the 1960s and 1970s, a Western intelligence service recruited a Communist who happened to be a confidant of senior CPSU leaders such as Boris Ponomarev as well as of top

Communist leaders in China and other countries. His handlers were not primarily concerned with these connections; they wanted to know what his own Communist Party was doing so they could neutralize the activity. Reports of his conversations with Communist luminaries for the most part remained on counterintelligence shelves and in counterintelligence safes, only rarely coming to the attention of policymakers and almost never reaching positive intelligence analysts who were working with inferior information. Only once or twice was the agent asked to pose telling questions to his powerful connections. In 1968, a careful reading of his reports—alas, retrospectively—indicated he had provided warning of the invasion of Czechoslovakia.

There are good and bad reasons for failures of this sort. On one hand, to protect delicate sources, the counterintelligence manager restricts access to their information or masks their high-level connections, and he is usually reluctant to burden sources with further, potentially compromising tasks. He may apply the need-to-know principle in self-defeating ways. For his part, the positive collector is reluctant not only to task counterintelligence sources but also to factor in information that does not show his collection in the best light. Hence national systems tend not to take full advantage of their counterintelligence sources. Information acquired from counterintelligence sources is rarely integrated into foreign intelligence collection and analysis. If a system is to exploit its sources fully, counterintelligence analysts have to be tasked to glean the nuggets from counterintelligence sources and to process them so that sources are protected—but so the value of the information is fully exploited. They must then pass the "take" to positive collectors and stand ready to receive feedback and tasks from them and their analysts. No matter how great the temptation, as a rule counterintelligence managers should not send nuggets exclusively to high-level policymakers. Just as in positive collection, there is some benefit to be gained from cross-checking other sources to screen for errors or deception.

Thus counterintelligence analysis has the potential to be a powerful multiplier. It can play a major role in helping counterintelligence managers formulate counterintelligence priorities and programs. It can help investigators, the "gumshoes," make sense of what they learn by picking out fruitful leads from dead ends. Then, when investigation or collection bears fruit, analysis assists managers and operators in determining how best to protect government secrets or exploit a foreign intelligence service.

Counterintelligence Collection

After analysis, the second essential component of counterintelligence is collection, which often takes the form of investigation. Indeed, many counterintelligence practitioners believe their work is little but investigation. Moreover, because investigation is a difficult, sensitive activity, counterintelligence investigators sometimes behave like detectives and jealously guard their "scoops." They tend not to pool information—for good security reasons and not-so-good reasons of parochial self-interest. As we have seen, this proclivity and the attitudes behind it do not make for first-class national counterintelligence.

Counterintelligence investigation tends to be more productive when it focuses on targets already identified as suspect by analysis. Focused collection, in turn, provides better, sometimes superior, information to analysts. In the postwar era, senior American counterintelligence managers have recognized this in fits and starts. But until the late 1980s it was not widely accepted at the most senior levels. Even then, some were more enthusiastic about focused, analytically driven collection than others. But even if the top management recognizes the need for this sort of collection, it is not easy to change the natural bent of investigators, who are at heart interviewers and people handlers. Rarely do investigators spend their time and energy reading and consulting with "unrealistic intellectuals," as they tend to think of them. It is not easy to mix two radically different professional cultures, but in this area of counterintelligence, interaction would be helpful.

Integration of Sources

In addition to more, and more focused, analysis, investigators benefit from the integration or sharing of diverse collection methods and sources. The counterintelligence community in democracies is fragmented in part by tradition and in part to keep any single group or entity from gaining control of government. But there are serious disadvantages to fragmentation. These could be overcome to a large extent by establishing all-source collection programs and coordinated priorities, and by training practitioners in diverse collection disciplines to work together.

Integration of human and technical collection is an obvious example. Imagery and sigint can be brought to bear on counterintelligence as on positive intelligence. One of the best illustrations is in the evolution of British counterintelligence. Peter Wright, the scientist with Britain's

MI5, describes how in the postwar era he gradually persuaded his operational and essentially humint counterintelligence colleagues to take advantage of technological and scientific thinking to make case officers more efficient. Among many examples cited by Wright is that the Soviets were able to exploit MI5 surveillance communication frequencies to neutralize British surveillance, while the British could use the same radio frequencies to identify KGB activity.[17] Fiction writers such as Tom Clancy may be exaggerating current U.S. technical capabilities and their integration with human sources, but several of his novels illustrate what can be accomplished when one is seeking to identify foreign spies, terrorists, and drug dealers. In *Patriot Games*, Clancy shows human agents providing one piece of the puzzle, satellite imagery another piece, and open sources still a third; then his hero—an analyst—puts them all together.

When counterintelligence collection integrates information from foreign and domestic operations, there can be significant benefits. Sometimes MI5 and MI6, or the CIA and the FBI, have shared information or collaborated on joint collection operations. But in the global environment of the late twentieth century—a world of economic interdependence, increasingly open borders, and the easy transfer of people, money, knowledge, and technology—broad-reaching investigation is more important than ever. In the 1990s it is routine to spot and assess an agent in one country and recruit and meet him in another. Watching foreign intelligence operatives in one country alone may not reap much reward, for they can easily slip through the cracks and vanish forever.

Countries obviously do not have the same counterintelligence capabilities or advantages abroad that they enjoy at home, but this limitation can be overcome to some extent by integrating technical and human techniques and open and secret sources, and by concentrating analysis on promising avenues of investigation. Imagine a foreign intelligence service seeking to identify American operatives and their agents. Should all known CIA offices in the United States and abroad be watched? All Americans traveling abroad? This would be a daunting, prohibitively expensive task. Instead, the foreign service would try to identify U.S. intelligence priorities through analysis and collection; assess what opportunities U.S. intelligence has to obtain the secrets it wants; determine the CIA's modus operandi and any patterns that it might exhibit; and finally, integrate and concentrate all collection capabilities on personnel and techniques likely to be employed in pursuit of U.S. intelligence goals.

The value of integrating open and secret sources is clear, and from time to time the effort is made. But it involves reading the esoteric writing of foreign political, economic, and military leaders. With the pressing day-to-day concerns, it is difficult for most counterintelligence managers and case officers to find time or opportunity to expand their professional knowledge base in this way. Further, counterintelligence officers have a more pronounced tendency than most to socialize or exchange views almost exclusively with their colleagues. Rarely do they spend time with nonintelligence specialists working on the same subject, for example, Iranian statecraft or nuclear proliferation. This can be attributed in part to security considerations, but it is also a natural tendency of professionals in an esoteric discipline—and this is by no means limited to counterintelligence professionals. Moreover, like other professionals, counterintelligence managers and case officers are busy—too busy to prevent valuable sources from slipping away. For this reason, if no other, they would benefit from more use of open sources.

Collection from Open Sources

In the future, counterintelligence managers will have to ensure that their services are blending open and secret sources. Some believe that counterintelligence collection has little to gain from studying open source literature—newspapers, journals, the slogans and rhetoric of demonstrators. Some intelligence officers even scoff at their colleagues who study the minutiae of political groups, or case histories, in a search for clues about the current and future behavior of secret services or terrorist groups. Many, if not most, operators prefer to rely on clandestine sources—wiretaps, phone intercepts, and penetration of foreign services. But to zero in on these techniques to the exclusion of open sources is to miss a significant opportunity to reconstruct the priorities and thinking and to understand the techniques of foreign intelligence operatives.

How, for example, would the United States ascertain which specific American technologies hostile services may be seeking? Perhaps by looking where the services themselves look, at one of the best open sources on new technology, the magazine *Aviation Week and Space Technology*. During the cold war, the Soviet embassy in Washington had a number of subscriptions to *Aviation Week*. A team of translators awaited each new issue and sped the results to Moscow, where the KGB and GRU and other intelligence services pored over the publication. If *Aviation Week* reported a particular industrial laboratory as the site of a new discovery, then the Soviet Academy of Sciences or a Soviet "scientific attaché" might well request meetings with Americans working on the premises. Nor would it be out of the ordinary for the Soviet sister-cities organization to suggest to its American counterpart that an arrangement between the American city where the lab was located and a small Soviet city might foster American-Soviet friendship. During the cold war, this pattern of collection would have produced many counterintelligence leads.

Open sources can also be useful in anticipating the direction of foreign covert action or, to use the Russian term, "active measures" programs. For years, intelligence services in the United States, Britain, France, and West Germany tried to find out how the CPSU and the KGB were attempting to discredit the United States and reduce its influence on the Eurasian continent, a Soviet priority since the end of World War II.[18] One of the major Soviet techniques was to draw on European and American agents of influence in the Western Communist parties, or in international fronts such as the World Peace Council and the World Federation of Trade Unions. To direct and fund these organizations of influence, Moscow maintained a relatively large apparatus of people and publications in the Soviet Union and at locations throughout the world. According to many former participants, after secretly deciding what specific themes and tactics to employ in a given year, the CPSU would send out its instructions in written and oral forms through the KGB and the international department of the CPSU. They, in turn, transmitted the instructions and resources to Western Communist parties and fronts. Usually it took some time, perhaps several months, for Moscow's instructions to filter out to the main organs of the apparatus. A primary method of transmitting the secret instructions was through publications of the international department, the parties themselves, and the fronts. By carefully reading these publications, knowledgeable observers were able to detect many of Moscow's covert action priorities and the techniques for implementing them. Today, similar efforts could be made to understand and anticipate, for example, Libyan or Iranian programs.[19]

Clandestine technical and humint sources can be used to confirm this kind of special "take" from open sources—and open sources can be used to confirm the information from clandestine sources. Open sources have been used this way in the past, sometimes with great effect. In 1945, Ben Mandel was a consultant to the U.S. Department of State's tiny section concerned with international Communism, EUR-X.[20] Reading through declarations of key foreign Communist leaders, Mandel noticed that the April 1945 issue of the French Communist

Party monthly *Cahiers du Communisme* contained a sharp attack on the leadership of the American Communist movement. The author was Jacques Duclos, a leader of the French Communist Party and member of the executive committee of the Comintern, the Soviet-controlled international of Communist parties. (Stalin had supposedly dissolved the Comintern in 1943 to foster an image of cooperation between the Communist and non-Communist world.) Mandel, who knew that Duclos had close ties to Moscow, reasoned that the article in all likelihood reflected a basic shift in its position with regard to the West. Duclos complained that American Communists were too soft on capitalism and on President Roosevelt's foreign policy, and he maintained that relations between the Communist world and the West were going to worsen. And so they did, in 1947. But in 1945 when his article appeared, the euphoria of wartime collaboration between the West and the Soviet Union was still strong. The United Nations was on the verge of drafting its charter in San Francisco, and the Nazis were heading toward final defeat. Aside from the observations of a few senior U.S. officials, among them Ambassador Averell Harriman, that Stalin was becoming more difficult, there were few overt or covert signs that the cold war would resume in earnest.

Mandel brought the article to the attention of his chief, Ray Murphy, who in turn tried to bring it to the attention of others. One of the few organizations in Washington interested in the article during that optimistic spring was the American Federation of Labor. In 1944 the AFL had set up the Free Trade Union Committee to continue Samuel Gompers's founding tradition of helping democratic union leaders who resisted all forms of dictatorship. The secretary of the committee was Jay Lovestone, a former head of the CPUSA who had known Duclos. Lovestone immediately recognized the significance of Duclos's article. He forwarded it to AFL president William Green and AFL secretary-treasurer George Meany. The AFL leadership was then apprised of what was pending, but still there remained few in Washington who believed that an intensive cold war was about to begin.[21] Overt "collecting"—subscribing to foreign theoretical journals, translating them, and reading them—can thus alert officials to change or continuity, which can be checked against other sources. But those officials have to be receptive to avail themselves of these opportunities.

Open sources are also helpful in counterterrorism. They can be used to anticipate circumstances likely to trigger an attack as well as to suggest what form it might take. They may even help identify the potential perpetrators of an attack. One French specialist and a Belgian police official describe how, in the 1980s, they anticipated the moves of Action Directe (France) and Fighting Communist Cells (Belgium) by carefully reading and analyzing their "strategic resolutions" (not the short factual communiqués but the long texts, ten to forty pages, with deadly boring Marxist-Leninist analyses). By understanding what was written—the equivalent of translating a foreign language—they were able to anticipate the terrorists' moves. The authors point out that analysis of the writing of groups such as the Irish Republican Army and of some Islamists yields important insights into their thinking and strategy.[22]

Another proponent of the use of open sources served for many years as a congressional investigator and later as a U.S. Information Agency official and scholar. Herbert Romerstein mentions specific murders and bank robberies that took place in the United States and that might have been prevented if the FBI had been reading specific open source publications in which people close to the terrorist perpetrators described their motives in detail and hinted broadly at the targets. Months later the FBI still did not know the motive for the murders.[23]

Open sources can facilitate counterintelligence recruitment by shedding light on the mind-set of a potential recruit. A case officer with detailed knowledge of the ideology of, and the ideological fissures inside, an organization may persuade a potential recruit that he understands his concerns. Indeed, in the previously cited case of CPSU official Boris Ponomarev's friend, recruited from inside a Western Communist Party in the 1950s, the fact that the handlers had information on trends inside the party (some of which was obtained from other agents, some from open sources) is what persuaded him to become an agent. He did not turn for money or excitement, but rather because he was unhappy about the direction of the international Communist movement. Western counterintelligence operators, aware of his disaffection, "worked" the recruit to keep him from leaving the party and then helped boost him high in its ranks.

Similarly, by keeping track of front groups and other types of organizations' activities through publications, counterintelligence specialists can learn of impending visits of foreign delegations (which include intelligence officers) to key installations or to people of interest to them. This tips off the counterintelligence service, which may be interested in the presence of a foreign intelligence officer in a particular place at a particular time, where he or she can be watched, assessed, and perhaps considered for recruitment.

Clandestine Collection from Human Sources

The most important counterintelligence information results from the integration of open source material with information gained from *secret* human and technical sources.

Penetrating an adversary's intelligence service, especially the counterintelligence units, is one of the most valuable counterintelligence collection techniques. Often it is also notoriously difficult. For example, if the United States had successfully penetrated KGB counterintelligence, Aldrich Ames would probably have been caught within months, if not a year or two. Intelligence services are usually on the lookout for their own weak spots, and they have a whole array of security procedures to combat penetration. Nevertheless, intelligence services do sometimes manage to scale the wall of security and run agents inside other services. A high-level penetration long predating Ames is Heinze Felfe, a senior West German Bundesnachrichtendienst (BND) officer in the late 1950s responsible for counterintelligence operations against the Soviets in East Germany. Felfe was actually a KGB mole who kept the Soviets informed of West German and American interests and operations and fed disinformation to the BND and CIA.[24]

One penetration technique is to plant junior officers inside a service and watch them rise. This is most successful when vetting procedures are slack, as exemplified by the case of the Soviet "Cambridge Comintern" (Kim Philby, Anthony Blunt, Guy Burgess, John Cairncross, and Donald Maclean) hired by British intelligence during World War II.[25] The case of Larry Wu-Tai Chin was mentioned earlier. Chin was the Chinese Communist plant who began work as a U.S. Army translator in 1943 and went on to the CIA as a translator who had access to agent reports. Eventually caught, in 1986 he was convicted of selling classified documents to China for over thirty years. And then there is the case of Karl Koecher, a trained Czech illegal, who was able to get hired as a CIA translator in 1973 after passing a polygraph and background investigation.[26]

Although recruiting a foreign intelligence officer differs only slightly from recruiting a nonintelligence officer, it is more difficult. If the target is an officer of an adversary service, he will be very guarded, because he knows he is being assessed and he is familiar with recruitment techniques. He is better able than a nonintelligence officer to avoid the web spun by recruiters. He knows not to accept "gifts" or sign "reports" for foreigners, and to report all meetings or contacts with nationals of adversary countries—especially those operating under official cover. Of course, he may stumble, succumb to financial temptation, or seek revenge against his service or his government—the apparent motives of CIA officer Aldrich Ames. Human beings are vulnerable. Moreover, skilled recruiters specialize in spotting such weaknesses. This is simpler to do in the recruiter's own country—where without too much trouble he can develop "access agents" and monitor movements and telephone calls—and much more difficult in the potential recruit's own country.

A Western counterintelligence officer described in an interview how a foreign intelligence officer was once recruited by a Western country's service. The service surrounded the target even when he was not at work. His telephone and car were bugged. His neighbors were asked to cooperate. The target's social life was monopolized by access agents or full-time counterintelligence officers. The service even went so far as to charter a yacht because the target liked to sail. A recruiter then befriended the target and made the boat available to him on weekends. The owner of the boat hosted parties on the vessel where every guest except the target was an intelligence officer or someone connected to the recruiter's service. Eventually the man succumbed to this hands-on treatment and became an agent.[27]

Foreign intelligence services will often look for new recruits among those perceived as most vulnerable. These may be lower-ranking code clerks, couriers, or secretaries, who, at lower salaries and with less prestige, are often more susceptible to money offers or psychological recruitment than senior officers. The East German HVA (the foreign intelligence component of the Ministry of State Security), one of the most effective intelligence services of the twentieth century, specialized in recruiting agents from (and planting them in) West German intelligence agencies, many of whom came from the most junior positions. Moscow too enjoyed successes in this area. One example was Jack Dunlap, a U.S. Army sergeant assigned to the NSA in 1958, first as a chauffeur for its chief of staff, then as a clerk-messenger. Because of, rather than in spite of, his low rank, Dunlap was in a position to sell highly classified information from all areas of his agency. Recruited sometime in 1960 by Moscow, Dunlap was caught when he left the Army and applied to the NSA as a civilian employee, for which he had to undergo a polygraph examination.[28]

Foreign intelligence services know that potential recruits may be less guarded in their actions abroad than on their home turf. This can be exploited by using a third country for the initial recruitment. Sharon Scranage, a young American CIA operations support assistant at the

CIA station in Ghana in the early 1980s, was recruited for Ghana by her lover, Michael A. Soussoudis, a relative of the Ghanaian leader.[29] Beneficiaries of the Scranage recruitment, in addition to the Ghanaians, were the Cubans and the East Germans, who helped train the Ghanaian service. When Scranage returned to the CIA in Washington and was assigned to other subjects, her lover was dispatched to Washington to obtain from her information that would have aided Soviet bloc interests. Instead she was caught and jailed.

Foreign intelligence officers can also be recruited through liaison relationships. In this sort of relationship there is a great deal of contact between individuals from the two services. Officers in liaison relationships socialize regularly and work on common projects against common adversaries, circumstances ripe for recruiting. While liaison officers are usually warned to be cautious, less caution may be exercised when dealing with a "friendly" service than with a hostile one.

In 1954, for example, an NSA cryptologist, Joseph Peterson, was arrested for passing sensitive communications intelligence (comint) information to the Dutch. During World War II, Peterson had worked closely with two Dutch cryptologists on Japanese diplomatic codes. After the war, the United States and the Netherlands ended their cryptological liaison, but Peterson continued feeding them information that included details of American success in breaking Dutch codes.[30] As for the United States, it has used liaison to court and develop penetrations of other services. In the early 1960s the French station chief in Washington, Philippe de Vosjoli, came to share the views of the CIA over those of his own service. After a while, he chose to resign from the French foreign intelligence service and live in the United States.[31] Another example may be Nazar Haro, the former head of the Mexican security service, who in the 1970s reportedly participated in a liaison relationship with the United States.[32]

This technique may sound relatively straightforward, but it has frequently been botched—usually because recruiters have weak counterintelligence skills. Their assessment of the target is poor, their knowledge of the target's service is limited, or they fall into a trap set by the service they are trying to penetrate. One informative case study is based on a Soviet GRU attempt to secure a Mirage jet through a suborned (but doubled) Lebanese pilot.[33] Another example was a failed attempt by the CIA to recruit Singapore intelligence officers.[34] They were led on by the Singapore security service, entrapped, and embarrassed.

Another successful way of recruiting foreign intelligence personnel is to infiltrate political support groups or fronts sympathetic to the politics of the foreign service. Many foreign services looking for recruits, notably the Soviets from the 1920s on, have hired selected sympathizers. When the individual performs well, he or she rises to a position equivalent to that of an operative in the foreign service. He or she may serve as a recruiter, develop subagents, and handle them for the foreign service. This kind of recruitment becomes almost as valuable as a foreign intelligence officer himself.

This tactic is useful in infiltrating terrorist organizations, that is, planting or recruiting someone inside a terrorist support group. Needless to say, this is a dangerous profession. The terrorists who actually plan the killing and the bombing observe the behavior of those who claim to support them, and on the basis of their observations decide which, if any, supporters they wish to include in their bloody projects. It can be relatively easy to penetrate a nascent movement or organization, as the French found in Algeria in 1959, and the United States found when it penetrated Students for a Democratic Society and various Communist and African-American groups in the 1960s and 1970s. As organizations mature, however, penetration becomes more difficult. The terrorist organization will not easily accept unknowns into its inner circle. It may demand loyalty tests, such as committing a murder, to which a plant will usually not submit. Patience may ultimately pay off, but many societies want fast results (and, of course, no involvement in criminal acts). Given these constraints, the generally preferred technique is to recruit someone already inside a terrorist organization.

An example of a successful recruit on the edge of a foreign service concerns a friend to senior CPSU leaders in the 1950s. A Western intelligence service became aware of the fact that a Communist living in a Western country was disillusioned with the CPSU and cultivated him. Like many others once loyal to the CPSU, he decided for political reasons to turn on it. The man never became a KGB officer, but the KGB entrusted him with some of its most sensitive communications equipment. He often met with KGB officers and was given large sums—millions over the years—to pass to local Communist parties as well as to other individuals and groups who supported specific Soviet objectives but who were not openly Communist. For decades, the man was also in contact with Western counterintelligence handlers almost every day. He was able to provide the West with detailed knowledge of KGB methods and techniques, knowledge that was invaluable in identifying and keeping track of KGB officers, their agents, and their active measures programs.

Defectors

Some of the most valuable counterintelligence human sources are volunteers from other services, that is, defectors, often referred to as walk-ins. They present tremendous opportunities—and a challenge. To take full advantage of the potential of defectors, they must be extremely well handled.

A well-documented illustration of good handling is that of Paul Thümmel, a German Abwehr (Nazi military intelligence) officer based in Dresden. One morning in March 1937, a blue envelope arrived on the desk of Frantisek Moravec, the chief of Czech military intelligence. The letter, mailed in Czechoslovakia, listed the kind of information that the sender could provide on the buildup of the German army on the Saxon border, on German defenses, on Sudeten Germans receiving covert support from the Nazis, and on German espionage in Czechoslovakia. The writer wanted what was then the fairly large sum of 100,000 Reichsmarks (approximately $70,000 in today's dollars).[35] Thümmel told the Czechs that he was opposed to the Nazis—as was his Serbian mistress—and that he needed money. As agent A-54, he provided first-rate positive and counterintelligence information from 1937 until he was first arrested by the Gestapo in 1941. He was released but rearrested some months later, and is believed to have been executed toward the end of the war. Although Thümmel occasionally supplied inaccurate analysis and tips, several scholars who have examined the records believe he was an excellent source. Indeed, from the time the Czech government was established in London (after the Nazis took over Czechoslovakia) until the early stages of the war, A-54 was regarded as the single best intelligence source the British had (through the Czechs).[36]

Another successful case of a well-handled walk-in, Pytor Popov, is reported in *Mole*, written by William Hood. Hood was one of the case officers who ran Popov, a GRU officer, after he wrote a letter volunteering his services to U.S. intelligence in November 1952. At first Popov provided details of the KGB and GRU order of battle, of GRU methods, and of some agents. Washington wanted him to report as well on Soviet foreign policy and political developments, but these were not his forte. According to Hood, his best intelligence reports were . . . in the military field—data he gleaned from the reserve officers' course he regularly attended and information elicited from high ranking officers stationed with the Soviet Central Group of Forces in East Germany. . . . Of less national importance than the military intelligence Popov was delivering but of great interest were his reports on the illegal support section. Never before had any Western service penetrated so deeply into the nerve center of Soviet secret operations. . . .

[The agent's reports] on GRU illegal agents were unique; there was nothing they could be compared with. At the time, Popov's counterintelligence reports were assayed as being "priceless."[37]

Based on Hood's account, Popov was handled well, but he made some mistakes that apparently led to his capture and execution.

Michael John Bettaney, an employee of MI5 who offered himself to the Soviets, did not succeed. At midnight on April 3, 1983, Bettaney personally delivered a letter to the residence of Arkady Grouk, whom Bettaney believed to be a KGB officer. In the letter, Bettaney volunteered his services, provided secret information on MI5 operations against the KGB, and suggested the Soviets reply through a dead letter box. Bettaney made three attempts in all, to no avail. He continued to collect MI5 secrets, which if passed on "would have put lives in danger," but before this could happen Bettaney was arrested, and in April 1984 he was convicted of offenses against Britain's Official Secrets Act.[38] It is unclear why the KGB rejected Bettaney's services and just how he was caught. But there is speculation that a senior KGB officer, Oleg Gordievsky, who was a British agent and had risen to become the deputy KGB resident in London, persuaded his KGB colleagues that Bettaney was an attempted MI5 plant and at the same time alerted MI5 to his treason.

How does a service handle a walk-in properly? Security is the first concern; the intelligence service must guard the defector's identity from within and without. He must not be overly taxed with missions that could lead to his discovery. He must be kept satisfied, both psychologically and materially, lest he return to his original service—and be used by it for deception. Finally, an extraction plan must be in place for the walk-in in case he is detected.

Despite the failure in the Bettaney case, the KGB handled its penetrations of British intelligence in model fashion during World War II and afterward, and has repeated that performance in more recent cases—Geoffrey Prime in Britain[39] and John Walker and Aldrich Ames in the United States. It appears, at least, to have treated several other walk-ins well in the 1970s and early 1980s: the NSA's Ronald Pelton, who gave away valuable U.S. methods to intercept Soviet communications, and Edward Lee Howard, who while being trained as a CIA case officer for the Moscow station gave away agents' identities and CIA techniques.

Handling walk-ins is not much different from handling positive collection agents. If the walk-in's own service is not making a special effort to watch its own intelligence officers, or if its tradecraft and security practices are sloppy, handling is a great deal easier. As we have noted, in World War II the British hired new personnel without taking proper security precautions. More recently, the Soviets were able to meet their British and American volunteers—Geoffrey Prime, John Walker, Christopher Boyce, Andrew Daulton Lee, and Ronald Pelton—with almost carefree abandon in Austria and Mexico City. Indeed, Pelton apparently stayed in the Soviet embassy compound in Vienna on one of his trips, and Norwegian Foreign Office official Arne Treholt was seen relaxing with his Soviet handlers in the same city.

For the purposes of counterintelligence (and other types of intelligence), the best defector is what is sometimes called a defector-in-place. He cannot risk extensive contact with his new service. While his information is regular and up-to-date, his situation limits debriefing and continuing assessment. The longer he remains in a position of trust, the more valuable he becomes. The former Romanian intelligence chief Ion Mihai Pacepa first visited the U.S. embassy in Bonn in early 1978 to announce that he wanted to defect. He did not actually do so until July of the same year and thus was able to gather even more valuable material than if he had defected earlier.[40]

Defection is not necessarily a passive event inspired by personal circumstance alone. An intelligence service can take offensive action to induce defection, for example by assessing which foreign intelligence officers have a political or personal propensity to change sides and then encouraging and facilitating their "move." One of the best-documented cases is that of Vladimir Mikhailovich Petrov, the KGB temporary resident in Australia who defected with his wife, Evdokia, also a KGB officer, in 1954. The Australian Security Intelligence Organization had managed to place one of its agents close to the Petrovs, and he encouraged and assisted in their defection.[41] The couple then provided a gold mine of information—one of the most important counterintelligence sources for the West in the mid-1950s.

A defector is particularly valuable just after he "comes in from the cold," at which time he is able to identify many of his former colleagues around the world, their operations, and sometimes even their agents—particularly his former service's agents in the newly adopted country. This information is extremely time-sensitive. The security service will need to act on it immediately to catch spies who may flee when the old service realizes that one of its officers has defected. Once the defector starts giving names, places, dates, and other information that can be used to identify agents, the service to which he has defected starts to neutralize hostile activities against itself and its allies. Intelligence services thus routinely withhold news of defections.

The immediate value of information should not obscure the potential value of defectors over the long term. They may be a treasure trove of knowledge on the modus operandi and ethos of their former service, providing information to analysts trying to understand how a foreign service operates—its strengths and weaknesses—and how these can be exploited. For example, information on the training programs of his former service may be revealing. What were the cover devices, the successful operations, put forward in training as classic? If several generations of officers have been taught that a particular type of operation is successful, it is likely that the new generation of recruits will receive the same lesson. According to defectors such as former KGB officer Ilya Dzhirkvelov, KGB personnel were schooled in political and intelligence deception operations such as the notorious and highly successful Trust in the 1920s. Hence it was not surprising that the KGB and the services it trained, such as the Polish and the Albanian, used the same trick of creating false opposition movements decade after decade during the cold war.[42]

Similarly, a KGB defector who worked with the Soviet press agency TASS would know which of the scores of TASS posts were usually reserved for KGB officers. He also would know methods of distinguishing KGB officers from regular correspondents, information that would help Western intelligence in the future focus its attention on KGB officers likely to be under TASS cover.

Yet many defectors to the West have pointed out that after their initial debriefing for the immediate "hot stuff," counterintelligence personnel showed relatively little interest in their broader knowledge of their own services. From the moment a defector indicates he or she wants to change sides, a defector needs attention—and many intelligence services are reluctant to provide it. At the outset, a defector's good faith needs to be checked. Is he who he says he is, genuine, or simply a plant sent to disinform and confuse? Then there is bargaining over the terms of his new life, and arranging for safe passage from the old country to the new. What does the defector want in exchange for cooperation? This is an important and delicate question. If it is not answered and the defector is poorly handled, the new service may find itself with a useless and perhaps ultimately counterproductive asset should he become disgruntled. What if he decides to reveal the identities of the agents and the modus operandi of his temporarily adopted service, denouncing it in a press conference for kidnapping and "terrorism," as several Russians such as Oleg Bitov and Vitali Yurchenko did in the 1980s? One of the few senior CIA officers who has written about the subject, Tom Polgar, says that many defectors change their minds and want to go home again. The defector, he comments, is "welcomed by Western intelligence services with clear recognition that the costs of handling and resettling [him] . . . can be high; in money, manpower, administrative inconvenience, and potential embarrassment should the erstwhile defector change his mind or turn out to be something quite different from what he was thought to have been."[43]

Arranging the extraction of a defector-in-place is the stuff of spy fiction. If the defector is allowed to travel outside his native country, this may be relatively easy, though sometimes hair-raising. More daring and risky is an escape from within the defector's home country. Victor Sheymov, a KGB Eighth Chief Directorate (communications) officer, was smuggled out of Moscow in 1980 with his wife and child. He purposely left clues in his apartment to suggest the whole family was dead. Sheymov explains that "the trick wasn't just to leave. The trick was to make it so the KGB would be led to think something had happened to me, that perhaps I was dead." Sheymov says the key to the plan was to "preview in your mind the KGB's investigation. If you know how it is done, you have a chance."[44] In 1990, following the exposure of his story, Moscow called the smuggling out of Sheymov's family "a subversive action by U.S. intelligence . . . a gross violation of rules of international law . . . in fact, an act of state terrorism."[45]

Sometimes defection can be much more complicated—as when in the early 1980s the French government allowed a potential Romanian defector to fake the assassination of a Romanian dissident in Paris. The purpose of the drama was to convince the Romanian Communist leadership of the defector's trustworthiness so that it would allow his family to join him in France. The family could then defect together. French counterintelligence cooperated and apparently the plan worked.[46]

Perhaps the hardest aspect of handling defectors, particularly politically oriented intelligence officers, is permanent resettlement. Most defectors are anxious to start a new life. They are given new identities and a lump sum in cash, and are set up in a new life. Many adjust well. Others never quite manage to. They may have been important figures in their old life, and comparatively well off. In their adopted society they are anonymous, not poor but not very well off, and they have to start new careers at a time when many begin thinking of retirement. They are cut off from old friends and family, and they are culturally isolated (particularly if they are concerned about their safety). Sometimes they become homesick. Some suffer from personal problems that may have been manifest before they arrived but that intensify in the new environment. Sometimes they are not trusted by their new service, and not even consulted when they could be helpful.

One way to keep defectors from returning to their native land or redefecting is to convince them that they can continue to contribute to the security of their new home. This has been done, on occasion, by finding defectors jobs in government or the private sector where they can write, speak, teach, and interact with scholars, journalists, and government officials who may be delighted to meet them. However, controllers or handlers are often reluctant to "allow" their "charges" these contacts lest it jeopardize their security.

Counterintelligence collection that involves seeding and recruiting in adversary intelligence services and handling and inducing defections is an especially attractive area of intelligence in a democracy. The government is not after its own citizens; rather, it is targeting foreign intelligence officers and services that are usually breaking the laws of the democracy, if not seeking to undermine it completely.

Physical Surveillance

Another important type of counterintelligence collection is the investigation and surveillance of foreign intelligence operators and their contacts around the world. As noted already, it is usually much easier to conduct investigations and surveillance in one's own country, much more difficult in a third country where local police and security services may not allow foreign intelligence officers to monitor the behavior of other services, and most difficult against a foreign service on its own territory.

The first priority is to identify hostile intelligence officers. One or more defectors may have identified a person as a former colleague. Analysts may have established a pattern or a profile of how intelligence officers differ from diplomats. Hence all the counterintelligence collectors have to do is gather a few facts about a given individual to see if he or she fits the profile. In the trade, this process is known as "making" the target. Making or unmaking new diplomats is a straightforward process. Making people under serious cover is an art unto itself.

The next priority is to watch activities of known or suspected intelligence officers. Given enough counterintelligence personnel and resources, this is not difficult. A blanket of surveillance over all suspects produces facts that speak for themselves. Thus it is not surprising that intelligence services such as the KGB and the Cuban and Chinese services, which have enormous manpower resources, are adept at this sort of work, while democracies, less willing to maintain thousands upon thousands of agents and officers, are less so. This is why it is important for services in democracies to seek guidance through analysis and by integrating open and secret collection techniques; but these services still need some surveillance capability.

It takes a bare minimum of six people and three cars just to follow one person twenty-four hours a day—overtly. To do covert surveillance around the clock requires at least twenty-four people and twelve cars. Covert surveillance at home, where the team knows the streets and countryside, secures the cooperation of local inhabitants, and blends in with the local population, is difficult enough; in a foreign country it is obviously much more demanding. Moreover, an adept professional is able to elude even good professional surveillance. He will lose his tail if he really wants to—usually confirming, however, that he is indeed "dirty."

Although surveillance of personnel and establishments may be a useful place to begin sniffing out foreign intelligence contacts, it is far from enough. Consider that in a single day in Washington, D.C., several hundred Americans and foreigners enter just one of several dozen foreign facilities known to harbor intelligence services targeting U.S. secrets: tourists seeking visas, journalists, scholars, businessmen with appointments, foreign diplomats consulting with their counterparts. A few, a very few each year, are "walk-ins" volunteering important information to foreign governments (such as Edward Lee Howard, Ronald Pelton, and John Walker at the Soviet embassy in the 1960s, 1970s, and 1980s) or otherwise signaling their willingness to collaborate in active measures. Most services, however, are reluctant to meet recruited agents in the embassy. Those who have walked in, and whom the service believes to be potentially valuable agents, can be put in the trunk of a diplomat's car and smuggled out without attracting the attention of the local security service—as was done with Pelton and Walker in the Soviets' Washington embassy. Thus photographing the traffic in and out of a foreign embassy may not provide much information in itself. Technical devices—such as bugs, wiretaps, audiovisual surveillance cameras, and chemical tracking devices planted in the cars, apartments, and diplomatic establishments used by foreign intelligence services—can be more helpful.[47]

In addition to trailing hostile intelligence personnel, counterintelligence collectors often keep an eye on the people and places that hostile services may be trying to penetrate. Again they need to be told where to look—which technologies and what type of individual a foreign government may be targeting. For example, counterintelligence operators are sometimes assigned to be on the lookout for unusual relationships between foreigners and people who have access to particular technology, or certain journalists or trade union leaders. These individuals in turn might be notified that they have been targeted by foreigners—diplomats or nondiplomatic personnel—to be recruited for active measures purposes.

In a democracy, some private citizens regard any questioning or contacts with counterintelligence, however benign, as an intrusion by the government into their private lives. They may refuse to answer questions or meet with counterintelligence personnel. Certainly those who have wittingly entered into a clandestine relationship with foreigners have an incentive to answer untruthfully. Others may believe that it is better to confess to a relationship, particularly if they have not committed a crime. Or, as part of an effort to redeem any transgressions, they may confess and offer to help their government. In some cases a person has not yet had contact with a foreign "diplomat"; simply inquiring about the proposed meeting may alert him to danger and may help prevent a recruitment.

Access Agents

Another method of identifying and keeping track of suspected intelligence personnel is to recruit people close to suspects, known in the jargon as "access agents." Counterintelligence operators can seek out secretaries, janitors, chauffeurs, interpreters, neighbors, or friends and request that they pass on information about the target's predilections and behavior. Although citizens in democracies do not have to cooperate with their counterintelligence service, many are quite willing to do so. It is seldom difficult to recruit access agents in a free society—provided the service tries.

If a trained counterintelligence recruiter who goes underground manages to pass himself off as an access agent, he can do far more than that.[48] The undercover recruiter can not only better assess his prey, he can pick the exact time the target is most vulnerable. Even if he is rebuffed—if, for example, the target is not interested—the counterintelligence professional may be able to bring it off in a way that does not reveal that he even tried, for example, by asking hypothetical questions. Moreover, if the recruiter learns that the target would be more susceptible to an official approach, he might arrange for such an approach to be made without alerting the target to the undercover officer's identity.

Double Agents

The double agent is one of the most important tools for investigation and exploitation. As noted earlier, during the cold war the United States sometimes used Americans who posed as spies for the Soviet bloc to uncover the identities of Soviet bloc intelligence officers, their taskings, and their patterns of activity. On the whole, however, the United States and some other services have preferred to use double agents for relatively short-term purposes—to learn the techniques (tradecraft) and current priorities of adversary services. The service would exploit the double agent and blow an operation to disrupt the foreign service. This method has its merits. Moreover, short-term operations fit in well with a particular type of bureaucratic culture such as the American intelligence community which, reflecting the larger society it serves, tends to want quick results. At any rate, it is extremely hard to run long-term double-agent operations in an open society where sources and information from agents can be checked and double-checked. To keep an operation going usually means giving away some good information, and hence it may become too costly.

But there are important advantages for collection and exploitation in longer-term double-agent operations. They can be used, for example, to keep a foreign service's positive collectors completely occupied and lull the service into believing it has a whole network of reliable agents and hence does not need to recruit many more. Long-term double agents can also be used to degrade a foreign service, or to feed it credible disinformation as part of a strategic deception. The service that recruits and falls for a long-term double agent will be most reluctant to admit it—even to itself. When their own counterintelligence people express doubts about an agent, the positive collectors will defend their valuable "asset."

The double agent's handlers then have the option of sowing confusion in the adversary's camp. By coordinating the tasking of several double agents, for example, they can add to the adversary's doubts about the first double agent, that is, blow their own agent to create tension inside the service.[49] If the double-agent handlers play their cards well, they may be able to take advantage of exposing one long-term double agent by using another long-term double agent or penetration to do the exposing. Inside the adversary service, this will enhance the career of the second, as he will be seen as a clever and courageous professional who was willing to stand up against prevailing wisdom. These, of course, are complicated and difficult games. But if counterintelligence managers know enough about the mind-set of their adversaries, and have a plan, they can use long-term double-agent assets to seriously disrupt another service.

Liaison

Counterintelligence managers can also liaise with foreign intelligence services to obtain information. Sometimes this works well. During the cold war the Soviet government apparently had an extensive network of liaison. And during World War II and the cold war, when they had major common and few conflicting interests, the United States and various Western services such as Britain's, France's, and Australia's exchanged biographic information and analysis on the modi operandi of their principal adversaries. For example, the former head of the French internal security service, Marcel Chalet, and the former French station chief in Washington, Philippe de Vosjoli, describe how Anatoliy Golitsyn's information about Soviet penetration led to the discovery that the top echelon of the French government and the French intelligence services were penetrated in the 1960s.[50]

More rarely, services will exchange information on their recruitment from or penetration of a foreign service. Even when services are close, such information is regarded as so precious and sensitive that it is reluctantly, and then only barely, shared within the originating intelligence community or with the government itself, let alone with foreigners.

Liaison services abroad, if they share common objectives, may tolerate or even facilitate surveillance of suspected foreign intelligence operations on their soil. They may help in setting up observation posts on foreign missions in their countries. They may even offer to conduct physical surveillance in areas where it would be difficult for a foreign surveillance team to operate, perhaps because of the team's obviously foreign appearance.[51]

In wartime, this kind of cooperation can be much more extensive. In South Vietnam, the United States sometimes was intimately involved with its ally's military and police surveillance of and operations against the Vietcong.[52] But there are risks in and costs of using liaison services. There is a quid pro quo—money, equipment, information, and sometimes reciprocal privileges on one's own soil. Furthermore, foreign services have their own interests. They may decide to sell the information they acquire from joint operations to others, perhaps even to the side under surveillance. Or it may be that after a major change in government, the new government, like Russia's in 1992, decides to reveal some of the secrets of the previous regime's liaison relationships. Or another service may be penetrated. Soon after World War II, no foreign service had closer liaison with American counterintelligence than the British—and probably few were more infiltrated by Soviet agents.

Another problem in liaison relationships can be the incompetence of a partner. There is no reason to establish liaison with an intelligence service that is ineffective. In the interwar years, French counterintelligence against the Soviets was inadequate for a variety of reasons, and it would have been useless—indeed, probably detrimental—for another service to liaise with the French at this time.[53] Liaison relations must be undertaken with an eye toward expedience and necessity, rather than mere diplomacy or convenience.

It should be noted that circumstances in which there is overwhelming danger from a common enemy and an alliance forms against that enemy, as in World War II and the cold war, are the exception, not the rule. More often, various forms of rivalry and collaboration coexist. Rivals may want to know some of each other's secrets or try covertly to influence each other, while at the same time seeking help through liaison with one another. This complicates counterintelligence collection through liaison, making it less effective. Liaison should be regarded as one of a number of useful collection methods, but it should not be the major avenue for collecting counterintelligence information.

Illegals

In the twentieth century, the dominant players in human intelligence collection, counterintelligence, and covert action increasingly came to be professional officers who enjoyed diplomatic immunity running agents who did not. There were important exceptions to this pattern, and it may well change in the future.

The Soviet Union from the 1920s on and Israel from the 1940s on relied heavily on officers under nonofficial cover, known as illegals. Although illegal intelligence officers are more vulnerable to psychological and physical danger, they are also more difficult for the adversary to identify and neutralize. Most intelligence services are able to fabricate documents or find ways to ensure that their illegals can gain relatively safe admission into target countries. Sometimes even this simple task is mishandled. There are hilarious cases—hilarious to outside observers—of the Germans during World War II sending illegals into Britain who were identified almost immediately, and of Moscow using the same cover for different illegals.[54] In general, though, once an illegal has stepped on shore or across the border, it is not easy to find him or her.

Apart from gathering information from a defector, one proven technique for identifying "unofficial" and illegal intelligence officers is to surveil those intelligence officers in an embassy who support illegals. Many services assign a small number of professionals in legal missions abroad to prepare for the recruitment, training, dispatch, and arrival of illegals, and to service illegals once they go to work. The support officer will, for example, prepare a legend—a false story—and documents for new illegals. If counterintelligence personnel can get just a hint of the name or legend, they will be in a position to trace the new arrival.

In his book *Mole*, William Hood tells how two GRU illegals who operated in the United States in the 1950s were identified. Pytor Popov, the GRU defector-in-place, was assigned to the East German station supporting illegals. Apparently he had helped service a GRU illegal on her way to the United States through Berlin. Popov told the CIA, which in turn told the FBI. The FBI followed her in New York, where she met a man—another illegal who seemed to be her husband. After some weeks under FBI surveillance, the pair vanished. (Some hypothesize that FBI surveillance may have tipped off the KGB that someone in the Soviet illegal support section was a CIA agent, and that this was one reason Popov came under suspicion.)[55]

Officers in charge of supporting illegals are on occasion tasked to pick up reports from illegals, or to provide them with money and letters from home. Surveilling a support officer clandestinely may well lead counterintelligence to the illegal, the way counterintelligence surveillance of intelligence officers can lead to the identification of their agents.

Sometimes illegals are identified through their communications with headquarters. Modern communications technology has made this much less likely. In the days when illegals used high-frequency radio sets, it was possible to identify the approximate locale of the intended receiver. If the counterintelligence service was listening in at the right time, it was often able to pinpoint the location of the transmitter. This happened many times in World War II. It may also have been the way the Syrians caught the Israeli illegal Eli Cohen just before he was to be named to a high post in the Syrian government in 1965. But that technology is obsolete. Agents can now beam a burst transmission straight up to a satellite for relay home. In the future other even simpler and more foolproof methods will be available. Counterintelligence will have to ride on the hope that the illegal makes personal contact with known support officers.

Some illegals expose themselves by recruiting agents, or by somehow arousing suspicion that they are intelligence officers (as may have been the case with Eli Cohen). But the most competent among them behave in ways that arouse little suspicion. They live quiet lives in a foreign country until they are needed, possibly in missions so sensitive that the employer service prefers to use officers with no legal connection to its government.

Or they may be activated to help deny their adversaries crucial information or critical computers at strategic junctures, for example, at the outset of war. Several Western European intelligence services were convinced that the Soviet Union trained scores of KGB and GRU officers to operate illegally in Western Europe in the event of war. Basing his estimate on the revelations of the Polish defector Mroz, Marcel Chalet states there were about one hundred illegals in France alone in the 1970s.[56] Just before the end of the cold war, the Swedish government produced an educational film to show how illegals might operate.[57] In one of the most chilling scenes, a female Spetznaz (a member of KGB or GRU special forces), an illegal, is given a ride by a Swedish woman of about the same age and description. In the course of the drive, the illegal suddenly stabs the woman and assumes her identity and job at a Swedish communications facility. The Spetznaz blows up the facility just before a surprise Soviet attack.

With little contact between support officers and illegal officers in the field, and few mistakes in clandestine tradecraft, it is difficult, in open societies at least, to catch illegals without the skilled analyses discussed earlier, for example, analyzing anomalous behavior or past patterns of operation.

Technical Counterintelligence

One of the great challenges for modern counterintelligence managers is the integration of technical and human operations. Technical and humint operators tend to come from different organizations and cultures. Moreover, most technical collection is positive, and few counterintelligence humint operators know much about it.

The essence of technical counterintelligence collection is learning through technical means what foreign intelligence services see, hear, and sense, what they know about one's own technical means, and how they are using this information. Which targets are foreign intelligence services trying to photograph, either from the ground or from space? Which communications do they seek to intercept? What are their electronic, signals, and communications intelligence capabilities? Additionally, how are foreign services trying to mislead about their capabilities and targets? Just as counterintelligence humint collection seeks to identify and monitor foreign intelligence officers and their agents, technical counterintelligence seeks to learn the priorities and capabilities of foreign technical collection systems.

For example, the United States is now faced with several foreign governments that have space-based platforms. In the future, other governments and even nongovernmental groups will have access to satellite imagery and electronic intercept capability. What are these foreign space satellites photographing every day? What U.S. communications channels are being targeted? What information can foreign intelligence collectors discover by monitoring defense contractors, military posts, and police and government installations? This is a job for skilled counterintelligence. Answering these questions not only bolsters security but also helps choose exactly what information, misleading or otherwise, to expose to a foreign service.

Technical collectors may assist their own counterintelligence humint operators by focusing on the humint capabilities of foreign services. Imagery can reveal a lot about the characteristics of the headquarters of foreign services and the movement of large numbers of various kinds of personnel. Sigint uncovers information about foreign intelligence contacts with offices or personnel at home and abroad. Even if foreign communication cannot be deciphered, message traffic patterns can reveal a lot.

Counterintelligence technical collectors, like humint collectors, benefit a great deal from combining the take from open, humint, and technical sources. An item published in a foreign journal on American technological research can put counterintelligence humint operators on the trail of a possible leak at a particular U.S. research facility. It would also be helpful to know if a foreign service was using its technical systems to photograph that research facility. Or it could be the other way around. The United States might notice foreign satellite interest in a given facility and begin to wonder why. Could there be a humint leak?

The utility of dovetailing open, humint, and technical counterintelligence collection in this way is not self-evident. For years, the United States did little such interdisciplinary work. Each counterintelligence discipline and organization was responsible to itself, each had its own priorities, each decided how to train its personnel and how much of its resource base would be directed to help sister counterintelligence services.

Some services emphasize some aspects of counterintelligence collection to the detriment of others, thus failing to take advantage of integrated collection. Open sources, not usually considered valuable, are rarely mined to the fullest. Some clandestine humint collection techniques are emphasized at the cost of others. In the United States in the 1950s and 1960s, there was some coverage of hostile foreign intelligence abroad, in the 1970s and early 1980s far too little. At almost no time, however, was there adequate coverage of collection by foreign technical systems—or of what Moscow, for example, knew about American technical capabilities. Even when some of this information was collected, it was not usually passed on to counterintelligence humint operators or analysts, let alone to positive analysts or those considering overall policy to influence or manipulate foreign adversaries.

Ideally, counterintelligence managers and operators need to make balanced use of all collection sources, and share and integrate counterintelligence collection. Human or technical means alone are not likely to be adequate. Information about foreign technical capabilities complements humint counterintelligence operations, and vice versa. Information from open sources is also useful to both humint and technical counterintelligence collection. Unless mission control and budget allocations mandate cooperation, joint training and doctrine, and mutual priorities, it is unlikely that the disciplines will be coordinated. In an era of scarce resources, this means that counterintelligence collection managers must lean heavily on analysis, thinking through all available techniques before deploying and integrating their resources.

Exploitation

The fruit of good counterintelligence collection and analysis is exploitation. Knowledge of foreign intelligence not only protects a service's own secrets and plans, it also helps unlock the secrets of others so that they can be manipulated to advantage. As pointed out earlier, effective counterintelligence gives policymakers and intelligence managers a decided advantage and access to further measures for weakening adversaries. Statesmen can choose to be purely defensive, drawing on counterintelligence simply to neutralize foreign intelligence threats. This in itself is helpful, but even more benefit is to be realized from the offensive use of the defense.

Good defense consists of efficiently managing security and countermeasures. *Security* means protecting the service's own secrets—intelligence, military, diplomatic—from unauthorized eyes and ears. As a discipline, security is often separate from *countermeasures*. Security managers tend not to see their work as thwarting a specific foreign service or weakening an adversary. They are not political, and it is not their job to focus on the antics of particular foreign intelligence services. Rather, their job is to ensure that only those who have a genuine need for access to particular secret documents, communications, technology, or buildings have that access, and that records are maintained as to who had access to what. For example, one of the security managers' major concerns is the trustworthiness of people who have access to secrets. They decide who should be given security clearances and what an individual's need-to-know is. These are difficult judgment calls.

Take the issue of who should be cleared to work in a particular agency, or who should have access to the most sensitive type of information. No one, or next to no one, is given access to all of the most sensitive information. Routinely, only those who have been investigated and found reliable, and whose reliability is confirmed by periodic reinvestigation, are allowed access to sensitive information. What should be the criteria for reliability? There is no simple answer. Choices have to be made, and they often prove expensive. Until now, each agency in the United States has answered such questions in its own way, and agencies on the whole have not often accepted each other's clearances. Policymakers and intelligence managers can continue this pattern, or they can insist on more general standards to reduce costs. They have the option of taking these choices out of the hands of security managers at individual agencies. For example, in the United States until the mid-1960s, questions about political reliability and loyalty were important in background investigations. By the 1970s they were deemed out-of-bounds in most agencies. But in the wake of the spy scandals of the 1980s, in which it became apparent that convicted spies such as the Walker-Whitworth ring had little personal loyalty to the United States, such questions resurfaced. Had there been a general, mandatory standard for individual agencies to adhere to, this sort of improvised fluctuation in security practice probably would not have occurred.

The minimum criterion in a background investigation is that a person is actually who he or she claims to be. A life is traced from birth through every change of school, address, and employment, and acquaintances of the subject are interviewed. If this is done properly, it prevents infiltration by first-generation illegals who have a good legend. It doesn't help with second-generation illegals such as Peter Hermann, the son of two KGB illegals. Peter was born in Western Europe, emigrated to the United States at an early age with his parents, and in the 1970s was attending Georgetown University's School of Foreign Service in anticipation of joining the State Department. Anyone checking his record would indeed have found that he was born where he said he was, went to school where he said he did, and so forth.[58] Another minimum criterion is character. Is the person responsible and loyal? Can he or she be expected to safeguard information? What sort of people does the person associate with? If the person abuses drugs or alcohol or engages in petty criminal acts, is he or she likely to behave irresponsibly with state secrets? Again, people who have known the candidate will help answer these questions, and police, tax, credit, and FBI records will be checked.

In U.S. intelligence agencies—as opposed to the White House and the Defense and State departments—major emphasis has come to be placed on polygraph examinations to help determine the accuracy of information the candidate and others have provided. Most foreign intelligence and security services are more skeptical of this method. They believe the polygraph is subjective, that it intrudes too far into a person's private life, that it makes mistakes, and that people can be trained to beat it.[59] In recent years, too, U.S. counterintelligence managers have grown less enthusiastic about the polygraph, but it is still the decisive instrument in the clearance process in intelligence agencies.

The person who fails to convince polygraph operators of his or her honesty is almost never granted a security clearance.

The "box" has its advantages. It does scare people and deters many from lying or misbehaving lest they later have to confess their sins. It does uncover information and deception. And it shields the security manager from criticism—after all, the decision about a candidate is made not by him but by a more or less objective mechanical device. When in doubt, the manager can err on the side of caution by resubmitting a candidate to the polygraph. This discourages responsibility. The security manager doesn't have to be sure, based on other criteria and through investigation, that his judgment is accurate. He can hide behind the lie detector. His mistakes—allowing people to pass because they beat the box, or screening out innocent people who cannot convince polygraphers that they are not being deceptive—for the most part go unrectified.

The next step in security defense is compartmentation. Compartmentation, or "need-to-know," means that while clearance makes the subject eligible to receive sensitive information in general, it entitles that person to none in particular. The subject is allowed access only to material required for work to which he or she has been specifically assigned. Just as potential damage to a ship is minimized by dividing its hull into watertight compartments, the damage that any disloyal or incompetent individual can do to an intelligence or military system is limited by restricting the information to which he or she might have access. If the information is too tightly restricted, however, few analysts or operators can use it. Security managers tend to err on the side of strict compartmentation.

In reality, this is difficult to enforce. Defectors and agents have been able to provide a great deal of information on subjects that they themselves were not handling because of what they learned from friends and colleagues, both formally and informally, in other parts of their former service.[60] Furthermore, as individuals rise higher in a service, they often gain access to more and more compartments. There is a natural tendency to share and make use of good information, as well as to bring in people with outside expertise for advice. Though the reasons for doing so may be honorable, when information is shared, compartmentation breaks down.

Similarly, security managers try to set up a system of accountability whereby a record is made of who receives what information. Then, if a breach of security takes place, and even if the breach becomes known years later, for example, through information provided by a defector, there is a method for tracking the leak. The system sometimes works, especially if information has been closely compartmentalized, and most especially if it has been distributed to recipients in individualized form. But much of the time accountability is defeated by the same factors that defeat compartmentation.

Security for installations, communications, documents, and information is as important as ensuring the reliability of people. After all, if a foreign intelligence service gets physical access to the typewriters, computers, communication equipment, or files inside an embassy—as there is strong reason to believe the Soviets did in much of the U.S. embassy in Moscow in the 1980s—this is almost as good as, and perhaps even better than, having a spy inside the compound. Spies cannot know everything. They are not on duty twenty-four hours a day, nor do they work in all sections of an embassy.

However, their access to embassy communications or facilities will severely compromise security as well as diplomatic and military secrets. It will also give away the predilections, interests, and vulnerabilities of embassy personnel and facilitate their recruitment by the foreign service.

Counterintelligence managers are increasingly concerned about automated information security. The future requirements of security in this area are hard to overestimate. Almost every governmental and nongovernmental organization the world over is confronted by unprecedented reliance on computers and automatic data processing. Even the dial tone in an ordinary telephone depends on a computer program. If anyone has unauthorized access to an information processing system, the whole system and its information are open to compromise and external manipulation. Non-security-related information systems have proved vulnerable to amateur hackers and sophisticated viruses. Security systems have to be protected against amateurs and determined professionals alike. Strategists agree that we are entering an age when the ability to wage and defend against "information war" may be one of the most powerful forces a country can muster.

The counterintelligence manager may decide that protecting secrets against unauthorized disclosure is not enough. He or she may decide to become more focused, and more political, and use knowledge of specific foreign intelligence threats to protect secrets. When the counterintelligence manager neutralizes a foreign threat in a defensive manner—that is, without seeking to destroy or interrupt the threat—it is known as a *countermeasure*. Just as there are security specialists, there are countermeasure specialists.

Countermeasures on the whole aim at thwarting hostile intelligence from a distance. Countermeasures against imagery, for example, would involve camouflage and concealment. Countermeasures against spies might entail controlling the movement and location of "foreign diplomats" in one's own country and requiring government employees to report contact with foreign diplomats.

Because some services expend enormous effort on technical collection, countermeasures to frustrate this effort can be worthwhile. In World War II the British, who knew that the Germans placed great confidence in air reconnaissance, used a variety of tricks, some provided by professional magicians, to arrange buildings, tents, and trucks in illusory combinations that would—and did—trip up German photoanalysts. After that war, the KGB and GRU strove mightily to deny information to Western intelligence technical collectors and mislead them about Soviet capability. More recently, in Operation Desert Shield (1990), the Iraqis managed, in part through countermeasures, to hide major nuclear facilities from U.S. aerial reconnaissance.

At the most basic level, denying foreign services any knowledge of technical intelligence capabilities and missions is ideal, if not usually the case. Even without leaks, foreign services will acquire some information from walk-ins and recruited agents as well as from their own observations and calculations. Given that few secrets can remain totally under wraps, an effort should be made to disguise one's capabilities and mislead foreigners. This is important in peacetime, even more so in a crisis or wartime when previously existing capabilities become especially vulnerable. Preparations should be made to protect and disguise the technical capabilities that will be used in wartime.

Controlling access by a foreign intelligence service is obviously beneficial. The Soviet services specialized in this. Almost two-thirds of the Soviet Union was completely out of bounds to foreigners until Gorbachev came to power. Border guards, not ordinary soldiers but a huge and integral part of the KGB's manpower, kept the Soviet people in and everyone else out. They monitored all ports, airports, and entry points. Further, the KGB's Second Chief Directorate monitored every single foreign installation and foreign person living in the Soviet Union. It kept files on foreigners and decided where they could live, where they could work, and where they could travel.

By contrast, for decades after World War II, the United States was relatively relaxed about border controls and the location and movement of foreign personnel in the United States. Responsibility was divided among the Department of State, the Immigration and Naturalization Service, Customs, and the Border Patrol—none of which had counterintelligence responsibilities until the early 1980s. Then the United States became more interested in security and countermeasures. The Office of Foreign Missions (OFM) was established in the Department of State, headed by James Nolan, a former senior FBI counterintelligence manager. His arrival was not generally welcomed by State Department diplomats, and upon retirement he was replaced by a career Foreign Service officer with no counterintelligence experience.[61]

The OFM came to regulate the buildings and movements of foreign government personnel to improve U.S. counterintelligence and limit the effectiveness of hostile intelligence services. They distributed distinctive license plates to foreign diplomats so that their cars could be easily identified—a standard security practice for decades in many foreign countries. These plates make diplomats stick out like sore thumbs outside the capital city, and even in certain neighborhoods within the city. For the United States in the mid-1980s, it was a major innovation that made it easier for the FBI to follow vehicles used by foreign intelligence services.[62]

Counterintelligence chiefs must make a variety of management decisions revolving around a central question: is it better to allocate resources to general security or countermeasures? There may be no manager for countermeasures, or countermeasures may be run by different managers competing for resources—in either case, defense is expensive. Here counterintelligence chiefs need help from analysts. Given general security considerations and specific threats and vulnerabilities, they have to decide between more locks and fences or more sophisticated information security systems. These decisions involve billions of dollars. Counterintelligence managers who invest wisely not only save on the security and countermeasures budget but also better protect their country. The choices don't stop at defense issues. Counterintelligence managers have to ask whether offensive operations are the most effective way to deter and neutralize foreign attempts to collect, manipulate, or steal technology, as well as to prevent their own intelligence operations from being neutralized and manipulated by foreign services.

On the Offensive

Counterintelligence managers draw on a variety of methods to deter, degrade, or disrupt foreign intelligence activities. (In the past, this was known as counterespionage.) They can pursue a top-driven strategy or overall plan to accomplish this mission, or they can operate in an ad hoc manner, much as the United States did for a good part of the cold war.

The first decision concerns *specific objectives*. To degrade the foreign service or activity? If so, how much? To neutralize a few operatives in their own country or in a given region? To completely destroy the effectiveness of the foreign service worldwide, and for an extended time?

After deciding on the objective, counterintelligence managers need to bring their analysts and collectors to bear on the requirements for carrying it out. This will involve identifying any opportunities to accomplish their purpose, that is, spotting vulnerabilities in a foreign service and capabilities that can be mobilized to exploit them. Do they know enough about the foreign service to do more than a little damage? Even if they know enough, do they have the assets—the penetration, the double agents, appropriate liaison with other countries, and the financial resources—to carry out the strategy? What are some of the consequences that might result from this strategy? Is the leadership of the foreign government likely to strike out in some unanticipated way? What contingencies should be planned for? Only after these questions have been answered can the managers actually decide on specific methods of neutralization and disruption and assign program priorities to individual agencies or branches.

The most common and straightforward technique of disruption is to expose or arrest foreign intelligence officers and their agents. (In the case of intelligence officers with diplomatic immunity, they would be declared *personae non gratae* and told to leave.) One argument in favor of this approach is that it might lead the foreign intelligence service to believe it has been more broadly penetrated than is the case. For example, if one or two officers in a diplomatic unit are left untouched while others are "burned" or expelled, the foreign service won't be sure whether the counterintelligence service has uncovered all its "legal" officers. Exposure and expulsion also shake up an illegal support apparatus in an embassy, particularly if the best, most experienced officers are exposed and the less effective are left behind.

Another option, usually considered more sophisticated, is to keep track of an identified intelligence officer and see where the trail goes—rather than to expel him and start all over again identifying and establishing the modus operandi of his replacement. It might also be preferable not to arrest him at all, because that might teach the foreign service to improve its operational security and thus foil further disruption efforts down the road.

An alternative method of neutralization, already mentioned, which also has its advantages and disadvantages, is to tie up and distract foreign intelligence officers with controlled double agents. The British did this to the Germans in World War II, and apparently the Cubans deceived the Americans this way in the 1970s and 1980s. This type of action, of course, requires patience, resources, and a great deal of skill. The British and the Cubans, for example, could have publicly arrested, executed, or expelled most of the German and American intelligence officers and their agents that were directed against them. Indeed, there were good arguments for doing so. Exposure could have been used to show how effective their own counterintelligence services were, and to discourage the foreign services, whose leadership could be portrayed as incompetent. It would also have served as a warning to citizens not to be tempted into working for a foreign service.

The opposite course, to maintain for years the charade that these agents were still effective, required great skill. The British availed themselves of wartime censorship and the suspension of normal democratic functions in a time of crisis. The disinformation they fed to the Nazis had to be good enough not to arouse suspicion, yet harmless enough that it would not compromise the British war effort in any significant way. The British, like the Cubans later, also had to handle their controlled sources deftly and make sure there was no penetration of or defection from their service that would blow the massive operation.

There are still other, if more difficult, ways to neutralize the activities of a foreign service—by planting agents inside the service, recruiting foreign intelligence officers from it, or causing some to defect. The home service learns about a foreign service's major operations and meanwhile plants the seeds of discontent and suspicion so that the foreign service doubts its purpose and competence and tears itself apart. The adverse effects may reach beyond the service all the way to the governing political system.

One such technique is to frame an intelligence officer. Whether or not the officer is guilty of having changed sides, he is made to look like a traitor to his service. This can be accomplished in a variety of ways: by depositing money in his bank account, sending him messages from a "foreign service" that seem part of a long-running clandestine correspondence, or creating circumstances suggesting that he is about to defect. It may be that more than the effectiveness of the intelligence officer is impaired; his service is likely to expend considerable energy rebuilding all the operations and security arrangements to which the intelligence officer was perhaps privy. If one can either genuinely recruit or, failing that, frame or spoil the operations of several intelligence officers simultaneously, the effect on the foreign service will be that much more devastating.

These methods, among others, were used by the United States and other services to neutralize the Romanian service in the 1970s. First, Western intelligence successes against Romanian operatives weakened morale inside the service, which led to pressure from Communist Party leader Nicolae Ceausescu for change. The change did not take place, and as we have seen, in 1978 Ion Pacepa, deputy chief of the service and also its acting director, defected. In September of that year, the Western press and diplomatic sources in Bucharest reported that General Pacepa's defection—he was perhaps the highest-ranking intelligence officer ever to defect—was followed by the greatest political purge in postwar Romania.

> A third of the ruling Council of Ministers was demoted. Twenty-two Ambassadors were replaced, and more than a dozen high-ranking security officers were arrested, while several dozen more simply vanished from sight in the turmoil. . . . In October 1978 with DIE [Romania's Department of External Information] officers throughout the West under investigation by counterintelligence services, Bucharest was fully engaged in a furious operation aimed at withdrawing most of the DIE legal and illegal officers, evidently to avoid further international embarrassment. Some of them chose freedom then and there, others later, and all reported that only hours after General Pacepa's disappearance the DIE entered a state of desperate confusion and soon began to disintegrate.[63]

Perhaps Pacepa was not the linchpin whose removal caused the DIE to fall apart. Western services may have employed double agents and other aggressive counterintelligence techniques to further the process. The result, Pacepa claims, was that "numerous investigating commissions, all directed by Elena [Nicolae Ceausescu's wife], started dissecting the DIE and its personnel. By the end of the year, Elena had reportedly disbanded the DIE and started to build a new organization on its ashes." This put a stop to heretofore successful Romanian collection and active measures and created tension inside the Romanian government that would build over the years until the fall of Ceausescu in

1989. In short, the roots of the destruction of the Romanian intelligence service—a vital linchpin in the entire political system—arguably are found in precisely the kind of counterintelligence advocated here: an *offensive* defense. This case illustrates how the strategic uses of counterintelligence can significantly advance a nation's security objectives.

Deception and Offensive Counterintelligence

Counterintelligence can also be used to help manage and manipulate the perceptions of a foreign service. Perception management is a policy decision. Heads of state have the option of using their intelligence and counterintelligence capabilities to reinforce a particular image that they want foreigners to have of their domestic or foreign policy. This will require a decision on which part of the intelligence bureaucracy to use: the covert action component or counterintelligence personnel. For example, they might want to give a more or less accurate or an essentially false—*deceptive*—image. In the late 1980s and early 1990s, Mikhail Gorbachev, for example, used the KGB's active measures apparatus to reinforce the perception in the West that he was in terrible trouble at home, and that the West could help him by going easy in its demands, siding with him against nationalities, and providing economic assistance. This image appears to have been essentially accurate—probably more so than Gorbachev realized and certainly more than he wanted. The KGB active measures program devoted considerable effort to reinforcing and exaggerating that image, and accordingly, the West was more sympathetic to Gorbachev than to his predecessors.[64]

Similarly, the Iranians in the 1980s and early 1990s used their covert action assets to reinforce the message that there were moderate as well as hard-line factions in Teheran, and that the United States could help empower the moderates through arms sales and economic assistance and by pressuring Israel on behalf of Palestinians and Lebanese Shiites.

When a head of state opts to manipulate the perceptions and behavior of foreign governments, the decision should be part of overall foreign policy. Intelligence agencies are not usually in a position to authorize this sort of plan unilaterally, because it involves much more than intelligence considerations, and because implementation of the plan is likely to involve not just counterintelligence but also other parts of the government. Even in the absence of a grand strategy, a prime minister or president could decide to influence foreign perceptions about his or her lack of strategy or about more limited aspects of his or her government's policy and capabilities.

Once there has been a decision to manipulate or deceive, the group charged with implementing the plan must be small and must have the authority to coordinate activities with other organizations necessary for its execution. For deception particularly, security is of the essence, as the British experience in World War II illustrates. The British set up a small, secure deception planning and coordination unit, known for most of the war as the London Control Section (LCS), in an underground bunker in Westminster. The LCS consisted of both intelligence and nonintelligence personnel who planned and coordinated the implementation of plans approved by Churchill. MI6, which was responsible for Ultra, humint, and counterintelligence abroad, was involved, along with MI5, which ran the Double-Cross network of captured German agents and was in charge of security in Britain. Military intelligence and other agencies such as the Political Warfare Executive were tasked to send out false, and combinations of true and false, messages to deceive the Nazis, which they often managed to do.[65]

In a democracy, especially during peacetime, the deceivers cannot mislead their own voters and legislators about policy either intentionally or even inadvertently. Elected officials are accountable to the electorate, and voters must be in a position to understand the overall aims or general direction of the nation's policy as well as the aims and capabilities of its adversaries. Because democratic governments cannot mislead their citizens as they seek to mislead adversaries, deception must take place primarily through secret intelligence channels. In normal peacetime circumstances, a democratic government cannot afford to plant intentionally false stories in the foreign media, since they are likely to be picked up by the media at home; the stories could "blow back" into the country and be read by—and mislead—domestic opinion leaders and politicians. But there are always circumstances in which foreign leaders can be given some true and some false information through intelligence channels without incurring this risk.

Deception requires creative planning and execution. Good perception managers tend not to be people enmeshed in the routine culture of a large bureaucracy. Studies of successful deception and *a priori* reasoning seem to suggest that it is better to employ amateurs outside the "system" for specific deception tasks—as the British did during World War II—than to rely exclusively on professional intelligence officers. Whoever they are, perception managers have to know a great deal about the worldview of those they are trying to manipulate, and they must recognize the human proclivity for self-deception. *Identifying* the prejudices of targets is the job primarily of positive collection and analysis. *Exploiting* this information is the job of counterintelligence practitioners and covert action specialists.

Counterintelligence specialists are the best equipped to know how and what the target's intelligence service "sees" and "hears." Hence they are in an advantageous position to craft and send out specially selected messages that can be passed along with maximum effectiveness. The target's intelligence collection and analytical capabilities have to be understood so that the target will actually pick up the message and then find it credible. What are the target's technical frequencies tuned into? What are its human agents interested in, and how can they be steered to the "right" themes?

Next, counterintelligence, working jointly with positive collection and with analysis, determines how the target is reacting to the crafted message. Can it be fine-tuned to play to the target's prejudices? This is the "feedback channel." One reason the British were so successful during World War II was that Ultra intercepts let them know how the Nazis perceived the false British messages. If the right messages were not getting through, they could be sent again or altered to ensure that subsequently they would come to the attention of the Germans and be found credible.

Finally, successful deception requires skilled practitioners to pass along messages. These personnel, who may work in the covert action branch of an intelligence service, the counterintelligence branch, or some other part of the government, are the equivalent of con men who can manipulate their "marks." The British did this in World War II in a sting operation known as Mincemeat. They created "the man who never was," Major Martin, a Marine courier ostensibly carrying top-secret invasion plans for the Allied landing in Greece in 1943. In fact the Allies were planning to land in the Central Mediterranean, Sicily. A British submarine dropped a body dressed in Marine uniform off the coast of Spain, knowing that the current would wash it ashore and that Spanish police would send the false documents to the Germans. By monitoring German communications, the British confirmed that the Germans had fallen for the ruse. This was just one of many "stings" the British used to mislead the Germans during World War II.[66]

Positive Intelligence

Counterintelligence has the potential to make a valuable contribution to positive intelligence. Because counterintelligence penetrates opposition intelligence services, counterintelligence managers can glean from their worldwide technical and human sources secret information for use in strategic planning and defense, as well as in crisis situations. The United States failed to do this when it ignored information suggesting an attack on Pearl Harbor was likely. In times of crisis counterintelligence sources can be tasked to report *any* possibly relevant information. For example, they might ask their agents in foreign intelligence services whether foreign services have given them any special tasking, or whether their well-placed friends or relatives have any special insights on the crisis. Counterintelligence sources are also routinely tasked to aid positive analysts and operators seeking insight into the activities, priorities, and mind-set of foreign governments and groups.

Managing a system so that counterintelligence can be applied to positive intelligence is not easy. On the one hand, counterintelligence managers want to be useful to policymakers and want to be recognized as significantly bolstering the overall intelligence effort. On the other hand, they perceive their primary mission as being, not positive intelligence, but neutralization and disruption of opposition services. They see the downside, perhaps too vividly, of using counterintelligence in positive intelligence: it diverts time, manpower, and money from the primary mission. Counterintelligence collectors and analysts have to be trained for and alerted and responsive to positive requirements. Moreover, the more widely disseminated the take from counterintelligence sources, the more likely the source will be blown. It takes first-class management at the top to balance competing incentives below and ensure that counterintelligence resources are fully exploited in the national interest rather than for parochial reasons.

Counterintelligence, then, is a strategic instrument available to states to protect themselves and advance their interests in the struggle for power, wealth, and influence.

Analysis supports counterintelligence policy choices and defensive and offensive operations. It guides counterintelligence operators in military and intelligence agencies so that their work is not left to serendipity or chance—laborious attempts to find needles in haystacks. Analysis is, in some respects, the queen of counterintelligence. It makes sense of the daily efforts of foreign governments to manipulate, to steal secrets and technology, and to thwart intelligence. It is also an important ingredient in the effort of counterintelligence operators a3nd positive collectors to do the same to foreign governments.

Counterintelligence collection is best done by counterintelligence managers who take advantage of the symbiotic relationship of overt, technical, and humint collection. As in positive collection, overt sources can guide human and technical collection. Or human and technical sources can guide (and enrich) overt collection. Counterintelligence collectors, more so than their positive intelligence counterparts, rarely appreciate each other's strengths, and they are more wary, in part for good security reasons, of sharing their counterintelligence take with each other, much less with liaison services, except when it directly concerns a spy operating in a foreign government. Hence, opportunities to combine the fruits of diverse collection sources often evaporate. Disincentives prevail over incentives.

But the end product, the mission of counterintelligence, is action—action to protect against foreigners and action to manipulate foreigners in the service of national goals. Not everyone will see it that way. Positive collectors and covert action operators, for example, may see security as trivial, annoying "police work." Security specialists will tend to believe their work is crucial and that it should override the general mission of the intelligence system—the mind-set that it is better not to distribute reports from agents or to allow risky operations lest they jeopardize security. In other words, security specialists tend to regard the security of sources and operations as the major end of intelligence.

The optimal solution lies somewhere in between. The absence of security invalidates the rest of intelligence work if it allows foreign penetration and manipulation. But total security hobbles intelligence operators by restricting their access to positive collection, analysis, and operations. Security is a necessary but not a sufficient condition for counterintelligence.

Countermeasures can be important but are not in themselves sufficient. Targeting and neutralizing the specific techniques of foreign intelligence services add an extra layer of protection on top of security, and they make a difference. But countermeasures activity is often viewed as an add-on to be indulged in when there has been a spy scandal and politicians are demanding that something be done, or when there are extra resources available. This discipline usually has few institutional advocates, and when there are no spy scandals and resources are limited, it is among the first to go.

By contrast, what used to be called counterespionage, aggressively pursuing and neutralizing a foreign service in both the human and technical realms, is often the exciting stuff of spy fiction and films. Unfortunately, it is not the ordinary work of counterintelligence operators in peacetime democracies. Few counterintelligence practitioners get a chance to develop and implement plans to neutralize a whole service, whether in a given area or worldwide. It takes vision, leadership, commitment, knowledge, and patience from the top of the counterintelligence establishment to do more than just arrest spies or run double-agent operations. Disrupting, neutralizing, or manipulating a foreign service does not usually bring counterintelligence practitioners public acclaim or even short-term private satisfaction, since it takes time, even years, to run its course. The successors of the counterintelligence leaders who design and develop the disruptive attack are likely to get the credit. Nevertheless, this is the mission—*to understand the total foreign intelligence threat rather than fragments of it, and to exploit that knowledge to undermine foreign intelligence operatives for advantage.*

The manipulation of foreign governments to reinforce more or less true images or to create false ones is not exclusively the job of counterintelligence. Customarily, counterintelligence targets opposition services but not other parts of a foreign government. Counterintelligence can play a key role in the manipulation process. Especially in democracies, counterintelligence has to be constrained when using overt intelligence channels to influence foreign perception, lest it pollute its own domestic political debate. Finally, if done right, counterintelligence contributes directly to positive collection, to analysis, and to covert action. Counterintelligence sources that have access to the thinking of foreign leaders and that understand the strengths and weaknesses of foreign societies are unique and valuable. Counterintelligence, in all its aspects, is essential to the symbiosis that makes for first-class intelligence.

6

IN PURSUIT OF EFFECTIVE INTELLIGENCE

Variables at Play

As the preceding chapters suggest, there is a disparity between *ideal* counterintelligence and covert action and how both have been practiced by the United States. This is, of course, not surprising. It is a rare government whose statecraft perfectly harmonizes theory with practice. But what specifically accounts for the gap? Why have American counterintelligence and covert action taken the particular forms they have? Is it possible to close the gap and use these two intelligence elements more effectively in the national interest?

A number of conditions define the setting in which intelligence operates and shape how intelligence is practiced at any given time in a state's history. At least four major variables are at play: the pace of modernization and technological innovation; government structure and bureaucratic culture; the perception of political circumstances; and the nature of the regime. Sometimes these variables are subject to human manipulation in the short term, over a period of several years. Others are not as amenable to change in the short term.

The Pace of Modernization and Technological Innovation

The first variable is the pace of modernization and technological innovation. Modernization, increasing control of nature and increasing human cooperation, leads to various technological innovations that enhance military, economic, and intelligence capabilities. Generally speaking, during periods of limited modernization, there is less need for intelligence; this is particularly true in the case of military intelligence. However, when there are new advances in weapons of war, there is a need both for intelligence on these developments and specialists who understand their significance.[1]

What happened in the nineteenth century illustrates this. The revolution in military affairs generated by the Industrial Revolution and the wars of French Revolution and empire greatly expanded the need for information on new foreign weapons, tactics, and command technology. Either ambassadors had to become experts in these matters or, more likely, experts had to be deployed. By the mid-nineteenth century, most European governments found it necessary to station military specialists in their foreign diplomatic missions, and by the end of the century most had created permanent military intelligence organizations.

As the pace of modernization quickened at the turn of the century, the military in various countries also began to develop special means of collecting information. As mastery of physics and the electromagnetic spectrum grew, reconnaissance moved from horseback or the top of a nearby hill to balloons, then aircraft, and finally space. Eavesdropping, no longer practiced solely by being in the next room or by bribing the courier, was accomplished by pulling electronic signals from the air and from space. Corps of professionals were formed to analyze and exploit esoteric data from these new modes of collection. Technical security subspecialties also arose to protect and disguise forces, materiel, and communications from the collection innovations of adversaries. Predictably, this in turn was followed by the advent of specialties whose function it was to uncover and neutralize an adversary's security measures.

These trends, especially during the cold war, greatly affected the conduct of U.S. intelligence. Attempts to gather information on "hard targets" behind an "Iron Curtain" resulted in remarkable and rapid advances in technical collection, as well as the means for sorting and analyzing the resulting masses of data. From the use of computers for cryptanalysis to satellite surveillance, American intelligence benefited enormously from modernization; in turn, modernization played a major role in determining the structure of the U.S. intelligence community and the emphasis given to certain aspects of intelligence.

Specifically, the rapid—and expensive—technical advances in collection took place at the expense of counterintelligence. Despite repeated episodes of U.S. technical collection systems being compromised by the KGB and GRU, Americans still tend to regard collection as a quasi-scientific endeavor in which data are gathered from afar much as images are picked up in space by the Hubble Telescope. Collection usually was not seen in the context of adversaries who knew that the United States has such capabilities, and who were willing to spend the time and money to deny access to the information and/or to deceive us.

Pride in U.S. technical collection capability has waned with the growing awareness of how successfully the Russians, Libyans, Iraqis, and North Koreans kept their programs and activities secret. Complicating matters is the fact that, with the widespread availability of powerful computing technologies, advances in encryption are likely to outpace efforts to decrypt. In short, in the future it is possible that U.S. intelligence will be able to see and hear more, but understand less.

This trend, combined with a reduction in the number of hard-target countries around the world and a stagnant if not depleted intelligence budget, suggests that U.S. intelligence may place less emphasis on costly technical collection programs, and may, as a result, be forced to reconsider the imbalance that has existed between collection and analysis on the one hand and counterintelligence on the other. If the appropriate lessons are drawn, America's intelligence community may become more sophisticated in its understanding of the possibilities and limitations of its capabilities.

Government Structure and Bureaucratic Culture

Whether the right lessons will be learned from recent U.S. experience is uncertain. That will ultimately depend on the willingness of the intelligence community's leaders to make changes in their bureaucracy's entrenched culture and behavior. Government structure and bureaucratic culture thus compose the second, leading variable in the shaping of intelligence.

In practice, the instruments of statecraft are often in the hands of bureaucratic managers rather than elected officials. The managers are the leaders of an army of civil servants who interpret legislation, issue and enforce regulations, define policy options, and carry out policymakers' decisions. Modern government seems to require an array of big bureaucracies; and any big bureaucracy routinely develops its own peculiar way of seeing and doing things. This is as true for the intelligence community as it is for the armed services or the Department of Labor.

A bureaucracy is also affected by the inevitable power struggles among its various branches. The specialist bureaucrat—whether he is a collector, an analyst, or a counterintelligence practitioner—is likely to view his branch as the one that puts others in the shade. The skillful orchestration of diverse intelligence perspectives may result in a balanced community of interests, or if not well conducted, in a fractured bureaucracy some of whose components are emphasized at the expense of others. Recruitment, training, and promotion of personnel will then come to reflect whichever parochial disciplines are dominant.

How have the different components of the American intelligence community interacted? A key factor in determining the interplay, especially in this area of government activity (by its nature less bound by the usual rules of civil service and detailed oversight), is strong leadership. William J. Donovan succeeded in persuading President Roosevelt to override a powerful military bureaucracy and thereby for the first time in U.S. history to establish a full-service intelligence capability. Although President Truman dismantled most of Donovan's structure in 1945, it resurfaced with the CIA's creation in 1947. OSS veterans, particularly Allen W. Dulles, Director of Central Intelligence in the 1950s, built upon this foundation. Dulles and his immediate successors supported collectors, counterintelligence practitioners, and covert action operators and saw to it that they collaborated, if not always harmoniously and effectively. Although counterintelligence was never first among equals, neither was it subordinated to the other elements.

Nevertheless, the centrifugal parochial tendencies that the centralized and unified CIA was designed to overcome were not obliterated entirely. By the 1970s, bureaucratic pressures within the agency, combined with the breakup of the foreign policy consensus and new CIA leadership, led to important changes in the relative power and relationships of its components. Under a succession of DCIs, counterintelligence and covert action were substantially downgraded—and some would say human collection was as well—while analysis and technical collection became dominant.

The parochial views of intelligence held by other components of the intelligence-policy community reinforced these trends. State Department officials and foreign service officers tended to view intelligence as essentially the collection of information, rather than analysis or action to influence other states; they saw themselves as the primary analysts and managers of the country's foreign affairs. Without a clandestine collection capability or a covert action arm, and with only a small counterintelligence branch, officials of the Defense Intelligence Agency had an equally constricted view of intelligence. It was intensified by the fact that, with the exception of Army intelligence, the armed services and their counterintelligence elements were housed in organizations, such as the Naval Investigative Service and the Air Force Office of Investigation, whose principal function was law enforcement in the military.

During the 1980s, some efforts were made to revive the former balance among intelligence elements. In particular, more attention and resources were devoted to counterintelligence and covert action. But on the whole the improvements did not go far. In the absence of focused attention by DCIs and support from successive administrations and the two congressional oversight committees, the reform process stalled. Permanently altering U.S. intelligence priorities will require sustained and courageous political-bureaucratic leadership.

Complicating any such effort is the structure of the U.S. intelligence community itself and its relationship to the U.S. political system. A British scholar has noted that key segments within the system have "greater independence . . . from direct political control" than similar agencies in other countries. For example, the CIA "is not, and never has been, a part of the State Department in the way in which the British Secret Service (SIS) is part of the Foreign and Commonwealth Office." Then there is the sheer complexity of the organization of U.S. intelligence: numerous agencies, bureaus, and departments involved in diverse and sometimes overlapping activities. The result is a lack of coherence and sometimes rather confused lines of responsibility and communication.[2]

Changing the ways of a long-established intelligence bureaucracy is exceedingly difficult in a democracy such as America's, much more so than in the relatively strong-party parliamentary political system that prevails in so many democracies. The modern American intelligence community has, through forty-five years of training and everyday operations, ingrained a professional ethos in its various arms that is not easily modified. Unlike the American military, which traditionally values its willingness to take orders from civilian leaders—to salute smartly and carry out those directives—American intelligence often takes pride in its objectivity and quasi-independence from policymaking.

In the past, this attitude was counterbalanced by the notion that intelligence components, especially the CIA, served as the executive's "eyes and ears." By and large, for most of the country's history, intelligence was the policy and administrative preserve of the president—his prerogative. Since the mid-1970s, however, this has not been the case. An evolving notion of separation of powers, the essential framework of the government's constitutional system, has brought intelligence more within the purview of the courts and the legislative branch. In the United States, intelligence policy and administration are treated more like administration and policy in other areas of government. In terms of separation of powers, the world of U.S. intelligence has been "normalized."

This means, of course, that the intelligence community has more than one master. It is sheltered from simple control by any one branch of government. This is both a strength and a potential weakness. Unless there is a clear and strongly held consensus about national security affairs in the post-cold-war era, it will be difficult, if not impossible, for an administration and Congress to agree that covert action and counterintelligence capabilities need substantial overhaul and upgrading. Different institutional and partisan perspectives and agendas will rule the day, impeding significant reform in these particular areas.

The Perception of Political Circumstances

The government's perception of the context in which it operates is another variable shaping the intelligence community. How leaders perceive the political circumstances they face has important implications for the practice of intelligence. Different governments employ the various elements of intelligence differently and attach different values to each.

The possibility of war is, of course, primary among political concerns; those who sense danger obviously behave differently from those who do not. From the Reformation until the Treaty of Westphalia (1648), Europe was torn by religious wars, and it is no coincidence that during that time, European ambassadors did little but set up secret networks for intelligence and subversion. The Western distinction between states at peace and at war was eclipsed, and intelligence became a much more common feature of government. At the end of the next century, Europe was buffeted by successive wars. Between 1789 and 1815, there was little respite. French consuls sent spies to penetrate the French émigré communities, while the monarchs of Europe came to look on the whole French nation—not just its army—as a threat. Revolutionary France teemed with foreign agents. After Napoleon's defeat, European monarchies saw themselves as still being at war with the secular nationalism that had been fueled by the Enlightenment and the French Revolution. The Holy Alliance of Russia, Austria, and Prussia sought to eliminate revolutionaries everywhere in Europe. None were more zealous in this regard than the czars of Russia. They sent so many agents into Europe to ferret out revolutionaries that other rulers sometimes feared the czars also had designs on them. During his exile in London in the mid-nineteenth century, the Italian Giuseppe Mazzini, a leader in the revolutionary republican Risorgimento, was closely watched and his mail was opened by British special agents. The Duke of Wellington argued that such methods were necessary to squelch the revolutionary menace.[3]

Overall, the nineteenth century was an era of limited conflict, and Western statesmen only slowly realized the need to develop significant intelligence capabilities. In the last decades of the century, the requirement for intelligence became more apparent. Statesmen and military commanders began to develop intelligence capabilities to anticipate much graver conflicts.[4]

Many twentieth-century intelligence systems in democracies have their origins in the tensions leading to World War I and the revolution in military technology that accompanied it. In the late nineteenth century, intelligence, where it existed, focused on military preparations, weaponry, logistics, topography, and troop movements. World War I enlarged the scope of intelligence enormously. Many elements of society now were perceived to have a direct or indirect bearing on the outcome of battle. Industry, science, medicine, railroad schedules and repairs, civilian morale—all came to be viewed as important, and hence fell under the purview of intelligence.

Following World War I, the rise of totalitarian political movements in Italy, Germany, and Russia led to the creation of the most widespread clandestine networks in Western history. The Bolsheviks and Nazis who secured and maintained power at home through a combination of organization, propaganda, and violence began to apply these methods abroad. Meanwhile, military innovation depended on specialized collection and analysis of the new developments.

As they perceived the danger of subversion and war increasing, Western democracies themselves began to develop a more systematic and organized approach to intelligence. Military forces still took priority over intelligence. It was not until war was just on the horizon that serious attempts were made to fund and integrate technical and human-source information into intelligence efforts, and to consider countermeasures. In the end, under pressure of actual war, Western democracies built large bureaucracies for the collection, protection, and analysis of intelligence of all types, and for conducting paramilitary and other secret operations aimed at influencing the course of events.

Broadly speaking, the history of U.S. intelligence has followed this pattern. Factoring in America's relative geopolitical isolation through-out much of its first hundred years and the historical anomaly of its civil war, U.S. interest in intelligence has risen and fallen with the per-ceived threat to its national interests from abroad. In particular, the two world wars fostered sharp increases in support for intelligence. The measures adopted during World War I were allowed to atrophy after the war, then were revived in new organizations and with new procedures just prior to and during World War II. Assuming that the peace achieved in 1945 would be the norm thereafter, the United States dismantled most of this intelligence infrastructure. But it was quickly built back up when President Truman, his administration, and key members of Congress came to believe that America's former ally the Soviet Union posed a significant military and political threat of indeterminate duration. The perception of threat changed, and, quite rapidly and decisively, so did the U.S. understanding of the role of intelligence in support of national security policies.

But Washington's view of the Soviet "menace" was not static. As discussed earlier, shifting perceptions during the four-plus decades of the cold war repeatedly altered the American practice of intelligence. By and large, the greater the perceived threat, the more support there was for intelligence and the more interest in bolstering covert action and counterintelligence. To the degree the Soviets were under-stood to pose an effective full-service intelligence threat, the United States strove to match or counter it. Washington's decision to match Moscow was not simply a reflexive imitation of Soviet ways. Rather, Moscow and Washington developed, not identical capabilities, but rather capabilities that paralleled one another offensively and defen-sively.

In the immediate post–cold–war security environment, the United States faces no competing superpower. Russia, a potential adversary in various parts of Eurasia, and likely to retain its nuclear arsenal and intelligence capabilities, will not be the superpower the Soviet Union was. For the most part, the United States will not have to worry about any single grave threat and an integrated hostile worldwide intelligence alliance. What it faces is a plethora of smaller, traditional and nontra-ditional threats. Some traditional threats may turn into major con-cerns, as in the cases of Iran, Iraq and North Korea, but over the next decade they are unlikely to be threats of the magnitude associated with Nazi Germany or the Soviet empire. Nevertheless, the sum of the whole of these smaller parts poses a major challenge.

To what extent a world of ad hoc crises and international surprises results in renewed intelligence capabilities remains to be seen. This renewed support, if it comes, may well be thrown behind collection and analysis rather than covert action and counterintelligence. Shortsighted as this may seem, history suggests that in the absence of a perceived clear and present danger, and with no consensus about what role the United States should play in the world, counterintelligence and covert action may well be little more than afterthoughts to policymakers and to the American public.

The Nature of the Regime

Although a country's geostrategic situation plays a critical role in determining its national security policies—Costa Rica's defense and intelligence requirements are not the same as Israel's—it is also true that a country's perception of the threats it faces and its definition of its national interest will vary from regime to regime. The nature of the regime is the last, and perhaps most important, variable in explaining the different ways in which intelligence is practiced and understood from state to state. The old adage that what one sees is determined in large part by where one sits is true, but incomplete. What one sees is also a product of eyesight. Not everyone's lenses are the same.

In general, governments will be either defensive or offensive in strategic posture. They see themselves either as "on the march" or satisfied with the status quo. The national security policies and the intelligence they need to support them will depend on which posture is taken.[5] For example, the perception that a country is on the defensive rather than the offensive means that a government will probably pay closer attention to its vulnerabilities and less attention to opportunities, even defensive opportunities, for taking action. A liberal democracy often will be slow to organize covert action capabilities, and it will be susceptible to "spy scares," believing that the very tolerance that defines its political life leaves it vulnerable to the intrigues of an aggressive adversary.

Of course, representative and autocratic governments do not fall neatly into one or the other strategic posture. Modern liberal democracies have tended to be status quo powers, but not always. Britain, the United States, and France have all had their imperial days. Conversely, Franco's Spain, Hoxha's Albania, and Somoza's Nicaragua were relatively pacific states vis-à-vis their neighbors.

Throughout history, most societies that have endured have been characterized by strong personal rule. The absence of a strong ruler has almost uniformly meant fragility and vulnerability. Indeed, a prime purpose of government has usually been to protect and enhance the power of the ruler, whether emperor, king, sultan, prince, chief, sheik, or general. When the legitimacy of the government is readily challenged, the ruler's relationship to the ruled is based on preserving and expanding power—with the ruler viewing the ruled as though they were actual or potential enemies. Security and counterintelligence become the paramount intelligence elements. Indeed, intelligence collection abroad—particularly, keeping track of exiles or a neighboring ruler's willingness to foment trouble in an adjacent state—is often only an extension of security concerns at home.

This century's infamous totalitarian governments were more thoroughgoing versions of traditional strongman rule. They too rejected the liberal notion that all who live peacefully within a country's borders are citizens or potential citizens; only members of the ruling party could aspire to a role in the regime's political life. The ruling party, with its large internal security forces, closed border policy, and ever-ready troops, was in a state of permanent war with the ruled and those it sought to rule.

Not surprisingly, intelligence in totalitarian societies differs in many ways from intelligence in most democratic societies.[6] In authoritarian and totalitarian systems, intelligence services are almost synonymous with security services. They are directed primarily at the local population, although little or no distinction is made between enemies at home and enemies abroad—both are kept track of, and both neutralized whenever possible. Potential domestic enemies are much closer—all about, in fact—and far outnumber possible foreign agents; therefore approximately 90 percent of the KGB's manpower, estimated at one time to be in excess of 500,000 (including troops and border police), was traditionally deployed against its own population, not against the capitalist enemy abroad.[7]

The contrast here, stemming from differences in the nature of government, is significant. The United States and Great Britain, for example, operating on different premises, usually focus approximately 95 percent of their intelligence effort on external threats.[8]

Further, few totalitarian rulers fully accept the modern concept of the sovereign equality of stable nation-states. Instead, adhering to the notion that a particular system is the only "correct" way of organizing society, they have sought to impose it on their neighbors whenever possible. Other states have been viewed, in effect, as aliens that if not removed would over time undermine the health of the revolutionary order. Nor have such governments accepted the mainstream Western concept of a sharp distinction between war and peace. Perpetually at war at home and abroad, the totalitarian ruler has employed whatever measures were deemed necessary to the survival of the regime. There have been few limits on the exercise of intelligence in totalitarian societies. Covert political action, in particular, has been a routine weapon.[9]

This general outline of the differences between the intelligence practices of democratic versus authoritarian regimes does not account for government systems that change over time, for governments that lie somewhere between democracy and authoritarianism or for weak states facing strong sub- or transstate threats, e.g., contemporary Russia, Turkey, Colombia, and Mexico. But it does suggest that a modern stable, liberal democracy like the United States will be less inclined to expand its covert action and counterintelligence capabilities than will an autocratic power or a weak, fragmented state. For one thing, the democracy will see less of a need to do so; equally important, it will be more attuned to the potential tension between covert action and counterintelligence on the one hand and the values of democratic, open societies on the other.

Putting the Pieces Together

This study began by distinguishing between the various elements of intelligence to clarify their functions. The elements exist in a symbiotic relationship. If one element is weakened or eliminated, the others are likely to be adversely affected. Counterintelligence and covert action, properly executed, require the assistance of collection and analysis, and to varying degrees vice versa. And each, in turn, is dependent on and reflects the guidance provided by policymakers.

Of course, no intelligence system is perfectly balanced. At various times, a state will emphasize one or more element over the others. And the fact that the United States gives shorter shrift to counterintelligence and covert action than might, in the abstract, seem optimal is not entirely negative. Too much emphasis on counterintelligence can, for example, impede collection and lead to domestic abuses. Similarly, too easy a reliance on covert action can generate operations based less on strategic soundness than on government failure to argue convincingly for politically sensitive policies.

The question that needs to be raised now is whether in the case of the United States the imbalance among the elements is too great. Has the prevailing bias against counterintelligence and covert action created a situation in which the country's statecraft and intelligence effort as a whole suffer? Certainly over the last few decades the disparity between what counterintelligence and covert action capabilities could be and what they are has grown. This made the struggle against the major adversaries of the time, the Soviet Union and its allies, more difficult and, probably, more costly. A key national security issue for the future is whether it is wise to allow the disparity to persist or to widen.

For the Foreseeable Future

The end of the cold war eliminated or reduced many of the threats that preoccupied the United States during much of the second half of the twentieth century. However, the end of the cold war did not bring with it an end to conflict. On the contrary, world politics continues as it has for much of mankind's existence. The types of units or actors that engage in world politics change. The issues and threats that concern these players vary. But contrary to some rather optimistic recent predictions that we are approaching the "end of history" or "perpetual peace," world politics, characterized by relatively low levels of government and relatively high expectations of conflict and violence, is likely to continue.[10] The United States faces an uncertain and dangerous world. States will continue to resort to armed conflict, to the production and dissemination of weapons of mass destruction, and to terrorism. This was exemplified in the Persian Gulf War of 1991 and crisis with Iraq in late 1994.

In addition, there is increasing recognition that the United States and indeed much of the interdependent global community face nontraditional challenges for which the state-centric paradigm that served reasonably well during the twentieth century no longer provides sufficient explanation and guidance.[11] Perhaps the most significant nontraditional challenge to United States interests is the increasing number of weak governments and the rise of the substate and transstate actors that are increasingly able to challenge local governments and to defy international control. These include ethnic and religious groups and organized criminals with high-level political connections.

The phenomenon is most apparent in what used to be called the Second World and Third World. Some states have disintegrated completely—in the Balkans, the Caucasus, Southwest Asia and Central Africa. In the Andes and parts of Mexico, Central America, and the Caribbean, governments have great difficulty imposing control over their territory. Disintegrative tendencies are also apparent in parts of the First World. For example, ethnic criminal, racial, and religious conflict has been increasing in parts of Europe, and governments there are finding it difficult to meet the challenge.

The end of the cold war not only did not bring an end to conflict, it did not bring an end to the requirements for a full-service intelligence capability. Not only will there continue to be a need for collection and analysis on traditional and nontraditional conflicts, there will also be a need for the symbiotically related elements of counterintelligence and covert action.

Today American governmental personnel and installations at home and abroad are the target of a hundred or more intelligence services of states and nonstate actors. Some states, for example Iraq, North Korea, Iran, and Sudan, are likely to be hostile to U.S. interests in particular regions of the world. Many other authoritarian governments will be hostile to U.S. interests within their own borders but not outside. Many hostile foreign intelligence services will try to thwart U.S. intelligence and, to some extent, to manage American perceptions. They will try to divert or deflect U.S. policy in their own countries, as well as to neutralize positive U.S. intelligence operations against them.

Other governments will be friendly to overall U.S. interests and will even cooperate on some issues, such as terrorism and organized crime. But even the services of many friendly governments will devote a portion of their resources to learning U.S. secrets, influencing U.S. perceptions, and preventing U.S. efforts to learn their secrets and influence their politics. All told, perhaps as many as 100,000 able human beings will earn their living trying to neutralize and outwit American intelligence. To advance its interests, the United States will need to do what prudent statesmen have done in different ways for centuries: ensure that counterintelligence is adequate to the task.

Also to be considered is the intelligence threat posed by nonstate actors such as large, skillful criminal groups, for example, the Colombian drug cartels, the Chinese Triads, and the Italian and Russian mafias, whose international reach sometimes extends as far as that of recognized sovereignties. These entities also engage in intelligence activities, such as attempting to penetrate law enforcement bodies and to covertly influence the decisions of their own and foreign governments.

The United States for a while may decide that the effort needed to counter activities of the state and nonstate actors is not worth the cost politically or bureaucratically. But that decision sooner or later may well backfire—whether in successful terrorist attacks in American cities, in compromise of U.S. intelligence programs in key regions of the Middle East or Eurasia, or in the inability of the United States to understand what is happening inside "counterintelligence states" and political-criminal groups in various regions of the world. Counterintelligence has been and will remain in the future a valuable strategic instrument. As history demonstrates, when properly understood and employed, counterintelligence can be used by a state not only to protect itself but also to advance its interests against those of its adversaries. The same is true for covert action.

The United States may continue not to avail itself of covert action as a regular supplement to policy. But even if covert action were regarded as a normal tool of American statecraft, it would not necessarily mean that there should be more covert action in the post-cold-war era. Covert action should not become a substitute for political consensus or well-conceived policy. Unless the United States can develop such a policy and forge a national consensus, not much should be expected from covert action. Effectively utilized, however, covert action, in conjunction with other military and foreign policy tools, may be able to play a valuable, even decisive, role in furthering U.S. interests in the face of traditional and nontraditional threats. There is a strong argument to be made for developing a covert action infrastructure that can be called on when needed as an adjunct to policy, and not as a last resort.

Letting counterintelligence and covert action capabilities lapse may not prove fatal, given the advantages the United States enjoys today with respect to the world's other powers. Nevertheless, diminished counterintelligence and covert action capabilities raise the cost of exercising that advantage by reducing the tools a president has on hand to address national security problems, short of waging war. Moreover, American dominance is unlikely to go untested forever; the Hitlers and Stalins of the world have not vanished with the end of the twentieth century. When the test does come, a weak U.S. counterintelligence and covert action capability could be much more than a mere hindrance. It might prove a catalyst for disaster—as it has for many others throughout world history.

America's interest in foreign affairs traditionally manifests itself in fits and starts. The recurring trend of engagement and withdrawal is now so ingrained in American history that it seems almost as natural as the seasons. And yet this cycle is neither inevitable nor desirable. Serious and sustained effort may make a difference. To enhance security, American intelligence needs to be revitalized. America's leaders can ill afford to be reluctant supporters of a full-service intelligence capability. Presidents and congressional leaders can start by acknowledging and articulating the contribution that intelligence, including counterintelligence and covert action, makes to maintaining national security. But this probably will not be enough. Presidential and congressional rhetoric and reform alone cannot eliminate the disparity between what counterintelligence and covert action capabilities are and what they might be. Modernization, bureaucratic culture, and threat perception cannot be easily managed even by vigorous, sustained leadership. Nevertheless, strong leadership and public understanding of why the disparity exits can go a long way toward reducing the intelligence deficit in the interest of future security.

Notes

Preface

1. William Hood, *Spy Wednesday* (New York: Norton, 1986), p. 64. A bit of exposition inserted into the author's fiction. In addition to his fiction, Hood is the author of the classic *Mole: The True Story of the First Russian Spy to Become an American Counterspy*, the story of the handling of a real-life Soviet double agent, Pytor Popov, in the 1950s (New York: W. W. Norton, 1982. Reprint, Washington, DC: Brassey's, 1993). Hood started his career in OSS in 1943 and retired from the CIA in 1975.

2. An example of a former practitioner's work is Christopher Felix's *A Short Course in the Secret War*, originally published in 1963. It has been reprinted several times, most recently by Madison Books (3rd ed., Lanham, MD, 1992). David Wise and Thomas Ross's *The Invisible Government* (New York: Random House, 1964) is an example of a journalistic exposé, and one of the first of the post–World War II U.S. intelligence system.

1. Neglected Elements in American Intelligence

1. For different perspectives on the definition of intelligence, see Abram N. Shulsky, *Silent Warfare: Understanding the World of Intelligence*, 2nd ed., rev. by Gary J. Schmitt (Washington, DC: Brassey's, 1993), pp. 1–3 and 189–92; Alexander Orlov, "The Theory and Practice of Soviet Intelligence," *Studies in Intelligence* 24.3:17; Sherman Kent, *Strategic Intelligence for American World Policy* (Princeton, NJ: Princeton University Press, 1949; reprint 1966), especially Kent's response to Orlov in the introduction to the 1966 edition; Bruce D. Berkowitz and Allan E. Goodman, *Strategic Intelligence for American National Security* (Princeton, NJ: Princeton University Press, 1989); Abram N. Shulsky and Jennifer Sims, "What Is Intelligence?" in Roy Godson, Ernest May, and Gary Schmitt, eds., *U.S. Intelligence at the Crossroads: An Agenda for Reform* (Washington, DC: Brassey's, 1995).

2. See, for example, Cord Meyer, *Facing Reality: From World Federalism to the CIA* (Lanham, MD: University Press of America, 1982); and Chapter 2 of Shulsky, *Silent Warfare*.

3. Shulsky, *Silent Warfare*, pp. 53–59.

4. There are many who believe that security and countermeasures are not, strictly speaking, part of counterintelligence. They see security and countermeasures as separate disciplines, supportive but not integral parts of counterintelligence. Some argue that this definition is too limited, that counterintelligence

should include the activity of countering threats posed to security by non-governmental forces with their own intelligence capabilities, such as terrorists or international organized crime. Others have an even more far-reaching definition, one with policy implications: counterintelligence is concerned with the overall objectives, vulnerabilities, and methods of adversary governments or organizations that use intelligence to enhance their interests; it is concerned with the way in which intelligence fits into their offensive and defensive strategies. Adversaries may include states or political movements controlled or significantly influenced by intelligence or counterintelligence, in which case counterintelligence assumes major responsibility for overall analysis of the others' intentions, priorities, and capabilities.

The best and most important recent illustration of such a state is the former Soviet Union. The Soviet leadership and the Communist Party of the Soviet Union, in their heyday, were influenced, if not dominated by, security and counterintelligence concerns. For them, counterintelligence and security were essential to protecting the regime against enemies at home and abroad. The KGB was one of the most prestigious and elite institutions in the country. As a result, the Soviet security service was intimately involved in policymaking and its implementation. Attempts to understand the internal workings and preoccupations of the KGB provided the United States and others with important insights not only into Soviet foreign policy but also into Soviet domestic preoccupations and the Soviet leaders' perception of their own vulnerabilities. That is, knowledge about the KGB was useful for protecting against the threats it posed as well as for explaining Soviet behavior and exposing opportunities to exploit Soviet vulnerability.

5. The 1991 nomination of Robert Gates as Director of Central Intelligence, for example, raised the question, publicly and privately, of whether the analysts were "taking over" from the covert action specialists who had been DCIs in the past—such as Allen Dulles, William Colby, and William Casey—and, if so, whether this was a desirable development. Gates's career had been spent as an analyst and National Security Council official.

6. These people might be key governmental or nongovernmental leaders who already enjoy status and material comfort. Few would risk their own lives or the lives of their family members for a small stipend or for clandestine romance. Some have done so however, when they saw their activities as part of a larger design to influence significant events.

7. The full story of Iraqi denial and deception is not available in print, but David Kay, the United Nations inspector who played a major role in discovering the extent of Iraq's weapons program after the Gulf War, has described his experiences in "Deception: Collection and the Lessons of Iraq," in Godson, May, and Schmitt, *U.S. Intelligence at the Crossroads*.

8. Kent, *Strategic Intelligence*, pp. 155–58; Graham Fuller, "Intelligence, Immaculately Conceived," *National Interest* 26 (Winter 1991–92), esp. pp.

96–97; Harold Ford, *Estimative Intelligence: The Purposes and Problems of National Intelligence Estimating*, rev. ed. (Lanham, MD: University Press of America, 1993); Ray Cline, *Secrets, Spies and Scholars: Blueprint of the Essential CIA* (Washington, DC: Acropolis Books, 1976).

9. U.S. Congress, Senate Select Committee to Study Governmental Operations with Respect to Intelligence Activities, chaired by Senator Frank Church (hereafter referred to as the "Church Committee"), *Final Report*, 94th Cong., 2nd sess., 1976, S.Rpt. 94–755; House Select Committee on Intelligence, chaired by Representative Otis Pike (the "Pike Committee"). The Pike Committee's final report was never published by the House, but a draft text was leaked to the *Village Voice* and later published by a British publishing house as *CIA: The Pike Report* (Nottingham: Spokesman Books, 1977).

10. Ernest Lefever and Roy Godson, *The CIA and the American Ethic: An Unfinished Debate* (Washington, DC: University Press of America for the Ethics and Public Policy Center, Georgetown University, 1985), p. 49. Figures taken from Church Committee, *Final Report*.

11. Kenneth G. Robertson, "The Study of Intelligence in the United States," in Roy Godson, ed., *Comparing Foreign Intelligence* (Washington, DC: Pergamon-Brassey's, 1988), p. 13.

12. Samuel F. Huntington, *American Politics: The Promise of Disharmony* (Cambridge, MA: Belknap, Harvard University Press, 1981), p. 191.

13. Huntington, *Promise of Disharmony*, p. 178.

14. Huntington, *Promise of Disharmony*, pp. 191–92. On the breakup of the foreign policy consensus, see Raymond L. Garthoff, *Detente and Confrontation: American-Soviet Relations from Nixon to Reagan* (Washington, DC: Brookings, 1985); John Lewis Gaddis, *Strategies of Containment: A Critical Appraisal of Postwar American National Security Policy* (New York: Oxford University Press, 1982); James N. Rosenau and Ole R. Holsti, "U.S. Leadership in a Shrinking World: The Breakdown of Consensuses and the Emergence of Conflicting Belief Systems," in G. John Ikenberry, *American Foreign Policy: Theoretical Essays* (Glenview, IL: Scott, Foresman, 1989); James A. Nathan and James K. Oliver, *United States Foreign Policy and World Order*, 4th ed. (Glenview, IL: Scott, Foresman, 1989), pp. 561–82; Cyrus Vance, *Hard Choices: Four Critical Years in Managing America's Foreign Policy* (New York: Simon & Schuster, 1983); Zbigniew Brzezinski, *Power and Principle: Memoirs of the National Security Adviser, 1977–1981* (New York: Farrar, Straus & Giroux, 1983); Henry Kissinger, *The White House Years* (Boston, MA: Little, Brown, 1979); and Norman Podhoretz, *Why We Were in Vietnam* (New York: Simon & Schuster, 1982).

15. See, for example, John Ranelagh, *The Agency: Rise and Decline of the CIA* (New York: Simon & Schuster, 1986); John T. Elliff, *The Reform of FBI Intelligence Operations* (Princeton, NJ: Princeton University Press, 1979); Robert

L. Borosage and John Marks, eds., *The CIA File* (New York: Grossman Publishers, 1976); Loch K. Johnson, *A Season of Inquiry* (Lexington, KY: University Press of Kentucky, 1985).

16. Since the late 1970s, CIA recruitment advertisements in newspapers throughout the country have never referred to counterintelligence or covert action. For example, an advertisement in the June 14, 1994, *Wall Street Journal* describes the CIA's Clandestine Service as "the cutting edge of American intelligence, an elite corps gathering the vital information needed by our policymakers to make critical foreign policy decisions."

Retired Air Force colonel John Macartney, commandant of the DIA's Defense Intelligence College (DIC) from 1984 to 1988, recalls that neither covert action nor counterintelligence was really considered the business of defense intelligence in the early 1980s, nor were they covered to any great extent in the DIC curriculum. In part, that was because covert action, and to some extent counterintelligence, were not functions of defense intelligence at that time.

17. Some general works that help correct that imbalance are Shulsky, *Silent Warfare*; Angelo Codevilla, *Informing Statecraft: Intelligence for a New Century* (New York: Free Press, 1992); Robin Winks, *Cloak and Gown: Scholars in the Secret War, 1939–1961* (New York: Quill, 1987); Rhodri Jeffreys-Jones, *The CIA and American Democracy* (New Haven, CT: Yale University Press, 1989); Roy Godson, ed., *Intelligence Requirements for the 1980s: Covert Action* (Washington, DC: National Strategy Information Center, 1981); Roy Godson, ed., *Intelligence Requirements for the 1980s: Counterintelligence* (Washington, DC: National Strategy Information Center, 1985); and Roy Godson, ed., *Intelligence Requirements for the 1980s: Intelligence and Policy* (Lexington, MA: Lexington Books, 1986). In addition, there have been a number of scholarly studies about individual episodes or aspects of intelligence.

18. The single best book on the Zimmermann telegram is Barbara Tuchman, *The Zimmermann Telegram* (New York: Macmillan, 1966).

19. For an account of Sorge's life and activities as a Soviet agent, see Gordon W. Prange with Donald Goldstein and Katherine V. Dillon, *Target Tokyo: The Story of the Sorge Spy Ring* (New York: McGraw-Hill, 1984); and F. W. Deakin and G. R. Storry, *The Case of Richard Sorge* (London: Chatto & Windus, 1966).

20. See *Soviet Acquisition of Western Technology* (Washington, DC: Department of Defense, April 1982) and *Soviet Acquisition of Militarily Significant Western Technology: An Update* (Washington, DC: Department of Defense, September 1985).

21. Much of this information can also be found in an article written by a senior French counterintelligence official under a pseudonym. See Henri Regnard, "L'URSS et le Renseignement Scientifique, Technique et Tech-

nologique," *Defense Nationale* 39 (December 1983): 107–21. For an account of the agent, "Farewell," and the information he provided, see Thierry Wolton, *Le KGB en France* (Paris: Bernard Grasset, 1986); Marcel Chalet and Thierry Wolton, *Les Visiteurs de l'Ombre* (Paris: Bernard Grasset, 1990); Christopher M. Andrew and Oleg Gordievsky, *KGB: The Inside Story of Its Foreign Operations from Lenin to Gorbachev* (London: Hodder & Stoughton, 1990); and Gordon Brook-Shepherd, *The Storm Birds: Soviet Postwar Defectors* (London: Weidenfeld & Nicolson, 1988).

22. Philip Hanson, "Soviet Industrial Espionage," *Bulletin of the Atomic Scientists* 43 (April 1987): 27. This is based upon his study of certain of the documents the French obtained from "Farewell."

23. House Committee on Armed Services, *Report of the Technology Transfer Panel of the Committee on Armed Services*, 98th Cong., 2nd sess., 1984, Committee Print, p. 17.

24. "Report on Soviet Use of the Media," in House Permanent Select Committee on Intelligence (hereafter "HPSCI"), *The CIA and the Media*, 95th Cong., 1st and 2nd sess., 1977–78, pp. 531–627; Charles A. Sorrels, *Soviet Propaganda Campaign Against NATO* (Washington, DC: Arms Control and Disarmament Agency, 1983). This focuses solely on intermediate range nuclear forces. The following documents are on active measures and forgeries which include examples taken from the neutron bomb and INF campaigns: Senate Committee on Foreign Relations, *Soviet Imperatives for the 1990s, Part 2, Soviet Active Measures*, 99th Cong., 1st sess., 1985, S.Hrg. 99–400; HPSCI, *Soviet Covert Action (The Forgery Offensive)*, hearings before the Subcommittee on Oversight, 96th Cong., 2nd sess., February 6 and 19, 1980; HPSCI, *Soviet Active Measures*, 97th Cong., 2nd sess., July 13–14, 1982.

25. Senate Foreign Relations, *Soviet Active Measures*; HPSCI, *Soviet Active Measures*; Clive Rose, *Campaigns Against Western Defense: NATO's Adversaries and Critics* (New York: St. Martin's Press, 1985); Richard Shultz and Roy Godson, *Dezinformatsia: Active Measures in Soviet Strategy* (Washington, DC: Pergamon-Brassey's, 1984).

26. One of the better secondary accounts is Richard L. Kugler, *Commitment to Purpose: How Alliance Partnership Won the Cold War* (Santa Monica, CA: Rand, 1993), pp. 373, 375–390.

27. The full and accurate story of Philby and the other British spies of that time is buried in the records of the American, British, and Soviet intelligence services, as well as with the spies themselves. But for other accounts (none definitive) of Kim Philby and other British spies, see Andrew Boyle, *The Fourth Man: The Definitive Account of Kim Philby, Guy Burgess and Donald Maclean and Who Recruited Them to Spy for Russia* (New York: Dial Press, 1979); Robert Cecil, *A Divided Life: A Personal Portrait of the Spy Donald Maclean* (London: Bodley Head, 1988); John Costello, *Mask of Treachery*

(London: Collins, 1988); Anthony Glees, *The Secrets of the Service: British Intelligence and Communist Subversion, 1939–1951* (London: Jonathan Cape, 1987); Bruce Page, David Leitch, and Phillip Knightley, *The Philby Conspiracy* (New York: Ballantine Books, 1981); Patrick Seale and Maureen McConville, *Philby: The Long Road to Moscow* (New York: Simon & Schuster, 1973).

28. For more information on the Albanian operation and Philby's role, see Nicholas Bethel, *Betrayed* (New York: Times Books, 1984).

29. Even if Philby himself did not supply the information, Albanian émigré groups in Europe from whom the resistance was drawn were heavily penetrated. Poor operational security practices probably would have doomed the operation without Philby and other double agents in the Albanian resistance. In his own account of the Albanian operation, written after he defected to Moscow, Philby makes no mention of his role in informing the KGB. Instead he attributes the failure to poor conception, bad planning, British-American infighting, and lack of resistance potential in a loyally Communist Albania. Philby writes, "The operation, of course, was futile from the beginning." See Kim Philby, *My Silent War* (New York: Grove Press, 1968), p. 197.

30. See testimony of Robert M. Gates before the House Committee on Foreign Affairs, *Post Cold War Intelligence*, 102nd Cong., 2nd sess., Committee Hearing, February 25, 1992.

31. At this point, the most authoritative statements available on the damage Ames did to U.S. interests can be found in "The Aldrich H. Ames Case: An Assessment of CIA's Role in Identifying Ames as an Intelligence Penetration of the Agency," Report of Frederick P. Hitz, CIA Inspector General, 21 October 1994; Senate Select Committee on Intelligence, "An Assessment of the Aldrich H. Ames Espionage Case and Its Implications for U.S. Intelligence," 1 November 1994 (including Hitz's statement to the Committee in appendix 4); and DCI R. James Woolsey, "The CIA and the Aldrich Ames Case," Statement to the Press at the U.S. House of Representatives, September 28, 1994.

32. John J. Dziak, *Chekisty: A History of the KGB* (Lexington, MA: Lexington Books, 1988), p. 47.

33. The organization's actual name was the Moscow Municipal Credit Association—thus, the Trust. It posed as a financial institution operating within the liberal economic environment of Lenin's New Economic Policy. The bogus group's clandestine name was the Monarchist Association of Central Russia. For more information about the Trust operation, see Geoffrey Bailey, *The Conspirators* (New York: Harper & Brothers, 1960); Dziak, *Chekisty*; George Leggett, *The Cheka: Lenin's Political Police* (Oxford: Clarendon Press, 1981).

34. One ironic aspect of the Trust operation was that British and French intelligence services were paying the Russian émigrés for the disinformation being

supplied them by the Cheka through the Trust. Allegedly, at one point, money paid to these sources by the West was used to cover the expenses of the deception operation itself. In short, the West was paying to be deceived (Bailey, *Conspirators*, p. 67).

35. For more information on Operation Fortitude, see Ralph Bennett, *Ultra in the West: The Normandy Campaign 1944–1945* (New York: Scribner's, 1980); F. H. Hinsley, et al., *British Intelligence in the Second World War*, 5 vols. (Cambridge, UK: HM Stationery Office, 1979–1988), vol. 3, pt. 2, pp. 44–65; J. C. Masterman, *The Double-Cross System in the War of 1939–1945* (New Haven, CT: Yale University Press, 1972), pp. 145–63; Ewen Montagu, *Beyond Top Secret Ultra* (New York: Coward, McCann & Geoghegan, 1978), reprint of *Beyond Top Secret U* (London: Peter Davies, 1977), pp. 151–56. For arguments about whether the Germans were really deceived, see the debate between Klaus-Jurgen Muller, "A German Perspective on Allied Deception Operations in the Second World War," *Intelligence and National Security* 2.3 (July 1987): 301–26; and Michael Handel, "Methodological Mischief: A Reply to Professor Muller," *Intelligence and National Security* 4.1 (January 1989): 161–64. Also see Michael Howard in F. H. Hinsley, ed., *British Intelligence in the Second World War: Strategic Deception*, vol. 5 (Cambridge, UK: HM Stationery Office, 1990).

36. For the opinions and actions of Louis XV and his foreign minister, Choiseul, regarding the American colonies, see C. H. Van Tyne, "French Aid Before the Alliance of 1778," *American Historical Review*, October 1925, pp. 20–40.

37. Samuel Flagg Bemis, *The Diplomacy of the American Revolution* (Bloomington, IN: Indiana University Press, 1957), p. 27. In March 1776, Vergennes wrote "Consideration on the Affairs of the English Colonies in America." He saw secret aid as a device to exhaust the English, as well to give France and Spain time to build up their armed forces in Europe. It would also move the focus of conflict away from the European continent, helping to avoid general European war. One month later he wrote "Reflections" as a practical plan of how to achieve these goals. See Orville T. Murphy, *Charles Gravier, Comte de Vergennes: French Diplomacy in the Age of Revolution, 1719–1787* (Albany, NY: SUNY Press, 1982), pp. 235–36.

38. Secret emissaries were sent to America, not only to keep the French government informed of the situation, but also to spread dissatisfaction among the colonists. Benjamin Franklin, speaking about France, declared in 1767 that "'the intriguing nation' was blowing up the coals between Great Britain and her colonies, and he, at that time, hoped to prevent her success." Van Tyne, "French Aid," p. 24.

39. Van Tyne, "French Aid," p. 39. Among those who advised the French monarch to provide the covert assistance was Baron de Beaumarchais. Beau-

marchais, the famous and wealthy author of renowned comedies (*The Barber of Seville* and *The Marriage of Figaro*) and a lover of intrigue, was to play a major role in helping the American Revolution. In the words of one historian, Beaumarchais advised Louis XVI that "the policy of governments is not the moral law of its citizens." Van Tyne, "French Aid," p. 38. He also remarked that "secrecy is the soul of [this] business, and that in politics a project once disclosed is a project doomed to failure." *Intelligence in the War of Independence*, a Bicentennial publication of the Central Intelligence Agency (Washington, DC: Central Intelligence Agency, 1976), p. 14.

40. Bemis, *Diplomacy of the American Revolution*, pp. 27–28, 39–40, 89; also J. B. Perkins, *France in the American Revolution* (Boston: Houghton Mifflin, 1911), pp. 58–59, 86.

41. At first, Spain's assistance was only financial, but during the summer of 1776, the governor of New Spain began to provide lethal assistance as well. He "privately" delivered twelve thousand pounds of gunpowder "out of the King's stores" to the Americans. *Intelligence in the War of Independence*, p. 15. This aid helped frustrate British plans to conquer Fort Pitt in the strategically important Ohio Valley. From New Orleans and Havana, gunpowder and other supplies supported George Rogers Clark's expedition into Indiana and Ohio, and from the "very secret service fund" of the Spanish governor came the means Clark used to capture Fort Kashoskia and Vincennes (*Intelligence in the War of Independence*, p. 15). Finally, Spain continued to provide secret financial assistance (totalling approximately $400,000 from 1776 through 1779). Bemis, *Diplomacy of the American Revolution*, pp. 91–93.

42. *Intelligence in the War of Independence*, p. 10. Archard de Bonvouloir, a French army officer, was a collector of intelligence who also sought to assure the Americans that the French had no interest in Canada and might be willing to assist the American colonists. His information confirmed to the French that the American rebels could succeed, but that they needed aid in order to reach victory. Murphy, *Comte de Vergennes*, p. 234; Van Tyne, "French Aid," pp. 36–37; Perkins, *France in the American Revolution*, pp. 45–48.

43. Van Tyne, "French Aid," p. 37; Bemis, *Diplomacy of the American Revolution*, pp. 36–37.

44. *Intelligence in the War of Independence*, p. 15.

45. Many scholars agree that the rebel victory at Saratoga in October 1777 was made possible only by secret French aid (Van Tyne, "French Aid," pp. 20, 40). O. W. Stephenson wrote, ". . . it may be stated with some degree of assurance that if it had not been for the great quantities of powder obtained by importations from France before the Saratoga campaign, the Revolution would have broken down long before that time." O. W. Stephenson, "The Supply of Gunpowder in 1776," *American Historical Review* 30.2 (January 1925): 281.

46. Murphy, Comte de Vergennes, pp. 247–51.

47. The British were probably aware that the French were secretly supporting the Americans. Edward Bancroft, the confidential secretary of Franklin and Deane in Paris, was a British agent. But the British did not want war with France, and, as they were not confronted with overt French involvement, they evidently chose to ignore the covert assistance. In this instance, plausible denial was apparently sufficient. Bemis, *Diplomacy of the American Revolution*, pp. 65–66; Van Tyne, "French Aid," p. 31.

48. Friedrich Katz, *The Secret War in Mexico* (Chicago, IL: University of Chicago Press, 1981), p. 327.

49. Jules Witcover, *Sabotage at Black Tom* (Chapel Hill, NC: Algonquin Books, 1989). See also Count Bernstorff, *My Three Years in America* (New York: Scribner's, 1920); Colonel W. Nicolai, *The German Secret Service*, trans. George Renwick (London: Stanley Paul, 1924); George Sylvester Vierick, *Spreading Germs of Hate* (New York: Horace Liveright, 1930).

50. Witcover, *Sabotage*, p. 82. Witcover notes that the German efforts became somewhat more professional after Captain Franz von Rintelen arrived in the United States in 1915.

51. M. L. Saunders and Philip Taylor, *British Propaganda During the First World War* (London: Macmillan, 1982), esp. pp. 167–208.

52. Arthur Willert, *The Road to Safety: A Study in Anglo-American Relations* (London: Derek Verschoyle, 1952), pp. 63–64. Willert was the Washington correspondent for the *Times* of London, and was the secretary of the British War Mission in the United States. Other key sources for the Wiseman story are the *Woodrow Wilson Papers*, edited by Arthur S. Link et al. (Princeton, NJ: Princeton University Press, 1966–1994); Edward Mandell House, *The Intimate Papers of Col. House, Arranged as a Narrative by Charles Seymour*, vol. 2 (Boston: Houghton Mifflin, 1928); W. B. Fowler, *British-American Relations, 1917–1918: The Role of Sir William Wiseman* (Princeton, NJ: Princeton University Press, 1969).

53. Even after declaring war on Germany, the Congress and the American public were reluctant to become heavily involved. Wiseman wrote to London explaining this reluctance, and apparently suggesting some "covert" assistance: "Any pronouncement [the Allied governments] can make which will help the President to satisfy the American people that their efforts and sacrifices will reap the disinterested reward they hope for, will be gratifying to him, and in its ultimate result serve to commit America yet more heartedly to the task at hand. . . . the Administration are ready to assist us to the limit of the resources of their country; but it is necessary for them to educate Congress and the Nation to appreciate the actual meaning of these gigantic figures. . . . The Allies will have to use patience, skill and ingenuity in assisting the Ameri-

can authorities to arrive at a solution of this one grave difficulty." House, *The Intimate Papers of Colonel House*, p. 31.

54. John Bruce Lockhart, "Sir William Wiseman, Bart—Agent of Influence," *RUSI Quarterly*, Summer 1989, p. 66.

55. Lockhart, "Sir William Wiseman," p. 67.

56. Original British document, quoted in Mary S. Lovell, *Cast No Shadow* (New York: Pantheon, 1992), p. 339.

57. David Ignatius, "How Churchill's Agents Secretly Manipulated the U.S. Before Pearl Harbor," *Washington Post*, Outlook, 19 September 1989. Ignatius says he was given the opportunity to peruse the official 423-page history of BSC, written in 1945, and to take notes on it. His account of the volume is similar to that of Mary Lovell. Lovell says that she was shown a copy by a source she refuses to identify. She also says that she has interviewed a number of the report's writers, all former BSC employees, who claim that almost all of the official papers of BSC were destroyed. Lovell, *Cast No Shadow*, pp. 346–47.

58. Lovell, *Cast No Shadow*, p. 341.

59. Thomas F. Troy, *Donovan and the CIA* (Washington, DC: Central Intelligence Agency, 1981), pp. 82–84.

60. Lovell, *Cast No Shadow*, p. 341.

61. Ignatius, "Churchill's Agents"; and Lovell, *Cast No Shadow*.

62. Few details have been made public on the role of British paramilitary activity. Apparently, it focused on protecting munitions and other goods against sabotage on U.S. soil. There was probably some violence (particularly in U.S. ports, necessary to counter Nazi agents). Later in the war, the United States apparently also made use of the Mafia for this purpose. See Rodney Campbell, *The Luciano Project* (New York: McGraw-Hill, 1977).

63. Michael Ledeen, *Western European Communism and American Foreign Policy* (New Brunswick, NJ: Transaction, 1987), pp. 1–49.

64. Roy Godson, *American Labor and European Politics* (New York: Crane, Russak, 1976), especially pp. 17–87. The bibliography cites studies of Communist infiltration of the European labor movement in the 1930s and 1940s. See also the bibliography in Ledeen, *Western European Communism*.

65. See F. Borkenau, *World Communism: A History of the Communist International* (Ann Arbor, MI: University of Michigan Press, 1962); Branko Lazitch, "Two Instruments of Control by the Comintern: The Emissaries of the ECCI and the Party Representatives in Moscow" and "Stalin's Massacre of the Foreign Communist Leaders," in M. Drashkovitch and Branko Lazitch, eds., *The Comintern: Historical Highlights* (New York: Praeger, 1966); Guenther Nollau,

International Communism and World Revolution: History and Methods (New York: Praeger, 1961; reprint, Westport, CT: Greenwood Press, 1975); Stefan T. Possony, "The Comintern as an Instrument of Soviet Strategy," in M. Drashkovitch, ed., *The Revolutionary Internationals, 1864–1943* (Stanford, CA: Stanford University Press, 1966); M. N. Roy, *The Russian Revolution* (Calcutta: Renaissance Publishers, 1949); Senate Committee on the Judiciary, *The Revival of the Communist International and Its Significance for the United States*, staff study, 86th Cong., 1st sess., Committee Print, 1959.

66. By 1948, total U.S. military forces stood at 1.4 million (approximately 10 percent of the wartime peak) and the majority were stationed on U.S. soil. By 1946, U.S. forces in Europe were down to 400,000. In contrast, Stalin had thirty divisions in Eastern Europe, thirty more on Russia's western border, and a total of at least 2.8 million in uniform (some estimates are as high as 4.6 million). See Charles Morris, *Iron Destinies, Lost Opportunities: The Arms Race Between the USA and the USSR, 1945–1987* (New York: Harper & Row, 1988). See also Matthew Evangelista, "Stalin's Postwar Army Reappraised," *International Security*, Winter 1982–83, pp. 110–29; Department of State, *Documents on Disarmament, 1945–1959*, vol. 1, 1945–1956 (Washington, DC: Government Printing Office, 1960).

67. Hugh Tovar, "Covert Action," in Roy Godson, ed., *Intelligence Requirements for the 1980s: Elements of Intelligence*, rev. ed. (Washington, DC: National Strategy Information Center, 1983), p. 73.

68. See Harry Rositzke, *The CIA's Secret Operations: Espionage, Counterespionage, and Covert Action* (New York: Reader's Digest Press, 1977); Sallie Pisani, *The CIA and the Marshall Plan* (Lawrence, KS: University Press of Kansas, 1991); and Burton Hersh, *The Old Boys* (New York: Scribner's, 1992). In addition, there are references to U.S. covert action in several books, but no detailed description of the covert action in Western Europe has been published. One of the best descriptions of a covert action country plan, but for the mid-1950s, can be found in William Colby with Peter Forbath, *Honorable Men: My Life in the CIA* (New York: Simon & Schuster, 1978), pp. 108–40. Colby, stationed in Rome in the 1950s, was responsible for U.S. covert action at the American embassy in Italy.

69. Gregory F. Treverton, *Covert Action: The Limits of Intervention in the Postwar World* (New York: Basic Books, 1987), pp. 203–4.

70. For example, note the slow-drip effect of Radio Free Europe/Radio Liberty in weakening Communist ideology in Eastern Europe and Russia. See the 1990 testimonials by then Czech president Václav Havel, then Polish prime minister Tadeusz Mazowiecki, then Hungarian prime minister–elect Jozsef Antall, the then Romanian foreign minister, and the then chairman of the Council of Estonia, quoted in Appendix 7 of Roy Godson with Richard Kerr

and Ernest May, "Covert Action in the 1990s," paper of the Working Group on Intelligence Reform (Washington, DC: Consortium for the Study of Intelligence, Working Group on Intelligence Reform, 1993), pp. 51–53.

2. Steps and Missteps: Covert Action Since 1945

1. See Nancy Lisagore and Frank Lipsius, *A Law unto Itself: The Untold Story of the Law Firm of Sullivan and Cromwell* (New York: Morrow, 1988), p. 47. This was later the firm of Allen and John Foster Dulles.

2. On the history of sporadic U.S. covert action since the American Revolution, see Stephen F. Knott, *Lifting the Veil: The Roots of American Covert Activity* (Ph.D. diss., Boston College, 1991). For a survey of secondary accounts, see G.J.A. O'Toole, *Honorable Treachery* (New York: Atlantic Monthly Press, 1991). There are also detailed accounts of specific activities in Mexico: see, for example, A. Brook Caruso, *The Mexican Spy Company: United States Covert Operations in Mexico, 1845–1848* (Jefferson, NC: McFarland, 1991); and Charles H. Harris and Louis R. Sadler, *The Border and the Revolution: Clandestine Activities of the Mexican Revolution, 1910–1920* (Silver City, NM: High Lonesome Books, 1988). For additional references to books and journals, see Neal H. Petersen, *American Intelligence 1774–1990: A Bibliographical Guide* (Claremont, CA: Regina Books, 1992).

3. Anthony Cave Brown, ed., *The Secret War Report of the OSS* (New York: Berkeley, 1976).

4. Omar Bradley, *A Soldier's Story* (New York: Holt, 1951), p. 536.

5. Arnold F. Rogow, *James Forrestal: A Study of Personality, Politics and Policy* (New York: Macmillan, 1963), pp. 144–45, n56.

6. The files of EUR-X disappeared. Inquiries at the National Archives revealed little about the existence of the organization or the location of its records. However, there are occasional references to the body. For example, an official CIA historian noted that when, in 1947, there were interagency disputes about the creation of a political warfare agency, one of the CIA's opponents remarked that "he didn't see how this would differ from what Murphy was doing at State." Arthur Darling, "The Central Intelligence Agency, an Instrument of Government, to 1950" (Washington, DC: National Archives, DCI Historical Series, December 1953), ch. 7, p. 53.

7. Darling is the best source on this bureaucratic struggle. See also Church Committee *Final Report*, bk. 4, pp. 9–25.

8. NSC 1/3 as quoted in *Foreign Relations of the United States, 1948*, vol. 3, *Western Europe* (Washington, DC: Government Printing Office, 1974), p. 778.

9. Church Committee *Final Report*, bk. 4, p. 29.

10. Darling and the Church Committee reports are the best sources on this period.

11. Text of NSC 10/2 is found in William M. Leary, ed., *The Central Intelligence Agency: History and Documents* (Tuscaloosa, AL: University of Alabama Press, 1984), pp. 131–34.

12. The existence of the OPC in the late 1940s was almost as secret as the Manhattan Project had been earlier. A standing joke concerned the young recruit who went into a drugstore one evening in search of a then-popular cure-all, APC tablets, but in some confusion asked for "OPC tablets." Appalled at his pronouncement of the forbidden initials, he promptly fled fearfully into the night.

13. The only book that details the role of Wisner is not flattering to him or the OPC. See Hersh, *Old Boys*.

14. Here again the popular ethos, and State Department prejudices, rose as an obstacle: former Foreign Service officers (FSOs) such as Maynard Barnes and Carmel Offie were willing to go to OPC, but James McCargar, who accepted Wisner's invitation to join his staff on the advice of Loy Henderson, "Mr. Foreign Service," believes that he was probably the only active-duty FSO ever assigned to permanent duty at OPC. Interview with James McCargar, May 19, 1993.

15. Church Committee *Final Report*, bk. 4, pp. 35–36.

16. British paramilitary covert activities had been set up early in the war in the Special Operations Executive (SOE) apart from the British foreign intelligence service, MI6. On the whole, this was viewed as a disaster. After the war the British did not repeat the experience. See F. H. Hinsley, ed., *British Intelligence in the Second World War*, vol. 2, ch. 15, esp. pp. 14–17; vol. 3, pt. 1, app. 1, esp. pp. 461–64. See also David Stafford, *Britain and European Resistance, 1940–1945: A Survey of the Special Operations Executive, with Documents* (Toronto: University of Toronto Press, 1980).

17. Hugh Tovar in Godson, *Elements of Intelligence*, p. 87. See also former OSO officer Harry Rositzke, *CIA's Secret Operations*, p. 163.

18. Author interview with James McCargar, May 19, 1993.

19. Church Committee *Final Report*, bk. 4, p. 37.

20. The OPC operations suffered major Soviet penetrations. In part this can be attributed to the weakness of OSO counterintelligence at the time, which failed to protect both OPC and OSO operations, particularly those inside the Sino-Soviet bloc.

21. Church Committee *Final Report*, bk. 4, p. 37.

22. There is not, so far as is known, a single, coherent document which might be described as "a covert action annex." There were, however, a variety of NSC directives that were translated by the covert action bureaucracies of the day, especially the Office of Policy Coordination (OPC), into what Harry Rositzke, in his 1977 book, referred to favorably, and in their aggregate, as the

"covert action annex to the Marshall Plan." Rositzke, *Secret Operations*, p. 158. For a brief description of these documents and their background, see the official CIA history, declassified in 1994, by Wayne G. Jackson, *Allen Welsh Dulles as Director of Central Intelligence, 26 February 1953–29 November 1961*, vol. 3, *Covert Activities* (Washington, DC: Central Intelligence Agency, July 1973). For a critical analysis, see Pisani, *CIA and the Marshall Plan*. For another critical view, see Hersh, *Old Boys*, which contains information so far unavailable elsewhere on OPC chief Frank Wisner and his senior staff. There is no detailed description on the public record of U.S. covert action in Western Europe during this period, which was large, far-reaching, and affected politics in many countries.

23. President Truman's role in setting up this pattern was obscured by his apparent denunciation of covert action years later. See Rositzke, *Secret Operations*, p. 151.

24. The documentation on U.S. policy in the late 1940s and 1950s is now fairly extensive. Both primary and secondary sources support this conclusion. The major primary sources include the NSC directives (many of which have now been declassified) and the memoirs of many of the participants. See, for example, NSC Directives 10, 20, and 68, as well as the memoirs of the presidents and many of their advisers, including George Kennan and Charles Bohlen. Secondary sources also, in the main, confirm these conclusions. Although a "New Left" revisionist school suggested that the U.S. leaders had a policy to overthrow Communist rule in Russia and Eastern Europe well before 1948, the overwhelming evidence of secondary accounts does not bear this out. It also does not support the conclusion that after World War II the United States was seeking, in the classical Wilsonian formulation, to promote global democracy. The United States was quite prepared to tolerate and even sometimes to assist nondemocratic regimes and political forces so long as they were perceived to be opposing Soviet global hegemony. The United States was prepared to work with the full spectrum of political forces from extreme right to extreme left when it was thought to be useful for balance-of-power purposes. The United States, for example, supported the Communist government of Yugoslavia in the late 1940s when Marshal Tito, Milovan Djilas, and other Communists stood up to Stalin, just as in the early 1970s it defended the People's Republic of China against possible Soviet nuclear attack. The United States in the 1950s also assisted Franco's Spain and Salazar's Portugal—both dictatorships of a different sort—when it sought their incorporation into the NATO alliance, as well as other dictatorships and authoritarian leaders when this was considered useful. Among the best secondary sources on American foreign policy in the postwar period are Gaddis, *Strategies of Containment*; Ernest May, *"Lessons" of the Past: The Use and Misuse of History in American Foreign Policy* (New York: Oxford University Press, 1975); and Stephen Ambrose, *Rise to Globalism: American Foreign Policy Since 1938* (New York: Penguin Books, 1988).

25. There is no study of the ethos or mind-set of U.S. covert action managers. However, the political background of most of these managers leads to the conclusion that they were domestic liberals in the post–World War II American political sense. Indeed, the more conservative CIA leaders, such as Allen Dulles, were proud of the fact that they harbored many American liberals who in their youth had flirted with Communism or with Communist fronts. Among those liberals who were prominent in the covert action world of the 1950s and 1960s and who have written about their work—some more discreetly than others—are Thomas Braden, "I'm Glad the CIA Is 'Immoral,'" *Saturday Evening Post*, May 20, 1967, pp. 9–13; Meyer, *Facing Reality*; Colby, *Honorable Men*; and William Colby with James McCargar, *Lost Victory: A Firsthand Account of America's Sixteen-Year Involvement in Vietnam* (Chicago, IL: Contemporary Books, 1989).

Also, the published congressional testimony of the Church Committee on covert action—the largest single source of documentation on U.S. covert action—reveals a pattern of support to the democratic center, left, and right. But it should be noted that the Church Committee often was selective with the information it published. For example, although it mentions support to labor organizations abroad, it does not discuss much detail. On the other hand, it goes into great detail on instances of support to military or "right-wing" forces on other occasions.

26. On this struggle inside the labor movement and CIA support for both camps, see Godson, *American Labor and European Politics*, and Braden, "I'm Glad the CIA Is 'Immoral.'" Another example of CIA involvement in political infighting in the nongovernmental sector involved the Congress for Cultural Freedom; see Peter Coleman, *The Liberal Conspiracy: The Congress for Cultural Freedom and the Struggle for the Mind of Postwar Europe* (New York: Free Press, 1989).

27. For an example of the approval and coordination process at the top, see Kermit Roosevelt, *Countercoup: The Struggle for the Control of Iran* (New York: McGraw-Hill, 1979). The DP (and British MI6) came up with a plan, code-named AJAX, to remove Iranian prime minister Mussadegh in 1953. The plan was taken to John Foster Dulles by the DP project manager, Roosevelt, and DCI Allen Dulles. Present were the Secretary of State; Undersecretary Walter Bedell Smith (who had recently been the DCI with Allen Dulles as his deputy); the director of policy planning, Robert Bowie; the deputy undersecretary, Robert Murphy; and several of State's specialists on the Middle East, as well as then Secretary of Defense Wilson. Roosevelt was pleased to have approval for his plan but shocked at the cavalier way the decision was made. As he put it, "Surely it deserved thorough examination, the closest consideration, somewhere at the highest level. It had not received such thought at this meeting. . . . At any rate, from that point forward, I was on my own. And that, I felt, was a good place to be. I could count on maximum support with, in

all probability, a minimum of interference. I had a good team with me, a fine venture to tackle." Roosevelt, *Countercoup*, pp. 18–19.

28. Church Committee *Final Report*. See also secondary sources, including Thomas Powers, *The Man Who Kept the Secrets: Richard Helms and the CIA* (New York: Knopf, 1979), which, while hostile to covert action, still maintains that the CIA was not a rogue elephant.

29. A notable example was Italy, where Ambassador Clare Boothe Luce and her minister-counselor of embassy, Elbridge Durbrow, later ambassador to South Vietnam, fought a rearguard action against, among others, William Colby, over the *apertura alla sinistra*, the "opening to the left." See Colby, *Honorable Men*.

30. Felix, *Short Course in the Secret War*, p. 7.

31. Donovan Pratt, "Counterintelligence Organization and Operational Security in the 1980s," in Godson, ed., *Counterintelligence*, pp. 230–31.

32. Angleton's judgment of the mid-1950s turned out to be correct. Not until Bettino Craxi took over the Italian Socialist Party in 1976 did it seriously attempt an organizational break with the Communists. See Angelo Codevilla, "The Opening to the Left," in Giovanni Sartori and Austin Ranney, eds., *Eurocommunism: The Italian Case* (Washington, DC: American Enterprise Institute, 1978).

33. This was the main thesis of the Church Committee *Final Report*, as well as of the Karalekas history of the CIA in Book 4 of the *Final Report*. Karalekas interviewed many former DI analysts as well as reviewing written histories. Not everyone shared all these views: some DI chiefs, for example, Ray Cline, did not. See his *Secrets, Spies, and Scholars*. But even Cline (for a variety of reasons) calls for the separation of the analysts from the clandestine services, particularly on the grounds that this would help analysis. This view, which is still widely held inside and outside the CIA, assumes that analysts and collectors are objective and without policy preferences. It should also be noted that in the 1990s the leadership of the Directorate for Intelligence, the CIA's analytic branch, began a program to make analysts aware of their own biases. See Joseph Nye, "Estimating the Future?" and Douglas MacEachin, "The Tradecraft of Intelligence: Challenge and Change at the CIA," in Godson, May, and Schmitt, *U.S. Intelligence at the Crossroads*.

34. Godson, *American Labor and European Politics*. Several chapters are devoted to the foreign policy perspectives of the AFL leaders and their activities before, during, and after World War II.

35. Braden, "I'm Glad the CIA Is 'Immoral.'"

36. "The Most Dangerous Man," National Affairs: Labor, *Time*, March 17, 1952.

37. On the relationship between the CIA and the American labor movement, see Godson, *American Labor and European Politics*, pp. 46–48.

38. There are no studies available on comparative U.S.-Soviet covert aid programs. Those most familiar with the information available from penetration of Soviet and European Communist Party activities believe Soviet aid was much more extensive than that of the United States for most of the postwar period. See, for example, Rositzke, *Secret Operations*, esp. p. 187; Meyer, *Facing Reality*, pp. 97–100; and Colby, *Honorable Men*, pp. 104–12 *passim*.

39. Few of the West European ministers of the interior or their internal security service chiefs have written books about their experiences. Some have described and denounced Soviet and Communist Party attempts to take over their countries, but they include very few comments about U.S. assistance to anti-Communists. See, for example, the memoirs of the French Socialist minister of the interior Jules Moch, *Rencontres avec Leon Blum* (Paris: Plon, 1970).

40. For example, in 1964, Congressman Wright Patman of the House Committee on the Problems of Small Business revealed the names of eight of the CIA's funding instruments. This jarred the Agency, but the disclosure did not create a major flap, and little was done to prevent the operational disaster when the media really went after the CIA in 1967. Church Committee *Final Report*, bk. 4, p. 185.

41. On the Philippines and following cases, there are memoirs of former participants as well as secondary works, based to some extent on interviews with former CIA participants. There are also secondary accounts extremely critical of the U.S. role in these incidents. Almost all of the memoirs and accounts based on interviews with the participants portray their role and tradecraft as very good. The secondary accounts are extremely critical of the U.S. policy and intervention. Very few of these authors, however, have examined the quality of U.S. covert action itself, as opposed to overall U.S. policy.

For example, see the memoir of the key former American participant in the Philippines, Edward Landsdale, *In the Midst of Wars: An American's Mission to Southeast Asia* (New York: Harper & Row, 1972); the analysis written by former CIA operative Douglas S. Blaufarb, *The Counterinsurgency Era: U.S. Doctrine and Performance, 1950 to the Present* (New York: Free Press, 1977); the basically favorable secondary account written by John Ranelagh, *The Agency*, pp. 224–26; and a critical secondary study by D. Michael Shafer, *Deadly Paradigms: The Failure of U.S. Counterinsurgency Policy* (Princeton, NJ: Princeton University Press, 1988), pp. 205–40.

42. Roosevelt, *Countercoup*; Ranelagh, *Agency*, pp. 260–64; and Treverton, *Covert Action*, pp. 44–83.

43. David Atlee Phillips, *The Night Watch: Twenty-five Years of Peculiar Service* (New York: Atheneum, 1977); Ranelagh, *Agency*, pp. 264–69; Treverton, *Covert Action*.

44. Blaufarb, *Counterinsurgency Era*, pp. 128–68; Colby, *Honorable Men*, pp. 191–202; Tovar, in Godson, ed., *Elements of Intelligence*.

45. Malcolm Wallop, "Covert Action: Policy Tool or Policy Hedge," *Strategic Review*, Summer 1984, pp. 9–16.

46. There is a paucity of well-documented studies of these operations, and relatively few undocumented descriptions of CIA operations to weaken or overthrow Communist governments, with the exception of accounts of the many operations against Castro in the 1960s, and some marginal works on the Albanian operation.

A few former chief CIA operatives have given interviews to journalists on this subject or discussed them in their writings, e.g., Rositzke, *Secret Operations*; and Franklin Lindsay, *Beacons in the Night: With the OSS and Tito's Partisans in Wartime Yugoslavia* (Stanford, CA: Stanford University Press, 1993). Lindsay is an OSS veteran who was in charge of OPC operations in Eastern Europe. For interesting tidbits, especially on OPC and later DP chief Frank G. Wisner, see Hersh, *Old Boys*.

In 1989 a British journalist published an account of Baltic operations based in part on interviews with former British intelligence and CIA officers, as well as KGB officers: Tom Bower, *The Red Web: MI6 and the KGB Master Coup* (London: Aurum, 1989).

47. Powers, *Richard Helms*, pp. 42–43; and Bower, *Red Web*.

48. The literature on the Bay of Pigs and other attempts to overthrow Castro is voluminous. Primary sources include memoirs of many former participants and some declassified documents, including postmortem analysis of what went wrong by U.S. officials. For an overview of the planning that went into the operation and its fallout, see Jackson, *Allen Welsh Dulles*, pp. 113–47. There also have been numerous interviews with some key U.S. officials such as then DDP Richard Bissell. The Church Committee also released studies based on CIA files of paramilitary activities and the assassination plots against Castro. See Church Committee, *Alleged Assassination Plots Involving Foreign Leaders*, 94th Cong., 1st sess., S.Rpt. 94–465 (Washington, DC: Government Printing Office, 1975). A number of scholars and journalists have also gone over much of this material. Some of the best sources are *Operation Zapata: The "Ultrasensitive" Report and Testimony of the Board of Inquiry on the Bay of Pigs* (Frederick, MD: University Publications of America, 1981); Phillips, *Night Watch*, pp. 85–111; Ranelagh, *Agency*; and Peter Wyden, *Bay of Pigs: The Untold Story* (New York: Simon & Schuster, 1979).

49. Powers, *Richard Helms*, p. 113.

50. Church Committee *Final Report*, bk. 4, pp. 47–48.

51. For example, Tad Szulc notes judgments by both the U.S. government and Castro that the CIA underestimated Cuban capabilities in preparing for the Bay of Pigs invasion. See Szulc, *Fidel: A Critical Portrait* (New York: Morrow, 1986), pp. 555, 557. More recently, Castro accused the CIA of orchestrating the assassinations of Trujillo in the Dominican Republic and Torrijos in Panama. See *Foreign Broadcast Information Service (FBIS)*, Latin America, May 21, 1990, pp. 4–5.

52. One critic of covert action operations in the halcyon days is Hugh Tovar, who was an operative with OSS, SSU, and OSO and a CIA station chief. He became chief of the covert action staff in the late 1960s. Unfortunately, Tovar does not provide many examples to bolster his case, and one former DO operative maintains that key details of the example he does cite, Indonesia in 1957–58, are inaccurate. Tovar in Godson, *Elements of Intelligence*, pp. 77–78.

53. For more on the relationship between the NSA and the CIA and its exposure in 1967, see William H. Chafe, *Never Stop Running: Allard Lowenstein and the Struggle to Save American Liberalism* (New York: Basic Books, 1993), pp. 104–10, 254–61.

54. Marcus Raskin, "A Short Account of International Student Politics and the Cold War with Particular Reference to the NSA, CIA, etc.," *Ramparts*, March 1967, pp. 29–39.

55. See Meyer, *Facing Reality*, pp. 85–109.

56. Cord Meyer discusses the Johnson administration's shocked reaction to the "scandal." One of the few politicians at the time to defend the CIA was Robert Kennedy, who had been an enthusiastic supporter of the projects. Richard Harris Smith, *OSS: The Secret History of America's First Central Intelligence Agency* (Berkeley, CA: University of California Press, 1972), p. 380.

57. Author interview with James McCargar, May 20, 1993.

58. On the growth of proprietaries and even CIA management's ambivalence toward them, see the Church Committee *Final Report*, bk. 1, pp. 205–51.

59. Indeed, in the late 1960s when CIA funding came to a halt, more or less, and Soviet funding did not, pro-Communist elements made major gains in democratic socialist circles, for example, the Socialist International. Where the U.S. government, or the CIA, kept its programs going—the radios broadcasting across the Iron Curtain—the slow drip had its effect. See Chapter 1, note 70.

60. On changes in dominant Washington culture and the decline of anti-Communism, see Norman Podhoretz, *Breaking Ranks: A Political Memoir* (New York: Harper & Row, 1979). See also the sources cited in Chapter 1, note 14.

61. Church Committee Hearings, vol. 7, *Covert Action*, p. 54.

62. Stansfield Turner, *Secrecy and Democracy: The CIA in Transition* (Boston, MA: Houghton Mifflin, 1985), p. 177.

63. See Brzezinski, *Power and Principle*. For background, see also Lawrence T. Caldwell and Alexander Dallin, "U.S. Policy Toward the Soviet Union," in Kenneth Oye, Donald Rothchild, and Robert Lieber, eds., *Eagle Entangled: U.S. Foreign Policy in a Complex World* (New York: Longman, 1979), pp. 215–23.

64. See Mark Lagon, *The Reagan Doctrine: Sources of American Conduct in the Cold War's Last Chapter* (Westport, CT: Praeger, 1994).

65. On the interagency struggles through the mid-1980s over increasing covert assistance to the Afghani Mujahideen, see George Schultz, *Turmoil and Triumph: My Years as Secretary of State* (New York: Scribner's, 1993), pp. 692, 1086–87; Mohammed Yousaf and Mark Adkin, *The Bear Trap: Afghanistan's Untold Story* (London: Leo Cooper, 1992), pp. 98, 180–82; Riaz Khan, *Untying the Afghan Knot: Negotiating Soviet Withdrawal* (Durham, NC: Duke University Press, 1991), pp. 85, 88, 169–72, 243–44; and Marin Strmecki, *Power Assessment: Measuring Soviet Power in Afghanistan* (Ph.D. diss., Georgetown University, 1994), pp. 144–46. Yousaf, a member of ISI, the Pakistani intelligence service, ran the Afghani support program from 1983 to 1987. Khan was the second-ranking member in the Pakistani team that negotiated the Geneva accords leading to Soviet withdrawal from Afghanistan.

66. For the text of the Hughes-Ryan Amendment and the relevant section of the National Security Act of 1947 to which it refers, see HPSCI, *Compilation of Intelligence Laws and Related Laws and Executive Orders of Interest to the National Intelligence Community, As Amended through March 1, 1981*, 97th Cong., 1st sess., Committee Print, March 1981, pp. 149–50.

67. Gary Schmitt, "Oversight—What for and How Effective?" in Godson, ed., *Intelligence and Policy*, pp. 130–31.

68. For background, see House Select Committee to Investigate Covert Arms Transactions with Iran and Senate Select Committee on Secret Military Assistance to Iran and the Nicaraguan Opposition, *Report of the Congressional Committees Investigating the Iran-Contra Affair*, 100th Cong., 1st sess., H.Rpt. 100–433 and S.Rpt. 100–216 (hereafter referred to as Iran-Contra Report); and Martha Cottam, "The Carter Administration's Policy Toward Nicaragua," *Political Science Quarterly*, Spring 1992, pp. 123–46. See also Roy Gutman, *Banana Diplomacy: The Making of American Policy in Nicaragua, 1981–1987* (New York: Simon & Schuster, 1988); Bob Woodward, *Veil: The Secret Wars of the CIA* (New York: Simon & Schuster, 1987); Constantine Menges, *The Twilight Struggle: The United States v. the Soviet Union Today* (Washington, DC: American Enterprise Institute, 1990); and Robert Pastor, *Condemned to Repetition: The United States and Nicaragua* (Princeton, NJ: Princeton University Press, 1987).

69. See sources above, esp. Iran-Contra Report, p. 27.

70. See Peter Kornbluh and Malcolm Byrne, eds., *The Iran-Contra Scandal: The Declassified History* (New York: New Press, dist. by Norton, 1993), p. 11;

Theodore Draper, *A Very Thin Line: The Iran-Contra Affairs* (New York: Hill & Wang, 1991); Constantine Menges, *Inside the National Security Council: The True Story of the Making and Unmaking of Reagan's Foreign Policy* (New York: Simon & Schuster, 1988); and Alexander Haig, *Caveat* (New York: Macmillan, 1984). On the differences between Carter's and Reagan's approach, see Cottam, "Carter Administration."

71. See Lagon, *Reagan Doctrine*, chs. 3 and 5, *passim*.

72. Then representative Harkin's amendment as quoted in the Iran-Contra Report, p. 395.

73. As quoted in Iran-Contra Report, p. 396.

74. Iran-Contra Report, pp. 32–35, and 396.

75. Iran-Contra Report, pp. 33–34. Iklé is quoted in Codevilla, *Informing Statecraft*, p. 268.

76. See Woodward, *Veil*, p. 256, for an (unsourced) account of a Shultz-Baker discussion on this topic. See also Jane Mayer and Doyle McManus, *Landslide: The Unmaking of the President, 1984–1988* (Boston, MA: Houghton Mifflin, 1988), pp. 15–17.

77. Iran-Contra Report, p. 406. After the election, Reagan moved away from the interdiction of arms to the FMLN in El Salvador as a formulation. In 1985, in a speech to the UN and in the State of the Union address, he embraced aid to anti-Communist guerrillas as a collective policy.

78. As quoted in Iran-Contra Report, p. 398. For different accounts of Reagan's rationale in signing the bill, see Iran-Contra Report, p. 491; and Draper, *Very Thin Line*, p. 27.

79. For an example of this reasoning regarding the Contra aid issue, see the memo from Robert Gates to William Casey quoted in Kornbluh and Byrne, *Iran-Contra Scandal*, pp. 45–49.

80. A clear-cut statement of this view can be found in an article by then deputy DCI Robert Gates, who became DCI in 1991: ". . . the CIA today finds itself in a remarkable position, involuntarily poised nearly equidistant between the executive and legislative branches." Robert Gates, "The CIA and American Foreign Policy," *Foreign Affairs* 66 (Winter 1987–88): 224–25.

81. The first major book naming names to be sold in many capitals was put out by the East German intelligence service and was ostensibly authored by Julius Marder: *Who's Who in the CIA*. See Ladislav Bittman, *The Deception Game* (Syracuse, NY: Syracuse University Research Corp., 1972), pp. 155–56. This was followed a few years later by Philip Agee's *Inside the Company: CIA Diary* (Harmondsworth, UK: Penguin Books, 1975), and then by magazines, such as *Covert Action Information Bulletin*, that allegedly specified which U.S. embassy personnel and nongovernmental organizations were working for U.S. intelligence.

Ladislav Bittman, a former Czech intelligence officer who specialized in disinformation, says the technique of naming names was an East German, Soviet, and Czech operation in which he participated. Bittman defected in 1968 and wrote several influential books on Soviet bloc active measures and disinformation. On the origin of naming names, see Ladislav Bittman, *The KGB and Soviet Disinformation* (Washington, DC: Pergamon-Brassey's, 1985), pp. 191–92; and Bittman, *Deception Game*, pp. 155–56.

82. The careers of two up-and-coming young social democratic leaders, the Norwegian Ola Teige and the Dane Jan Hackkerup, both then secretaries of the International Union of Socialist Youth, were ruined. Teige, according to a former colleague, shot himself.

83. Church Committee *Final Report*, bk. 1, pp. 157–59.

84. When the United States was moderately successful, as in the long-drawn-out struggle in Afghanistan in the 1980s, it was not because the United States had many people to do the covert action job. Rather, the United States was able to join in a covert coalition with others, in which the United States was the provider and the others the actors. According to Mohammed Yousaf, the man who ran the actual war inside Afghanistan (and inside the USSR), the Pakistani intelligence service benefited from U.S. (and other) money, training, equipment, and intelligence. But it was the Pakistanis, rather than U.S. personnel, who did the work inside Afghanistan. See Yousaf and Adkin, *Bear Trap*; also Steve Coll, "Anatomy of a Victory: CIA's Covert War in Afghanistan," *Washington Post*, July 19, 1992; and Steve Coll, "In CIA's Covert Afghan War Where to Draw Line Was Key," *Washington Post*, July 20, 1992.

85. Some observers of these developments have dubbed them "the Foreign Service's revenge"—the U.S. Foreign Service being one of the great bastions of insistence on "generalists."

86. Church Committee *Final Report*, bk. 4, pp. 32–33.

87. Other countries, among them Libya and Iran, have for years secretly and not so secretly helped build up forces friendly to them in the West Bank and/or the Persian Gulf.

88. On KGB training and the lessons KGB officers learn from past successes such as the Trust, see Ilya Dzhirkvelov, *Secret Servant: My Life with the KGB and the Soviet Elite* (New York: Harper & Row, 1987), pp. 40–63. Given the fact that several generations of young KGB officers were shown that Trust operations were successful, it is not surprising that such operations were continued from the 1920s to the 1980s.

89. Take as an example U.S. assistance to Polish labor. Although the full record is still not available, both Carl Bernstein, a journalist and a Reagan critic, and Edwin Meese, Reagan's Attorney General, have maintained that President Reagan mobilized all the instruments of statecraft, including the

CIA, to collaborate with the Vatican and various trade union elements to keep the Polish Solidarity movement alive after the imposition of martial law in Poland in 1981. See Meese's description, including his approving citation of Bernstein, in Edwin Meese III, *With Reagan: The Inside Story* (Washington, DC: Regnery Gateway, 1992), pp. 170–71.

Another example of a successful program was covert support to the Mujahideen in Afghanistan from the late 1970s through the 1980s. See Marin Strmecki, *Power Assessment*.

90. One manifestation of this view is "The Need to Know: The Report of the Twentieth Century Fund Task Force on Covert Action and American Democracy" (New York: Twentieth Century Fund Press, 1992).

91. For an example of this type of policymaking, see Haig, *Caveat*, pp. 128–29. This kind of thinking was often prevalent in dealing with post–World War II ruling Communist parties. For another example of this perspective, see the comments of a former undersecretary of state cited in "Need to Know," p. 37.

92. The Task Force on Covert Action and American Democracy was a nongovernmental project of the Twentieth Century Fund. Its report was published in 1992.

93. See Ernest May, "Covert Action in the 1990s," in Godson, May, and Schmitt, *U.S. Intelligence at the Crossroads*.

3. Building and Rebuilding: Counterintelligence Since World War II

1. See, for example, Witcover, *Sabotage at Black Tom*; and Joan M. Jensen, *Army Surveillance in America, 1975–1980* (New Haven, CT: Yale University Press, 1991), pp. 160–80.

2. Nathan Glazer, *The Social Basis of American Communism* (Westport, CT: Greenwood Press, 1974), pp. 38–89.

3. Church Committee *Final Report*, bk. 2, pp. 21–36. Also, James Kirkpatrick Davis, *Spying on America: The FBI's Domestic Counterintelligence Program* (New York: Praeger, 1992), pp. 2–31.

4. Church Committee *Final Report*, bk. 2, pp. 25–28; Jensen, *Army Surveillance*, pp. 211–30; and Jeffrey M. Dorwart, *Conflict of Duty: The U.S. Navy's Intelligence Dilemma, 1919–1945* (Annapolis, MD: Naval Institute Press, 1983), pp. 111–25.

5. Robert J. Lamphere and Tom Shachtman, *The FBI-KGB War* (New York: Random House, 1986), pp. 19–41.

6. Ian Sayer and Douglas Botting, *America's Secret Army: The Untold Story of the Counter Intelligence Corps* (London: Grafton-Collins, 1989), pp. 268–364.

7. See Chapter 2 for the development of the postwar consensus on U.S. containment policy in the late 1940s and the breakup of that consensus in the 1960s.

8. Dziak, *Chekisty*, pp. 2–4.

9. See William Odom, "Who Controls Whom in Moscow," *Foreign Policy* 19 (Summer 1975): 109–23; and Abdurakhman Avtorkhanov, "The Soviet Triangular Dictatorship: Party, Police, and Army: Formation and Situation," *Ukrainian Quarterly* 34.2 (1978): 135–53.

10. There is a fairly extensive literature on the integration of Soviet bloc intelligence. Most of it is derived from the writings of Soviet bloc defectors and former American and other Western intelligence practitioners who share the major interpretation of the defectors. See, for example, the books of defectors such as Bittman, *Deception Game*; and Ion Mihai Pacepa, *Red Horizons: Chronicles of a Communist Spy Chief* (Washington, DC: Regnery Gateway, 1987).

11. There is a large body of literature by scholars and participants and counterintelligence practitioners on this relationship. For an overview on the KGB use of the CPUSA, see Herbert Romerstein and Stanislav Levchenko, *The KGB Against the "Main Enemy"* (Lexington, MA: Lexington Books, 1989).

12. On the early years and the tradition of the Cheka, see Leggett, *Cheka*; and Dziak, *Chekisty*.

13. In the U.S. intelligence community, an "illegal" is a professional intelligence officer who adopts a completely false identity and does not operate under official cover. Not only does the illegal claim that he is not an intelligence officer, but his personal identity papers, travel documents, and résumé are usually all false. "Legal" operatives often will not declare their real profession, but they will use their real name or at least official documents, such as passports, that utilize some true details. Most legals, whether using their real name or not, operate under official cover.

14. On Soviet illegals operating in the United States, for example, see Romerstein and Levchenko, *Main Enemy*.

15. There is no detailed study of the postwar Western intelligence alliance. On the origin of the U.S.–UK relationship, see Bradley E. Smith, *The Ultra Magic Deals* (Novata, CA: Presidio Press, 1993). Among the studies that deal with the subject are Jeffrey T. Richelson and Desmond Ball, *The Ties That Bind: Intelligence Cooperation Between the UKUSA Countries* (Boston, MA: Allen & Unwin, 1985). See also Christopher Andrew, "The Growth of Intelligence in the English Speaking World," Working Paper #83 of the International Security Studies Program of the Wilson Center for International Scholars (Washington, DC: nd).

16. See Lamphere and Shachtman, *FBI-KGB War*; and Peter Wright, *Spycatcher: The Candid Autobiography of a Senior Intelligence Officer* (New York: Viking, 1987).

17. National Security Council Intelligence Directive No. 5, declassified June 1, 1976.

18. See W. Raymond Wannall, "Setting Straight the FBI's Counterintelligence Record," *World & I*, January 1987, p. 176. Wannall is a retired assistant director of the FBI's Intelligence Division. The description here of the directives governing counterintelligence in the United States is drawn from Wannall's article, although bits and pieces of the directives can be found in the Church Committee *Final Report*.

19. Wannall, "Setting Straight," p. 176.

20. Wannall, "Setting Straight," p. 176.

21. Wannall, "Setting Straight," p. 176.

22. Even the more liberal members in Congress were not very interested in the intrusive techniques being used by the FBI. This was to change in the 1960s. For example, see William W. Keller, *The Liberals and J. Edgar Hoover* (Princeton, NJ: Princeton University Press, 1989). On the evolution of congressional interest in intelligence, see essays by Roy Godson in Lefever and Godson, *CIA and the American Ethic*.

23. The name of the division of the FBI concerned with counterintelligence and security changed over the decades. In the mid-1990s, it became known as the National Security Division. It is referred to here as the Intelligence Division.

24. Both ran afoul of the Director shortly after Hoover's death, and both in effect were fired.

25. In World War II, emerging from the Bureau's counterintelligence activities in the western hemisphere, the FBI developed a positive intelligence program in Latin America, having secured Roosevelt's agreement that the Bureau rather than the OSS was responsible for intelligence and counterintelligence in that region. Stanley E. Hilton, *Hitler's Secret War in South America, 1939–1945* (New York: Ballantine Books, 1981), pp. 191–223.

26. William C. Sullivan, *The Bureau: My Thirty Years in Hoover's FBI* (New York: Norton, 1979), p. 163.

27. Church Committee Hearings, vol. 6, p. 348.

28. W. Mark Felt, *The FBI Pyramid from the Inside* (New York: G.P. Putnam's Sons, 1979), p. 31. Some FBI officials with wartime experience in these kinds of interviews believe Felt was exaggerating.

29. The literature on the internal security investigation is fairly extensive. A great deal of data was made public in the Church Committee hearings. In addition, several scholars, congressional investigators, and others who were critical of FBI practices also have analyzed the data. Among them: Athan Theoharis, *Spying on Americans: Political Surveillance from Hoover to the Huston Plan* (Philadelphia, PA: Temple University Press, 1978); Davis, *Spying on America*; and Elliff, *Reform of FBI Intelligence Operations*.

30. Church Committee *Final Report*, bk. 3, p. 49.

31. Information on Bureau techniques and strengths and weaknesses in the first few decades of the postwar period is derived from interviews with former senior officials of the period. These interviews were conducted in the spring of 1993.

32. Church Committee *Final Report*, bk. 3, p. 434, n221; Davis, *Spying on America*, p. 30. See also Sullivan, *Bureau*; and Felt, *FBI Pyramid*. Basically informants are double agents, i.e., they work for two sides, but their true loyalty is to one side. Not all informants operate clandestinely on behalf of two parties, i.e., an informant in the CPUSA might be overt in his affiliation with the CPUSA, but operate secretly for the FBI.

33. Felt, *FBI Pyramid*, p. 348.

34. See, for example, Hood, *Mole*, pp. 202–56.

35. The most famous case is the Soviet illegal who used the name Rudolph Abel and was arrested in 1957, convicted, and exchanged for U-2 pilot Gary Powers in 1962. But there were other much less known cases. See, for example, Sullivan, *Bureau*, pp. 163–65.

36. For example, Abel was identified only because of his coworker Reino Haynahan, a Finn who had become a Soviet agent, defected in Paris in 1957. See Sullivan, *Bureau*, pp. 180–81.

37. See, for example, note 39 on surveillance of Soviet illegal agents.

38. Felt, *FBI Pyramid*, pp. 105–9; Theoharis, *Spying on Americans*, pp. 111–12. One former senior Bureau official claimed that one reason for Hoover's action was that the White House would not provide written requests for the use of sensitive intrusive techniques.

39. Sullivan, *Bureau*, pp. 179–80.

40. Church Committee *Final Report*, bk. 2, p. 62, n238.

41. Apparently the product of this mail surveillance, or "coverage" in intelligence usage, at times was valuable. For example, the FBI was told that Soviet illegal agents in the United States who wished to meet their Soviet principals were under instruction to send a communication from the United States to a particular address in the Soviet Union. According to the Church Committee, the coverage was useful but it did not lead to the actual identification of any foreign illegal agents. Church Committee *Final Report*, bk. 3, pp. 624–25, 632–33. Interviews with former FBI officials indicate that the coverage was more effective than the Church Committee concluded.

42. Church Committee *Final Report*, bk. 2, pp. 58–59.

43. Lamphere and Shachtman, *FBI-KGB War*, p. 86.

44. Lamphere and Shachtman, *FBI-KGB War*, pp. 161–62.

45. Church Committee Hearings, vol. 2, p. 68.

46. Author interview with Sam Papich, a former senior FBI official, September 21, 1993.

47. J. Edgar Hoover, *Masters of Deceit: The Story of Communism in America and How to Fight It* (New York: Holt, Reinhart Winston, 1958); and J. Edgar Hoover, *A Study of Communism* (New York: Holt, Reinhart & Winston, 1962).

48. Sullivan, *Bureau*, pp. 88–93.

49. Some former Bureau officials, while acknowledging the violation of security, especially by field officers, believe it was more than compensated for in the cooperation, cross-fertilization, and comradery among Bureau offices.

50. Sullivan apparently was concerned about Soviet penetration of FBI offices. See Sullivan, *Bureau*, pp. 188–91.

51. It is difficult to know how effective Bureau surveillance was. One indication is that the KGB warned its people that the Bureau was effective and that it was dangerous to regularly meet agents in the United States. Further, as the decades passed, the KGB moved its meetings with U.S. agents abroad, for example, to Mexico City or Vienna, to avoid Bureau surveillance.

52. Internal memorandum cited by Wannall, "Setting Straight," p. 168.

53. Memorandum cited by Wannall, "Setting Straight," pp. 168.

54. Many of the details of COINTELPRO against Old Left groups (i.e., the CPUSA and the SWP), the New Left (SDS, PLP), and groups deemed extremist (the KKK, the Nation of Islam, and the Black Panthers) are available in both the Church Committee hearings and in secondary accounts previously cited. One or two books favorable to the Bureau's program also have been published by journalists, e.g., Don Whitehead, *Attack on Terror: The FBI Against the Ku Klux Klan in Mississippi* (New York: Funk & Wagnall, 1970). Few memoirs of Bureau and Justice Department officials discuss these programs.

55. This technique was known as the "snitch jacket." Church Committee *Final Report*, bk. 3, p. 46. One of the most effective uses of it against the CPUSA that has come to light is the case of a trusted CPUSA leader, William Albertson. See Morton Halperin, Jerry J. Berman, Robert Borosage, and Christine M. Marwick, *The Lawless State* (New York: Penguin, 1976), pp. 115–16. Apparently, in 1989 the U.S. government paid Albertson's widow $170,000 as compensation for wrecking Albertson's career.

56. Davis, *Spying on America*, pp. 33–51.

57. Information on the perception of CIA officials about the roles of counterintelligence and the counterintelligence staff in the first few decades after World War II is based on discussions with over thirty senior CIA officials from

both the counterintelligence staff and the DO divisions. This includes most of the relevant senior CI staff officials and many DO division chiefs and former chiefs of station, and several of the DOs and assistant DOs of the period. These conversations took place throughout the 1980s, and many of the officials were interviewed on the subject several times. Several former members of the counterintelligence staff have written about their experiences, and these accounts have confirmed the basic substance of the interviews. See, for example, the essays by Norman Smith and Donovan Pratt in Godson, *Counterintelligence*.

58. One of the few sources on the techniques and utility of penetrating Communist parties can be found in Rositzke, *Secret Operations*, pp. 84–100. Rositzke at one point headed up the international Communist division.

59. Church Committee *Final Report*, bk. 3, pp. 559–679.

60. The counterintelligence staff study of the Rote Kapelle was declassified and published as a book in 1979. See *The Rote Kapelle: The CIA's History of Soviet Intelligence and Espionage Networks in Western Europe, 1936–1945* (Washington, DC: University Publications of America, 1979).

61. One of the overviews of a country's foreign intelligence system was found in the U.S. embassy when it was taken over by the Iranians in 1979. It was subsequently published in several places. See, for example, "Israeli Foreign Intelligence and Security Services," March 1979, reprinted in *Counterspy*, May–June 1982, pp. 34–54.

62. Ronald Kessler, *Spy vs. Spy* (New York: Pocket Books, 1988), pp. 232–40.

63. A special group examined the cases of employees who were all suspected security risks. The group consisted of representatives from the Office of Security, the Office of Personnel, and the DP. Author interview with Sam Halpern, November 1, 1994.

64. Several journalists have written books about the mole hunt in the CIA in the late 1960s. Among them is Tom Mangold, *Cold Warrior* (New York: Simon & Schuster, 1991). The main theme of this book and details of cases, however, are not correct. See, for example, William Hood, James Nolan, and Samuel Halpern, "Myths Surrounding James Angleton: Lessons for American Counterintelligence," in Godson, May, and Schmitt, U.S. *Intelligence at the Crossroads*.

65. The best description of Soviet penetration can be found in Hayden B. Peake, "Soviet Espionage and the Office of Strategic Services (OSS)" (September 1988 revision of paper delivered at the Conference on World War II and the Shaping of Modern America, Rutgers University, New Brunswick, NJ, April 4–6, 1986). For an illustration of how the security system could operate, see the fictionalized account written by a former CIA employee, Sylvia Press, *The Care of Devils* (New York: Beacon, 1958; reprint, Bantam, 1966). Another

illustration, albeit one-sided, can be found in a book by writer and activist Penn Kimball, *The File* (San Diego, CA: Harcourt Brace Jovanovich, 1983).

66. An example was Cord Meyer. See his memoir, *Facing Reality*. Another was Carmel Offie; see next note.

67. One example of DO overruling the Office of Security was in the case of Frank Wisner, who worked with Carmel Offie when the Office of Security, the FBI, and Senator McCarthy all wanted Offie terminated. A gossipy account can be found in Hersh, *Old Boys*, esp. pp. 252–55 and 441–48.

68. The former head of the counterintelligence staff research branch considered this highly desirable. See Pratt in Godson, *Counterintelligence*, p. 234. Perhaps the first U.S. government exposure of specific Soviet global disinformation activities can be found in the testimony of Richard Helms, then the chief of operations, before a Senate committee. See Senate Committee on the Judiciary, *Communist Forgeries*, Committee Hearings, 87th Cong., 1st sess., June 2, 1961. Another CIA report, "The Soviet and Communist Bloc Defamation Campaign," was given to a prominent member of the House Armed Services Committee, Representative Melby Price, and published in the *Congressional Record*, September 28, 1965, pp. 25391–93. This type of analysis was used to neutralize Soviet disinformation throughout the world. See, for example, Colby, *Honorable Men*, p. 244. This effort at public education was sidetracked for more than a decade, but became the basis of a major educational program of the U.S. government in the late 1970s and 1980s.

69. Winks, *Cloak and Gown*, pp. 411–13, analyzes alternative explanations of how the speech was obtained and disseminated.

70. There is a consensus that the dissemination of the speech had a major impact on support for Soviet Communists throughout the world. For a CIA view of its import, see Rositzke, *Secret Operations*, p. 97.

71. Pratt in Godson, *Counterintelligence*, p. 243.

72. One of the best illustrations of the schism between the divisions and the counterintelligence staff can be found in Colby, *Honorable Men*, pp. 243–45. Colby, a former OSS paramilitary operator, was an OPC recruit who rose to become a division chief, DO, and later DCI. For his account of the distinction between his own covert action perspective and the mentality of collection and counterintelligence, see his *Lost Victory*, p. 121.

73. See, for example, Rositzke, *Secret Operations*, p. 147.

74. Unfortunately, Angleton did very little public writing about counterintelligence matters and often was very cryptic in conversations. The two most useful accounts of his thinking in print are Winks, *Cloak and Gown*, who devotes a chapter to "The Theorist: James Jesus Angleton," pp. 332–439; and Edward J. Epstein, *Deception: The Invisible War Between the KGB and the CIA* (New York: Simon & Schuster, 1989), especially pt. 1, "The State of Mind," pp. 9–110.

75. I am grateful to Tim Naftali for this observation. For more on X-2, see T. J. Naftali, *X-2 and the Apprenticeship of American Counterespionage, 1942–1944*, Ph.D. diss., Harvard University, 1993.

76. One of the few discussions of the CIA's views of the pros and cons of using double agents during these years can be found in Rositzke, *Secret Operations*, pp. 123–26.

77. The DO was closely involved with the development of technology to support humint operations, with some applications of technology "on the ground." The DO and the counterintelligence staff were little involved in protecting or exploiting NSA and the National Reconnaissance Office for counterintelligence purposes. See, for example, the comments of several retired and then serving intelligence officials in Godson, *Counterintelligence*, especially inferences on pp. 13–94 and 224–25.

78. The idealists have not written a great deal. One of the few who has is Angleton's chief of operations, Newton "Scotty" Miler. See, for example, his essay in Godson, *Elements of Intelligence*, and his comments in Godson, *Counterintelligence*, vol. 3 of the same series. Angleton and others did encourage a few writers and journalists, such as Edward J. Epstein, to make their case.

79. See, for example, Epstein, *Deception*, or Winks, *Cloak and Gown*. Even some of the DO's first generation were "idealistic" and influenced writers such as John Ranelagh, *Agency*; and Tom Powers, *Richard Helms*. Both of these authors, but especially Ranelagh, acknowledge their debt to them. Powers's book is especially interesting as he lambastes covert action but is almost completely uncritical of the quality of the CIA's counterintelligence.

The best-known journalists who carry this message are David C. Martin, *Wilderness of Mirrors* (New York: Harper & Row, 1980); Tom Mangold, *Cold Warrior*; and David Wise, *Molehunt: The Secret Search for Traitors That Shattered the CIA* (New York: Random House, 1992). These books also acknowledge their debt to former DO operators, especially Leonard McCoy.

80. Mangold, *Cold Warrior*, pp. 30, 51.

81. Codevilla, *Informing Statecraft*, p. 156.

82. Sayer and Botting, *America's Secret Army*, p. 19.

83. In reality, years before, the Carter White House, with a vice president and several staff who had all worked on the Church Committee, had begun to take steps to improve White House control of counterintelligence and to improve interagency cooperation on counterintelligence matters. But on the whole the Carter NSC was little concerned with counterintelligence.

84. The text of EO 12036 is available in HPSCI, *Compilation of Intelligence Laws*, pp. 215–30.

85. See "The Aldrich H. Ames Case," Report of Frederick P. Hitz, CIA Inspector General, October 21, 1994.

86. George Kalaris and Leonard McCoy, "Counterintelligence," in Roy Godson, ed., *Intelligence Requirements for the 1990s: Collection, Analysis, Counterintelligence and Covert Action* (Washington, DC: Consortium for the Study of Intelligence, National Strategy Information Center, 1989), p. 135.

87. Kenneth deGraffenreid's response to Kalaris and McCoy is in Godson, *Intelligence Requirements for the 1990s*, p. 147.

88. Senate Select Committee on Intelligence, *Meeting the Espionage Challenge: A Review of United States Counterintelligence and Security Programs*, 99th Cong., 2nd sess., S.Rpt. 99–522, pp. 38–58.

4. Handmaiden of Policy: Principles of Covert Action

1. There are, however, distinctions to be made among the "exceptionalists." In general, one school decries the use of covert action on practical grounds. They believe that separation of powers and the pluralism mandated by the American constitutional system is not so constructed as to permit successful covert action. An example of this line of thinking can be found in Ernest May, "Covert Action in the 1990s," in Godson, May, and Schmitt, *U.S. Intelligence at the Crossroads*. A second school bases its position on moral and ethical grounds, alleging that covert action violates our democratic norms. See Borosage and Marks, eds., *CIA File*. There is yet a third position that asserts that the results of covert action are at the best marginal and, even when successful, not worth the risk. For this view, see Treverton, *Covert Action*; and Turner, *Secrecy and Democracy*.

2. Elizabeth was inconsistent in her aid to rebel and opposition groups in Spain, and her efforts were largely unsuccessful. See Conyers Read, *Mr. Secretary Walsingham and the Policy of Queen Elizabeth*, 3 vols. (Cambridge, MA: Harvard University Press, 1925); and J. B. Black, *The Reign of Elizabeth, 1558–1603* (Oxford, UK: Clarendon, 1959). On the French efforts to aid the American revolution, see Chapter 1.

3. This particular failure was in large part due to the blatant lack of consonance between action and policy, which became evident when it all became public. Initiatives of this sort, which contradict declared policy, are very risky. But they are not always failures. An example of a successful covert initiative contrary to declared policy was the Nixon-Kissinger approach to Communist China.

4. See Uri Bialer, "The Iranian Connection in Israel's Foreign Policy, 1948–1951," *Middle East Journal* 39.2 (Spring 1985): 292–315.

5. Paul Smith, Jr., *Political War* (Washington, DC: National Defense University Press, 1989), pp. 62, 68.

6. On Parvus, see Z.A.B. Zeman, *The Merchant of Revolution: The Life of Alexander Israel Helpland (Parvus), 1867–1924* (New York: Oxford University Press, 1965).

7. Hugh Tovar, "Covert Action," in Godson, ed., *Intelligence Requirements for the 1990s*, p. 220.

8. One of the best available sources on this mission is Charlie A. Beckwith, *Delta Force* (New York: Dell, 1983).

9. Rosemary Devonshire Jones, *Francesco Vettoci: Florentine Citizen and Medici Servant* (London: Athlone Press, 1972), pp. 11–12.

10. See Colby, *Lost Victory*.

11. Black, *Reign of Elizabeth*, p. 171.

12. The principle of long-term penetration of the leadership of enemies by impostors even has a tradition in Polish literature. The poem *Konrad Wallenrood*, by the most famous Polish poet, Adam Mickiewicz (1798–1855), is the story of a Lithuanian impostor who takes on the identity of the real Wallenrood after his death. The impostor then infiltrates the Teutonic Knights and leads them to defeat in revenge for their persecution of his fellow Lithuanians. In the period between the two world wars, "Wallenroodism" was a term of art used by the Polish intelligence service.

13. See Charles O. Hucker, "Hu Tsung-hsien's Campaign Against Hsü Hai, 1556," in *Chinese Ways and Warfare*, Frank Kierman, Jr., and John Fairbanks, eds. (Cambridge, MA: Harvard University Press, 1974), pp. 273–307.

14. After World War II, one of the premier scholars of the warlord era, James Sheridan, interviewed some of the Japanese involved. See Sheridan, *Chinese Warlord: The Career of Feng Yü-hsiang* (Stanford, CA: Stanford University Press, 1966).

15. James Westfall Thompson and Saul K. Padover, *Secret Diplomacy: Espionage and Cryptography, 1500–1815* (New York: Ungar, 1963), pp. 91–92.

16. The story of the chevalier has been told in several books. See Octave Homberg and Fernand Jousselin, *D'Eon de Beaumont, His Life and Times*, trans. Alfred Rieu (London: M. Secker, 1911); Edna Nixon, *Royal Spy: The Strange Case of the Chevalier d'Eon* (New York: Reynal, 1965); Ernest Alfred Vizetelly, *The True Story of the Chevalier d'Eon* (London: Tylston and Edwards and AP Marsden, 1895). Apparently, the chevalier spent the last twenty-five years of his life in England living as a woman, having been shunned by the French government. He died in 1810 in poverty, and the controversy in London over the chevalier's true sex were dispelled when he was declared a man following his death. Havelock Ellis coined the term "eonism" to describe what is now called transvestitism in his work *Studies in the Psychology of Sex, vol. 3, pt. 2, Eonism and Other Studies* (New York: Random House, 1936).

17. Jock Haswell, *Spies and Spymasters: A Concise History of Intelligence* (London: Thames & Hudson, 1977), pp. 53–54.

18. Philippe Thyraud de Vosjoli, *Lamia* (Boston, MA: Little, Brown, 1970); and Leon Uris, *Topaz: A Novel* (New York: Bantam, 1968).

19. Francis Dvornik, *Origins of Intelligence Services* (New Brunswick, NJ: Rutgers University Press, 1974), p. 11.

20. Thompson and Padover, *Secret Diplomacy 1500–1815*, pp. 226–28.

21. Even as late as 1989, a pro-Soviet American clergyman was arrested for bringing Soviet money into the United States to support Moscow's activities here.

22. Rose Mary Sheldon, "Spying in Mesopotamia," *Studies in Intelligence* (offprint; nd), pp. 10–11.

23. Lawrence C. Soley and John S. Nichols, *Clandestine Radio Broadcasting: A Study of Revolutionary and Counterrevolutionary Electronic Communication* (New York: Praeger, 1987), p. 42. Another source on American clandestine broadcasting that the Germans believed reduced the effectiveness of their troops is Cave Brown, *Secret War Report of the OSS*, ch. 9, pp. 525–40.

24. One of the criticisms of OSS covert propaganda was that General William Donovan hired general lawyers as managers for creative public relations executives, writers, and artists. Apparently the lawyers were too conservative in style and too rigid in procedure to utilize the creative talent. In contrast to the British in Elizabethan times or in World War I, the U.S. commanders were not self-made men who could adapt themselves to most circumstances, or talented writers who knew how to appeal to their target audience.

25. The French had such a boost for their paramilitary operations against the British in the British colonies on the Atlantic seaboard during the American Revolution. Lloyd George and the British—even the Germans with Holweg and Nicolai—had men of this quality.

26. Known also as the Ismailian Nizaris; the word "assassin" is the European version of *hashishin*, from their reputed habit of using hashish before their murders.

27. David Rapoport, "Fear and Trembling: Terrorism in Three Religious Traditions," *American Political Science Review* 78.3 (September 1984): 666.

28. See Callum MacDonald, *The Killing of S.S. Obergruppenführer Reinhard Heydrich* (New York: Free Press, 1989).

29. Edward Burman, *The Assassins* (Wellingborough, UK: Crucible, 1987), pp. 100–1, 126–27.

30. Rapoport, "Fear and Trembling," pp. 660–64.

31. See Richard A. Horsley, "The Sicarii: Ancient Jewish Terrorists," *Journal of Religion* 59.4:435–58; Rapoport, "Fear and Trembling," p. 669–81.

32. The target must be the leadership. The average militiaman in the terrorist network will be harder to deter, given the harsh and dangerous slums from which he emerges in, say, Beirut or the Palestine refugee camps in Lebanon. For many of the "soldiers" working for a terrorist organization, living in moderate hotels, or marrying European women, and earning $1,000–2,000 a month is a much more comfortable and less dangerous existence than living in Lebanon.

33. Some European specialists believe that the Jordanians may have helped entrap the Syrians in this affair.

34. This was known as Operation Bleutie. See Yves Courrière, *La Guerre d'Algerie*, bk. 3, *L'heure des Colonels* (Paris: Fayard, 1974). For more information on French intelligence in Algeria, and particularly the high caliber of French intelligence officers, see Alistair Horne, *A Savage War of Peace: Algeria, 1954–1962* (New York: Viking, 1978).

35. Rapoport, "Fear and Trembling," p. 663.

36. Youssef M. Ibrahim, "Arabs Say Deadly Power Struggle Has Split Abu Nidal Terror Group," *New York Times*, November 12, 1989, p. 1.

37. Documentation on covert manipulation of terrorist movements is extremely hard to come by. One journalist who appears to have had access to some material is Patrick Seale. See his *Abu Nidal: A Gun for Hire* (New York: Random House, 1992).

38. On the role of resistance movements in the twentieth century see the work of British historian M.R.D. Foot, especially his *Resistance* (London: Eyre Methuen, 1976).

39. On the British experience in Malaya, see Sir Robert Thompson, *Defeating Communist Insurgency: The Lessons of Malaya and Vietnam* (New York: Praeger, 1966). On experiences in Kenya, see Randall Heather, "Intelligence and Counter-Insurgency in Kenya, 1952–1956," in *Intelligence and National Security*, July 1990, pp. 57–83. On the French experience, see Roger Trinquier, *Modern Warfare: A French View of Counterinsurgency* (New York: Praeger, 1964). On the U.S. experience, see Colby, *Lost Victory*; Dale Andrade, *Ashes to Ashes: The Phoenix Program and the Vietnam War* (Lexington, MA: Lexington Books, 1990); Stuart Herrington, *Silence Was a Weapon: The War for the Vietnam Village, a Personal Narrative* (Novato, CA: Presidio Press, 1982); and Orrin DeForest and David Chanoff, *Slow Burn: The Rise and Bitter Fall of American Intelligence in Vietnam* (New York: Simon & Schuster, 1990).

40. See Richard Shultz, *The Soviet Union and Revolutionary Warfare* (Stanford, CA: Hoover Institution, 1988), pp. 64–67, 173–78.

41. Mark Mayo Boatner III, *Encyclopedia of the American Revolution* (New York: McKay, 1976); John McAuley Palmer, *General von Steuben* (New Haven, CT: Yale University Press, 1937); Charles J. Peterson, *The Military Heroes of the Revolution* (Philadelphia, PA: Jas. B. Smith, 1858); Horst Ueberhorst, *Friedrich Wilhelm von Steuben, 1730–1794* (Baltimore, MD: Heinz Moos Publishing, 1983); Neil Young, "Clandestine Aid and the American Revolutionary War: A Reexamination," *Military Affairs* 43.1 (February 1979): 26–30.

42. Michael Yardley, *T.E. Lawrence: A Biography* (New York: Stein & Day, 1987), 106–7. On T. E. Lawrence, see also John E. Mack, *A Prince of Our Disorder* (Boston, MA: Little, Brown, 1976); T. E. Lawrence, *Seven Pillars of Wisdom: A Triumph* (Garden City, NY: Garden City Publishing, 1938); B. H. Liddell-Hart, *T. E. Lawrence in Arabia and After* (London: Jonathan Cape, 1934).

43. See Leggett, *Cheka*; Lennard D. Gerson, *The Secret Police in Lenin's Russia* (Philadelphia, PA: Temple University Press, 1976) and Richard Pipes, *The Russian Revolution* (New York: Knopf, 1990).

44. Colby, *Lost Victory*, pp. 133, 147.

45. For an example of how the UK and the United States did it successfully, see Roosevelt, *Countercoup, passim*.

46. Roosevelt, *Countercoup*, p. 15.

47. From Stephenson's foreword to the BSC's official history, "British Security Coordination (BSC): An Account of Secret Activities in the Western Hemisphere, 1940–1945," quoted in Ignatius, "Churchill's Agents," p. C2.

48. Troy, *Donovan and the CIA*, pp. 54–55.

49. Andrew, "Growth of Intelligence," pp. 22–23.

50. See MacDonald, *Reinhard Heydrich*. See also Warren E. Frank, "An Insider's Analysis," *Foreign Intelligence Literary Scene*, 8.5 (1989).

51. Mary Ellen Reese, *General Reinhard Gehlen: The CIA Connection* (Fairfax, VA: George Mason University Press, 1990).

52. Bittman, *Deception Game*, pp. 142–44.

5. Offensive Defense: Principles of Counterintelligence

1. DCI Webster, for example, created a CIA Counterintelligence Center in 1988 to mobilize and coordinate counterintelligence capabilities inside the CIA, and to integrate the CIA's counterintelligence work with the FBI and DoD more fully. Secretary of Defense Cheney in 1991 approved the Plan for Restructuring Defense Intelligence. This created a new position, the deputy assistant secretary of defense for counterintelligence. The idea was that a single manager should coordinate the DoD central and individual services' offen-

sive and defensive counterintelligence activities within the United States and around the world. This person also was to improve the DoD's cooperation with the FBI, CIA, and other agencies as well as private-sector contractors who provide DoD with most of its technology and other equipment. In the mid-1980s, the White House also created a point of coordination in the director of intelligence programs, and the DCI established his own small staff as director of the intelligence community. This was complemented by high-level working groups of CI managers that began to meet regularly to coordinate U.S. resources.

2. Read, *Mr. Secretary Walsingham; Intelligence in the War of Independence*; Dziak, *Chekisty*; Bernard Porter, *Plots and Paranoia: A History of Political Espionage in Britain, 1790–1988* (Boston, MA: Unwin Hyman, 1989). This is not to say it is necessary to create an authoritarian system and adopt the techniques used by these governments. Counterintelligence can be brought together with other elements to achieve strategic purposes.

3. On the London Control Section staff, see Charles G. Cruickshank, *Deception in World War II* (Oxford, UK: Oxford University Press, 1979); Ronald Wheatley, *Operation Sea Lion: German Plans for the Invasion of England, 1939–1942* (Oxford, UK: Clarendon Press, 1958); and Anthony Cave Brown, *Secret War Report*. For the story of how Jasper Maskelyne, one of Britain's leading magicians, was employed to create illusions to fool the Nazis, see David Fisher, *The War Magician* (New York: Coward-McCann, 1983).

4. For information on Golitsyn, see Chalet and Wolton, *Les Visiteurs de l'Ombre*. Oleg Gordievsky's story is mostly told in Andrew and Gordievsky, *KGB: The Inside Story*.

5. Kenneth deGraffenreid in Godson, ed., *Intelligence Requirements for the 1990s*, p. 151.

6. Philippe Bernet, *SDECE Service 7, L'Extraordinaire Histoire du Colonel LeRoy-Finville et de ses Clandestins* (Paris: Presses de la Cité, 1980). For apparent British successes against the French, Egyptian, and Commonwealth countries, see Wright, *Spycatcher*.

7. The Department of Defense, in cooperation with the Department of Energy, submits to the armed services committees of the Senate and House a classified and unclassified plan for the development of twenty technologies considered "most essential to develop in order to ensure the long-term qualitative superiority of U.S. weapons systems." This list and the technologies on it are obviously major targets of hostile intelligence for both strategic and economic reasons. The first unclassified report was issued in the spring of 1989: Department of Defense for the Senate Committee on Armed Services, *Critical Technologies Plan: Response to Public Law 100–456, The National Defense Authorization Act, Fiscal Year 1989, of 29 September 1988* (Washington, DC: Department of Defense, 1989).

8. On the Venona breaks, see Lamphere and Schactman, *FBI-KGB War*, ch. 5. For the Norwegian use of Venona, see Ornulf Tofte, *Spaneren* (Oslo: Guldendal Forlarget, 1987).

9. Senate Select Committee on Intelligence, *Report on Security at the United States Missions in Moscow and Other Areas of High Risk*, 100th Cong., 1st. sess., September 9, 1987, S.Rpt. 100–154, p. 6.

10. William S. Sessions, "The Evolving Threat: Meeting the Counterintelligence Challenges of the 1990s: A Strategic Issue Facing Our Nation," *American Intelligence Journal* 10.2 (Summer/Fall 1989): 21.

11. Sessions, "Evolving Threat," p. 21.

12. In the past, the U.S. and other Western governments have taken into their services individuals who were plants. For example, the CIA hired Larry Wu-Tai Chin as a staff officer and Karl Kocher as a contract employee.

13. Department of Defense, *Soviet Military Power: An Assessment of the Threat, 1988* (Washington, DC: Government Printing Office, 1988), pp. 59–62. See also "Soviet Gambit May Change '90s Balance," *Disinformation: Soviet Active Measures and Disinformation Forecast* 7 (Fall 1987): 1; and "Nuclear Weapons: Major Soviet Deception," *Disinformation: Soviet Active Measures and Disinformation Forecast* 9 (Summer 1988): 1. See Codevilla, *Informing Statecraft*, pp. 332–33, on the discovery of this facility.

14. Wright, *Spycatcher*, p. 139.

15. This method of identification and counterintelligence detection was actually used by the Norwegian intelligence services, which noted which KGB officers were being promoted to the rank of general. The promotion patterns in the KGB helped identify which parts of residencies and which officers were most successful, thus guiding Norwegian counterintelligence in its search for Soviet penetrations. See Tofte, *Spaneren*.

16. Zwy Aldouby and Jerrold Ballinger, *The Shattered Silence: The Eli Cohen Affair* (New York: Coward, McCann & Geoghegan, 1971), pp. 325–26.

17. For discussion of RAFTER, the code name for this technique, see Wright, *Spycatcher, passim*.

18. Some of their findings are made public. In the United States this has included hearings in both the Senate and the House, as well as interagency reports. For congressional hearings, see "Report on Soviet Use of the Media," in HPSCI, *The CIA and the Media*, pp. 531–627; HPSCI, *Soviet Covert Action (The Forgery Offensive)*; HPSCI, *Soviet Active Measures*; and Senate Committee on Foreign Relations, *Soviet Active Measures*.

For executive branch studies, see Arms Control and Disarmament Agency, *Soviet Propaganda Campaign Against NATO* (October 1983); Arms Control and Disarmament Agency, pub. 122, *The Soviet Propaganda Campaign Against the U.S. Strategic Defense Initiative* (Washington: Arms Control and

Disarmament Agency, August 1986); Department of State, pub. 9630, *Active Measures: A Report on the Substance and Process of Anti-U.S. Disinformation and Propaganda Campaigns* (Washington, DC: Department of State, August 1986); Department of State, pub. 9536, *Contemporary Soviet Propaganda and Disinformation: A Conference Report* (Washington, DC: Department of State, March 1987); Department of Justice, *Soviet Active Measures in the United States 1986–1987* (Washington, DC: Department of Justice, June 1987); Department of State, pub. 9627, *Soviet Influence Activities: A Report on Active Measures and Propaganda, 1986–1987* (Washington, DC: Department of State, August 1987); U.S. Information Agency, *Soviet Active Measures in the Era of Glasnost*, prepared for the House Committee on Appropriations (Washington, DC: U.S. Information Agency, June 1988); and Department of State, pub. 9720, *Soviet Influence Activities: A Report on Active Measures and Propaganda, 1987–1988* (Washington, DC: Department of State, August 1989). The State Department also releases a series of "Foreign Affairs Notes" on this subject, many of which can be found in the Senate hearings, *Soviet Active Measures*, cited above.

Elsewhere, the West German Bundesminister des Innern (Interior Ministry) annually released its *Verfassungsschutzbericht*, which reported on threats to the West German constitution, including the activities of East Germany with respect to West Germany, such as the West German Communist Party. In London, the Foreign and Commonwealth Office prepared "Background Briefs" on the subject of Soviet attempts to influence NATO decision-making.

19. For the accounts of former Eastern bloc officials involved with these activities, see Bittman, *Deception Game*; Bittman, *KGB and Soviet Disinformation*; Dzhirkvelov, *Secret Servant*; Stanislav Levchenko, *On the Wrong Side: My Life in the KGB* (Washington, DC: Pergamon-Brassey's, 1988); Pacepa, *Red Horizons*; and Jan Sejna, *We Will Bury You* (London: Sidgwick & Jackson, 1982).

For a detailed discussion of the apparatus and techniques involved in Soviet active measures campaigns, see Shultz and Godson, *Dezinformatsia*. For information on the CPSU International Department, see Department of State, pub. 9726, *The International Department of the CC CPSU Under Dobrynin* (Washington, DC: Department of State, September 1989). For an example of an ID publication used to provide directions to foreign Communist parties, see the monthly journal *World Marxist Review* (also known as *Problems of Peace and Socialism*). This journal was distributed out of Prague and appeared in over twenty languages.

For background to almost one hundred different Soviet fronts or influence groups, see Clive Rose, *The Soviet Propaganda Network: A Directory of Organizations Serving Soviet Foreign Policy* (New York: St. Martin's Press, 1988). For Soviet descriptions of some of these same groups, see E. M. Primakov and A. I. Vlasov, eds., *What's What in World Politics: A Reference Book* (Moscow: Progress Publishers, 1986). These fronts often produced their own regular publications. Two examples are the World Peace Council's monthly paper,

Peace Courier, and the World Federation of Trade Unions' monthly magazine, *World Trade Union Movement*.

20. Mandel had been a member of the CPUSA, but in the late 1920s he "defected" to join the Right Communist Opposition under the former CPUSA leader Jay Lovestone. The Lovestonites disbanded in the late 1930s, but remained very anti-Stalinist. Mandel was skilled at reading CP publications and was hired by Ray Murphy, the head of EUR-X.

21. Author interviews with Jay Lovestone and Ben Mandel in 1968 and 1972.

22. The French specialist, Christian de Bongain, writes under the name of Xavier Raufer and teaches at the French Institute of Criminology, as well as for the French government. In his quarterly publication of the French Institute of Criminology, *Notes et Etudes*, de Bongain publishes the results he and European police specialists have obtained from using these techniques. *Notes et Etudes*, Institut de Criminologie, nos. 10, 11, and 12 (1989).

23. Herbert Romerstein, "What Information Should Be Collected and How Should Collection Be Organized?" in Roy Godson, ed., *Intelligence Requirements for the 1980s: Domestic Intelligence* (Lexington, MA: Lexington Books, 1986), pp. 107–37.

   In a specific response to Romerstein, a leading FBI specialist did not deny Romerstein's contentions, but asserted that the Privacy Act of 1974 had prevented the FBI in 1980 and 1981 from collecting and retaining the relevant open source publications.

24. Hood, *Mole*, pp. 267–68.

25. Cecil, *Divided Life*; Costello, *Mask of Treachery*; Glees, *Secrets of the Service*; F. H. Hinsley and C.A.G. Simkins, *British Intelligence in the Second World War*, vol. 4, *Security and Counterintelligence* (Cambridge, England: HM Stationery Office, 1990).

26. Senate Select Committee on Intelligence, *Meeting the Espionage Challenge*; Suzanne Cavanagh, *Individuals Arrested on Charges of Espionage Against the United States Government, 1966–1987*, CRS Rpt. 87-320GOV, April 20, 1987 (Washington: Congressional Research Service, Library of Congress, 1987).

27. For an example of how the FBI apparently used a similar ploy, see the story about Boris Yuzhin by Ralph Blumenthal, "A Graying Onetime Double Agent Returns to Scenes of Old Intrigue," *New York Times*, July 17, 1994, p. 14. Yuzhin, a KGB officer in San Francisco in the early 1980s, allowed himself to be recruited by the FBI. Subsequently betrayed by Aldrich Ames, Yuzhin was sent to the gulag, later released, and now lives in the United States.

28. James Bamford, *The Puzzle Palace* (New York: Penguin Books, 1983), pp. 196–200.

29. Senate Select Committee on Intelligence, *Meeting the Espionage Challenge*; Cavanagh, *Individuals Arrested*.

30. Bamford, *Puzzle Palace*, pp. 173–77.

31. De Vosjoli, *Lamia*.

32. In 1982, Haro was identified by the U.S. attorney in San Diego, William Kennedy, as having been recruited by the CIA. Kennedy complained that the United States was refusing to indict Nazar Haro for involvement in a car theft ring in 1982 because he was a CIA agent. Kennedy was dismissed by the Justice Department for making the remarks, which, according to the *Washington Post*, then Attorney General William French Smith called "highly prejudicial to the interests of the United States." William Branigin and Michael Isikoff, "Newly Named Mexican Officials Linked to Drugs," *Washington Post*, January 7, 1989, p. A-1.

33. Morvan Duhamel, *Duel d'Espions pour un Mirage* (Paris: Editions France-Empire, 1971).

34. As told in Joseph Burkholder Smith, *Portrait of a Cold Warrior* (New York: Putnam's, 1976), pp. 202–4.

35. Frantisek Moravec, *Master of Spies: The Memoirs of General Frantisek Moravec* (Garden City, NY: Doubleday, 1975), pp. 57–58. Moravec was chief of Czech military intelligence before and during World War II.

36. Christopher Andrew, *Her Majesty's Secret Service: The Making of the British Intelligence Community* (New York: Penguin Books, 1987), pp. 463; MacDonald, *Reinhard Heydrich*.

37. Hood, *Mole*, pp. 210–11.

38. Report of the Security Commission, May 1985, Cmnd 9514 (London: HM Stationery Office, 1985), p. 11.

39. Report of the Security Commission, May 1983, Cmnd 8876 (London: HM Stationery Office, 1983), p. 2.

40. For Pacepa's story, see Pacepa, *Red Horizons*.

41. See Robert Manne, *The Petrov Affair* (New York: Pergamon Press, 1987). See also the memoirs of the agent himself in Michael Bialoguski, *The Petrov Story* (London: Heinemann, 1955), American edition *The Case of Colonel Petrov* (New York: McGraw-Hill, 1955).

42. Dzhirkvelov, *Secret Servant*.

43. Thomas Polgar, "Defection and Redefection," *International Journal of Intelligence and Counterintelligence* 1.2 (1986): 34 (In the 1980s the United States was plagued with at least three defectors who threatened redefection. One, Yurchenko, actually did so. Two others, Rudi Hermann and Anatoli Bogaty, threatened to do so, but did not go through with it.) See *News and Views from the USSR*, Soviet Embassy, Washington, DC, October 7, 1987, and October 27, 1987.

A U.S. Senate report on handling defectors stated that "our society is not fully and productively integrating these individuals into the mainstream of

American life. Nor, as a result, are we fully utilizing their talents and analytical skills." Senate Permanent Subcommittee on Investigations of the Committee on Governmental Affairs, *Federal Government's Handling of Soviet and Communist Bloc Defectors*, 100th Cong., 2nd sess. (Washington, DC: Government Printing Office, 1988), p. 3.

44. David Ignatius, "'Major' KGB Defector to U.S. Breaks 10 Years of Silence," *Washington Post*, March 2, 1990, p. A1. See also Sheymov's memoir, *Tower of Secrets: A Real Life Spy Thriller* (New York: HarperCollins, 1994). Apparently this same philosophy governed the escape of Oleg Gordievsky (a KGB resident in London, who had gone over to the British in 1974) from Moscow in 1985. See the introduction to Andrew and Gordievsky, *KGB: The Inside Story*.

45. George Lardner, Jr., "Soviet Union Denounces KGB Defector Sheymov," *Washington Post*, March 13, 1990, p. A13.

46. Matei Pavel Haiducu, *J'ai Refusé de Tuer: Un Agent Secret Roumain Revel les Dessous de "L'Affaire"* (Paris: Plon, 1984).

47. Wright, *Spycatcher*; Harvey Barnett, *Tales of the Scorpion* (Boston, MA: Allen & Unwin, 1988).

48. One of the best descriptions of this, with specific examples, is to be found in Ilya Dzhirkvelov's *Secret Servant*. Dzhirkvelov is one of a handful of KGB specialists who did this kind of work and the only officer of the Second Chief Directorate who has written extensively on how he was able to influence foreigners, surround them with agents, and even recruit some of them.

49. Even if the KGB had tried, it probably could not have caused more disruption than the fight that erupted inside U.S. and British intelligence over the bona fides of the defectors Golitsyn and Nosenko in the 1960s, and double agents known as "Fedora" and "Top Hat," among others.

50. Chalet and Wolton, *Les Visiteurs de l'Ombre*; de Vosjoli, *Lamia*.

51. Relatively few former CIA or other officials who have written memoirs discuss the details of these liaison relationships. Exceptions include those who wanted to damage their former service, such as Philip Agee. But even those who are very critical of their services are much less forthcoming about their liaison relationships, particularly for counterintelligence surveillance. See the bestseller by Peter Wright, *Spycatcher*, or the almost unknown work by Melvin Beck *Secret Contenders* (New York: Sheridan Square, 1984). One person who does discuss liaison is Joseph Smith, a CIA case officer for many years. In the course of describing his covert action (not counterintelligence) work in the Philippines in *Portrait of a Cold Warrior*, Smith states that the Philippine National Intelligence Bureau of Investigation, at the request of the United States, bugged the telephone of an American believed to be a criminally corrupt financier of Filipino politicians. "The tapes of his phone conversations were regularly read by some of us in the station for various reasons. I read them to try to pick up leads on political deals. . . ." Smith, *Portrait*, p. 294.

52. See Herrington, *Silence Was a Weapon*. However, some CIA veterans are highly critical of the Agency's Far Eastern division failure to provide adequate CI protection in the 1960s and 1970s.

53. See, for example, Wolton, *Le KGB en France*, ch. 1.

54. See Masterman, *Double-Cross System*. See also Dan Raviv and Yossi Melman, *Every Spy a Prince: The Complete History of Israel's Intelligence Community* (Boston, MA: Houghton Mifflin, 1990); and Chalet and Wolton, *Les Visiteurs de l'Ombre*, pp. 73–74.

55. Hood, *Mole*, pp. 212–15.

56. Chalet and Wolton, *Les Visiteurs de l'Ombre*, p. 83.

57. The film is titled *Forebudet* and was produced by Forsvarets Laromedelscentral in Stockholm. The defection of Oleg Lyallin in the early 1970s also revealed a major illegal sabotage operation in the UK. See Chapman Pincher, *The Secret Offensive: Active Measures, a Saga of Deception, Disinformation, Subversion, Terrorism, Sabotage and Assassination* (London: Sidgwick & Jackson, 1985).

58. For the Peter Hermann story, see John Barron, *KGB Today: The Hidden Hand* (New York: Berkeley Books, 1985), pp. 278–314.

59. For an interesting discussion of why the British are reluctant to use the polygraph, see the Report of the Security Commission, May 1983, CMND 8876 (London: HM Stationery Office, 1983), pp. 36–38.

60. Jonathan Pollard, a U.S. Office of Naval Intelligence analyst convicted of spying for Israel in the 1980s, was able to obtain documents that were not necessary for his own work and passed them to Israeli intelligence.

61. The Senate Select Committee on Intelligence report accompanying the appropriations authorization for U.S. intelligence activities for FY 1991 reported that in early 1990, President Bush lifted travel controls on Polish diplomats based on a State Department recommendation submitted without prior consultation with the FBI or CIA. Calling this decision "questionable," the report stated that "counterintelligence-related controls administrated by the Office of Foreign Missions (OFM) should not be modified without an assessment of the impact from the FBI and other appropriate elements of the intelligence community." It went on to call for the intelligence community to submit a detailed analysis of foreign intelligence activities in the United States to the president and the committee. Thus any changes in OFM policies should be explained with specific reference to this analysis. See Senate Permanent Select Committee on Intelligence, Report to Accompany S.2834, 101st Cong., 1st sess., S.Rpt. 101–358.

62. Another countermeasure that was contemplated in the 1980s, after the spy scandals of that era, was a presidential decision in November 1985 that ordered individual agencies to ensure that their employees reported contact

with personnel from foreign countries believed to be operating major intelligence programs against the United States. Individuals were to report to their security officers any facts or circumstances "which appeared to (1) indicate any attempt or intention to obtain unauthorized access to proprietary, sensitive or classified information, (2) which appear to offer reasonable potential for such, or (3) indicate the possibility of continued professional or personal contacts." NSDD-197, issued November 1, 1985.

The purpose of this countermeasure, were it to be fully implemented, would be not only to increase the security awareness of the millions of Americans who would be required to report those contacts, but also to establish the pattern of foreign intelligence behavior and contacts with Americans, so that it could be neutralized in individual cases and in a more systematic fashion. This presidential decision, however, was fully implemented in only some agencies and ignored completely by others.

63. Pacepa, *Red Horizons*, pp. 424–25.

64. See "Priorities for '89: Political, Military & Economic," in *Disinformation: Soviet Active Measures and Disinformation Forecast* 11 (Winter 1989): 1.

65. Howard, *British Intelligence in the Second World War*, vol. 5.

66. Ewen Montagu, *The Man Who Never Was* (Philadelphia, PA: Lippincott, 1954); and Howard, *British Intelligence in the Second World War*, vol. 5, pp. 88–92. For a critique of strategic deception capabilities by two former senior U.S. officials, see Godson, *Intelligence and Policy*, pp. 109–13.

6. In Pursuit of Effective Intelligence

1. There has been little application of the literature on modernization and technological innovation to intelligence. For a historical perspective, see Alfred Vagts, *The Military Attaché* (Princeton: Princeton University Press, 1967); Thomas A. Fergusson, *British Military Intelligence, 1870–1914* (Frederick, MD: University Publications of America, 1984); and David Kahn, *Hitler's Spies: German Military Intelligence in World War II* (New York: Macmillan, 1978). Now the United States and other countries are wrestling with the latest revolutions in technology and their implications for intelligence. See, for example, William Odom, *America's Military Revolution* (Washington: American University Press, 1993); and both Robert Kohler, "The Intelligence Industrial Base: Doomed to Extinction?" and James Fitzsimonds, "Intelligence and the Revolution in Military Affairs," in Godson, May, and Schmitt, *U.S. Intelligence at the Crossroads*.

2. Robertson, *British and American Approaches to Intelligence*, p. 249.

3. Thompson and Padover, *Secret Diplomacy*; Haswell, *Spies and Spymasters*; and Christopher Andrew, "Dechiffrement et Diplomatie: Le Cabinet noir du Quai d'Orsay Sous La Troisième Republique," *Relations Internationales* 3.5 (1976): 51–55.

4. Andrew, *Her Majesty's Secret Service*; Andrew, "Dechiffrement et Diplomatie"; and Andrew, "The Mobilization of British Intelligence for the Two World Wars," in N. F. Dreisziger, *Mobilization for Total War* (Ontario: Wilfred Courier Press, 1981), pp. 89–110. See also Hinsley et al., *British Intelligence in the Second World War*, vol. 1; Ernest May, ed., *Knowing One's Enemies: Intelligence Assessment Between the Two World Wars* (Princeton: Princeton University Press, 1984); W. C. Beaver, *The Development of the Intelligence Division and Its Role in Aspects of Imperial Policymaking, 1854–1901* (D.Phil. diss., Oxford University, 1976); Vagts, *Military Attaché*; and Fergusson, *British Military Intelligence, 1870–1914*. For a summary of nineteenth-century German military intelligence, see Kahn, *Hitler's Spies*, esp. ch. 2 and its footnotes. On U.S. intelligence, see Jeffrey M. Dorwart, *The Office of Naval Intelligence: The Birth of America's First Intelligence Agency, 1865–1918* (Annapolis, MD: Naval Institute Press, 1979); and Rhodri Jeffreys-Jones, *American Espionage: From Secret Service to CIA* (New York: Free Press, 1977).

5. The distinction between the strategy and requirements of states on the offensive versus the defensive has not been well explicated. One of the few books to do this is George Quester, *Offense and Defense in the International System* (New Brunswick, NJ: Transaction Books, 1988).

6. Angelo Codevilla first made this general point to me in a long conversation one night in Wyoming.

7. There is considerable knowledge about the Soviet intelligence system in the public domain, and two major bibliographies on Soviet intelligence. See Raymond Rocca and John Dziak, *Bibliography on the Soviet Intelligence and Security Service* (Boulder, CO: Westview Press, 1985); and Michael Parrish, *Soviet Security and Intelligence Organizations, 1917–1990: A Bibliographic Dictionary and Review of the Literature in English* (Westport, CT: Greenwood Press, 1992). See also Congressional Research Service, Library of Congress, *Soviet Intelligence and Security Services: A Selected Bibliography of Soviet Publications*, 2 vols. (Washington, DC: Government Printing Office, 1972–75).

8. The U.S. intelligence community is organized in such a way that intelligence responsibilities are shared by multiple organizations, and there is no concentration of power, authority, or capabilities in any one entity. U.S. intelligence is under the control of both the executive and the legislative branches, and the heads of the various agencies report to different commanders and members of the cabinet. The organizational arrangements ensure that intelligence cannot play a major role in domestic affairs, and many activities are proscribed by law.

9. Interestingly, despite the vast expenditure on intelligence collection in totalitarian regimes, intelligence analysis has been far less significant than in other states. Initially, it appears, this was the case because powerful figures such as Lenin, Stalin, and Hitler did not take seriously analysis that differed from their own assessments of situations. Given their personal power, it was

hardly safe for intelligence officers to continue to press views at variance with the leadership. In the Soviet Union, after Stalin's death, intelligence was likely to be tailored in a mundane and predictable effort to curry favor with the leadership of the party and governing circles.

10. Francis Fukayama, *The End of History and the Last Man* (New York: Free Press, 1992). There have also been a rash of books and articles on the decrease in conflict associated with the predicted increasing democratization of the world. Propounded by Enlightenment philosophers such as Immanuel Kant many years ago, this "idealistic," neo-Wilsonian view has resurfaced again. See, for example, Bruce Russett, *Grasping the Democratic Peace* (Princeton, NJ: Princeton University Press, 1993); and Rudolph J. Rumel in Priscilla M. Jensen, ed., "Speaking about Democracy and Peace," *United States Institute of Peace Journal* 3 (1990): 3.

11. Zbigniew Brzezinski, *Out of Control: Global Turmoil on the Eve of the Twenty-first Century* (New York: Scribner's, 1993); Daniel Patrick Moynihan, *Pandaemonium: Ethnicity in International Politics* (New York: Oxford University Press, 1993); and Samuel Huntington et al., *The Clash of Civilizations: The Debate* (New York: Council on Foreign Relations Press, 1993) are perhaps the best known of many works by scholars, journalists, and policymakers that have called attention to the growing inadequacy of a state-centric approach to world politics.

Glossary of Terms and Abbreviations

active measures Soviet leaders and KGB operators used this term for covert operations to achieve political objectives, using propaganda, agents of influence, forgeries, and other forms of covert disinformation.

AFL American Federation of Labor. The major national federation of American trade unions, created at the end of the nineteenth century. Merged with another federation created in the 1930s, the Congress of Industrial Organizations (CIO), to become the AFL-CIO in 1955.

AFOSI Air Force Office of Special Investigation. The section of the Air Force that is concerned with both criminal and counterintelligence investigations.

America First An isolationist lobby to keep the United States out of World War II.

analysis Refers both to the intellectual processing (in order to identify significant facts and derive conclusions therefrom) of raw intelligence information to make it more intelligible and meaningful and to the products of that processing. See Chapter 1.

ASA Army Security Agency. A precursor to the National Security Agency, ASA was a branch of the War Department during World War II responsible for signals intelligence.

BSC British Security Coordination. The covert British organization in the United States before and during World War II. The BSC assisted American anti-Nazi counterintelligence operations and extensively used covert propaganda and other means to influence American public opinion to support the British war effort.

CIC Counter Intelligence Corps. The Army's first counterintelligence agency, created in 1917. It sought to protect the U.S. military from espionage, sabotage, and subversion both at home and abroad.

CIG Central Intelligence Group. Created by President Truman in January 1946, it was overseen by the National Intelligence Authority and was meant to coordinate departmental intelligence efforts. It was succeeded by the Central Intelligence Agency in 1947.

COI Office of the Coordinator of Information. America's first centralized intelligence organization, created by President Roosevelt in 1941 and headed by William Donovan. Succeeded in 1942 by the Office of Strategic Services (see OSS, below).

COINTELPRO An FBI program which began in 1956 to disrupt and disorganize the CPUSA and the Old Left, and later expanded to achieve the same results in the New Left and black nationalist groups.

collection The gathering of valued information from open, technical, and human sources, much of it by clandestine means.

counterintelligence The identification, neutralization, and exploitation of the intelligence activities of adversaries. The effort by a nation's intelligence services to protect their secrets, to prevent themselves from being manipulated, and (sometimes) to exploit the intelligence activities of others for their own benefit. Here, it includes security procedures, countermeasures, and active counterintelligence.

covert action The attempt by a government or group to influence events in another state or territory without revealing or acknowledging its own involvement. Covert action includes propaganda, political action, paramilitary operations, and intelligence assistance.

CPSU Communist Party of the Soviet Union, the ruling party from 1917 to 1991.

CPUSA Communist Party of the United States of America, or Communist Party USA.

DCI Director of Central Intelligence. Appointed by the president and confirmed by the Senate, the DCI has three official functions. He is the president's principal adviser on intelligence, the head of the intelligence community, and the director of the CIA.

DI Directorate for Intelligence. The main element of the CIA, responsible for analyzing and producing finished intelligence. The head of this element is the deputy director for intelligence and is also called the DI, or the DDI.

disinformation Deliberately false information used to discredit an adversary or to mislead a foreign government or disrupt its operations.

DO Directorate for Operations. The element of the Central Intelligence Agency responsible for foreign intelligence collection, counterintelligence abroad, and covert action. Also called the Clandestine Service. DO also refers to the deputy director for operations, the head of this directorate, also called the DDO.

"Double-Cross" The British counterintelligence operation during World War II of turning or doubling German intelligence agents. It was used especially to feed the Germans false information.

DP Directorate for Plans. The office and title of deputy director for plans existed in the CIA from December 1950. It was responsible for overseeing the Office of Special Operations (OSO) and the Office of Policy Coordination (OPC). OSO was responsible for clandestine collection and counterintelligence abroad, and OPC was responsible for covert action abroad. Both offices merged in 1952 and became known as the Clandestine Service, and in 1973 its name was changed to the Directorate for Operations (DO).

DS&T Directorate for Science and Technology. The element of the Central Intelligence Agency responsible for applying science and technology to intelligence, principally collection. DDS&T refers to the deputy director for science and technology, the head of this element.

EUR-X A small group founded in the 1930s State Department under the direction of Ray Murphy. It specialized in analyzing the international Communist movement and, in the 1940s and 1950s, encouraged sophisticated Foreign Service officers to do all they could to help anti-Stalinist elements abroad.

FMLN The Salvadoran Front Farabundo Martí para la Liberación Nacional (Farabundo Martí Front for National Liberation). A Marxist-Leninist-led revolutionary movement in El Salvador.

FUSAG The First U.S. Army Group. An entirely fictional army group, supposedly commanded by General Patton and supposedly headquartered in East Anglia in the UK, facing the Pas de Calais in France. Used as part of Operation Fortitude to deceive the Germans in World War II as to the location and timing of the D-Day invasion.

GKNT The Soviet State Committee for Science and Technology.

GRU The Soviet General Staff Intelligence Organization, the military collection branch that ran agents abroad from the 1920s through the 1980s.

HPSCI House Permanent Select Committee on Intelligence. The House of Representatives' oversight committee, founded in 1977.

Hughes-Ryan Amendment The 1974 congressional amendment appended to the Foreign Assistance Act of 1961 increased congressional oversight of covert action by requiring the president to certify to the congressional committees in a finding that covert operations abroad were important to national security.

human intelligence (humint) Intelligence information gathered from human, rather than technical, sources.

IG-CI Interagency Group for Counterintelligence. A subcommittee of the Senior Interagency Group for Intelligence (see SIG-I, below).

IG-CM and Security Interagency Group for Countermeasures and Security. Another subcommittee of the Senior Interagency Group for Intelligence.

information warfare Information warfare (or infowar) seeks to influence adversaries by denying information, or by influencing, degrading, and/or destroying adversary information systems. It also includes denying, negating, or turning to friendly advantage adversary efforts to destroy, disrupt, and/or deny information.

intelligence assistance   A type of covert action, intelligence assistance is aid to the intelligence service of another group or government beyond normal liaison. It attempts to influence events or decisions in other countries by training personnel, providing material or technical assistance, or passing information to achieve intended effects.

ISI   The Pakistani intelligence service that worked with the CIA on covert action programs in Afghanistan during the 1980s.

KGB   The Soviet Committee for State Security. The main Soviet internal and external intelligence service. Had many different names since its creation as the Cheka in 1917.

Mossad   Israel's foreign intelligence service.

NSCID 5   National Security Council Intelligence Directive 5, 1948. The presidential decision that gave the DCI and the CIA primary responsibility for counterintelligence abroad.

ONI   Office of Naval Intelligence. Created in 1882 to provide the Navy with information on foreign naval developments.

OPC   Office of Policy Coordination. Created in 1948 to conduct covert action primarily in support of the containment policy. Under the auspices of the CIA, but maintained an autonomous existence until turf battles led to its merger with the OSO as the Clandestine Service in 1952.

OSD   Office of the Secretary of Defense.

OSO   Office of Special Operations. The clandestine collection and counterintelligence branch of the SSU, CIG, and of the newly formed CIA in 1947. Merged with the OPC as the Clandestine Service in 1952.

OSS   The Office of Strategic Services. Established in 1942 by President Roosevelt out of the Office of the Coordinator of Information (COI) to collect and analyze strategic intelligence and conduct counterintelligence and covert action abroad. Disbanded by President Truman in 1945. The OSS was the first "full-service" centralized intelligence agency, conducting collection, analysis, counterintelligence, and covert action.

paramilitary operations   A type of covert action that involves the use of force. This includes support for, or defense against, terrorism, resistance movements, insurgents, and other unconventional forces.

PFIAB   The President's Foreign Intelligence Advisory Board. Established first in the Eisenhower administration, PFIAB was disbanded in 1977 and reconstituted in 1981. The PFIAB is composed of private citizens who, at the behest of the president, review the performance of U.S. intelligence agencies.

PFLP-GC   Popular Front for the Liberation of Palestine–General Command. A Palestinian terrorist group headed by Ahmad Jibril.

political action   A type of covert action that uses political means (e.g., advice, agents of influence, material support) to influence foreign events. Such efforts can be directed at foreign governments, as well as at nongovernmental entities such as labor, youth, intellectual, and religious movements.

positive intelligence   Valued information about foreign developments and activities. Positive intelligence is usually obtained by positive intelligence collectors, but sometimes counterintelligence information can provide important positive insights.

propaganda   A type of covert action that uses words, symbols, and other psychological techniques to influence foreign developments. In the latter half of the twentieth century, most propaganda was directed at influencing the mass media.

SCC   Special Coordination Committee. Created in 1978 by President Carter under the National Security Council to deal inter alia with the oversight of sensitive intelligence activities, such as covert action, which were undertaken on presidential authority.

SIG-I   Senior Interagency Group for Intelligence. A committee of the National Security Council in the Reagan presidency that included the DCI, the assistant to the president for national security affairs, the directors of the FBI and the NSA, the deputy secretaries of state and defense, the deputy attorney general, and the chairman of the Joint Chiefs of Staff. Coordinated and monitored interagency intelligence work.

signals intelligence (sigint)   Intelligence derived from electronic signals, including electronic communications, telemetry, and person-to-person communications.

SIS   Britain's Secret Intelligence Service, also known as MI6, responsible for clandestine collection, counterintelligence, and covert action abroad.

SOE   Special Operations Executive. Britain's organization for paramilitary covert activity during World War II.

SSCI   Senate Select Committee on Intelligence. The Senate's intelligence oversight committee, created in 1976.

SSU   Strategic Services Unit. This office of the War Department carried out collection, counterintelligence, and limited covert action operations when the OSS was disbanded in 1945.

SWP   Socialist Workers Party. A Trotskyite American political group infiltrated by the FBI.

tradecraft   The methods and operations that intelligence professionals use.

"Trust"   A false opposition movement. A Soviet counterintelligence program created in the early 1920s to identify opponents of the Bolshevik regime and to feed false intelligence to the West. See Chapter 1.

"Ultra"   The generic name for the products of Allied operations to intercept and decode German electronic communications during World War II.

VPK   The Soviet Military Industrial Commission. The VPK collected and prioritized requirements from key defense industries and then passed those requirements on to "acquisition" organizations such as the GKNT, which in turn tasked the GRU and the KGB to acquire them.

X-2   The branch of the OSS responsible for counterintelligence. X-2 veterans, particularly James Angleton, played significant roles in the development of the DDP's counterintelligence operations. Also referred to as OSS-X2. See Chapter 3.

Bibliography

Books

Agee, Philip. *Inside the Company: CIA Diary*. Harmondsworth, UK: Penguin Books, 1975.

Aldouby, Zwy, and Jerrold Ballinger. *The Shattered Silence: The Eli Cohen Affair*. New York: Coward, McCann, 1971.

Ambrose, Stephen. *Rise to Globalism: American Foreign Policy Since 1938*. New York: Penguin Books, 1988.

Andrade, Dale. *Ashes to Ashes: The Phoenix Program and the Vietnam War*. Lexington, MA: Lexington Books, 1990.

Andrew, Christopher. *Her Majesty's Secret Service: The Making of the British Intelligence Community*. New York: Penguin Books, 1987.

Andrew, Christopher, and Oleg Gordievsky. *KGB: The Inside Story of Its Foreign Operations from Lenin to Gorbachev*. London: Hodder & Stoughton, 1990.

Bailey, Geoffrey. *The Conspirators*. New York: Harper & Brothers, 1960.

Bamford, James. *The Puzzle Palace*. New York: Penguin Books, 1983.

Barnett, Harvey. *Tales of the Scorpion*. Boston, MA: Allen & Unwin, 1988.

Barron, John. *KGB Today: The Hidden Hand*. New York: Berkeley Books, 1985.

Beck, Melvin. *Secret Contenders*. New York: Sheridan Square, 1984.

Beckwith, Charlie A. *Delta Force*. New York: Dell, 1983.

Bemis, Samuel Flagg. *The Diplomacy of the American Revolution*. Bloomington, IN: Indiana University Press, 1957.

Bennett, Ralph. *Ultra in the West: The Normandy Campaign, 1944–1945*. New York: Scribner's, 1980.

Berkowitz, Bruce D., and Allan E. Goodman. *Strategic Intelligence for American National Security*. Princeton, NJ: Princeton University Press, 1989.

Bernet, Philippe. *SDECE Service 7, L'Extraordinaire Histoire du Colonel LeRoy-Finville et de ses Clandestins*. Paris: Presses de la Cité, 1980.

Bernstorff, Count. *My Three Years in America*. New York: Scribner's, 1920.

Bethel, Nicholas. *Betrayed*. New York: Times Books, 1984.

Bialoguski, Michael. *The Petrov Story*. London: Heinemann, 1955. American ed., *The Case of Colonel Petrov*. New York: McGraw-Hill, 1955.

Bittman, Ladislav. *The Deception Game*. Syracuse, NY: Syracuse University Research Corp., 1972.

———. *The KGB and Soviet Disinformation*. Washington, DC: Pergamon-Brassey's, 1985.

Black, J. S. *The Reign of Elizabeth, 1558–1603*. Oxford, UK: Clarendon Press, 1959.

Blaufarb, Douglas S. *The Counterinsurgency Era: U.S. Doctrine and Performance, 1950 to the Present*. New York: Free Press, 1977.

Boatner, Mark Mayo, III. *Encyclopedia of the American Revolution*. New York: McKay, 1976.

Borkenau, F. *World Communism: A History of the Communist International*. Ann Arbor, MI: University of Michigan Press, 1962.

Borosage, Robert L., and John Marks, eds. *The CIA File*. New York: Grossman Publishers, 1976.

Bower, Tom. *The Red Web: MI6 and the KGB Master Coup*. London: Aurum, 1989.

Boyle, Andrew. *The Fourth Man: The Definitive Account of Kim Philby, Guy Burgess and Donald Maclean and Who Recruited Them to Spy for Russia*. New York: Dial Press, 1979.

Bozeman, Adda. *Strategic Intelligence and Statecraft*. Washington, DC: Brassey's, 1992.

Bradley, Omar. *A Soldier's Story*. New York: Holt, 1951.

Brook-Shepherd, Gordon. *The Storm Birds: Soviet Postwar Defectors*. London: Weidenfeld & Nicolson, 1988.

Brzezinski, Zbigniew. *Power and Principle: Memoirs of the National Security Adviser, 1977–1981*. New York: Farrar, Straus & Giroux, 1983.

———. *Out of Control: Global Turmoil on the Eve of the Twenty-first Century*. New York: Scribner's, 1993.

Burman, Edward. *The Assassins*. Wellingborough, UK: Crucible, 1987.

Calvocoressi, Peter. *Top Secret Ultra*. New York: Pantheon, 1980.

Campbell, Rodney. *The Luciano Project*. New York: McGraw-Hill, 1977.

Caruso, A. Brook. *The Mexican Spy Company: United States Covert Operations in Mexico, 1845–1848*. Jefferson, NC: McFarland, 1991.

Cave Brown, Anthony, ed. *The Secret War Report of the OSS*. New York: Berkeley, 1976.

Cecil, Robert. *A Divided Life: A Personal Portrait of the Spy Donald MacLean*. London: Bodley Head, 1988.

Chafe, William H. *Never Stop Running: Allard Lowenstein and the Struggle to Save American Liberalism*. New York: Basic Books, 1993.

Chalet, Marcel, and Thierry Wolton. *Les Visiteurs de l'Ombre*. Paris: Bernard Grasset, 1990.

Cline, Ray. *Secrets, Spies and Scholars: Blueprint of the Essential CIA*. Washington, DC: Acropolis Books, 1976.

Codevilla, Angelo. *Informing Statecraft: Intelligence for a New Century*. New York: Free Press, 1992.

Colby, William, with Peter Forbath. *Honorable Men: My Life in the CIA*. New York: Simon & Schuster, 1978.

Colby, William, with James McCargar. *Lost Victory: A Firsthand Account of*

America's Sixteen-Year Involvement in Vietnam. Chicago, IL: Contemporary Books, 1989.

Coleman, Peter. *The Liberal Conspiracy: The Congress for Cultural Freedom and Struggle for the Mind of Postwar Europe*. New York: Free Press, 1989.

Costello, John. *Mask of Treachery*. London: Collins, 1988.

Courrière, Yves. *La Guerre d'Algerie*. Bk. 3, *L'heure des Colonels*. Paris: Fayard, 1974.

Cruickshank, Charles G. *Deception in World War II*. Oxford, UK: Oxford University Press, 1979.

Davis, James Kirkpatrick. *Spying on America: The FBI's Domestic Counterintelligence Program*. New York: Praeger, 1992.

Deakin, F. W., and G. R. Storry. *The Case of Richard Sorge*. London: Chatto & Windus, 1966.

DeForest, Orrin, and David Chanoff. *Slow Burn: The Rise and Bitter Fall of American Intelligence in Vietnam*. New York: Simon & Schuster, 1990.

de Vosjoli, Philippe Thyraud. *Lamia*. Boston, MA: Little, Brown, 1970.

Dorwart, Jeffrey M. *Conflict of Duty: The U.S. Navy's Intelligence Dilemma, 1919–1945*. Annapolis, MD: Naval Institute Press, 1983.

———. *The Office of Naval Intelligence: The Birth of America's First Intelligence Agency, 1865–1918*. Annapolis, MD: Naval Institute Press, 1979.

Draper, Theodore. *A Very Thin Line: The Iran-Contra Affairs*. New York: Hill & Wang, 1991.

Duhamel, Morvan. *Duel d'Espions pour un Mirage*. Paris: Editions France-Empire, 1971.

Dvornik, Francis. *Origins of Intelligence Services*. New Brunswick, NJ: Rutgers University Press, 1974.

Dzhirkvelov, Ilya. *Secret Servant: My Life with the KGB and the Soviet Elite*. New York: Harper & Row, 1987.

Dziak, John. *Chekisty: A History of the KGB*. Lexington, MA: Lexington Books, 1988.

Elliff, John. *The Reform of FBI Intelligence Operations*. Princeton, NJ: Princeton University Press, 1979.

Ellis, Havelock. *Studies in the Psychology of Sex*. Vol. 3, pt. 2, *Eonism and Other Studies*. New York: Random House, 1936.

Epstein, Edward J. *Deception: The Invisible War Between the KGB and the CIA*. New York: Simon & Schuster, 1989.

Felix, Christopher. *A Short Course in the Secret War*. 3rd ed. Lanham, MD: Madison Books, 1992. Orig. pub., New York: Dutton, 1963.

Felt, W. Mark. *The FBI Pyramid from the Inside*. New York: G. P. Putnam's Sons, 1979.

Fergusson, Thomas A. *British Military Intelligence, 1870–1914*. Frederick, MD: University Publications of America, 1984.

Fisher, David. *The War Magician*. New York: Coward-McCann, 1983.

Foot, M. R. D. *Resistance*. London: Eyre Methuen, 1976.

――――. *SOE: The Special Operations Executive 1940–46*. London: BBC, 1984.

Ford, Harold. *Estimative Intelligence: The Purposes and Problems of National Intelligence Estimating*. Rev. ed. Lanham, MD: University Press of America, 1993.

Fowler, W. B. *British-American Relations, 1917–1918: The Role of Sir William Wiseman*. Princeton, NJ: Princeton University Press, 1969.

Fukayama, Francis. *The End of History and the Last Man*. New York: Free Press, 1992.

Gaddis, John Lewis. *Strategies of Containment: A Critical Appraisal of Postwar American National Security Policy*. New York: Oxford University Press, 1982.

Garthoff, Raymond L. *Détente and Confrontation: American-Soviet Relations from Nixon to Reagan*. Washington, DC: Brookings, 1985.

Gerson, Lennard D. *The Secret Police in Lenin's Russia*. Philadelphia, PA: Temple University Press, 1976.

Glazer, Nathan. *The Social Basis of American Communism*. Westport, CT: Greenwood Press, 1974.

Glees, Anthony. *The Secrets of the Service: British Intelligence and Communist Subversion, 1939–1951*. London: Jonathan Cape, 1987.

Godson, Roy. *American Labor and European Politics*. New York: Crane, Russak, 1976.

Godson, Roy, ed. *Comparing Foreign Intelligence*. Washington, DC: Pergamon-Brassey's, 1988.

――――, ed. *Intelligence Requirements for the 1980s: Analysis and Estimates*. Washington, DC: National Strategy Information Center, 1980.

――――, ed. *Intelligence Requirements for the 1980s: Counterintelligence*. Washington, DC: National Strategy Information Center, 1980.

――――, ed. *Intelligence Requirements for the 1980s: Covert Action*. Washington, DC: National Strategy Information Center, dist. by Transaction Books, 1981.

――――, ed. *Intelligence Requirements for the 1980s: Clandestine Collection*. Washington, DC: National Strategy Information Center, dist. by Transaction Books, 1982.

――――, ed. *Intelligence Requirements for the 1980s: Elements of Intelligence*. Rev. ed. Washington, DC: National Strategy Information Center, 1983.

――――, ed. *Intelligence Requirements for the 1980s: Domestic Intelligence*. Lexington, MA: Lexington Books, 1986.

――――, ed. *Intelligence Requirements for the 1980s: Intelligence and Policy*. Lexington, MA: Lexington Books, 1986.

――――, ed. *Intelligence Requirements for the 1990s: Collection, Analysis, Counterintelligence and Covert Action*. Washington, DC: Consortium for the Study of Intelligence, National Strategy Information Center, 1989.

Godson, Roy, Ernest May, and Gary Schmitt, eds. *U.S. Intelligence at the Crossroads*. Washington, DC: Brassey's, 1995.

Gutman, Roy. *Banana Diplomacy: The Making of American Policy in Nicaragua, 1981–1987*. New York: Simon & Schuster, 1988.

Haiducu, Matei Pavel. *J'ai Refusé de Tuer: Un Agent Secret Roumain Revel les Dessous de "L'Affaire."* Paris: Plon, 1984.

Haig, Alexander. *Caveat*. New York: Macmillan, 1984.

Halperin, Morton, Jerry J. Berman, Robert Borosage, and Christine M. Marwick. *The Lawless State*. New York: Penguin Books, 1976.

Harris, Charles H., and Louis R. Sadler. *The Border and the Revolution: Clandestine Activities of the Mexican Revolution, 1910–1920*. Silver City, NM: High Lonesome Books, 1988.

Haswell, Jock. *Spies and Spymasters: A Concise History of Intelligence*. London: Thames & Hudson, 1977.

Herrington, Stuart. *Silence Was a Weapon: The War for the Vietnam Village, a Personal Narrative*. Novato, CA: Presidio Press, 1982.

Hersh, Burton. *The Old Boys*. New York: Scribner's, 1992.

Hilton, Stanley E. *Hitler's Secret War in South America, 1939–1945*. New York: Ballantine Books, 1981.

Hinsley, F. H., et al. *British Intelligence in the Second World War*. 5 vols. Cambridge, UK: HM Stationery Office, 1979–1990.

Homberg, Octave, and Fernand Jousselin. *D'Eon de Beaumont, His Life and Times*. Trans. Alfred Rieu. London: M. Secker, 1911.

Hood, William. *Mole: The True Story of the First Russian Spy to Become an American Counterspy*. New York: W. W. Norton, 1982. Reprint, Washington, DC: Brassey's/Macmillan, 1993.

———. *Spy Wednesday*. New York: Norton, 1986.

Hoover, J. Edgar. *Masters of Deceit: The Story of Communism in America and How to Fight It*. New York: Holt, Reinhart & Winston, 1958.

———. *A Study of Communism*. New York: Holt, Reinhart & Winston, 1962.

Horne, Alistair. *A Savage War of Peace: Algeria, 1954–1962*. New York: Viking, 1978.

House, Edward Mandell. *The Intimate Papers of Colonel House, arranged as a narrative by Charles Seymour*. 3 vols. Boston, MA: Houghton Mifflin, 1928.

Howard, Michael. *British Intelligence in the Second World War: Strategic Deception*, vol. 5. Cambridge, UK: HM Stationery Office, 1990.

Huntington, Samuel. *American Politics: The Promise of Disharmony*. Cambridge, MA: Belknap Harvard University Press, 1981.

Huntington, Samuel, et al. *The Clash of Civilizations: The Debate*. New York: Council on Foreign Relations Press, 1993.

Jeffreys-Jones, Rhodri. *American Espionage: From Secret Service to CIA*. New York: Free Press, 1977.

————. *The CIA and American Democracy*. New Haven, CT: Yale University Press, 1989.

Jensen, Joan M. *Army Surveillance in America, 1975–1990*. New Haven, CT: Yale University Press, 1990.

Johnson, Loch K. *A Season of Inquiry*. Lexington, KY: University Press of Kentucky, 1985.

Jones, Rosemary Devonshire. *Francesco Vettoci: Florentine Citizen and Medici Servant*. London: Athlone Press, 1972.

Kahn, David. *Hitler's Spies: German Military Intelligence in World War II*. New York: Macmillan, 1978.

Kahn, Riaz. *Untying the Afghan Knot: Negotiating Soviet Withdrawal*. Durham, NC: Duke University Press, 1991.

Katz, Friedrich. *The Secret War in Mexico*. Chicago, IL: University of Chicago Press, 1981.

Keller, William W. *The Liberals and J. Edgar Hoover*. Princeton, NJ: Princeton University Press, 1989.

Kent, Sherman. *Strategic Intelligence for American World Policy*. Princeton, NJ: Princeton University Press, 1949. Reprint, 1966.

Kessler, Ronald. *Spy vs. Spy*. New York: Pocket Books, 1988.

Kimball, Penn. *The File*. San Diego, CA: Harcourt Brace Jovanovich, 1983.

Kissinger, Henry. *The White House Years*. Boston, MA: Little, Brown, 1979.

Kornbluh, Peter, and Malcolm Byrne, eds. *The Iran-Contra Scandal: The Declassified History*. New York: New Press, dist. by Norton, 1993.

Kugler, Richard L. *Commitment to Purpose: How Alliance Partnership Won the Cold War*. Santa Monica, CA: Rand, 1993.

Lagon, Mark. *The Reagan Doctrine: Sources of American Conduct in the Cold War's Last Chapter*. Westport, CT: Praeger, 1994.

Lamphere, Robert J., and Tom Shachtman. *The FBI-KGB War*. New York: Random House, 1986.

Landsdale, Edward. *In the Midst of Wars: An American's Mission to Southeast Asia*. New York: Harper & Row, 1972.

Lawrence, T. E. *Seven Pillars of Wisdom: A Triumph*. Garden City, NY: Garden City Publishing, 1938.

Leary, William M., ed. *The Central Intelligence Agency: History and Documents*. Tuscaloosa, AL: University of Alabama Press, 1984.

Ledeen, Michael. *Western European Communism and American Foreign Policy*. New Brunswick, NJ: Transaction, 1987.

Lefever, Ernest, and Roy Godson. *The CIA and the American Ethic: An Unfinished Debate*. Washington, DC: University Press of America for the Ethics and Public Policy Center, Georgetown University, 1979.

Leggett, George. *The Cheka: Lenin's Political Police*. Oxford, UK: Clarendon Press, 1981.

Levchenko, Stanislav. *On the Wrong Side: My Life in the KGB*. Washington, DC: Pergamon-Brassey's, 1988.

Liddell-Hart, B. H. *T. E. Lawrence in Arabia and After*. London: Jonathan Cape, 1934.

Lindsay, Franklin. *Beacons in the Night: With the OSS and Tito's Partisans in Wartime Yugoslavia*. Stanford, CA: Stanford University Press, 1993.

Link, Arthur, et al., eds. *Woodrow Wilson Papers*. Princeton, NJ: Princeton University Press, 1966–1994.

Lisagore, Nancy, and Frank Lipsius. *A Law unto Itself: The Untold Story of the Law Firm of Sullivan and Cromwell*. New York: Morrow, 1988.

Lovell, Mary. *Cast No Shadow*. New York: Pantheon, 1992.

MacDonald, Callum. *The Killing of S.O. Obergruppenführer Reinhard Heydrich*. New York: Free Press, 1989.

Mack, John E. *A Prince of Our Disorder*. Boston, MA: Little, Brown, 1976.

Mangold, Tom. *Cold Warrior*. New York: Simon & Schuster, 1991.

Manne, Robert. *The Petrov Affair*. New York: Pergamon Press, 1987.

Martin, David C. *Wilderness of Mirrors*. New York: Harper & Row, 1980.

Masterman, J.C. *The Double-Cross System in the War of 1939–1945*. New Haven, CT: Yale University Press, 1972.

Mattingly, Garrett. *Renaissance Diplomacy*. New York: Russell & Russell, 1955. Reprint, 1970.

May, Ernest, ed. *Knowing One's Enemies: Intelligence Assessment Between the Two World Wars*. Princeton, NJ: Princeton University Press, 1984.

———. *"Lessons" of the Past: The Use and Misuse of History in American Foreign Policy*. New York: Oxford University Press, 1975.

Mayer, Jane, and Doyle McManus. *Landslide: The Unmaking of the President, 1984–1988*. Boston, MA: Houghton Mifflin, 1988.

Meese, Edwin, III. *With Reagan: The Inside Story*. Washington, DC: Regnery Gateway, 1992.

Menges, Constantine. *Inside the National Security Council: The True Story of the Making and Unmaking of Reagan's Foreign Policy*. New York: Simon & Schuster, 1988.

———. *The Twilight Struggle: The United States v. the Soviet Union Today*. Washington, DC: American Enterprise Institute, 1990.

Meyer, Cord. *Facing Reality: From World Federalism to the CIA*. New York: Harper & Row, 1980. Reprint, Lanham, MD: University Press of America, 1982.

Moch, Jules. *Rencontres avec Léon Blum*. Paris: Plon, 1970.

Montagu, Ewen. *Beyond Top Secret Ultra*. New York: Coward, McCann & Geoghegan, 1978. Reprint of *Beyond Top Secret U*. London: Peter Davies, 1977.

———. *The Man Who Never Was*. Philadelphia, PA: Lippincott, 1954.

Moravec, Frantisek. *Master of Spies: The Memoirs of General Frantisek Moravec*. Garden City, NY: Doubleday, 1975.

Morris, Charles. *Iron Destinies, Lost Opportunities: The Arms Race Between the USA and the USSR, 1945–1987*. New York: Harper & Row, 1988.

Moynihan, Daniel Patrick. *Pandaemonium: Ethnicity in International Politics*. New York: Oxford University Press, 1993.

Murphy, Orville T. *Charles Gravier, Comte de Vergennes: French Diplomacy in the Age of Revolution, 1719–1787*. Albany, NY: SUNY Press, 1982.

Nathan, James A., and James K. Oliver. *United States Foreign Policy and World Order*. 4th ed. Glenview, IL: Scott, Foresman, 1989.

Nicolai, Colonel W. *The German Secret Service*. Trans. George Renwick. London: Stanley Paul, 1924.

Nixon, Edna. *Royal Spy: The Strange Case of the Chevalier D'Eon*. New York: Reynal, 1965.

Nollau, Guenther. *International Communism and World Revolution: History and Methods*. New York: Praeger, 1961. Reprint, Westport, CT: Greenwood Press, 1975.

Odom, William. *America's Military Revolution*. Washington, DC: American University Press, 1993.

Operation Zapata: The "Ultrasensitive" Report and Testimony of the Board of Inquiry on the Bay of Pigs. Frederick, MD: University Publications of America, 1981.

O'Toole, G.J.A. *Honorable Treachery*. New York: Atlantic Monthly Press, 1991.

Pacepa, Ion Mihai. *Red Horizons: Chronicles of a Communist Spy Chief*. Washington, DC: Regnery Gateway, 1987.

Page, Bruce, David Leitch, and Philip Knightley. *The Philby Conspiracy*. New York: Ballantine Books, 1981.

Palmer, John McAuley. *General Von Steuben*. New Haven, CT: Yale University Press, 1937.

Parrish, Michael. *Soviet Security and Intelligence Organizations, 1917–1990: A Bibliographic Dictionary and Review of the Literature in English*. Westport, CT: Greenwood Press, 1992.

Pastor, Robert. *Condemned to Repetition: The United States and Nicaragua*. Princeton, NJ: Princeton University Press, 1987.

Perkins, J. B. *France in the American Revolution*. Boston, MA: Houghton Mifflin, 1911.

Petersen, Neal H. *American Intelligence 1774–1990: A Bibliographical Guide*. Claremont, CA: Regina Books, 1992.

Peterson, Charles J. *The Military Heroes of the Revolution*. Philadelphia, PA: Jas. B. Smith, 1858.

Philby, Kim. *My Silent War*. New York: Grove Press, 1968.

Phillips, David Atlee. *The Night Watch: Twenty-five Years of Peculiar Service*. New York: Atheneum, 1977.

Pincher, Chapman. *The Secret Offensive: Active Measures, a Saga of Deception, Disinformation, Subversion, Terrorism, Sabotage and Assassination*. London: Sidgwick & Jackson, 1985.

Pipes, Richard. *The Russian Revolution*. New York: Knopf, 1990.

Pisani, Sallie. *The CIA and the Marshall Plan*. Lawrence, KS: University Press of Kansas, 1991.

Podhoretz, Norman. *Breaking Ranks: A Political Memoir*. New York: Harper & Row, 1979.

———. *Why We Were in Vietnam*. New York: Simon & Schuster, 1982.

Porter, Bernard. *Plots and Paranoia: A History of Political Espionage in Britain, 1790–1988*. Boston, MA: Unwin Hyman, 1989.

Powers, Thomas. *The Man Who Kept the Secrets: Richard Helms and the CIA*. New York: Knopf, 1979.

Prange, Gordon, with Donald Goldstein and Katherine V. Dillon. *Target Tokyo: The Story of the Sorge Spy Ring*. New York: McGraw-Hill, 1984.

Press, Sylvia. *The Care of Devils*. New York: Beacon, 1958. Reprint, New York: Bantam, 1966.

Primakov, E. M., and A. I. Vlasov, eds. *What's What in World Politics: A Reference Book*. Moscow: Progress Publishers, 1986.

Quester, George. *Offense and Defense in the International System*. New Brunswick, NJ: Transaction Books, 1988.

Ranelagh, John. *The Agency: Rise and Decline of the CIA*. New York: Simon & Schuster, 1986.

Raufer, Xavier, ed. *Notes et Etudes*, Institute de Criminologie, Paris: 10, 11, and 12.

Raviv, Dan, and Yossi Melman. *Every Spy a Prince: The Complete History of Israel's Intelligence Community*. Boston, MA: Houghton Mifflin, 1990.

Read, Conyers. *Mr. Secretary Walsingham and the Policy of Queen Elizabeth*. 3 vols. Cambridge, MA: Harvard University Press, 1925.

Reese, Mary Ellen. *General Reinhard Gehlen: The CIA Connection*. Fairfax, VA: George Mason University Press, 1990.

Richelson, Jeffrey T., and Desmond Ball. *The Ties That Bind: Intelligence Cooperation Between the UKUSA Countries*. Boston, MA: Allen & Unwin, 1985.

Rocca, Raymond, and John Dziak. *Bibliography on the Soviet Intelligence and Security Service*. Boulder, CO: Westview Press, 1985.

Rogow, Arnold F. *James Forrestal: A Study of Personality, Politics, and Policy*. New York: Macmillan, 1963.

Romerstein, Herbert, and Stanislav Levchenko. *The KGB Against the "Main Enemy."* Lexington, MA: Lexington Books, 1989.

Roosevelt, Kermit. *Countercoup: The Struggle for the Control of Iran*. New York: McGraw-Hill, 1979.

Rose, Clive. *Campaigns Against Western Defense: NATO's Adversaries and Critics*. New York: St. Martin's Press, 1985.

———. *The Soviet Propaganda Network: A Directory of Organizations Serving Soviet Foreign Policy*. New York: St. Martin's Press, 1988.

Rositzke, Harry. *The CIA's Secret Operations: Espionage, Counterespionage, and Covert Action*. New York: Reader's Digest Press, 1977.

The Rote Kapelle: The CIA's History of Soviet Intelligence and Espionage Networks in Western Europe, 1936–1945. Washington, DC: University Publications of America, 1979.

Roy, M. N. *The Russian Revolution*. Calcutta: Renaissance Publishers, 1949.

Russett, Bruce. *Grasping the Democratic Peace*. Princeton, NJ: Princeton University Press, 1993.

Saunders, M. L., and Philip Taylor. *British Propaganda During the First World War*. London: Macmillan, 1982.

Sayer, Ian, and Douglas Botting, *America's Secret Army: The Untold Story of the Counter Intelligence Corps*. London: Grafton-Collins, 1989.

Schultz, George. *Turmoil and Triumph: My Years as Secretary of State*. New York: Scribner's, 1993.

Seale, Patrick. *Abu Nidal: A Gun for Hire*. New York: Random House, 1992.

Seale, Patrick, and Maureen McConville. *Philby: The Long Road to Moscow*. New York: Simon & Schuster, 1973.

Sejna, Jan. *We Will Bury You*. London: Sidgwick & Jackson, 1982.

Shafer, D. Michael. *Deadly Paradigms: The Failure of U.S. Counterinsurgency Policy*. Princeton, NJ: Princeton University Press, 1988.

Sheridan, James. *Chinese Warlord: The Career of Feng Yü-hsiang*. Stanford, CA: Stanford University Press, 1966.

Sheymov, Victor. *Tower of Secrets: A Real Life Spy Thriller*. New York: HarperCollins, 1994.

Shulsky, Abram N. *Silent Warfare: Understanding the World of Intelligence*. 2nd ed., rev. by Gary J. Schmitt. Washington, DC: Brassey's, 1993.

Shultz, Richard. *The Soviet Union and Revolutionary Warfare*. Stanford, CA: Hoover Institution, 1988.

Shultz, Richard H., and Roy Godson. *Dezinformatsia: Active Measures in Soviet Strategy*. Washington, DC: Pergamon-Brassey's, 1984.

Smith, Bradley E. *The Ultra Magic Deals*. Novata, CA: Presidio Press, 1993.

Smith, Joseph Burkholder. *Portrait of a Cold Warrior*. New York: Putnam's, 1976.

Smith, Paul Jr. *Political War*. Washington, DC: National Defense University Press, 1989.

Smith, Richard Harris. *OSS: The Secret History of America's First Central Intelligence Agency*. Berkeley, CA: University of California Press, 1972.

Soley, Lawrence C., and John S. Nichols. *Clandestine Radio Broadcasting: A Study of Revolutionary and Counterrevolutionary Electronic Communication*. New York: Praeger, 1987.

Stafford, David. *Britain and European Resistance, 1940–1945: A Survey of the Special Operations Executive, with Documents*. Toronto: University of Toronto Press, 1980.

Sullivan, William C. *The Bureau: My Thirty Years in Hoover's FBI*. New York: Norton, 1979.

Szulc, Tad. *Fidel: A Critical Portrait*. New York: Morrow, 1986.

Theoharis, Athan. *Spying on Americans: Political Surveillance from Hoover to the Huston Plan*. Philadelphia, PA: Temple University Press, 1978.

Thompson, James Westfall, and Saul K. Padover. *Secret Diplomacy: Espionage and Cryptography, 1500–1815*. New York: Ungar, 1963.

Thompson, Sir Robert. *Defeating Communist Insurgency: The Lessons of Malaya and Vietnam*. New York: Praeger, 1966.

Tofte, Ornulf. *Spaneren*. Oslo: Guldendal Forlarget, 1987.

Treverton, Gregory F. *Covert Action: The Limits of Intervention in the Postwar World*. New York: Basic Books, 1987.

Trinquier, Roger. *Modern Warfare: A French View of Counterinsurgency*. New York: Praeger, 1964.

Tuchman, Barbara. *The Zimmermann Telegram*. New York: Macmillan, 1966.

Turner, Stansfield. *Secrecy and Democracy: The CIA in Transition*. Boston, MA: Houghton Mifflin, 1985.

Ueberhorst, Horst. *Friedrich Wilhelm von Steuben, 1730–1794*. Baltimore, MD: Heinz Moos Publishing, 1983.

Uris, Leon. *Topaz: A Novel*. New York: Bantam, 1968.

Vagts, Alfred. *The Military Attaché*. Princeton, NJ: Princeton University Press, 1967.

Vance, Cyrus. *Hard Choices: Four Critical Years in Managing America's Foreign Policy*. New York: Simon & Schuster, 1983.

Vierick, George Sylvester. *Spreading Germs of Hate*. New York: Horace Liveright, 1930.

Vizetelly, Ernest Alfred. *The True Story of the Chevalier d'Eon*. London: Tylston and Edwards and AP Marsden, 1895.

Wheatley, Ronald. *Operation Sea Lion: German Plans for the Invasion of England, 1939–1942*. Oxford, UK: Clarendon, 1958.

Whitehead, Don. *Attack on Terror: The FBI Against the Ku Klux Klan in Mississippi*. New York: Funk & Wagnall, 1970.

Willert, Arthur. *The Road to Safety: A Study in Anglo-American Relations*. London: Derek Verschoyle, 1952.

Winks, Robin. *Cloak and Gown: Scholars in the Secret War, 1939–1961*. New York: Quill, 1987.

Wise, David. *Molehunt: The Secret Search for Traitors that Shattered the CIA*. New York: Random House, 1992.

Wise, David, and Thomas Ross. *The Invisible Government*. New York: Random House, 1964.

Witcover, Jules. *Sabotage at Black Tom*. Chapel Hill, NC: Algonquin Books, 1989.

Wolton, Thierry. *Le KGB en France*. Paris: Bernard Grasset, 1986.

Woodward, Bob. *Veil: The Secret Wars of the CIA*. New York: Simon & Schuster, 1987.

Wright, Peter. *Spycatcher: The Candid Autobiography of a Senior Intelligence Officer*. New York: Viking, 1987.

Wyden, Peter. *Bay of Pigs: The Untold Story*. New York: Simon & Schuster, 1979.

Yardley, Michael. *T. E. Lawrence, a Biography*. New York: Stein & Day, 1987.

Yousaf, Mohammed, and Mark Adkin. *The Bear Trap: Afghanistan's Untold Story*. London: Leo Cooper, 1992.

Zeman, Z.A.B. *The Merchant of Revolution: The Life of Alexander Israel Helpland (Parvus), 1867–1924*. New York: Oxford University Press, 1965.

Articles and Monographs

Andrew, Christopher. "Dechiffrement et Diplomatie: Le Cabinet noir du Quai d'Orsay Sous la Troisième République." *Relations Internationales* 3:5 (1976): 37–64.

———. "The Mobilization of British Intelligence for the Two World Wars." In N. F. Dreisziger, *Mobilization for Total War*. Ontario: Wilfred Courier Press, 1981.

———. "The Growth of Intelligence in the English Speaking World." Working Paper #83. International Security Studies Program. Wilson Center for International Scholars. Washington, DC, nd.

Avtorkhanov, Abdurakhman. "The Soviet Triangular Dictatorship: Party, Police, and Army: Formation and Situation." *Ukrainian Quarterly* 34.2 (1978): 135–53.

Bialer, Uri. "The Iranian Connection in Israel's Foreign Policy, 1948-1951." *Middle East Journal* 39:2 (Spring 1985): 292–315.

Blumenthal, Ralph. "A Graying Onetime Double Agent Returns to Scenes of Old Intrigue." *New York Times*, July 17, 1994, p. 14.

Braden, Tom. "I'm Glad the CIA Is Immoral." *Saturday Evening Post*, May 20, 1967.

Branigin, William, and Michael Isikoff. "Newly Named Mexican Officials Linked to Drugs." *Washington Post*, January 7, 1989, p. A1.

Caldwell, Lawrence T., and Alexander Dallin. "U.S. Policy Toward the Soviet Union." In Kenneth Oye, Donald Rothchild, and Robert Lieber, eds., *Eagle Entangled: U.S. Foreign Policy in a Complex World*. New York: Longman, 1979.

Codevilla, Angelo. "The Opening to the Left." In Giovanni Sartori and Austin Ranney, eds., *Eurocommunism: The Italian Case*. Washington, DC: American Enterprise Institute, 1978.

Coll, Steve. "Anatomy of a Victory: CIA's Covert War in Afghanistan." *Washington Post*, July 19, 1992, p. A1.

———. "In CIA's Covert Afghan War Where to Draw Line Was Key." *Washington Post*, July 20, 1992, p. A1.

Cottam, Martha. "The Carter Administration's Policy Toward Nicaragua." *Political Science Quarterly*, Spring 1992, pp. 123–46.

Evangelista, Matthew. "Stalin's Postwar Army Reappraised." *International Security*, Winter 1982–83, pp. 110–29.

Frank, Warren E. "An Insider's Analysis." *Foreign Intelligence Literary Scene* 8.5 (1989).

Fuller, Graham. "Intelligence, Immaculately Conceived." *National Interest* 26 (Winter 1991–92): 95–99.

Gates, Robert. "The CIA and American Foreign Policy." *Foreign Affairs* 66 (Winter 1987–88): 215–30.

Godson, Roy, with Richard Kerr and Ernest May. "Covert Action in the 1990s." Paper of the Working Group on Intelligence Reform. Consortium for the Study of Intelligence, Working Group on Intelligence Reform, Washington, DC, 1993.

Handel, Michael. "Methodological Mischief: A Reply to Professor Muller." *Intelligence and National Security* 4.1 (January 1989): 161–64.

Hanson, Philip. "Soviet Industrial Espionage." *Bulletin of the Atomic Scientists* 43 (April 1987): 25–29.

Heather, Randall. "Intelligence and Counter-Insurgency in Kenya, 1952–1956." *Intelligence and National Security*, July 1990, pp. 57–83.

Horsley, Richard A. "The Sicarii: Ancient Jewish Terrorists." *The Journal of Religion* 59.4:435–58.

Hucker, Charles O. "Hu Tsung-hsien's Campaign Against Hsü Hai, 1556." In Frank Kierman, Jr., and John Fairbanks, eds., *Chinese Ways and Warfare*. Cambridge, MA: Harvard University Press, 1974.

Ibrahim, Youssef M. "Arabs Say Deadly Power Struggle Has Split Abu Nidal Terror Group." *New York Times*, November 12, 1989, p. 1.

Ignatius, David. "How Churchill's Agents Secretly Manipulated the US Before Pearl Harbor." *Washington Post*, Outlook, September 19, 1989.

———. "'Major' KGB Defector to US Breaks 10 Years of Silence." *Washington Post*, March 2, 1990, p. A1.

"Israeli Foreign Intelligence and Security Services." *Counterspy*, May–June 1982, pp. 34–54.

Jensen, Priscilla M., ed. "Speaking About Democracy and Peace." *United States Institute of Peace Journal* 3 (1990): 3.

Lardner, George, Jr. "Soviet Union Denounces KGB Defector Sheymov." *Washington Post*, March 13, 1990, p. A13.

Lazitch, Branko. "Two Instruments of Control by the Comintern: The Emissaries of the ECCI and the Party Representatives in Moscow." In Milorad Drashkovitch and Branko Lazitch, eds., *The Comintern: Historical Highlights*. Published for the Hoover Institution on War, Revolution and Peace, Stanford University. New York: Praeger, 1966.

———. "Stalin's Massacre of the Foreign Communist Leaders." In *The Comintern: Historical Highlights*.

Lockhart, John Bruce. "Sir William Wiseman, Bart—Agent of Influence." *RUSI Quarterly*, Summer 1989, pp. 63–67.

"The Most Dangerous Man." National Affairs: Labor. *Time*, March 17, 1952.

Muller, Klaus-Jurgen. "A German Perspective on Allied Deception Operations in the Second World War." *Intelligence and National Security* 2.3 (July 1987): 301–26.

"The Need to Know: The Report of the Twentieth Century Fund Task Force on Covert Action and American Democracy." New York: Twentieth Century Fund Press, 1992.

"News and Views from the USSR." Embassy of the Union of Soviet Socialist Republics. October 7, 1987, and October 27, 1987.

"Nuclear Weapons: Major Soviet Deception." *Disinformation: Soviet Active Measures and Disinformation Forecast* 9 (Summer 1988): 1.

Odom, William. "Who Controls Whom in Moscow." *Foreign Policy* 19 (Summer 1975): 109–23.

Orlov, Alexander. "The Theory and Practice of Soviet Intelligence." *Studies in Intelligence* 24.3.

Peake, Hayden B. "Soviet Espionage and the Office of Strategic Services, (OSS)." September 1988 revision of paper read at the Conference on World War II and the Shaping of Modern America, at Rutgers University, New Brunswick, NJ, April 4–6, 1986.

Polgar, Thomas. "Defection and Redefection." *International Journal of Intelligence and Counterintelligence* 1.2 (1986): 29–44.

Possony, Stefan T. "The Comintern as an Instrument of Soviet Strategy." In M. Drashkovitch, ed., *The Revolutionary Internationals, 1864–1943*. Stanford, CA: Stanford University Press, 1966.

"Priorities for '89: Political, Military and Economic." *Disinformation: Soviet Active Measures and Disinformation Forecast* 11 (Winter 1989): 1.

Rapoport, David. "Fear and Trembling: Terrorism in Three Religious Traditions." *American Political Science Review* 78.3 (September 1984): 658–77.

Raskin, Marcus. "A Short Account of International Student Politics and the Cold War with Particular Reference to the NSA, CIA, etc." *Ramparts*, March 1967, pp. 29–39.

Regnard, Henry. "L'URSS et le Renseignement Scientifique, Technique et Technologique." *Defense Nationale* 39 (December 1983): 107–21.

Rosenau, James N., and Ole R. Holsti. "U.S. Leadership in a Shrinking World: The Breakdown of Consensus and the Emergence of Conflicting Belief Systems." In G. John Ikenberry, *American Foreign Policy: Theoretical Essays*. Glenview, IL: Scott, Foresman, 1989.

Sessions, William S. "The Evolving Threat: Meeting the Counterintelligence Challenges of the 1990s: A Strategic Issue Facing Our Nation." *American Intelligence Journal* 10.2 (Summer/Fall 1989): 19–23.

Sheldon, Rose Mary. "Spying in Mesopotamia." *Studies in Intelligence*. Cass Series, offprint, nd.

"Soviet Gambit May Change '90s Balance." *Disinformation: Soviet Active Measures and Disinformation Forecast* 7 (Fall 1987): 1.

Stephenson, Orlando W. "The Supply of Gunpowder in 1776." *American Historical Review* 30.2 (January 1925): 271–81.

Van Tyne, C. H. "French Aid Before the Alliance of 1778." *American Historical Review*, October 1925, pp. 20–40.

Wallop, Malcom. "Covert Action: Policy Tool or Policy Hedge." *Strategic Review*, Summer 1984, pp. 9–16.

Wannall, W. Raymond. "Setting Straight the FBI's Counterintelligence Record." *World and I*, January 1987, pp. 167–77.

Young, Neil. "Clandestine Aid and the American Revolutionary War: A Re-Examination." *Military Affairs* 43.1 (February 1979): 26–30.

Dissertations

Beaver, W. C. *The Development of the Intelligence Division and Its Role in Aspects of Imperial Policymaking, 1854–1901.* D.Phil. diss., Oxford University, 1976.

Knott, Stephen. *Lifting the Veil: The Roots of American Covert Activity.* Ph.D. diss., Boston College, 1991.

Naftali, Timothy J. *X-2 and the Apprenticeship of American Counterespionage, 1942–1944.* Ph.D. diss., Harvard University, 1993.

Strmecki, Marin. *Power Assessment: Measuring Soviet Power in Afghanistan.* Ph.D. diss., Georgetown University, 1994.

Government Documents

Arms Control and Disarmament Agency. Publication 122. *The Soviet Propaganda Campaign Against the US Strategic Defense Initiative.* Washington, DC: Arms Control and Disarmament Agency, August 1986.

———. *Soviet Propaganda Campaign Against NATO.* Washington, DC: Arms Control and Disarmament Agency, October 1983.

Cavanagh, Suzanne. *Individuals Arrested on Charges of Espionage Against the United States Government, 1966–1987.* CRS Rpt. 87-320GOV, April 20, 1987. Washington, DC: Congressional Research Service, Library of Congress, 1987.

Congressional Record. 89th Cong., 1st sess., September 28, 1965.

Congressional Research Service. Library of Congress. *Soviet Intelligence and Security Services: A Selected Bibliography of Soviet Publications.* 2 vols. Washington, DC: Government Printing Office, 1972–75.

Darling, Arthur. "The Central Intelligence Agency, an Instrument of Government, to 1950." Washington, DC: National Archives, DCI Historical Series, December 1953.

Department of Defense. *Critical Technologies Plan: Response to Public Law 100-456, the National Defense Authorization Act, fiscal Year 1989, of 29 September 1988.* Washington, DC: Department of Defense, 1989.

———. *Soviet Acquisition of Western Technology.* Washington, DC: Department of Defense, April 1982.

————. *Soviet Acquisition of Militarily Significant Western Technology: An Update*. Washington, DC: Department of Defense, September 1985.

————. *Soviet Military Power: An Assessment of the Threat, 1988*. Washington, DC: Government Printing Office, 1988.

Department of Justice. *Soviet Active Measures in the United States 1986–1987*. Washington, DC: Department of Justice, June 1987.

Department of State. Publication 9630. *Active Measures: A Report on the Substance and Process of Anti-U.S. Disinformation and Propaganda Campaigns*. Washington, DC: Department of State, August 1986.

————. Publication 9536. *Contemporary Soviet Propaganda and Disinformation: A Conference Report*. Washington, DC: Department of State, March 1987.

————. *Documents on Disarmament, 1945–1959*. Vol. 1, *1945–1956*. Washington, DC: Government Printing Office, 1960.

————. Publication 9726. *The International Department of the CC CPSU Under Dobrynin*. Washington, DC: Department of State, September 1989.

————. Publication 9620. *Soviet Influence Activities: A Report on Active Measures and Propaganda, 1986–1987*. Washington, DC: Department of State, August 1987.

————. Publication 9627. *Soviet Influence Activities: A Report on Active Measures and Propaganda, 1987–1988*. Washington, DC: Department of State, August 1989.

Foreign Broadcast Information Service (FBIS), Latin America, May 21, 1990.

Foreign Relations of the United States, 1948. Vol. 3, *Western Europe*. Washington, DC: Government Printing Office, 1974.

"The Aldrich H. Ames Case: An Assessment of CIA's Role in Identifying Ames as an Intelligence Penetration of the Agency." Report of Frederick P. Hitz, CIA Inspector General. Washington, DC: Central Intelligence Agency, October 21, 1994.

Intelligence in the War of Independence. Washington, DC: Central Intelligence Agency, 1976.

Jackson, Wayne G. *Allen Welsh Dulles as Director of Central Intelligence, 26 February 1953–29 November 1961*. 5 vols. Washington, DC: Central Intelligence Agency, July 1973.

Report of the Security Commission, May 1983. CMND 8876. London: HM Stationery Office, 1983.

Report of the Security Commission, May 1985. CMND 9514. London: HM Stationery Office, 1985.

Sorrels, Charles A. *Soviet Propaganda Campaign Against NATO*. Washington, DC: U.S. Arms Control and Disarmament Agency, 1983.

Troy, Thomas F. *Donovan and the CIA*. Washington, DC: Central Intelligence Agency, 1981.

U.S. Congress. House. Committee on Armed Services. *Report of the Technology Transfer Panel of the Committee on Armed Services*. 98th Cong., 2nd sess., 1984. Committee Print.

U.S. Congress. House. Committee on Foreign Affairs. *Post Cold War Intelligence*. 102nd Cong., 2nd sess., February 25, 1992.

U.S. Congress. House. Permanent Select Committee on Intelligence. *The CIA and the Media*. 95th Cong., 1st and 2nd sess., 1977–78.

———. *Compilation of Intelligence Laws and Related Laws and Executive Orders of Interest to the National Intelligence Community, as Amended Through June 8, 1993*. 103rd Cong., 1st sess., July 1993. Committee Print.

———. *Soviet Covert Action (The Forgery Offensive)*. 96th Cong., 2nd sess., February 6 and 19, 1980.

———. *Soviet Active Measures*. 97th Cong., 2nd sess., July 13–14, 1982.

U.S. Congress. House. Select Committee on Intelligence. *CIA: The Pike Report*. Nottingham: Spokesman Books, 1977.

U.S. Congress. House. Select Committee to Investigate Covert Arms Transactions with Iran and Senate Select Committee on Secret Military Assistance to Iran and the Nicaraguan Opposition. *Report of the Congressional Committees Investigating the Iran-Contra Affair*. 100th Cong., 1st sess., 1987. H.Rpt. 100–433 and S.Rpt. 100–216.

U.S. Congress. Library of Congress. Congressional Research Service. *Soviet Intelligence and Security Services: A Selected Bibliography of Soviet Publications*. 2 vols. Washington, DC: Government Printing Office, 1972–75.

U.S. Congress. Senate. Committee on Foreign Relations. *Soviet Imperatives for the 1990s*. Part 2, *Soviet Active Measures*. 99th Cong., 1st sess., 1985. S.Hrg. 99–400.

U.S. Congress. Senate. Committee on the Judiciary. *Communist Forgeries*. Committee Hearings. 87th Cong., 1st sess., June 2, 1961.

———. *Revival of the Communist International and Its Significance for the United States*. Staff Study. 86th Cong., 1st sess., 1959. Committee Print.

U.S. Congress. Senate. Select Committee on Intelligence. "An Assessment of the Aldrich H. Ames Espionage Case and Its Implications for US Intelligence." 103rd Cong., 2nd sess., November 1, 1994.

———. *Meeting the Espionage Challenge: A Review of United States Counterintelligence and Security Programs*. 99th Cong., 2nd sess., October 3, 1986. S.Rpt. 99–522.

———. *Report to Accompany S.2834, Authorizing Appropriations for Fiscal Year 1991 for the Intelligence Activities of the U.S. Government, the Intelligence Community Staff, the Central Intelligence Agency Retirement and Disability System, and for Other Purposes*. 101st Cong., 1st sess. S.Rpt. 101–358.

———. *Report on Security at the United States Missions in Moscow and Other Areas of High Risk*. 100th Cong., 1st sess., September 9, 1987. S.Rpt. 100–154.

U.S. Congress. Senate. Permanent Subcommittee on Investigations of the Committee on Governmental Affairs. *Federal Government's Handling of Soviet and Communist Bloc Defectors*. 100th Cong., 2nd sess. Washington, DC: Government Printing Office, 1988.

U.S. Congress. Senate. Select Committee to Study Governmental Operations with Respect to Intelligence Activities. *Alleged Assassination Plots Involving Foreign Leaders*. 94th Cong., 1st sess. S.Rpt. 94–465. Washington, DC: Government Printing Office, 1975.

———. *Final Report*. 4 vols. 94th Cong., 2nd sess., 1976. S. Rpt 94–755.

U.S. Information Agency. *Soviet Active Measures in the Era of Glasnost*. Prepared for the House Committee on Appropriations. Washington, DC: U.S. Information Agency, June 1988.

Index

Abu Nidal, 164
Access agents, 218–19
Action Directe, 206
Adams, John, 65
Adams, Samuel, 65
Afghanistan, 52, 53, 60
  Mujahideen resistance in, 165, 172
  Soviet invasion of, 8
AFOSI. *See* Air Force Office of Special
    Investigation.
Africa, 53, 142
Agent Identities Act (1982), 195
Agents of influence, 135–45, 204
  Israeli, 141
  Soviet, 141
Air America, 130
Air Force Office of Special Investigation
    (AFOSI), 99, 245
Albania, 14, 46–47, 86
Al-Banna, Sabri, 164
Algeria, 171
Algerian National Liberation Front,
    163
Allen, Richard, 53, 105
Allende, Salvador, 45, 125
Ambassadors, intelligence officers vs.,
    137–38
America First, 24
American Bar Association, 82
American Civil Liberties Union, 102
American Federation of Labor, 24,
    42–43, 68, 205
Ames, Aldrich, 115, 119, 188, 197
  competency of, 113
  motives, 208
Analysis, 2, 81–82
  counterintelligence, 187–200
  covert action and, 133
Angleton, James, 34, 87–88, 94
  controversy about, 111
  doctrine of intelligence, 91–92

managers, 112
  retirement of, 102
Angola, 53, 60, 168
Anhouse, Sidek, 145
Arafat, Yassir, 164
Army Security Agency, 81
Assassination, 63, 159–61
A Study of Communism, 82
Australia, 178
Australian Security Intelligence Organi-
    zation, 213
Aviation Week and Space Technology, 203

Baker, James, 53
Ball, George, 189
Bay of Pigs, 38, 47–48, 54
Beaumarchais, Pierre-Augustin de, 123
Belmont, Alan, 74, 80
Bently, Elizabeth, 68
Bettaney, Michael J., 212
Bissell, Richard, 39
Bitov, Oleg, 215
Bloch, Felix, 114
Blunt, Anthony, 207
Boland, Edward, 56
Bosnia-Herzegovina, 131
Boyce, Christopher, 213
Brackenridge, Hugh, 156
Braden, Tom, 43
Bradley, Omar, 28, 152
Brennan, C. D., 74
British Secret Intelligence Service (M15),
    81
British Secret Intelligence Service (M16),
    14, 81
British Security Coordination, 23–24,
    178
Bryce Report, 156
Brzezinski, Zbigniew, 52
Bureau of Diplomatic Security, 110
Burgess, Guy, 145, 207

Cahiers du Communisme, 205
Cairncross, John, 207
"Cambridge Comintern," 207
Carroll, Joe, 99
Carter, James E., Jr., 52, 55, 100
   call for threat analysis, 112
   covert action and, 58
   Executive Order 12036, 105
   FBI appointee, 107
Case officers, 61–63, 128
Casey, William, 53, 57, 58, 105, 112
Castro, Fidel, 47, 160, 176
Ceausescu, Elena, 234–35
Ceausescu, Nicolae, 234–35
Central America, 53, 120
   U.S. policy in, 55–58
Central Intelligence Agency, 30
   Clandestine Service of. *See* Direc-
      torate of Operations.
   communist infiltration of, 103–4
   counterintelligence, 85–95, 111–15
      education program, 90
      failures of, 90, 94, 114
      sources for, 88
   covert action and, 41
   creation of, 244
   Directorate for Plans (DP), 35
   executive branch and, 62, 245
   expenditures, 51
   infiltration of, 89
   lack of information in, 48
   Office of Policy Coordination. *See*
      Office of Policy Coordination.
   in postwar Europe, 44
   press and, 62
   research teams, 93
   secret funding relationships of, 48
   Soviet penetration of, 91
   State Department and, 245
Central Intelligence Group, 29
Chalet, Marcel, 220, 223
Cheka, 16
Chile, 26, 45
Chin, Larry Wu-Tai, 89, 207
China, 1, 143–44, 153
Chinese People's Liberation Army, 153
Church Committee, 101
   report (1976), 7, 35, 64

Churchill, Winston, 23, 236
CIA. *See* Central Intelligence Agency.
CIC. *See* Counter Intelligence Corps.
Clark, William, 53, 105
Clarridge, Duane, 57
Cohen, Eli, 141, 197
COINTELPRO, 84
Colby, William, 112, 137, 176
Cold War, 24–26
   FBI and, 74
   U.S. covert action in, 64
Collection of information, 1–2, 5
   counterintelligence, 201–26
   dovetailing in, 225
   FBI, 76–81
   from humint sources, 98, 118, 204,
      207–11
   technology, 105, 242
Colombian drug traffic, 132, 158
Communism, 153
   covert action and, 121
   Marshall Plan and, 43
   opposition by U.S. labor leaders to,
      42
   as rational for covert action, 35–39
   weaknesses of, 151
Communist Information Bureau, 25
Communist Party, Soviet Union, 141,
   153–54
Communist Party USA, 70, 84–85
   cipher break, 83
   leaders, framing, 84–85
   membership in, 77
   USSR exploitation of, 82
Congress. *See* U.S. Congress.
Contras, 170, 172. *See also* Nicaragua.
Cooper, Samuel, 156
Coordinator of Information, 28, 178
Coplon, Judith, 81
Costa Rica, 170
Counterdeception analysis, 192–95
Counterintelligence, 2, 7
   analysis, 187–200
      anomalous behavior, 196–97
      assessing vulnerability in, 190–91
      counterdeception analysis and,
         192–95
      pattern, 195

positive intelligence and, 199–200
   target and, 191–92
   triage of targets in, 188–90
Army, 100
authority for, 66–67
British, 186, 195
central function of, 15
CIA's, 85–95, 111–15
collection, 201–26
   access agents in, 218–19
   defectors and, 211–16
   double agents in, 219–20
   illegals in, 221–24
   integration of sources in, 201–3
   liaison services in, 220–21
   from open sources, 203–6
   physical surveillance in, 216–18
covert action and, 5
developing, 13
effective, 184
executive branch and, 72
FBI, 74–85
FDR directive on, 72
foreign vs. domestic, 72
German, 9–10
ineffective, results of, 9–18
KGB, 70
   masters of, in history, 185
military, 95–99, 115–17. *See also*
   Counter Intelligence Corps.
modus operandi, 231–37
national strategy and, 184
Normandy invasion and, 17
offensive, 231–37
   deception and, 235–37
policymakers and, 4, 9
positive intelligence and, 237–38
postwar, shaping of, 69
technical, 224–26
U.S.
   evolution of, 117
   FBI as premier, 69
   postwar, 69
   staff, first, 112
   weakness of, 115
USSR use of, 10–11, 70
in World War I, 9–10
in World War II, 17

Counterintelligence Center, 113
   staff of, 114
Counter Intelligence Corps, 95–98
   agent recruitment, 96
   Intelligence Directive no. 5 (NSC)
      and, 97
   OSS-X2 and, 96
   positive intelligence section, 97
Counter Intelligence Corps (CIC), 68
Countermeasures, 226
   goal of, 230
Counterterrorism, 180–83
Coups d'état, 175–77
Covert action, 2–3, 5–6
   activities in, 3
   agents of influence in
      history of, 143–45
   analysis and, 133
   as an instrument of policy, 39
   assassination as part of, 159–61
   British, U.S. entry in World War II
      and, 23–24
   Carter and, 58
   case officers for, 128
   channels, information and, 4
   Cold War and, 24–26
   communications and, 129
   communism and, 35–39, 121
   counterintelligence and, 5
   deep-cover officers in, 126
   effective, prerequisites for, 123–24
   financial support for, 147–51
   first principles, 121–22
   foreign policy and, 254
   funding for, 59
   goals of, 134
   helping organizations in, 145–47
   history of, 19–26
   infrastructure, 126–30
   intelligence assistance in, 3
   Iran hostage rescue and, 130
   labor unions and, 42–43
   material support for, 129–30
   other elements of intelligence and,
      132–34
   paramilitary, 3, 130, 134, 158–9
      special forces for, 173–75
   as part of U.S. policy, 39–41

Covert action (*continued*)
　personnel for, 126–28
　　technical, 128
　policymakers and, 9
　political activity and, 3, 135–51
　　agents of influence in, 135–45
　prejudice against, 27
　propaganda and, 3, 151–58
　question of values in, 130–32
　terrorism as part of, 161–64
　"threshold doctrine" and, 52
　U.S.
　　and Afghanistan, 26
　　and Central America, 55–58
　　and Chile, 26
　　and Cuba, 26
　　exceptionalist school of, 64–65
　　foreign policy and, 39–41
　　and Greece, 35
　　and Guatemala, 26
　　halcyon days of, 42–45
　　history of, 64–65
　　and Iran, 26
　　and Italy, 31, 35
　　lack of support, 50
　　missteps of, 46–49
　　and Nicaragua, 57–58
　　and Philippines, 26
　　and Poland, 26, 47
　　in the 1990s, 58–65
　　and Western Europe, 26, 31, 35
　U.S. Congress and, 53–55
　U.S. Constitution and, 65
　U.S. control of Panama Canal and, 27
CPUSA. *See* Communist Party, USA.
Croatia, 131
Cuba, 26, 166. *See also* Bay of Pigs.
Czechoslovakia, 153
　Communist coup in, 32
　intelligence service, 178–79
　　military, 211

DCI. *See* Director of Central Intelligence.
DDP. *See* Director for Plans.
Deaver, Michael, 53
Deep-cover officers, 60, 126
Defectors, 211–16
Defense Intelligence Agency, 115, 244
Defense Investigative Service, 115

Demetrius, 140
Department of Defense, 67, 80, 102
　counterintelligence and, 106
Department of Justice, 66–67
Diplomats, 110
　expulsion of Soviet, 111
Directorate for Plans (DP), 35–36
Directorate for Science and Technology,
　93, 113
Directorate of Operations, 53, 63, 86, 113
Director of Central Intelligence (DCI),
　29
　role of, 72
　Smith as, 35
　special assistant for counterintelli-
　　gence, 106
DO. *See* Directorate of Operations.
Dodd, Christopher, 56
Donovan, William, 23, 28, 123, 178
　development of U.S. intelligence and,
　　244
Double agents, 78–79, 109, 116
　in counterintelligence collection,
　　219–20
DP. *See* Directorate for Plans.
Drug traffic, 189
DS&T. *See* Directorate for Science and
　　Technology.
Dubinsky, David, 42
Duclos, Jacques, 205
Dulles, Allen, 35, 244
Dunlap, Jack, 208
Dzerzhinsky, Felix, 185
Dzhirkvelov, Ilya, 214

Eisenhower, Dwight D., 47, 73
Elizabeth I, 123
Ellis, Charles, 178
El Salvador, 56, 158
Emergency Detention Act (1950), 77
Ervin, Sam, 102
d'Estaing, Giscard, 148
EUR-X, 29
Executive Order 12036, 105
Executive Order 12333, 105

Fatah Revolutionary Council, 164, 182
FBI. *See* Federal Bureau of Investigation
　　(FBI).

Federal Bureau of Investigation (FBI),
    23, 67
  analysis by, information, 81–82
  "black bag" jobs, 80
  civil rights monitoring, 100
  Cold War and, 74
  collection of information by, 76–81
  communist infiltration of, 103–4
  counterintelligence, 74–85, 107–11
    field offices of, 108
    training for, 109–10
  defensive surveillance techniques,
    109
  double agents, 78–79
  information exploitation, 82–85
  public education program, 82–83
  recruitment of foreign officers, 79
Felfe, Heinze, 207
Felt, Mark, 77, 80
Ferri-Pisani, Pierre, 43–44
Fighting Communist Cells, 206
FitzGerald, Desmond, 39
Ford, Gerald, 100
Foreign Agents Registration Act, 67
Foreign Assistance Act (1961), 54
Foreign Service officers, 40
Forgery, 155
Forrestal, James, 29, 43
Forty Committee, 38
Fouche, Joseph, 185
Franklin, Benjamin, 20
Free Trade Union Committee, 43, 205
Fuchs, Klaus, 11, 81

Gasperi, Alcide de, 31
Gates, Robert, 15
Geer, Jim, 106
German counterintelligence, 9–10
Germany, 9–10, 131, 152, 157–58
Ghana, 209
Gold, Harry, 81
Goldberg, Arthur, 42
Golitsyn, Anatoliy, 102, 145, 187, 220
Gondomar, Count of, 135
Gorbachev, Mikhail, 235
Gordievsky, Oleg, 187, 212
Gouzenko, Igor, 68
Graffenreid, Kenneth de, 114, 188
Greece, 35

Green, William, 42, 205
Greenglass, David, 11
Grimes, Dan, 106
Grouk, Arkady, 212
5412 Group (1955), 38
GRU, 192, 196, 211
  special forces, 175
  World War II espionage, 89
Guatemala, 26, 45, 177
Gubetchev, Valentin, 81
Guerrilla movements, 164–70
Guevara, Che, 124

Hall, James, 114
Harkin, Tom, 56
Haro, Nazar, 209
Harriman, Averell, 205
Harrison, George, 42
Hathaway, Gus, 106
Helms, Richard, 39
Heydrich, Reinhard, 160
Hillenkoetter, Roscoe, 30, 35
Hitler, Adolf, 152, 159
Honduras, 170
Hood, William, 211
Hoover, J. Edgar, 23, 67, 72
  death of, 101
  Sullivan and, 82
  U.S. Air Force and, 99
House, Edward M., 136
House Permanent Select Committee on
    Intelligence, 56
House Un-American Activities Commit-
    tee, 67
Howard, Edward Lee, 15, 213
Hoxha, Enver, 46
Hughes-Ryan Amendment (1974), 54,
    101
Humint collection operations, 98, 118,
    204, 225
Hungary, 153
Huntington, Samuel, 8
Hussein, Saddam, 15, 176

IG-CI. See Interagency Group for Coun-
    terintelligence.
IG-CM. See Interagency Group for
    Countermeasures and Security.
Ignatius, David, 24

Ikl, Fred, 53, 57
Illegals, 221–24
    definition of, 222
    identification of, 222
    second generation, 227
Influence-peddling, 148–49
Information, 1
    accuracy of, determining, 227
    automated, 229
    covert action channels and, 1
    exploitation of, 82–85, 226–40
Intelligence. *See also* Counterintelligence;
        Covert Action.
    alliances, 177–80
    American. *See* U.S. Intelligence.
    Army, 95–98, 109, 115–17, 245
    Chinese, 1
    counterinsurgency, 165–66
    definition of, 1
    in democratic societies, 250
    elements of, 1–3
        covert action and other, 132–34
        integrating the, 3–6
        neglected, 6–9
    full-service, 1
        analysis in, 2, 81–82
        collection of information in, 1–2
        counterintelligence in, 2
        covert action in, 2–3
        elements of, 1–3
    as information, 1
    Navy, 98–99, 109, 116–17, 245
    positive, 97, 199–200, 237–38
    Soviet. *See* GRU; KGB.
    in totalitarian states, 250
    World War I and development of,
        247–48
Intelligence Directive no. 5, 72, 104
Intelligence Identities Protection Act
        (1982), 43
Intelligence officers, ambassadors vs.,
        137–38
Intelligence support, 177–80
Interagency Group for Counterintelli-
        gence (IG-CI), 106
Interagency Group for Counter-
        measures and Security (IG-
        CM), 106

Interdepartmental Intelligence Confer-
        ence, 72
International Congress for Cultural Free-
        dom, 50
International politics, shifts in, 51–52
Iran, 26, 38, 131, 143
    extrication of Jews from, 122
    hostages in, 8, 130
    Mussadegh government, 126–27
    as safe haven, 170–71
Iran-Contra affair, 57, 121
Iraq, 131
    extrication of Jews from, 122, 134
    as safe haven, 171
Iraqi nuclear weaponry, 14–15, 193, 230
Ishida, Hirohide, 145
Israel, 135, 160
    agents of influence from, 141
Italy, 31, 35

Japanese Socialist Party, 145
Jibril, Ahmad, 180
Johnson, Lyndon B., 100
Jones, Noel, 106

Kalaris, George, 106, 112, 114
Kelly, Merrill, 106
Kennan, George, 32
Kennedy, John F., 47, 73, 100
    Martin Luther King and, 84
Kennedy, Robert F., 73, 84
Kerensky, Aleksandr, 124, 176
KGB, 111, 192, 196, 211
    Communist Party USA and, 70
    counterintelligence, 70
    defectors from, 214
    Japanese Socialist Party and, 145
    Line PR, 108
    Line X, 108, 109
    modus operandi, 71
    postwar activity, 97
    Soviet politics and, 69
    special forces, 175
    U.S. Intelligence vs., 69
    use of unilateral penetration by, 180
Khomeini, Ayatollah, 52
Khrushchev, Nikita, 90
King, J. C., 61
King, Martin Luther, 84

Kissinger, Henry, 100
Koecher, Karl, 207
Korean War, 33
Kreesat, Marwan, 181
Krieger, Richard, 106
Ku Klux Klan, 84
Kuusinen, Otto, 159

Labor leaders, 42
Ladd, D. M. Mickey, 74
Laird v. Tatum, 102
Lalas, Steven, 114
Lamphere, Robert, 81
Laos, 45, 166
Lawrence, T. E., 124, 169–70
Lawrence of Arabia. *See* Lawrence, T. E..
Lebanon, 171
Lee, Andrew Daulton, 213
Lee, Arthur, 20
Levchenko, Stanislav, 145
Liaisons services, 220–21
Libya, 131, 143, 171, 181
Lithuania, 47
London Control Section, 236
Lost Victory, 137
Lovell, Mary, 24
Lovestone, Jay, 205
Loyalty and Security Program, 77
Loyola, Ignatius, 139–40

Maclean, Donald, 145, 207
Magsaysay, Ramon, 38
Mandel, Ben, 204–5
Marshall, George, 30
Marshall, Thurgood, 84
Marshall Plan, 25
    communism and, 43
Mass media, covert propaganda and, 156
Masterman, J. C., 199
Masters of Deceit, 82
May, Alan Nunn, 11
May, Ernest, 65
McCargar, James, 41
McCarran Act (1950), 78
McCarthy, Joseph, 70
Meany, George, 42, 205
Mexico, 53, 143, 189
Meyer, Cord, 50
Military Industrial Commission, 11

Miller, Richard, 110
Mitterand, Francois, 11
Mole, 211, 222
Moravec, Frantisek, 211
Morton, Desmond, 23
Mossad, 135
Mujahideen resistance, 165, 170, 172
Murphy, James, 92
Murphy, Ray, 29, 205

National Association for the Advance-
    ment of Colored People, 84
National Revolutionary Council, 198
National Security Act (1947), 30, 107
National Security Council (NSC), 30
    counterintelligence mechanism in, 105
    directives, 72, 104
        to DP, 38
National Students Association, 50
Nation of Islam, 84
Naval Investigative Service, 245
Nazi military intelligence, 211
Nazi Party, 131
Nenni, Pietro, 41
New York Times, The, 101
Nicaragua, 52, 53, 165
    covert action in, 57, 167
    Sandinistas in, 54
    U.S. aid to, 54, 55–58, 60, 166–67
Nixon, Richard M., 100
Nolan, James, 106, 231
Noriega, Manuel, 138
Normandy invasion, 192
North Atlantic Treaty Organization, 18
North Korea, 143
Nosenko, Yuri, 89, 92
    NSC. *See* National Security Council.

OCI. *See* Office of the Coordinator of
    Information.
Office of Foreign Missions, 110, 231
Office of Naval Intelligence, 98–99
Office of Policy Coordination (OPC), 32,
    41, 54
    in Asia, 33
    in Chile, 45
    counterintelligence protection, 86
    failures, 86, 90
    funding of, 35

Office of Policy Coordination (*continued*)
  headquarters, 33
  initial agenda of, 35
  in Lithuania, 47
  OSO and, 87, 91
  in Poland, 47
  Soviet bloc penetration of, 86
Office of Security, 90, 93, 112
  function, 86
Office of Special Operations (OSO), 32
  OPC and, 87, 91
  Staff C of, 86
Office of Special Projects (OSP), 32
Office of Strategic Services (OSS), 23, 28, 67
  black radio broadcasts, 23, 157
  CIC and, 96
  X-2 branch, 85, 95, 96
Office of the Coordinator of Information (OCI), 23
Office of the Secretary of Defense, 115
Official Secrets Act, 212
Oman, 168
OPC. *See* Office of Policy Coordination.
Operation Desert Shield, 230
Operation Double-Cross, 17
Operation Fortitude, 17-8
Operation Frolic, 153
Operations Coordinating Board (1953), 38
Organizations, covert action of, 145–47
OSO. *See* Office of Special Operations.
OSP. *See* Office of Special Projects.
OSS. *See* Office of Strategic Services.

Pacepa, Ion Mihai, 213, 234
Page, Edward, 31, 34
Pakistan, 170
Palestine Liberation Organization, 135, 164
Panama, 138
Paramilitary activity, 3, 158–59
  Air America in, 130
  covert, 169–70. *See* Guerrilla movements.
  cross-cultural factors in, 169–70
  guerrilla movements and. *See* Guerrilla movements.

history of, 158–59
  material support for, 171–73
  in Southeast Asia, 51
Parvus, Gustav, 124
Pathe, Pierre, 145
Pelton, Ronald, 213
Penkovsky, Oleg, 89, 90, 93
People's Republic of China, 103
Peterson, Joseph, 209
Petrov, Evdokia, 213–14
Petrov, Vladimir Mikhailovich, 213–14
PFIAB. *See* President's Foreign Intelligence Advisory Board.
Philby, Harold A. R. ("Kim"), 14, 207
Philippines, 38, 45
Physical surveillance, 216–18
Pike Committee report (1976), 7
PLO. *See* Palestine Liberation Organization.
Poland, 20, 47, 86, 152
Polgar, Tom, 215
Policymakers, 4
  counterintelligence and, 9
  covert action and, 9
Political action, 3
Pollard, Jonathan, 184
Polygraph, 227–28
Ponomarev, Boris, 199, 206
Pontecorvo, Bruno, 11
Popov, Pytor, 89, 93, 211–12
Popular Front for the Liberation of Palestine, 164, 180, 182
Popular Movement for the Liberation of Angola, 168
Portuguese revolution, 127
Positive intelligence, 97, 199–200, 237–38
President's Foreign Intelligence Advisory Board (PFIAB), 104, 105
Prime, Geoffrey, 213
Propaganda, 3, 167
  black, 154–56
    forgery as form of, 155
    history of, 154–56
  covert, 151–58
    black vs. gray, 151–52
    mass media and, 156
    overt vs., 151

radio broadcating and, 152–53
  types of, 156
  gray, 151–52, 154
  in World War I, 22
  in World War II, 154
Psychological Strategy Board (1951), 38

Radio 1212, 157
Radio Ba Yi, 153
Radio broadcasts, 152
  black, 157
  ghosting, 152
  snuggling, 152
Radio Free Europe, 51
Radio Free Japan, 153
Radio Liberty, 51
Ramparts, 50
Reagan, Ronald, 53, 55
  Executive Order 12333, 105
  expulsion of Soviet diplomats, 11
  FBI appointee, 107
  Nicaraguan covert action and, 57
Resistance movements, 164–70
  U.S. support for, 173
  Rocca, Ray, 89
  Romania, 213
  Department of External Information,
    234
  OSS mission to, 33
  support for guerrilla activity, 166
  Romerstein, Herbert, 206
  Roosevelt, Franklin D., 123, 136
  foreign policy, 205
  use of counterintelligence, 67, 72
Rote Kapelle, 89
Ruritania, 123, 124–25

Sadat, Anwar, 160
Safe haven, 170–71
Samozista National Guard, 165
Sandinistas, 54–56
SAVAK, 138, 177
SCC. *See* Special Coordination Commit-
  tee.
Scranage, Sharon, 208–9
Second Continental Congress, 20
Security defense, 226–28
  of automated information, 229
Senate Intelligence Committee, 118

Senior-level interagency intelligence com-
  mittee (SIG-I), 106
Sessions, William, 107
Shackley, Theodore, 137
Shah of Iran, 38
  security system, 138
Shakespeare, William, 123
Sherwood, Robert, 123
Sheymov, Victor, 215
Shiite terrorists, 170
Showers, Donald ("Mac"), 106
SIG-I. *See* Senior-level interagency intel-
  ligence committee.
Sigint collection, 224
Sigismund, 140
Smith, Walter Bedell, 35
Smith Act (1940), 78
Society of Jesus, founding of, 139
SOE. *See* Special Operations Executive.
Son Tay raid, 174
Sorge, Richard, 10
Souers, Sidney B., 29
Soussoudis, Michael A., 209
South Africa, 143
South West Africa People's Organization,
  166
Sovit Academy of Sciences, 203
*Soviet Acquisition of Militarily Significant
  Western Technology*, 11
Soviet secret service, 16
Soviet Trust, 16
Special Coordination Committee (SCC),
  105, 115
Special forces, 173–75
Special Group (1961), 38
Special Operations Executive (SOE), 34
Special political action, 2
SSU. *See* Strategic Services Unit.
Stalin, Josef, 159
Stanhope, James, 136
State Committee for Science and Tech-
  nology (GKNT), 12
Stephenson, William, 23, 136, 178
Strategic Services Unit (SSU), 28, 68
Subversive Activities Control Board, 78
Sullivan, William C., 74, 75, 80
  Hoover and, 82
Syria, 162, 171

TASS, 214
Technology, intelligence collection, 5, 105, 224–25
Terrorism, 161–64
  combating, 163–64
  counter, 180–83
  history of, 161–62
  Syrian, 162
Thailand, 86
"Threshold doctrine," 52
Thümmel, Paul, 211
Tolson, Clyde, 74
Torpy, Charles, 106
Tovar, Hugh, 106, 127–28
Treaty of Dover, 144
Treholt, Arne, 145, 156–57, 213
Triple agents, 133
Trotsky, Leon, 160
Trotskyite Socialist Workers Party, 83
Truman, Harry S., 29, 73, 244
  Loyalty and Security Program, 77
  replaces Hillenkoettter as DCI, 35
  veto of McCarran Act, 78
Turner, Stansfield, 52, 58, 106, 112
Twentieth Century Task Force, 65

Union of Soviet Socialist Republics
  acquisition of U.S. technology by, 10–12
  agents of influence from, 141
  in Angola, 168
  counterintelligence in, 10–12
  in El Salvador, 168
  in Nicaragua, 168
  postwar intelligence network, 70
  preparation for nuclear attack, 194–95
  support for guerrilla activity, 166
  U.S. embassy, 190
United Farm Workers, 84
United States
  Afghanistan and, 60, 172
  Angola and, 60
  anti-communism in, 52, 68
  Congress of. See U.S. Congress.
  control of Panama Canal, 27
  counterintelligence. See Counterintelligence.

  Laotian support, 166
  Moscow embassy, 190
  in Nicaragua, 55–58, 60, 166–67
  resistance assistance from, 173
  SAVAK and, 177
  Soviet spying in, 68
U.S. Air Force, 99, 117
U.S. Army, 95–98, 109, 115–17, 245
U.S. Congress, 53–55, 73
  covert action and, 53–55
U.S. Information Agency, 151, 206
U.S. Intelligence, 7, 202. See also Central Intelligence Agency.
  bureaucracy, 69
  history of, 27, 248
  Iraqi nuclear arms and, 14–15
  KGB vs., 69
  national security and, 255
U.S. Navy, 98–99, 109, 116–17, 245
U.S. Supreme Court, 78
USSR. See Union of Soviet Socialist Republics.

Vance, Cyrus, 52
Vang Pao, 166
Vietnam War, 100, 152–53
Voice of Democratic Kampuchea, 153
Voice of the Malayan Revolution, 153
Voice of the People of Burma, 153
Volksender Drei, 152
Vosjoli, Philippe de, 209, 220

Walker, Barbara, 118, 184
Walker, John, 118, 187, 213
Walker-Whitworth ring, 188, 197
Walsingham, Francis, 185
Warsaw Pact, 197
Washington, George, 185
Watson, R. W. Seton, 157
Weapons, 14-5, 130
Webster, William, 107, 110, 112
White, Harry Dexter, 145
Willert, Arthur, 21
Wilson, Woodrow, 21, 136
Wiseman, William, 21-2, 125, 136
Wisner, Frank G., 33, 35
  chief lieutenants, 33
Woll, Matthew, 42
World Federation of Trade Unions, 204

World Peace Council, 204
World War I
  counterintelligence in, 9–10
  covert action in, 20–22
  propaganda in, use of, 22
  U.S. entry into, 9–10
World War II
  clandestine broadcasts during, 152
  counterintelligence in, 67, 72, 85, 96

gray propaganda during, 154
  X-2 in, 87
Wright, Peter, 195, 201–2
Wu Tai Chin, Larry, 89

Yugoslavia, 153
Yurchenko, Vitali, 215

Zohra, Tadjer, 163

About the Author

R OY GODSON is associate professor of government at Georgetown University and coordinator of the Consortium for the Study of Intelligence. For over twenty years he has taught courses in national security and foreign policy; U.S. and foreign intelligence; and international relations and international law. From 1980 to 1981 he served on President Reagan's Transition Team for the Central Intelligence Agency. Since 1982, he has served as a consultant to the National Security Council, the President's Foreign Intelligence Advisory Board, and related programs and agencies of the United States government. Dr. Godson has also testified numerous times before the House and Senate Intelligence Committees. He has written, coauthored, and edited many scholarly articles and eighteen books including *Security Studies for the 1990s; Intelligence Requirements for the 1990s; Comparing Foreign Intelligence*; and the seven-volume series *Intelligence Requirements for the 1980s*.

CPSIA information can be obtained
at www.ICGtesting.com
Printed in the USA
BVOW09s1117110517
483823BV00001B/41/P

9 780765 806994